ONE WEEK LOAN

Films re
have bee
ent succ
history,
and in

From
issues of
ways in
raise and
and cultu
past in a
the visua
depiction
films suc
what per
which th
response
reapprais

Contribu
Fidelma
T. Mural   ık,

Editors: **Claire Monk** is Lecturer in Media Studies at De Montfort University.
Amy Sargeant is Lecturer in the History of Film and Visual Media at Birkbeck
College, University of London.

British Popular Cinema
Series editors: Steve Chibnall and I. Q. Hunter
De Montfort University, Leicester

At a time when there is a growing popular and scholarly interest in British film, with new sources of funding and notable successes in world markets, this series explores the largely submerged history of the UK's cinema of entertainment.

The series rediscovers and evaluates not only individual films but whole genres, such as science fiction and the crime film, once dismissed or undervalued but now celebrated in some quarters as important contributions to our cinematic heritage.

This series offers the opportunity for both established cineastes and new writers to examine long-neglected areas of British film production or to develop new approaches to more familiar territory. The books will enhance our understanding of how ideas and representations in films relate to changing gender and class relations in post-war Britain, and their accessible writing style will make these insights available to a much wider readership.

Books in the series:

British Crime Cinema
Edited by Steve Chibnall and Robert Murphy

British Science Fiction Cinema
Edited by I. Q. Hunter

British Horror Cinema
Edited by Steve Chibnall and Julian Petley

British Historical Cinema
The history, heritage and costume film

Edited by
Claire Monk and Amy Sargeant

London and New York

First published 2002
by Routledge
11 New Fetter Lane, London EC4P 4EE

Simultaneously published in the USA and Canada
by Routledge
29 West 35th Street, New York, NY10001

Routledge is an imprint of the Taylor & Francis Group

© 2002 Claire Monk and Amy Sargeant for selection and editorial matter;
individual chapters © the contributors

Typeset in Perpetua by
The Running Head Limited, Cambridge
Printed and bound in Great Britain by
TJ International Ltd, Padstow, Cornwall

British Library Cataloguing in Publication Data
A catalogue record for this book is available from the British Library

Library of Congress Cataloging in Publication Data
British historical cinema : the history, heritage, and costume film / edited by Claire
Monk and Amy Sargeant.
    p. cm. — (British popular cinema)
  Includes bibliographical references and index.
    1. Historical films—Great Britain—History and criticism. I. Monk, Claire, 1963– II.
Sargeant, Amy, 1962– III. Series.

PN1995.9.H5 B75 2001
791.43'658'0941—dc21   2001038714

ISBN 0–415–23809–9 (hbk)
ISBN 0–415–23810–2 (pbk)

Contents

Illustrations

Contributors

Stephen Bourne is the author of *Black in the British Frame*, his award-winning history of black British film and television, recently published in a revised, updated edition (Continuum, 2001), and *Brief Encounters: Lesbians and Gays in British Cinema 1930–71* (Cassell, 1996). He is currently undertaking PhD research on gay representation in British television drama at De Montfort University.

Alan Burton is a Lecturer in Media Studies at De Montfort University. He has published on aspects of British film history in *Film History: An International Journal* and the *Journal of Popular British Cinema*, and is co-editor with Tim O'Sullivan and Paul Wells of *The Family Way: The Boulting Brothers and British Film Culture* (Flicks Books, 2000) and *Liberal Directions: Basil Dearden and Post-War British Film Culture* (Flicks Books, 1997).

James Chapman is Lecturer in Film and Television History at The Open University. He is author of *The British at War: Cinema, State and Propaganda, 1939–1945* (1998), *Licence To Thrill: A Cultural History of the James Bond Films* (1999) and *Saints and Avengers: British Adventure Series of the 1960s* (2002), all published by I. B. Tauris. He is also co-editor with Anthony Aldgate and Arthur Marwick of *Windows on the Sixties: Exploring Key Texts of Media and Culture* (I. B. Tauris, 2000), and with Christine Geraghty of Issue 4 of the *Journal of Popular British Cinema* (2001) on the theme of 'British Film Culture and Criticism'. He is currently writing a survey history of film and society in the twentieth century for Reaktion Books.

Nicholas J. Cull is Professor of American Studies at the University of Leicester. He has written widely on issues of film and history, particularly in the *Historical Journal of Film, Radio and Television*. He is the author of *Selling War: British Propaganda and American 'Neutrality' in World War II* (Oxford University Press, 1995).

Fidelma Farley lectures in Film Studies at the University of Aberdeen. She is the author of *Anne Devlin* (Flicks Books) and *This Other Eden* (Cork University Press), and has also published articles on women and Irish cinema, contemporary Northern Irish films, and Scottish and Irish cinema.

Sheldon Hall is a lecturer and former journalist who teaches film studies at Sheffield Hallam University. He has contributed to *Studying Film* (BFI/WEA, 1990), *The Movie Book of the Western* (Studio Vista, 1995), *Unexplored Hitchcock* (Cameron and Holliss, 2000) and *The Films of John Carpenter* (Flicks Books, 2001). He is currently working on a number of projects developed from his doctoral research on widescreen blockbusters of the 1950s and 1960s.

Jane Kingsley-Smith lectures in Shakespeare and Renaissance Literature at the University of Hull. She has published work on *The Tempest*, *Shakespeare in Love* and Shakespeare's sources, and is currently researching banishment in Shakespeare's plays.

Kara McKechnie is a Lecturer in Dramaturgy at the University of Leeds, Bretton Hall campus. She is currently completing her PhD on the work of Alan Bennett at De Montfort University, Leicester.

Claire Monk is a Lecturer in Media Studies at De Montfort University. She has contributed to *Sight and Sound* since the early 1990s, has written widely on 1980s and 1990s British cinema, including heritage cinema, and is currently completing PhD research on British heritage-film audiences. Her work appears in *Journal of Popular British Cinema*, *Cineaste*, Ginette Vincendeau (ed.) *Film/ Literature/Heritage: A Sight and Sound Reader* (BFI, 2001), Robert Murphy (ed.) *British Cinema in the 1990s* (BFI, 2000), Justine Ashby and Andrew Higson (eds) *British Cinema: Past and Present* (Routledge, 2000), Steve Chibnall and Robert Murphy (eds) *British Crime Cinema* (Routledge, 1999), and Colin MacCabe and Duncan Petrie (eds) *New Scholarship from BFI Research* (BFI, 1996).

T. Muraleedharan is a Lecturer in the Department of English, St Aloysius College, Elthuruth, affiliated to the University of Calicut, Kerala, Southern India. His chapter in this book draws upon doctoral research on race and gender in the British Raj films of the 1980s. He has also contributed to R. Frankenberg (ed.), *Displacing Whiteness: Essays in Social and Cultural Criticism* (Duke University Press, 1997) and to Ruth Vanita (ed.) *Queering India: Same-Sex Love and Eroticism in Indian Culture and Society* (Routledge, forthcoming).

Tim O'Sullivan is Principal Lecturer and Reader in Media Education and Cultural Studies at De Montfort University, Leicester, where he is also head of the Department of Media and Cultural Production. His recent publications on British cinema include *The Family Way: The Boulting Brothers and British Film Culture* (Flicks Books, 2000) and *Liberal Directions: Basil Dearden and Post-War British Film Culture* (Flicks Books, 1997), both co-edited with Alan Burton and Paul Wells.

James Quinn is a television producer specialising in history and current affairs. He has published work on both British history and British cinema, and has completed a PhD thesis on the British historical film.

Amy Sargeant is a Lecturer in the History of Film and Visual Media at Birkbeck College, University of London. She has written extensively on silent cinema and especially screen performance in the silent period. She has contributed to the *Journal of Popular British Cinema*, the *International Journal of Heritage Studies* and *Film Studies* and to Andrew Higson and Justine Ashby (eds) *British Cinema: Past and Present* (Routledge, 2000). She is currently working on *A Critical and Interpretative History of British Cinema*, commissioned by the BFI.

Acknowledgements

We should like to begin by thanking Steve Chibnall for his initial invitation to contribute a volume on British period cinema to the British Popular Cinema series. Our particular gratitude, however, is reserved for James Chapman, who was the original co-editor of this volume with Claire Monk before exceptionally seductive competing opportunities – to publish studies of the James Bond films and British adventure television series of the 1960s – understandably lured him away from the project. James's input was of crucial importance in shaping the book in its early stages of development, and we particularly wish to acknowledge that the participation of a number of the contributors whose work appears here was secured through his efforts rather than our own.

Friends, colleagues, our contributors and not least our publisher will already know that – due to an array of personal circumstances and professional commitments both mundane and unanticipated – the gestation and completion of *British Historical Cinema* have been lengthier than we might have hoped. This book has been completed without research grants or research leave, and we particularly wish to thank our editors at Routledge, Rebecca Barden and Alistair Daniel, for their monumental patience, their enthusiasm and support for the book, and their constant willingness to dispense guidance and soothe editorial crises. Thanks are equally due to all our contributors for their resilience and goodwill. Claire Monk would also like to thank Brian Watson for his loving support – and both of us thank him for his practical help beyond the call of duty.

Special thanks for assistance with stills illustrations are due to Steve Chibnall as keeper of the British Cinema and Television Research Group archive, De Montfort University, to Nina Harding at BFI Stills, Posters and Designs, and to Ben Spencer at Merchant Ivory Productions.

Every effort has been made to obtain permissions to reproduce copyright material. If in any cases we or our contributors have failed to give proper acknowledgement, we apologise in advance, and invite copyright holders to inform us of the oversight.

This book is dedicated to the memory of Barbara Monk (1923–2000) and John Monk (1916–76). The latter (known as Harold Monk in his youth) worked as an assistant electrician in British film studios in the London/Hertfordshire area between 1932 and 1938, but known details are scant beyond those preserved in the form of family anecdotes. If by some slender chance this book is read by anyone who remembers him from that time, Claire Monk would be delighted to hear from them care of the publisher Routledge.

Claire Monk and Amy Sargeant
London, June 2001

1 Introduction

The past in British cinema

Claire Monk and Amy Sargeant

In contrast with some of the earlier volumes in this series, *British Historical Cinema* cannot plausibly claim to focus on a hitherto little-known or neglected genre of British cinema. On the contrary, British films set in 'the past' – recent or distant, actual or imagined and, most obviously, those which can be designated as belonging to the historical or costume genres – have been central to the popularity, commercial success – and exportability – of British cinema since its earliest decades. Indeed, British period films have often been closely equated in the eyes of the world – many would say too closely – with Britain's 'national cinema' itself. But, more than this, deep-rooted notions of Britain, and especially England, as an 'old country' (Wright 1985) – as a nation whose identity resides crucially in the narratives, myths, landscapes and material and cultural artefacts of its past and which somehow has 'more history' than others[1] – have meant that Britain and Britishness have all too often been defined and represented predominantly in terms of the nation's past – not least by filmmakers.

Against this background, the very popularity of British period films with audiences, and their prominent success as one of British cinema's most reliable exports – from *The Private Life of Henry VIII* (Alexander Korda, 1933) to *Shakespeare in Love* (John Madden, USA, 1999) – has often proved a double-edged sword. (And already, the act of listing these 'British' export hits brings us to one of the many complexities of British period cinema, namely its consistent debt to international personnel and US co-production funding or big-studio distribution.) Throughout much of the history of British cinema, British period films have been highly visible, much enjoyed – but also highly scrutinised, whether by critics, professional historians or representatives of the state. Their widely perceived status as projections of 'the nation' or 'the national past' has placed upon them a heavy burden of representation – although it is the view of this book's editors that in the case of many films this linking of British period films with 'the national' is overstated. As Alan Lovell has observed, the 'persistent linking of British film production with the question of national identity is odd' (Lovell 1997: 241); and we would argue that the critical – and wider – discourses around British period films constitute an extreme case of this oddness. Equally, British period films have been burdened and constrained by the widespread and strongly held belief that the central duty of films set in the past is to document historical fact – or at least the material world of the period depicted – as faithfully as known sources permit. As will be explored further throughout this introduction, this too is a view that many of our contributors reject, in some cases vehemently.

These strictures have made period films one of British cinema's most contested strands, and in specific cases – notably the Gainsborough Studios costume melodramas of the 1940s (Harper 1994; Cook 1996a) and the 'heritage films' of the 1980s and 1990s (Higson 1993 and 1996b; see also Claire Monk, Chapter 12) – they have become targets of official or critical attack. These attacks have variously targeted the 'inauthenticity' of period films' depictions of the past; their perceived aesthetic excess or vulgarity contravening the dominant values of realism and restraint championed by an elite British film-critical culture; or the ideological or hegemonic character of their uses of 'the past' or representations of 'the nation'.

British cinema's representations of the past have often provoked polarised reactions – in the process, often instructively exposing the fissures between elite critical taste agendas and the preferences of popular audiences. However, relatively few areas of British period cinema have received sustained and engaged critical consideration, nor has a great diversity of critical approaches been in evidence.

There is now no shortage of literature on the flamboyant, sensual, but historically highly 'inauthentic' Gainsborough melodramas, and their particular appeals to the working-class female audiences who devoured them in preference to Second World War realism or the middle-class restraint of *Brief Encounter* (David Lean, 1945) (Aspinall and Murphy [eds.] 1983; Harper 1987 and 1994; Cook 1996a, 1996b and 1997). Nor has there been any shortage of debate identifying, condemning, defending, reappraising – and, in the case of Claire Monk's chapter here, querying – the emergence of the 'heritage film' as the dominant form of British period cinema since the 1980s (see Chapter 12 for a full bibliography). Indeed, as Monk notes, heritage-film criticism 'has become as effective a commodity in the academy as heritage films have been in the cinema'.

But, beyond these areas, British period cinema encompasses an extraordinary spectrum of genres, themes, aesthetics and approaches which remain relatively unexplored. Given that some of these facets merit extended coverage beyond the space limits of this volume, and that – like all editors – we have been inclined to capitalise on our contributors' preoccupations, this collection does not seek to present a comprehensive, nor necessarily 'representative', survey of British period films or genres. Its 'project' is that it seeks to make a modest contribution to the opening up of this field, and – less modestly – to shake up the debate around British period films and to stimulate a reappraisal of the terms in which they are discussed and evaluated.

Figure 1.1 'One of British cinema's most contested strands': the official and critical vilification of the Gainsborough Studios melodramas such as *Madonna of the Seven Moons* (1944), exemplifies the extreme critical scrutiny to which British period and costume films have often been subjected.

Source: British Cinema and Television Research Group archive, De Montfort University (GFD/Gainsborough).

Certain concerns surface recurrently in the contributions to this volume which suggest directions in which the critical discussion of British period films might fruitfully be reappraised and developed. First, many of our contributors are concerned to emphasise, and analyse, the *multiplicity* of period film genres and the distinctions between them. Several contributors resist the blanket use of the term 'historical film' as a catch-all genre label (see especially Quinn and Kingsley-Smith, Chapter 11), seeking instead to move towards a more complex and less reductive mapping of 'films set in the past'. Sheldon Hall discusses *Zulu* (Cy Endfield, 1964) with reference to a range of popular genres not unique to period cinema (Chapter 8); and Claire Monk questions the usefulness and coherence of the heritage film as a genre category outside the highly specific cultural and political circumstances which formed 'the heritage-film idea' (Chapter 12).

Second, and following on from this, a number of our contributors move away from (or at least, bracket) the discursive framework which conceives of British period films as always centrally engaged in projecting 'the nation' or 'the national past' to focus instead on the pleasures offered to audiences by specific films (*Zulu* in Hall's chapter) or cycles (Merchant Ivory's adaptations from the novels of E. M. Forster in Monk's).

Third, most of our contributors work from within a clear understanding that historical films *are films* – indeed, are an important part of popular cinema – rather than an errant and inevitably flawed species of historical documentation. Neither we – nor, we think, our readers – are in need of Pierre Sorlin's patient explanation to historians seeking to use film (factual or fictional) as a source that what we see on screen is a construction, 'the result of a subjective choice' (Sorlin 2001: 28) – nor do our readers need reminding that a 'historical' film will often be a work of pure entertainment and pure fiction.

This volume is, then, as interested in questions of pleasure, filmic and genre conventions and audience responses – and in the avowedly fictional and the inauthentic – as it is in the relation of historical films to empirical events. These emphases set *British Historical Cinema* apart from much recent published work on 'the historical film' (see, for example, Rosenstone 1995 and many of the essays collected in Landy [ed.] 2001) in ways which we believe to be fruitful.

However, our contributors are equally concerned to analyse seriously the relationships between British period films of various genres and decades, the historical past and the present in which the films were produced. Most are concerned with the manner in which a historical past, actual or imagined, is appropriated in subsequent representations, or in the ways in which the represented past is specifically modern in its political and social resonance: see especially Fidelma Farley (Chapter 9), Amy Sargeant (Chapters 2 and 13) and Kara McKechnie (Chapter 14). Many draw comparisons between the representation of history in older and newer media: see Farley, Sargeant, and Nicholas J. Cull (Chapter 7). Kara McKechnie argues that the use of visual material, for instance official portraits, as a source for the costumes for *Elizabeth* (Shekhar Kapur, 1998), may render these representations more widely accessible, but equally notes that these sources are themselves coded, allegorical depictions. While McKechnie identifies 'getting it right' as one of the specific traits of post-1980s British period filmmaking, other contributors locate it as a longstanding trait of 'quality' British cinema and a regrettably pervasive criterion mobilised by the tradition of 'quality' film criticism in Britain (see Ellis 1996).

Several contributors are concerned with the representation on film of historical figures and/or events which can be classed as belonging to 'official' British history and which have become established as significant (if frequently problematic) points of reference when traditional notions of 'Britishness' or the nation are invoked: monarchy, heroic figures and the myths constructed around them, the nation at war. James Chapman's contribution (Chapter 6) is the first of three dealing with representations of the British monarchy on film (see also McKechnie; Quinn and Kingsley-Smith). It is also unusual in this volume in that it is concerned with the documenting of a supposedly 'historic' event at the time of its enactment: the feature-film documentary of the coronation of Elizabeth II, *A Queen Is Crowned* (Castleton Knight, 1953). Chapman discusses how *A Queen Is Crowned* displays 'an array of cultural and historical motifs' which make it more than just a filmed record of the coronation. In so doing, it employs historic evocation, quotation, panoply and ritual to construct a specific vision of 'the national heritage' which remains familiar today, as well as to register significance to its contemporary audience. Chapman notes especially the heralding by *A Queen Is Crowned* of 'a second Elizabethan age'. Citing Arthur Marwick (1996) and Asa Briggs (1979), he suggests also that the popularity of the monarchy at the time was demonstrated by the purchase of television sets on which to watch coverage of the coronation. In an episode narrating the life of the playwright Joe Orton in 1953, Stephen Frears's bio-pic *Prick Up Your Ears* (1987) suggests that the broadcasting of such public events can carry a significance for individual viewers which is entirely personal – in Orton's case, in ways which somewhat subvert their national importance.

Both Alan Burton and Amy Sargeant contribute chapters which address war as a significant event in public and personal history. Sargeant (Chapter 2) considers Maurice Elvey's *Nelson* (1919) as an adaptation of Robert Southey's biography of the British admiral – whose victories during the Napoleonic Wars culminating in the Battle of Trafalgar in 1805, assured British naval supremacy and made him a national hero – and as an ambitious pictorial epic which draws parallels between the defence of national, imperial and commercial interests in 1805 and at the outset of the Great War of 1914–18. Elvey's film, Sargeant argues, should be regarded as much in a broader context of nineteenth- and twentieth-century historiography and iconography as in its immediate function as triumphal propaganda (which has been the focus of most existing interpretative writing on the film: see Higson 1995). She places the celebration of Nelson as an immortal hero against current debates at the turn of the twentieth and twenty-first centuries regarding the propriety of public monuments and the politics of who, or what, should be commemorated.

Points about the politics, ethics and iconography of monuments are also made by Alan Burton (Chapter 3) in his survey of British cinema's shifting attempts to 'imagine' the experience of the Great War from Maurice Elvey's *Comradeship*, made immediately after the war in the same year as *Nelson*, to recent films of the 1990s. Burton notes that, in contrast with US depictions such as *All Quiet on the Western Front* (Lewis Milestone, USA, 1930) or Stanley Kubrick's *Paths of Glory* (USA, 1957), British films about the conflict have often focused on its psychological impacts and personal dramas rather than the direct physical experience of combat in the trenches – for reasons of budget, perhaps. His discussion is driven by a concern with the inadequate representation and acknowledgement of the contribution made to the war by the 'ordinary working-class Tommy' – cinematically, and in public memorials – and with the continuing official refusal to pardon and memorialise the British servicemen executed during the war for 'failing to do their duty' (often due to terror or exhaustion). He focuses centrally on the depiction of the working and officer classes in four films: *King and Country* (Joseph Losey, 1964), *Oh! What a Lovely War* (Richard Attenborough, 1969), *Regeneration* (Gillies MacKinnon, UK/Canada, 1997) and *The Trench* (William Boyd, UK/France, 1999) – most of them notable precisely for their rejection of a memorialising tradition.

Tim O'Sullivan's contribution (Chapter 5) is the second in the volume focusing on films produced in a period neglected in discussions of British historical cinema: the immediate post-Second World War years. In contrast with James Chapman's discussion of the filming of a highly public event belonging to 'official history', however, O'Sullivan focuses on two films which are markedly not concerned with significant, exceptional individuals but rather with 'the nature of "everyman" [and his] possibilities for advancement within modern society': *The History of Mr Polly* (Anthony Pelissier, 1949) and *The Card* (Ronald Neame, 1952). O'Sullivan writes from a position of personal affection and nostalgia for his chosen films. However, they are of wider interest precisely because of their apparent marginality in a number of respects – and, therefore, their non-conformity with the dominant frameworks within which British period cinema tends to be discussed. Both films were adapted from popular Edwardian novels (by H. G. Wells and Arnold Bennett respectively) but are neither much-remembered nor highly regarded today – indeed, they date precisely from the period when, in Sue Harper's analysis, the British costume film was in terminal decline (Harper 1994), as were British cinema attendances. As O'Sullivan notes, neither of the films' male protagonists is a 'known or "real" historical [figure]. Their life-stories and tales of the "unknown" and "unexpected" are not . . . even loosely based on a recognised historical person, fact or myth'. In the context of the 'depressed, austere and turbulent post-war environment' in which both films were produced, promoted and released, however, he argues that their appropriations of popular Edwardian fictions performed very specific functions for the post-Second World War male returning to the uncertainties of a transformed civilian world – while putting the post-war 'everywoman' firmly back in her place in a restored male-centred hierarchy. Both films offered male viewers a nostalgic escape into a pre-modern past – but, anticipating the social changes of the later 1950s, they also question the determining power of history and social structure over the individual.

A significant strand of chapters in the book are concerned expressly with Britain's relations and conflicts with other nations, or with Britain's history of national self-aggrandisement through Empire (Cull, Muraleedharan, Farley, Hall). Although Sheldon Hall begins his discussion of *Zulu* by explicitly alerting the reader to his viewing position as 'a white English male born in the year of *Zulu*'s initial release', other contributors write from an emphatically postcolonial perspective (and, in two cases, expressly from the perspective of the formerly colonised).

In her discussion of *Ryan's Daughter* (David Lean, 1970) (Chapter 9), Fidelma Farley observes the extent to which 'pastness' is crucial to British cinema's depictions not merely of Irish *history* but of Ireland *per se*. Farley argues that 'Ireland and the Irish are consistently placed by British films in an atemporal, essentially presocial realm, one which lacks the social, political and economic structures of modern, advanced civilisation'. She notes that the Irish landscape is rendered in these films in terms of a highly symptomatic wildness. But, given the history of this land as a source of conflict between Britain and Ireland, it simultaneously 'carries political meanings and functions as a site of danger and violence'. Farley notes that Irish characters – especially women – are equated in the films with the passionate unpredictability of their natural environment and presented as more sensual than the English. Significantly, however, in *Ryan's Daughter* it is the passive, eroticised and invalided male body of the English soldier Major Doryan (Christopher Jones) that stands for the demise of Empire.

Farley also draws a comparison between *Ryan's Daughter* – a commercial and critical disaster which prompted a fifteen-year withdrawal from filmmaking for Lean – and his 1984 film *A Passage to India* – critically received as marking a triumphal return, but also Lean's final film. T. Muraleedharan (Chapter 10) discusses *A Passage to India* in some detail in the context of 1980s British cinema's representations of the Raj, with comparative reference to *Heat and Dust* (James Ivory, 1982). Both Farley and Muraleedharan are concerned with the tropes deployed in their chosen films to personify the political relationship between the coloniser and the colonised, as well as the (perhaps inevitably) Anglocentric perspective Lean brings to the colonial relationship. Farley suggests that the otherness of the colonised is more immediately apparent when they are non-white. Muraleedharan suggests that the strategies adopted have the effect of representing colonialism as benign and dutiful. While acknowledging that this effect may not have been consciously sought by the films' makers, his concern is to 'make known my reading of, and my feelings about' these films as a postcolonial citizen of independent India, and thus to reclaim 'a history that is mine as well'.

Muraleedharan locates *A Passage to India* and *Heat and Dust* in relation to the post-1960s fashion for white European counter-migration (typically through extended foreign travel) in search of the exotic and strange. He notes the importance in both films of this trope of 'reverse migration' by young white women *to* India (Adela in *A Passage to India*; in *Heat and Dust*, Anne in the early-1980s strand of the narrative and her aunt Olivia in the colonial 1920s). For both Adela and Olivia, the other is attractive precisely *because* it is threatening: a fascination which we feel is similarly present in the more recent *Hideous Kinky* (Gillies MacKinnon, 1999), adapted from Esther Freud's novel, which drew upon Freud's child's-eye perspective on her hippy mother's adventures in Morocco in the 1960s. Muraleedharan's analysis explores the gendered workings of this trope of migration and their implications in the context of the colonial past. He argues that both *A Passage to India* and *Heat and Dust* figure the colonial relationship as a male friendship, but that in both films the 'sensual woman's fascination for the exotic Orient' becomes somehow accountable for breaking this up. Hence British womanhood is held accountable for the loss or degradation of colonial power.

Stephen Bourne's contribution (Chapter 4) is similarly informed by his personal cultural identity and history – in Bourne's case, as a Londoner from a family which blends black Caribbean and white British ancestry. His chapter explores a history which is almost invisible in British films: the history of black settlers and their descendants within Britain. As Bourne observes, this history has been traced back to at least 1555 – almost four centuries before the arrival in Britain of the *Empire Windrush* in 1948 – yet continues to be virtually ignored by British cinema. This invisibility extends to British films set in the present as well as those set in the past: in a notorious recent example, the highly profitable hit comedy-romance *Notting Hill* (Roger Michell, 1999) takes its title from the district of London most famous for its black community but portrays the area as inhabited entirely by whites.

Bourne's revealing account of British period cinema's rare acknowledgements of the black presence in the nation's past suggests that the growth of Britain's racially mixed communities and increased awareness of issues of race and representation have not brought progress in cinematic representation. Where Elvey's 1919 *Nelson* acknowledged the service of black sailors at Trafalgar, the Dark Lady of the Sonnets was notably absent from 1999's *Shakespeare in Love*. Bourne discusses Jack Gold's *The Sailor's Return* (1978) as a rare instance of a British period literary adaptation featuring a black central protagonist, the African princess Tulip (Shope Shodeinde) who settles in Victorian rural Dorset as the wife of the sailor Targett (Tom Bell). This film also failed to find a theatrical release.

The overwhelming 'whiteness' of British period cinema documented by Bourne raises the uncomfortable question of whether there is something specifically 'white' about the address and appeal of certain period film genres. Is the reliable whiteness of the past these films depict part of the known – if unspoken and for some viewers perhaps not even conscious – appeal of British period-genre films to certain sectors of a predominantly white audience? Bourne observes, however, that British period television drama – generally seen by larger and demographically broader audiences than period cinema releases – has in recent years been far more progressive than British cinema in integrating black citizens into the narration of the nation's past.

Bourne demonstrates how representations of the past on film impact upon social behaviour in the present by citing the example of *Zulu* as a source of racist name-calling in South London schools. A more extended discussion of *Zulu* is offered by Sheldon Hall (Chapter 8) – from a very different perspective, for Hall writes as a longstanding fan of the film. He argues that *Zulu* is a more complex film than its immediate appropriation by certain sections of white Britain at its release, and the subsequent attacks directed at it by hostile critics, might suggest. While agreeing that *Zulu* presents historical events from a highly selective, partial, white perspective, he argues that the effects of this are more ambivalent than has sometimes been claimed – and defends this strategy of selectivity for its *narrative* effectiveness within the structures of popular genre cinema. Hall boldly claims that it is the prerogative of cinematic representations to be appraised by criteria quite apart from their supposed correspondence to actual events, arguing that 'film-makers, like other artists, are entitled to as much latitude as they care to take in adapting the raw material of history to the demands of dramatic narrative'. While itemising some of the plentiful respects in which *Zulu* 'gets it wrong' historically, he is interested more to establish how *Zulu* accords with and departs from the conventions of a range of filmic and non-filmic genres.

Questions of genre – and specifically, the distinguishing characteristics of different period film genres – are explored more systematically by James Quinn and Jane Kingsley-Smith (Chapter 11) with reference to the reception of a particular film, Kenneth Branagh's 1989 filming of Shakespeare's *Henry V*. Quinn and Kingsley-Smith establish that Branagh's *Henry V* was received as both historical and contemporary at the time of its release. It conveys, in Patrick Wright's terms, a distinctly modern past, responding to its own context as expediently as did Laurence Olivier's adaptation of 1945 (Wright 1985: 2). Quinn and Kingsley-Smith suggest that Branagh's *Henry V* is indeterminate in its genre placing and that it draws upon a range of conventions derived variously from the history film, the heritage film and the 'Shakespeare film'. Given the status of *Henry V* as a 'Shakespeare film', debates among critics about 'authenticity' were concerned as much with fidelity to source text – and conflicting conceptions (among Shakespeare scholars) of what that might mean – as they were with the indication of a particular period in the past.

Kara McKechnie's contribution (Chapter 14) is concerned more expressly with the representation of the monarchy and, like Quinn and Kingsley-Smith, draws connections between the production of films dealing with past monarchs and events involving their successors. She quotes the actress Cate Blanchett's comments on the experience of playing and filming *Elizabeth*: 'It was incredible to begin filming two days after [Princess Diana's] death. The first line of the shoot was "The Queen is dead. Long live the Queen!" And it was just very odd, very odd.' Like Quinn and Kingsley-Smith too, McKechnie notes that Nicholas Hytner's *The Madness of King George* (1995) exploits and develops the use of Shakespeare's *King Lear* in his own staging of the source play, contemplating broader questions of kingship as performance in a film which itself renders the exotic – the lives of the rich, famous and infamous – as familiar (see Vivian Sobchak 1996: 18). McKechnie is interested in the ways in which monarchical bio-pics may be opportunistically tailored to suit perceived social purposes at the time of their production, especially in response to crises of the monarchy or state. She discusses in particular the differing purposes served by the representations of Queen Victoria in Herbert Wilcox's 1937 *Victoria the Great* and its 1938 successor *Sixty Glorious Years* (which sought to bolster both the institution of the monarchy and the institution of the family immediately after the 1936 Abdication of Edward VIII) in comparison with the recent *Mrs Brown* (John Madden, USA/UK/Ireland, 1997).

In 'Camping on the Borders' (Chapter 7), Nick Cull turns to the lowbrow *Carry On* costume films with their joyously vulgar piercing of the pretensions of the 'quality' historical drama and its reverence for verisimilitude. A remarkable number of the *Carry Ons* plundered the riches of British history or parodied the British and American historical films of the series' 1960s and early-1970s heyday. As Cull notes, their project was to mock 'great moments' from British history and, simultaneously, 'the stylistic devices used by mainstream historical films to establish their authenticity' through the punning use of archaic language, free play with fragments of reported speech, use of clichéd locations, imagery and stock footage, and so forth. Importantly, following Harper (1994) and Alison Light (1991), Cull suggests that the *Carry On* films used the past in multiple ways: as a zone of escape in which rich costumes added a level of pleasure, but equally as a device for commenting on both the present and the foreignness of the past. In *Carry On* the past became once again an exotic territory in which fantasies could be indulged – not least through the devices of (overtly unconvincing) disguise and masquerade in which nationality, race, sexuality and gender become blatantly performative. Cull notes particularly the films' wanton anachronisms and patent self-reflexivity, their acknowledgement of 'the present viewing the past with the advantages of hindsight'.

We would argue that these traits in the historical *Carry Ons* invite a fruitful comparison with the consciously experimental, self-reflexive treatment of history in Peter Watkins's *Culloden* (BBC-TV, 1965), Trevor Griffith's *Hope in the Year Two* (BBC-TV, 1994) and Ken McMullen's *Zina* (1985) and *1871* (1990); with Derek Jarman's highly stylised treatment of historical subjects with reference to the present in *Caravaggio* (1986) and *Edward II* (1991); and equally with the contemporaneities and excesses of Ken Russell's period films from *Women in Love* (1969) to *The Devils* (1971, designed by Jarman). This strand of films which are knowingly visually 'inauthentic' and blatantly contemporary in their treatment of history – whether this takes the form of politically inspired (and would-be Brechtian) attempts to prompt critical engagement on the part of present-day viewers or the 'vulgarity' of Russell and the *Carry Ons* – stands, we think, as the great 'repressed' of British *period* cinema, equally absent from general critical-historical discussions and from political-aesthetic debates. It is to our regret that we have had to defer more detailed discussion of this strand – and, likewise, of the wider neglected British period cinema of the 1960s and 1970s, when such excesses flourished – for future exploration.

The current partiality and incompleteness of existing critical accounts of British period cinema is also a point of reference for Claire Monk (Chapter 12) in her

Figure 1.2 A film ill-served by dominant critical debates: *Angels and Insects* (1995). Victorian working-class naturalist William Adamson (Mark Rylance) shows a rare butterfly to his patron's daughter Eugenia (Patsy Kensit) – who is protecting the aristocratic gene pool through incestuous couplings with her brother, in a film which makes much play with the ideas of Darwinism and eugenics.

Source: British Cinema and Television Research Group archive, De Montfort University (Playhouse International Pictures).

discussion of the debate around so-called 'heritage films' which has emerged in Britain since the late 1980s/early 1990s. The term 'heritage film', and a set of critical discourses identifying, characterising and criticising the films said to constitute the heritage 'genre', has risen to sufficient academic prominence that, increasingly, virtually all discussion of post-1979 British period films takes place within a 'heritage' critical framework.

One of the dangers of this dominance is that it marginalises films which do not neatly fit the 'heritage' critical template – such as *Angels and Insects* (Philip Haas, UK/USA, 1995), a visually striking adaptation from a prestigious literary source (A. S. Byatt's novella *Morpho Eugenia*) which is nevertheless centrally shaped by an acute and critical historical consciousness of Victorian England as a class society. Another is that heritage-film criticism severs the British period films of the Thatcher years from their 1960s and 1970s precursors (both cinematic and in the form of British television's numerous period literary adaptations) – thus repressing many continuities and complexities. (We would add that this artificial break also ignores the importance of the 1960s and 1970s as the decades in which many viewers of post-1979 period films – including this volume's editors – developed their taste

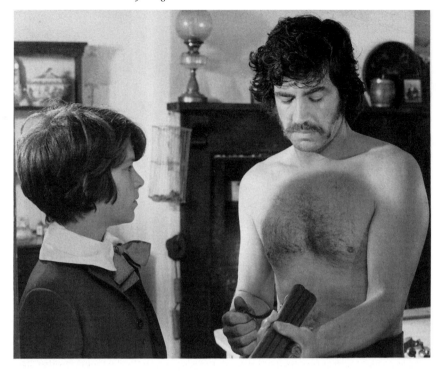

Figure 1.3 Dominic Guard as the young message-carrier of the title with farmer Alan Bates
in *The Go-Between* (1970). An example from a critically neglected phase of British period film production which merits fresh consideration – for its connections with the post-1979 'heritage' cinema as much as for its apparent distinctions
from it.

Source: British Cinema and Television Research Group archive, De Montfort University
(EMI/World Film Services).

for period screen fictions.) Even brief consideration of British period films of the
1970s reveals as much ambiguity and disagreement around their politics, authenticity and aesthetics as there has been around the heritage films of the 1980s onwards. To cite one example, while Joseph Losey's *The Go-Between* (1970, adapted
from L. P. Hartley's 1953 novel), the tale of a doomed affair between the daughter of a wealthy rural family (Julie Christie) and a farmer (Alan Bates), is often
constructed by critics as the antithesis of heritage cinema – it is widely seen as an
exemplary critique of 'the destructive side of the English class system' (Geoff
Andrew 1989: 231) – others have dismissed it as precisely 'the sort of prettified,
literary pomp that passes for intelligent cinema in Britain' (David Thomson 1994:
453).

Monk, like Quinn and Kingsley-Smith, is concerned in part with issues of
generic definition in British period cinema – and to emphasise the extreme generic
variety of the British period film as well as its often complex national/cultural

origins. She argues, however, that 'heritage films' lack coherence as a body of films, and are more usefully understood as a critical construct. Her chapter critically reviews the terms in which heritage films have been defined and the claims made about them, but focuses particularly on the methodological underpinnings of the British heritage-film debate and its highly specific origins. For Monk, these origins – as a reactive response to the viciously combative cultural and political climate fostered in 1980s Britain under Margaret Thatcher's Conservative government – make it questionable whether the heritage film as originally defined in the early 1990s has continuing usefulness as a critical or descriptive category in the Blairite 2000s. Monk suggests that new critiques are needed which are directly responsive to developments in recent British period films and to the changed industrial, cultural and political conditions in which films are produced and circulated since the election of Tony Blair's New Labour government in May 1997.

In 'The content and the form' (Chapter 13), Amy Sargeant takes up the challenge of analysing recent period films in terms other than those dictated by the heritage debate by focusing on the myriad devices used to invoke 'pastness' in three films set within the living memory of audiences: *Scandal* (Michael Caton-Jones, 1989), *The Cement Garden* (Andrew Birkin, UK/Germany/France, 1992) and *Velvet Goldmine* (Todd Haynes, UK/USA, 1998). Sargeant considers the stylistic devices which are habitually employed in period reconstruction and explores distinctions between received notions of history proper and the merely historical. She is interested particularly in the coherence of various materials across a range of media in a variety of applications. She considers the viewer's sense of time in our relationship with the past, and discusses the treatment of known, invented and archetypal characters in her chosen films. All three films depict pasts – the 1960s and 1970s – and engage with subjects some distance away from the material traditionally associated with 'the British historical film'. We are proud to have travelled that distance in this volume, and hope that our readers will find it an equally stimulating journey.

Note

1 The 'more history' perception was reported by Susan Condor as one of the findings of her recent survey, 'National history, national heritage: young people's representations of the national past', presented in a paper of the same title at the 'Relocating Britishness' conference, University of Central Lancashire, Preston, UK, June 2000.

Bibliography

Andrew, G. (1989) '*The Go-Between*' [review] in T. Milne (ed.) *The Time Out Film Guide*, Harmondsworth: Penguin.

Aspinall, S. and Murphy, R. (eds) (1983) *BFI Dossier No. 18: Gainsborough Melodrama*, London: BFI.

Briggs, A. (1979) *The History of Broadcasting in the United Kingdom* IV: *Sound and Vision 1945–55*, Oxford: Oxford University Press.

Cook, P. (1996a) *Fashioning the Nation*, London: BFI.

—— (1996b) 'Neither here nor there: national identity in Gainsborough costume drama' in A. Higson (ed.) (1996a): 51–65.

—— (ed.) (1997) *Gainsborough Pictures*, London: Cassell.

Ellis, J. (1996) 'The quality film adventure: British critics and the cinema, 1942–1948' in A. Higson (ed.) (1996a): 66–93.

Harper, S. (1987) 'Historical pleasures: Gainsborough costume melodrama' in C. Gledhill (ed.) *Home Is Where the Heart Is: Studies in Melodrama and the Woman's Film*, London: BFI: 167–96.

—— (1994) *Picturing the Past: The Rise and Fall of the British Costume Film*, London: BFI.

Higson, A. (1993) 'Re-presenting the national past: nostalgia and pastiche in the heritage film' in L. Friedman (ed.) *British Cinema and Thatcherism: Fires Were Started*, London: University College London Press: 109–29.

—— (1995) 'The victorious re-cycling of national history: *Nelson*' in K. Dibbets and B. Hogenkamp (eds) *Film and the First World War*, Amsterdam: Amsterdam University Press: 108–15.

—— (ed.) (1996a) *Dissolving Views: Key Writings on British Cinema*, London: Cassell.

—— (1996b) 'The heritage film and British cinema' in A. Higson (ed.) (1996a): 232–48.

Landy, M. (ed.) (2001) *The Historical Film: History and Memory in Media*, New Brunswick, NJ: Rutgers University Press.

Light, A. (1991) *Forever England: Femininity, Literature and Conservatism between the Wars*, London: Routledge.

Lovell, A. (1997) 'The British cinema: the known cinema?' in R. Murphy (ed.) *The British Cinema Book*, London: BFI: 235–43.

Marwick, A. (1996) *British Society Since 1945*, third edition, Harmondsworth: Penguin.

Rosenstone, R. A. (1995) *Revisioning History: Film and the Construction of a New Past*, Princeton, NJ: Princeton University Press.

Sobchak, V. (ed.) (1996) *The Persistence of History: Cinema, Television and the Modern Event*, London: Routledge.

Sorlin, P. (2001) 'How to look at an "historical" film' in M. Landy (ed.): 25–39.

Thomson, D. (1994) *A Biographical Dictionary of Film*, London: André Deutsch.

Wright, P. (1985) *On Living in an Old Country*, London: Verso.

2 Do we need another hero?

Ecce Homo and *Nelson* (1919)

Amy Sargeant

Little England and the Great British Empire

> On Sunday evenings the names were read of old boys killed in action during
> the week. There was seldom, if ever, a Sunday without its necrology. The
> chapel was approached by a passage in which their photographs were hung in
> ever-extending lines. I had not known them, but we were all conscious of
> these presences. It was not uncommon for preachers to refer to the sacrifices
> which were being made for our benefit. This did not seem humbug. It is said
> that an exhortation of this kind now rouses derision. It was not so in 1917.
>
> (Waugh 1964: 113)

Evelyn Waugh's memories of the beginning of his education at Lancing College
serve as a cautionary introduction to the following discussion of Maurice Elvey's
1919 *Nelson: The Story of England's Immortal Naval Hero*. Whereas Waugh records
and urges respect for the sacrifice of many, Elvey's film refers to a single exemplary figure, celebrated as a national hero. Like Robert Southey's 1813 *Life of
Nelson*, the film explicitly sets forth Nelson's career as a suitable inspirational
model. H. E. Marshall's *Our Island Story: A Child's History of England* tells stories of
the old country to the children of empire, 'lest we forget', and similarly appropri-
ates Southey's description of events and reported speech at Trafalgar. Admiral Sir
Robert Freemantle appears in Elvey's film as himself, recounting the history of the
naval fleet of the British Empire from King Alfred to the present via the Armada
and Napoleon, and offers a copy of Southey to a boy about to enter Osborne Naval
College. Nelson, the boy is told, showed indomitable spirit against all odds: 'And',
as a defender of freedom, 'to this very day, Nelson sweeps the seas', the epilogue
concludes.

Furthermore, Waugh reminds us that the past should be understood as the past,
distinctly unlike the present, even while we remain critical of the uses for which
a past may be invoked for present purposes. In his paradigmatic critique of
nineteenth-century Whig history, Herbert Butterfield suggests that the historian,

'instead of being moved to indignation by something in the past which at first seems alien and perhaps even wicked to our own day', should make 'the effort to bring this thing into a context where it appears natural . . . showing its relation to other things which we do understand' (Butterfield 1965: 17).

Much of Elvey's film is blatantly propagandistic, including images familiar from a variety of media during the First World War: a Teutonic gauntleted hand stretches out to seize a globe; Dreadnoughts are seen in action. Nelson was again invoked during the Second World War, with Robert Austin producing a series of posters resembling coloured woodcuts, including Pitt's 1804 speech concerning Britain's defence of its own safety and its example to other nations 'now bending under the iron yoke of tyranny' and Nelson's prayer on the eve of Trafalgar. Alexander Korda's *That Hamilton Woman* (USA, 1941), and Carol Reed's *The Young Mr Pitt* (1942) drew the 'obvious parallel between the taut political situation of 1793 and 1939 when England faced ambitious conquerors on the other side of the channel', and Reed similarly paraphrases Nelson's prayer and his letter to Emma Hamilton.[1] The theatre critic James Agate complained that the analogy of Then with Now 'is made clear to us with an almost unnecessary degree of insistence', with Napoleon haranguing the Paris populace in the film paralleling his modern prototype screaming: 'Must the enthusiastic crowd waiting outside number 10 Downing Street to welcome Pitt resemble so closely the crowds which cheered Mr Chamberlain in 1938?' (Agate 1942: 68).

According to the press book, *That Hamilton Woman* was Winston Churchill's favourite film.[2] As Waugh suggests, at a later date it may be all too easy to dismiss these images and the patriotic sentiments which they endorse. However, I intend here to discuss Elvey's film in a broader context of popular representations of Nelson's heroism in nineteenth- and twentieth-century history writing and iconography, indicating a more complicated and less immediate set of concerns than the bald term 'propaganda' might imply. Indeed, as Jacques Ellul has observed, propaganda tends to mobilise established notions rather than invent and impose new ones, frequently confirms rather than coerces, integrates rather than agitates; and as Foulkes adds, education can in some senses thus 'be seen as a pre-propagandist process through which facts are interpreted according to the symbols which express a group's collective ideas about its past and its future' (Ellul 1973: 15, 26; Foulkes 1983: 10). Furthermore, war remembered, as Patrick Wright observes, may have a 'quickening' effect, especially in subsequent times of war (Wright 1985: 24). The persistence of Nelson, as an heroic figure, resides in the conjunction of Romantic Individualism, Patriotic Duty and Historical Destiny; he epitomises both the 'manly virtues' extolled by Gibbon and the more 'feminine' qualities of tenderness and affection (Gibbon 1802: IV 144, 272).

I should also like to salvage the subsequent reputation of the film from Rachael Low's damnation of it as 'extremely primitive' (Higson 1995: 109; Low 1997: 238). Certainly Calthrop's make-up becomes increasingly crude as Nelson sinks into decrepitude. But the quantity of intertitles and the unintegrated iconography of which she complains serve, I shall contend, as particularly resonant quotations which reiterate a specific national history at a given moment. Given the recent debate of the status of Trafalgar Square as a memorial to historical heroes and proposals for an October bank holiday marking Nelson's demise, discussion of the 1919 commemorative film might seem particularly pertinent.

Like Elvey's hagiographic *The Life Story of Lloyd George* (1918), *Nelson* is episodic in structure, largely following Southey's chronology and chapter outlines: his humble birth in a Norfolk parsonage (used as a location for the film), his boyhood (including his enlisting with his uncle, his sickness, his fearless encounter with a polar bear); his excursion to the West Indies and meeting with his future wife in Jamaica; proceeding to his famous campaigns (the storming of Bastia, the fall of Calvi, the battles of St Vincent, the Nile and Copenhagen); alongside his personal struggle with infirmity, injury and decline and his successive professional and social promotion and accumulation of aristocratic titles and military honours, culminating in his apotheosis at Trafalgar (again, filmed aboard the *Victory* itself). The bronze reliefs at the base of Nelson's column in London are selectively devoted to the battles of St Vincent, the Nile ('I will take my turn with my brave fellows', says Nelson to the surgeon), Copenhagen and Trafalgar (where Nelson gives the famous signal 'England expects').

Nelson's column aggrandises its subject to heroic status and rouses the onlooker's soul by reference to Classical sources and precedent: the shaft and capital are copied from one of the Corinthian columns of the temple in Rome built by Augustus to Mars Ultor; the reliefs are cast from captured French cannon. Similarly, its Antique exemplar, Trajan's column in Rome, exhibits exact representations of the Dacian victories of its founder (Gibbon 1802: I 76).[3] At the time of the great French war, says Trevelyan, 'the comparison of the Roman Senate fighting Hannibal was in the mind of every educated man' (Trevelyan 1926: 579). Nelson dies a death which is not only good (the stoic resignation and self-possession of 'they've done for me at last, Hardy') but also ideal: at the supreme moment of catharsis, the death of the hero is amplified by the vanquishing of the foe; the agony of witnessing the death of the hero is coupled with the ecstasy of triumph. 'No boy', said Benjamin West, commenting on his own 1806 rendition of Nelson's death, 'would be animated by a representation of Nelson dying like an ordinary man. His feelings must be roused and his mind influenced by a scene great and extraordinary. A mere matter of fact will never produce the effect' (Abrams 1985: 206). But Nelson is celebrated as much for his relationship with the common man as for his position as an exceptional individual and for his defence of British mercantile interests (arguably war by other means) as he is celebrated as a military hero.

Like Elvey's *The Flag Lieutenant* (1926), the 1919 film is a composite of materials, comprising location and studio dramatised re-enactments of Nelson's life interspersed with Freemantle's reading with the boy, footage of battleships, model

Figure 2.1 Malvina Longfellow, former artists' model, poses as Emma, Lady Hamilton –
mistress of Nelson – in the *Bioscope*'s advertising supplement for *Nelson* (1919).
Source: BFI.

shots, animated diagrams, stylised mask shots (the view framed as if through a gun
hatch; a heart framing a view of the *Victory* to convey England's love of its hero),
cartouches presenting Nelson in the manner of Nelson memorabilia, overlaid
titles ('Will no one bring Hardy to me' and 'Thank God I have done my duty'
emanate from his own lips), inserts (a copy of Nelson's famous last letter to
Emma) and intertitles (conveying datelines, reported speech, commentary and
location; 'the position of the fleets at 1 p.m.' is inscribed as if on a school room
blackboard). Perhaps the execution and technique of the film failed to match its
ambition; perhaps the first version, destroyed in a fire before release, was more
carefully realised than its substitute, completed in less than seven weeks (Warren
1937: 123). Certainly it was well received by the trade press at the time: '*Nelson*
is one of the most spectacular, most artistic and one of the greatest British films
ever produced' says the reviewer for *The Kinematograph and Lantern Weekly*; the
Bioscope endorses *The Times* critic's recommendation of the film 'to every man,
woman and child of the Empire' (*The Kinematograph and Lantern Weekly* 1918: 54;
Bioscope 1919: 28).

Southey and Elvey are keen to stress the authenticity of their historical representations. Furthermore, Low Warren claims that Denis Calthrop (more so than
Cecil Hardwicke in 1926, Laurence Olivier in 1941 or Stephen Haggard in 1942)

bore a close physical resemblance to Nelson himself (Warren 1937: 123); and *The Kinematograph and Lantern Weekly* praised his impersonation of 'the great little Admiral' as 'one of the finest pieces of character acting the British screen has ever seen' (*KLW* 1918: 54). Permission was given by the navy for filming in Portsmouth and in the cockpit of the *Victory* (most of the guns, we are advised in an intertitle, are those actually used at Trafalgar) and Eliot Stannard's scenario was carefully vetted by Admiral Mark Kerr, 'Britain's most famous Admiral', who also provided a foreword to the film's souvenir programme:

> It is well for us all if we recall Nelson in our minds and to the minds of others at this time. It is still better if we never forget him, for he is the most shining example of patriotism in our history, as well as the most perfect embodiment of duty that the chronicles have given us. Patriotism cannot be dismissed as purely a sentiment, it is equally with duty a virtue and also a commercial asset; it is the spirit which binds the Empire together and makes it strong enough to keep its place in the world. It should be born in the home, thrive in the State, and reach its final growth in the Empire. In addition to Lord Nelson's work for the Empire, was the spirit he left in the Royal Navy, and it is to this spirit and his teachings of comradeship that we largely won our success in the Great War that has just been concluded.

The characterisation, costuming and composition of the shots of Nelson's death, as in *That Hamilton Woman*, seem to owe much to the epic paintings of West and especially of Arthur William Devis, who witnessed the actual event (Mitchell 1967: 269).[4] Southey cites diaries, reported speech frequently matched by Elvey's film, autographed letters (and reproduces Nelson's signature at various stages of his career, before and after the loss of his right arm) and official documents, to which he claims he was allowed privileged access. His *Life of Nelson* is dedicated to the Secretary of the Admiralty and is further authorised, one might contend, by Southey's own status as Poet Laureate from 1813. Broadley's and Bartlett's 1906 account of Trafalgar (authorised by the correspondence of Hardy, a selection of relics, navy lists of serving officers and a midshipman's 'remark book') and that of the Hubbacks (drawn from the letters between Jane Austen and her brothers) endorse the description and sentiments set out by Southey.[5] But whereas the reactionary Southey condemns Napoleon, 'the recreant Gaul' or 'perfidious Corsican', and the French in general in equal measure ('The French', he says, 'have never acted a generous part in the history of the world'), the later histories and the film versions of Nelson's life are more circumspect and discriminating. Southey is pleased to recount Nelson's own antagonism towards France but allows his differentiation between causes: 'I hate a Frenchman: they are equally objects of my detestation, whether royalists or republicans: in some points I believe the latter are the best' (Southey 1813: I 149).

Elvey's film, in the wake of the Franco-British wartime alliance, reduces Napoleonic France to a cipher in its opening allegorical sequence (the emperor appears as a medallion, swathed in the tricolour) then shows Napoleon strident in ten-gallon boots with his arms *like that* ordering the fleet to sea. Napoleon as a despotic tyrant is distinguished from France. The French high command is cut against the readily identifiable figures of Pitt and Wellington (in cockaded hat and boots). *The Young Mr Pitt* gives us a ghastly mob of ill-kempt *sans-culottes* and a silhouetted guillotine, the name of Napoleon is portentously presented but Talleyrand (Napoleon's sophisticated foreign minister) is shown as a Frenchman who recognises the threat which the Emperor's 'mad ambition' poses to the liberty of the European states, and warns the British government accordingly. Elvey devotes much space to Nelson's defence of Naples and the Neapolitan court against Imperial expansion.

England expects

In the century between the Battle of Trafalgar and *Nelson: The Story of England's Immortal Naval Hero*, significant moments in the history and the Nelson myth had been perpetuated in a variety of media: ballads (which Southey cites); verses by Tennyson, a later Poet Laureate, and others (which Marshall cites); textiles, ceramics, jewellery, paintings, prints, panoramas, lantern slides and stage performances.[6]

William Archer, in 1912, observed that theatre audiences were resistant to representations which challenged the received wisdom: 'Nero is bound to fiddle while Rome burns, or the audience will know the reason why . . . [an audience] wants to see Napoleon Napoleonising. For anomalies and uncharacteristic episodes in Napoleon's career we must go to books; the playhouse is not the place for them' (Archer 1912: 192). At the launch of *Nelson* in 1919, the Alhambra Theatre in London greeted diplomats from the Allied nations and representatives of the Admiralty and the American navy with bunting, and flags signalled Nelson's message, 'England expects that every man shall do his duty', conveyed as an animated intertitle in the film itself. Mark Kerr, it may be noted, makes no distinction between England and the British Empire. Elvey recounts the familiar tale of the Battle of the Nile, with Nelson insisting that the surgeon attend first to those more critically injured than himself and remaining on deck in spite of a serious wound to his forehead, and couples this with a boy reciting Felicia Hemans's infamous (and often lampooned) *Casabianca*, 'The boy stood on the burning deck . . .'. For the honour of England, Nelson orders that the drowning men from the decimated foreign fleet be saved. Having held fire on the *Redoubtable* it is from this ship which the fateful shot is fired at Trafalgar. Nelson's superior humanity is shown in the generosity which he extends to the enemy.

Elvey's film invokes common knowledge of events and draws upon the usual repertoire of images but also employs an awareness of familiarity in its use of foreshadowing and presentiment. Before Trafalgar, Napoleon comments upon the withering of flower petals as an omen of disaster: 'We dare not risk fighting Nelson again', says a French admiral. Napoleon, echoing Nelson's trepidation before battle, declares portentously: 'We need not fear – he will not take to the sea again.' Elvey's film, like Southey, uses historical foreshadowing in its emplotment of events. As a child, Nelson is seen to be fearless (eagerly ascending to the top of a very tall tree: 'the boys said I was afraid to go so high') and is shown boldly fighting a polar bear (here rendered pantomimically with sheets and tea chests serving as arctic rocks): '"Sir," said he', when reprimanded by the Captain for his trespass, 'pouting his lip, as he was wont to do when agitated, "I wished to kill the bear, that I might carry the skin to my father"' (Southey 1813: I 16). 'That encounter', Arthur Mee's *Children's Encyclopedia* informs us, 'was a forecast of all Nelson's seafaring life. Whatever the odds he advanced to the attack, and not only did he know no fear, but had the power of inspiring others with his own bravery' (Mee 1925: 143). At school, as in Abel Gance's *Napoleon* (France, 1927), the boy is seen to be father to the man, displaying the qualities of bravery and decisive leadership by which his later career will be distinguished: 'Nelson's first appearance as an Admiral' is witnessed in the dormitory, where he dons a paper cocked hat and puts a rolled tube card telescope to his eye. Returning home in 1776, stricken with malaria, the weakly Horatio falls delirious and 'sees his future greatness predicted' in visions of Alfred, Drake and Boadicea. A radiant orb flickers across the screen, 'suspended in his mind's eye', as Southey says, bearing with it 'a prophetic glory' (Southey 1813: 23). Linda Colley describes Nelson's own memoir of these events as 'a blend of euphoric bravery and beguiling egotism' (Colley 1992: 182):

> After a long and gloomy reverie, in which I almost wished myself overboard, a sudden glow of patriotism was kindled within me and presented my king and country as my patron. Well then I will be a hero! and confiding in Providence will brave every danger!
>
> (Southey 1813: 23)

However, Nelson fulfils not only his individual destiny but is made to answer a pattern of national encounters with adversaries, his own littleness and frailty (like that of Pitt) corresponding to the inferior number of British troops (so at Agincourt, so at Trafalgar, so at the River Plate) and to the smallness of the island which dares to resist conquest from the Continent. 'When Lord Nelson was passing over the quay at Yarmouth, to take possession of the ship to which he had been appointed', says Hazlitt, 'the people exclaimed, "Why make that little fellow a captain?" He thought of this when he fought the battles of the Nile and Trafalgar'. The same sense of personal insignificance which made this naval commander great in action, says Hazlitt (for whom Napoleon was a yet greater hero), made him a fool in love

Ah where, & ah where, is my gallant Sailor gone?   } DIDO, in Despair! { Hes gone to fight ỹ Frenchmen, t'loose t'other Arm & Eye.
He's gone to Fight the Frenchmen, for George upon the Throne.   And left me with the old Antique, to lay me down & Cry.

Figure 2.2 Emma, Lady Hamilton, formerly famous for her 'Classical' attitudes and as
         artists' model to Reynolds and Romney, pictured by James Gillray in 1801 as
         Dido in Despair.

Source: Courtesy of the Trustees of the British Museum.

Summers's 1926 film, the *Bioscope* tells us, 'merely touches upon' the complica-
tions of Nelson's private life (*Bioscope* 1926: 29). Elvey is understandably circumspect in his representation of the *ménage* for fear of compromising Nelson's
exemplary image. Certainly he is shown to be more saintly than the historical
record warrants and the illegitimacy of his 'adopted' daughter Horatia (for whose
welfare he is concerned in his final testament) passes unmentioned.

  Low Warren says that 'even the greatest propaganda picture would not be
complete without a touch of romance' and that therefore the historical figure of
Lady Hamilton was introduced as a participator in Nelson's joys and sorrows.
Korda casts Lady Nelson as acidic and dowdy opposite Vivien Leigh's glamorous
and sumptuously costumed Emma. In both films, Emma is seen to be a more
entertaining companion, revelling in Nelson's celebrity and playfully mimicking
his adventures by holding a mock telescope to a mock blind eye. In 1919, Elvey
explains Nelson's separation from his wife with a long intertitle: 'like most men of
his generation, Nelson craved for a warm-hearted appreciative response. Unfortunately his wife lacked the power to supply this . . .', contrasting this with Emma's
'impulsive and sympathetic heart', 'deeply affected [by] The Scarred Sailor . . .
how different from when she saw him last'. On his deathbed at Merton, William

Hamilton lays his hand over those of Emma and Horatio as if blessing their union; Nelson is, he says, quoting from Southey, 'the most loyal and truly brave character I have ever known'. But both *Nelson* and *That Hamilton Woman* present Horatio as the focus of romantic interest as much as Emma. Elvey locates the *Victory* at 'The Heart of England', framing the shot in a heart-shaped mask. Korda structures his film as a flashback, opening with a now destitute Emma, forsaken by England, looking back upon her more glorious past, and closing with Emma's collapse as she hears of Nelson's death: ultimately it is his story rather than hers.

Elvey's introduction of Lady Hamilton allows *Nelson* to adopt some of the characteristics of the costume film, matching such releases of the early 1920s as Elvey's *Bleak House* (1920), *Bonnie Prince Charlie* (C. C. Calvert, 1923), *Flames of Passion* (Graham Cutts, 1922) and *Young Lochinvar* (Will Kellino, 1923). High-brow snobbery against British costume productions was especially directed in the late 1920s against the popular success *Nell Gwynne* (Herbert Wilcox, 1926). In an Early editorial for *Close-Up*, Norman McPherson vent forth. The limited sensibility and narrow grounds of his disapproval are now commonplace:

> Then I ask you to think of Nell Gwynne, that bright and glittering specimen of culture and good breeding. Here, as accurate as the Georgian panelling our eye could not miss, we learn that the inimitable Nell entered State Banquets by sliding down the banisters at the moment when dessert was served, would jazz to where her monarch fed beside a Lady Castlemaine that none but a British censor could unblushingly permit and tossing herself athwart the Royal table, think of something bright and girlish, such as pulling his moustache or throwing a rotten plum at a nobleman. Now, films like this must be excessively harmful.
>
> (McPherson 1927: 12)

Where Elvey shows Nelson accompanied by a bulldog at his heel, Emma is attributed with a King Charles spaniel. Malvina Longfellow's profile is shown to good advantage in a picture hat of the style later to be adopted as the Gainsborough company logo. The Queen of Naples's bosom plims and falls appropriately with her growing anxiety at the threat of invasion and her husband's apparent incapacity to avert disaster; Emma displays a cleavage into which, inevitably, folded letters are deposited . . .

'Though God knows I need rest'

As Admiral Kerr's programme note reminds the audience in 1919, patriotism consists not only in a nation's conduct in external political affairs but is 'born in the home', grounded in the sentiments prompted by locality and the domestic. *The Kinematograph Weekly* review claims that Elvey 'spared no pains to find settings that for sheer beauty could surely not be equalled throughout the rest of England', in selecting his location for Merton, the house which Nelson bought for himself and the Hamiltons in 1801. Elvey shows him returning intermittently between campaigns. Nelson and Emma are seen walking their dogs down a long avenue of trees, across well-groomed lawns, among orderly flower-beds. British Imperial patriotism is here identified with an idiosyncratically English view of the domestic picturesque: Emma reads Nelson's last letter at a leaded window inset with a heraldic crest. Merton is all ease and tranquillity: as Nelson and Emma pause on the ornamental bridge over the lake, their figures are mirrored in the completely still water. Merton is both peace and beauty. When Napoleon orders his fleet to sea, Nelson knows that he must leave again, though he would sooner stay and fondly longs for the day when he might return and remain. 'England calls. Can you be ready in three days?' Pitt asks Nelson; 'I am ready now, Sir', he replies. Emma is distraught, torn by conflicting emotions, falling to her knees and clutching him to her. She is fearful of the fate which she anticipates but recognises the call of duty and glory which Nelson must obey.

Poor Parker

Southey remarked in a letter soon after Trafalgar: 'You will have heard of Nelson's most glorious death. The feeling it occasioned is highly honourable to the country' (Dennis 1894: 178). Francis Austen wrote to his sister to inform her of the tragedy. The nation's hero 'only lived long enough to know his fleet successful':

> In a public point of view I consider his loss as the greatest which could have occurred; nor do I hesitate to say there is not an Admiral on the list so calculated for command of a fleet as he was. I never heard of his equal, nor do I expect again to see such a man. To the soundest judgement he united prompt decision and the speedy execution of his plans; and he possessed in a superior degree the happy talent of making every class of persons pleased with their situation and eager to exert themselves in forwarding the public service.
>
> (Hubback 1906: 156)

Southey and A. L. Rowse dub Nelson 'the darling' of England and for Trevelyan his 'is the best loved name in English ears' (Southey 1813 II: 232; Rowse 1944: 15; Trevelyan 1926: 578). Marshall quotes Tennyson: 'This island loves thee well, thou famous man/The greatest sailor since our world began' (Marshall 1905: 453). Southey and subsequent historians recount anecdotes which testify to Nelson's affection for and loyalty to individual officers. Captain Parker, his leg having been shattered, was mourned deeply:

I beg that his hair may be cut off and given me; it shall be buried in my grave. Poor Mr Parker! What a son has he lost! If I were to say I was content I should lie; but I shall endeavour to submit with all the fortitude in my power. His loss has made a wound in my heart, which time will hardly heal.

(Southey 1813 II: 177, 254; Trevelyan 1926: 578)

Mee says that Collingwood always remained 'a hero to his valet' (Mee 1933: 1049). Elvey has Nelson's servant confronting his master after the loss of his arm: 'You ain't never going to die, Sir', he says, wiping a tear from his eye; 'I couldn't bear it'. Nelson is deemed a hero as much for his kindness as for his wisdom as a strategist and bravery as a warrior 'ever in the forefront of battle'. From his percentage of the spoils which he plundered, Nelson amassed great personal wealth but was extravagant and gave generously. Reputedly, he ensured that his men received their just rewards from the Admiralty. 'But he loved his men better than honours', Elvey tells us; 'Roll call after battle: Nelson's concern was always for his gallant men' and the admiral is shown visiting the wounded below deck. Nelson is seen to be a leader of men but in his affinity with the men is simultaneously one of them. Elvey effectively dramatises the comparison by showing a sailor in the cockpit expiring as victory is announced and immediately prior to Nelson himself. Nelson, as a hero, was thus distinguished from Wellington:

There is more in our relation to him than can be accounted for by his genius and our obligation. For Marlborough was unpopular and there was an element of fear in the respect and admiration felt for the Iron Duke. Indeed, Wellington's complete devotion to public service was rooted in a noble but not very lovable aristocratic pride, which made him live reserved as a man apart, saving him indeed from the mistakes and loss of dignity into which Nelson sometimes fell on shore. But Nelson entered straight into the common heart of humanity.

(Trevelyan 1926: 578)

Furthermore, the emphasis on Nelson's humble origins and the personal odds which he overcame, suggest that such heroism is is a worthy ambition for anybody. As the Osborne College recruits finish reading Southey, one declares, 'There will never be another hero like Nelson'; but an intertitle interjects, 'What about Jack Cornwell?' and we are shown the man who has answered the call, standing between the guns on a modern battleship, directly addressing the camera.

Ecce Homo (Behold the Man)

In recent years, there have been a number of proposals for the fourth corner of Trafalgar Square, empty since inauguration in 1841. The plinth is currently occupied by Bill Woodrow's bronze *Regardless of History*, showing a head crushed by a book, held by a leafless tree. Rachel Whiteread, characteristically, suggested the inverted transparent shell of the plinth itself, thereby questioning, possibly subverting, the elevation of individuals to heroic status; perhaps there is nothing or no one now worth elevating. For the passer-by at street-level, it should be said, Nelson the man is less immediately apparent than the colossal column and bell on which he perches and Landseer's bronze lions couchant which defend the sealord's honour. From July 1999 to January 2000, Mark Wallinger presented a figure of Christ, cast in white marble resin from life from the body of a friend. Indicating the proximity of both the National Gallery and South Africa House, Wallinger himself said that the sculpture celebrated Jesus 'not as a deity but as a political leader of an oppressed people. He hoped that the public would see the sculpture as a symbol of the pain of the recent past with its record of religious and racial intolerance' (Strong 1999: 27; MacGregor 2000: 194).

Controversy over the work divided between critics questioning its religious propriety and those who claimed that this life-size figure, standing on the plinth with the trepidation of a swimmer on the edge of the top diving-board, was somehow unsuitable for the pomp and grandeur of its location. Sir Roy Strong, former director of the Victoria and Albert Museum, complained that 'only people totally ignorant of the square's very definite theme could have chosen something so glaringly inappropriate' (Strong 1999). However, the celebration of the humanity of Christ is nothing new. Both the Classicist Gibbon and the Romantic Hazlitt promoted this re-evaluation of a historic individual. Gibbon finds most exemplary 'His mild constancy in the midst of cruel and voluntary sufferings, his universal benevolence, and the sublime simplicity of his actions and character' (Gibbon 1802: II 392). For Hazlitt:

> [Leaving religious faith quite out of the question], there is something in the character of Christ of more sweetness and majesty, and more likely to work a change in the mind of man, by the contemplation of its idea alone, than any to be found in history, whether actual or feigned. This character is that of a sublime humanity, such as was never seen on earth before, nor since.
>
> (Hazlitt 1970: 411)

Meanwhile, there have been attempts to supply a more authentic representation of the physiognomy of the 'real' Jesus, based on archaeological data and advanced forensic techniques.

What seems most significant to me is that all the proposals for a new companion for Nelson have engaged with questions of humanist and political value, with expectations of history and the heroism displayed by the square's resident statuary; they have all responded to a sense of place, albeit not in a manner designed to secure universal approval. All the proposals, but especially Wallinger's *Ecce Homo*,

I think, urge a public appraisal of the values which the statues and the site embody. It may be too complacent to deride, and simply ignorant to deny, this history, but perhaps this figure will prompt a timely re-examination of just what we choose to remember and what sentiments and virtues we commemorate when we render heroes immortal.

Acknowledgements

With thanks to Rina Prentice, National Maritime Museum, Greenwich; Henrietta Sitwell, Royal Society of Arts; Hugo Chapman, British Museum; Tim Wilson, Ashmolean Museum Oxford.

Notes

1 Robert Donat archive, John Rylands Library, Manchester; cuttings book 4: *Los Angeles Daily News*, 25 March 1943.
2 *That Hamilton Woman* press book, British Film Institute Special Materials collection.
3 Likewise, Jacques Gondoin's Vendôme column in Paris, commissioned by Napoleon to glorify the campaigns of 1805–7, is styled after Trajan's column and bears reliefs made from the metal of Russian and Austrian cannon.
4 Mitchell notes West's change of location from the cockpit to the deck in spite of his familiarity with the primary evidence of Devis and of Beatty's 1807 *Authentic Narrative of the Death of Lord Nelson*; Mitchell reports that Nelson himself imagined his death portrayed by West.
5 Such logbooks are now the source material for popular historical research into the lives of the lower ranks on board: see *Teaching History*, July 1991: 4.
6 For Trafalgar panoramas see *Panoramania!* (Hyde 1988: 66). For stage presentations of sea battles (including celebration of the British Navy's legendary founder, King Alfred) see *Garrick and de Loutherbourg* (Bough 1990: 31). For paintings and a vast collection of memorabilia, see the Nelson display at the National Maritime Museum in Greenwich and de Loutherbourg's *Battle of the Nile* in Tate Britain. The Victoria and Albert Museum, London, and the Ashmolean Museum in Oxford both have examples of mourning rings and other Nelson commemorative jewellery.
7 *That Hamilton Woman* conspicuously uses the Romney portraits and Emma's 'attitudes' (showing her posing in Greek drapery) and suggests that Sir William acquired her as his wife merely as a beautiful object, to add to his extensive collection of Antique treasures.

Bibliography

Abrams, A. (1985) *The Valiant Hero: Benjamin West and Grand-Style History Painting*, Washington, DC: Smithsonian Institute Press.
Agate, J. (1942) 'Myself at the picture', *Tatler and Bystander*, 15 July 1942.
Archer, W. (1912) *Play-Making*, London: Chapman and Hall.
Bioscope (1919) '———' [review of *Nelson*], 30 January 1919: 28.
—— (1926) '———', [review of *Nelson*], 23 September 1926: 29.
Bough, C. (1990) *Garrick and de Loutherbourg*, Cambridge: Chadwyck-Healey.

Broadley, A. M. and Bartlett, R. G. (1906) *The Three Dorset Captains at Trafalgar*, London: John Murray.

Butterfield, H. (1965) *The Whig Interpretation of History* [1931], New York: W.W. Norton.

Churchill, W. (1957) *A History of the English-Speaking People* III, London: Cassell.

Colley, L. (1992) *Britons: Forging the Nation, 1707–1837*, London: Pimlico.

Dennis, J. (1894) *Robert Southey: The Story of His Life Written in His Letters*, London: George Bell.

Ellul, J. (1973) *Propaganda: The Formation of Men's Attitudes*, translated by Konrad Kellen and Jean Lerner, New York: Alfred A. Knopf.

Foulkes, A. P. (1983) *Literature and Propaganda*, London: Methuen.

Gibbon, E. (1802) *The History of the Decline and Fall of the Roman Empire* [1776], London: Cadell and Davies.

Hazlitt, W. (1970) 'The Indian Jugglers' [1821]; 'On Different Sorts of Fame' [1817]; 'Jesus Christ' [1820], all in Ronald Blythe (ed.) *William Hazlitt: Selected Writings*, Harmondsworth: Penguin.

Higson, A. (1995) 'The victorious re-cycling of national history: *Nelson*' in K. Dibbets and B. Hogenkamp (eds) *Film and the First World War*, Amsterdam: Amsterdam University Press: 108–15.

Hubback, J. H. and Hubback, E. C. (1906) *Jane Austen's Sailor Brothers*, London: John Lane.

Hyde, R. (1988) *Panoramania!* London: Trefoil.

The Kinematograph and Lantern Weekly (1918) [review of *Nelson*] 26 December 1918: 54.

Langford, P. (2000) *Englishness Identified*, Oxford: Oxford University Press.

Low, R. (1997) *The History of the British Film* IV, London: Routledge.

Macaulay, T. B. (1977) *Napoleon and the Restoration of the Bourbons* [1831], (ed.) Joseph Hamburger, London: Longman.

MacGregor, N. (2000) *The Image of Christ*, London: National Gallery.

McPherson, N. (1927) editorial comment, *Close-Up* 3: 12.

Marshall, H. E. (1905) *Our Island Story: A Child's History of England*, London: T. C. and E. C. Jack.

Mee, A. (1925) *The Children's Encyclopedia*, London: The Educational Book Co.

Mee, A. (1933) *Arthur Mee's 1000 Heroes* II, London: Amalgamated Press.

Mitchell, C. (1967) 'Benjamin West's *Death of Nelson*' in Douglas Fraser, Howard Hibbard and Milton J. Lewine (eds) *Essays Presented to Rudolf Wittkower*, London: Phaidon.

Rowse, A. L. (1944) *The English Spirit: Essays in History and Literature*, London: Macmillan.

Sellar, W. C. and Yeatman, R. J. (1963) *1066 and All That* [1930], London: Methuen.

Southey, R. (1813) *Life of Nelson*, London: John Murray.

Strong, R. (1999) 'Is this a fitting place for a statue of Jesus Christ? Sir Roy Strong gives his verdict', *Daily Mail*, 22 July 1999: 27.

Trevelyan, G. M. (1926) *History of England*, London: Longmans, Green and Co.

Warren, L. (1937) *The Film Game*, London: T. Werner Laurie.

Waugh, E. (1964) *A Little Learning*, London: Chapman and Hall.

Wright, P. (1985) *On Living in an Old Country*, London: Verso.

3 Death or glory?

The Great War in British film

Alan Burton

'Perhaps it is the protest of the old that will bring things to an end.'

Captain Rivers, *Regeneration* (1997)

The inscription on the Victory Medal, issued in Britain soon after the war of 1914–18 in Europe had ended, provided the official view of its meaning: it had been 'The Great War for Civilisation'. Alternative interpretations had emerged, however, during the course of the war, such as that expressed in *Counter Attack* (1918), a book of war poems by a young infantry officer, Siegfried Sassoon. In a further brave and notorious outburst, Sassoon criticised the conduct and purpose of the war in a document drawn up with Bertrand Russell and Middleton Murray. This was published in *The Times* and the *Daily Mail* in July 1917 and led the authorities to question Sassoon's mental state (Hynes 1990: 174–5).

Cultural historian Samuel Hynes has shown in great detail how British artists of the time struggled to 'imagine' the awesome nature of total war; and how by the late 1920s the British literary elite – through memoirs, novels and, perhaps above all else, poetry – promoted a view of the conflict as wholly traumatic and catastrophic (Hynes 1990). Sassoon, for example, wrote of the 'veritable gloom and disaster of the thing called Armageddon . . . a dreadful place, a place of horror and desolation which no *imagination* could have invented' (quoted in Warner 1979: 42, emphasis added). The terrible suffering and privations endured by the soldiers and the unparalleled number of British casualties – the war left 750,000 British military dead and over one million ex-servicemen in receipt of post-war disability pensions – prompted some commentators to grasp for Biblical metaphors and invoke apocalyptic rhetoric to help them to conceive of and convey the conflict's horrific scale. While Sassoon invoked the terrors of Armageddon to bring his experiences to the public, for others, the shattering impact of the war was expressed in the popular epithet 'The Deluge' (Marwick 1965). For the ordinary soldier, many of whom condemned the intense fighting of the Western Front in the harshest terms, to be called back into a major battle was – in the documented words of one private, Jack Sweeny – little short of a return to 'Hell' (quoted in Brown 1978: 125).[1]

More than eight decades after the conflict, it has become enshrined in popular memory that the sacrifice of the Great War was futile, that ordinary soldiers were considered expendable by incompetent senior officers, with the conflict encapsulated in the terrible experience of the rat-infested trenches (Fussell 1975). However, it should be borne in mind that this viewpoint stands in contrast to an entrenched tradition of memorialising and remembrance that seeks to validate the sacrifices of the Great War. In a further, recent, elaboration, revisionist historians have gone a long way towards challenging some of the myths: arguing for the necessity of the war; acknowledging the skill that the British Army eventually brought to the conduct of modern industrialised warfare; and finding little evidence that large numbers of soldiers became disillusioned during the war itself. Indeed, one military historian has recently reassessed the Allied offensive of 1918 as 'the greatest victory in British military history' (Sheffield 1996: 60).

This 'new history' has been prompted by the professional concerns of empirical historians, and generally cannot be explained in terms of an ideological agenda motivated by a patriotic or militaristic bias. The desire has been to replace myth with 'good' history, while acknowledging that for many servicemen, including many who served with distinction, the experience of the war could be terrible and traumatic. There is a considerable disjuncture, then, between the 'cultural' historical perspective on the Great War – which has privileged the voices of a dissident officer class as expressed through elite literary forms – and the revised politico-military perspective. As G. D. Sheffield has recently concluded: 'At bottom, the media obsession with a handful of unrepresentative soldiers reflects the fact that British perceptions of the First World War too often stem from literary rather than historical sources' (Sheffield 1996: 65). A third historiographical strand concentrates on the experiential dimension of the Great War. Here, historians seek to give voice to the ordinary soldier and acknowledge his service on the front line (Brown 1978; Winter 1979) – again, in contrast to the 'cultural' history's elite emphasis.

This essay seeks to consider how British films have approached the Great War, how they have 'imagined' for popular audiences the meaning of the terrible conflagration, and how they have set about representing that experience through cinematic and narrational techniques. Film historian Michael Paris has noted popular culture's often ambiguous treatment of the First World War, where we are as likely as not to find justification for the great sacrifice made, and this presented in heroic terms. The treatment of the war in popular histories and *Boy's Own* adventures contrasted with that found in high literary mediations. These popular forms clearly served a social and psychological need for a nation coming to terms with its loss;[2] but they were never allowed the latitude of expression accorded to elite forms. This was nowhere more evident than in the commercial cinema, which had to conform to the strictures of a censorship code that promoted a patriotic out-look and denied an honest treatment of tragic loss in the war (Paris 1999).

The first British films to deal with the war typically voiced little criticism. Maurice Elvey's *Comradeship* (1919), for example – a traditional tale of a British soldier doing his duty – has none of the haunting, accusative qualities of Abel Gance's contemporaneous, pacifist *J'Accuse* (France, 1919). The 'official' British version of the war was best expressed by a series of popular war reconstructions produced by H. Bruce Woolfe for British Instructional Films during the 1920s. These included *The Battle of Jutland* (1921), *Ypres* (1925), *Mons* (1926) and *The Battles of the Coronel and Falkland Islands* (1927), productions which celebrated British military acumen and, according to one reviewer, saw war as 'an elaborate and permissible [boys'] adventure' (Bryher, *Close-Up*, July 1927, quoted in Kelly 1997a: 62). Some protest was raised against the pro-war sentiments of such films, as with the campaign against war pictures mounted by the Women's International League in the late 1920s. In Britain, the protest was joined by the Women's Co-operative Guild, which passed a resolution in 1928 condemning 'the large number of films glorifying war'.[3]

Some First World War films of the 1920s did court controversy. Most notably Herbert Wilcox's *Dawn* (1928), the story of Nurse Edith Cavell – shot by the Germans as a spy – which ran into difficulties with the British Board of Film Censors and censors in other nations over questions of diplomatic relations and good taste (Robertson 1984: 15–28). However, such films nevertheless singularly lacked the critical perspective of the war literature. A more ambivalent treatment of the war was offered by the celebrated film adaptation of R. C. Sherriff's play *Journey's End* (James Whale, USA/UK, 1930). The release of this early talkie co-incided with several other important films critical of the war, notably *All Quiet on the Western Front* (Lewis Milestone, USA, 1930) and *Westfront 1918* (G. W. Pabst, Germany, 1930). These, however, expressed much clearer anti-war sentiments.

While Whale's *Journey's End*, perhaps uniquely for the time, established the iconography – and introduced the sounds – of trench life, it also typified the class bias of British cinema of the period. There was, of course, a wider cultural tend-ency to reflect the experience of the Great War through the officer class. The war poets were all commissioned servicemen, and R. C. Sherriff was invalided out of the army after the Battle of Ypres in 1917 with the rank of captain. In both play and film, the emphasis was on officers nobly enduring the responsibilities, futility and horrors of war. Contemporary reviewers praised the film, and some later critics have sensed an anti-war message in its portrayal of war as hell (see Kelly 1997a: 65–75).

However, *Journey's End*'s protagonist Stanhope (Colin Clive), the senior officer in a front-line dugout, a shattered man taken to drink, is more concerned with his own personal failings than with articulating a wider condemnation of the war. What is centrally at stake in the film is the officer's fitness for duty – a duty that is never fundamentally called into question. While some popular cinema of the time could articulate a 'war is hell' philosophy and reveal the danger and stress of combat, this never contradicted an acceptance of the war as necessary. In this respect, it is interesting to note telling similarities between the fictional Stanhope and the real-life Sassoon: Stanhope, like Sassoon, becomes increasingly frustrated by the war, and is similarly awarded the Military Cross for gallantry. However, where Sassoon rebelled (throwing his Military Cross into the Mersey), his fictional counterpart stoically endures and does his duty until release in heroic death.[4]

Like Stanhope, Edgar Doe (Carl Harbord), the young officer protagonist of *Tell England* (Anthony Asquith/Geoffrey Barkas, 1931 – another British Instructional production), finds his nerves shattered and relies on drink to get through. He too recovers his purpose and is fatally wounded in an attack against Turkish mortars in the costly Dardanelles campaign. As in *Journey's End*, the *mise-en-scène* and dialogue offer a powerful evocation of the dirt, pain and carnage of First World War combat, again narrated through the experience of the officer class. One significant scene questions the very sentiment of the couplet cited in the film's title ('Tell England, ye who pass this monument/We died for her, and here we rest content' – originally a memorial inscription to soldiers who fell in the Boer War, and itself derived from an Ancient Greek tribute to the heroic Spartans at Thermopylae). Doe, in anguish, cries three times: 'This is what I'd like to tell England!' His outcry is followed by a montage of stark images of battle and death, a strategy which, as Andrew Kelly observes, contradicts an easy dismissal of the film as simplistically patriotic (Kelly 1997a: 76). Ultimately, though, *Tell England* extols the British class system: if modern war is unpleasant, young gentlemen, forged in the public schools, can nonetheless be counted upon to make the ultimate sacrifice and do their duty.

Australian scholar W. D. Routt criticises *Tell England* as 'a compounded act of disinheritance' in its effacement of the Australasian contribution to the campaign (Routt 1994: 66). He also offers a more complex interpretation of the film than previous critics who tended to read the film monolithically in terms of patriotism and duty. Instead, Routt alerts us to the film's 'multiple expositions', characterising it as simultaneously 'artistic, committed, sexy, evil' (Routt 1994: 67–8) – self-consciously artistic, ambiguous in its treatment of moral issues arising out of the war, and resplendent with 'improper' sexual and familial subtexts. Routt's evaluation serves as a warning not to dismiss all of the early Great War films as simple and naïve in their depiction of repression among their upper-class officers. In this connection, it is worth noting that the best-selling 1922 source novel by E. Raymond has been assessed by Malcolm Smith as 'a homo-erotic celebration of middle-class English youth' (Smith 1995: 181) and that the film's director Asquith was gay. Indeed, a number of cultural historians have now come to see the war principally in terms of masculine duty and sexuality, two issues but part of a continuing discourse on art and national identity (Smith 1995: 178).

Following the Second World War, British cinema's narratives of the Great War became more complex and challenging, explicitly adopting the 'multiple expositions' that had, perhaps tentatively, informed *Tell England*. One important reason for this was the nature and meaning of the more recently fought conflict. The justification for Britain's engagement in the Second World War was never questioned as it had been in the case of the earlier war: few within the Western democracies doubted that fundamental values of civilisation had been at stake. The national cinema of the 1950s celebrated the Second World War as 'Britain's finest hour'. This was mythologised in terms which stressed the quiet heroism of the Army, Royal Navy and Royal Air Force (although still predominantly in terms of the officer class) in such films as *The Dam Busters* (Michael Anderson, 1954) and *The Cruel Sea* (Charles Frend, 1953). If filmmakers wanted to challenge war, then it was necessary to do so in relation to a more distant conflict – and few were more suited than the Great War, around which such a potent myth of futility and waste had developed. Four post-1945 films speak eloquently of that myth and at least one of them stands as a masterpiece of anti-war cinema. It is with such films that British cinema began to conform more obviously with aspects of the dominant 'cultural' view of the First World War and in some measure aid the consolidation of the myth. The remainder of this essay will consider four key British films of the Great War from two contrasting decades – *King and Country* (Joseph Losey, 1964), *Oh! What a Lovely War* (Richard Attenborough, 1969), *Regeneration* (Gillies MacKinnon, UK/Canada, 1997) and *The Trench* (William Boyd, UK/France, 1999) – and the ways in which they imagine the conflict.

There are considerable aesthetic differences between the pair of films produced in the 1960s and the two produced in the 1990s. Both *King and Country* and *Oh! What a Lovely War* are more stylistically and narratively complex than the later films and their formal qualities form a crucial part of their meditation on the conflict. Joseph Losey directed *King and Country* shortly after the critical success of *The Servant* (1963), and produced another intimate and claustrophobic drama. The film's 'richly anticipatory' prologue (Palmer and Riley 1993: 23) and extensive use of non-diegetic cut-ins contribute to a complex narration in which an authorial concern with hypocrisy and injustice are firmly established. The opening sequence juxtaposes details of monuments memorialising the dead of the Great War: a bronze figure of Peace descending (on the Wellington Arch at Hyde Park in London), the Royal Artillery Monument, and a detail from that monument – the boots of a soldier. But as the scene cuts to documentary photographs of the carnage of the war, it becomes clear that the intent is not honorific but ironic and belongs to an anti-monumentalising tradition: what is being depicted is brutal, not noble.

The original release prints of *King and Country* were sepia-tinted to give the visual quality of old photographs, and the film clearly interrogates the tensions between history and memory, representation and lived reality. Memorialising symbols – the rhetorical expression of the crudest official historical discourse – are juxtaposed with the harshest experiential evidence: documentary images depicting the terrible experience of the Western Front. The process of representation is revealed for what it is, and its character exposed for interrogation. In keeping with his Brechtian sensibilities, Losey continues throughout the film to punctuate the narrative with non-diegetic inserts or images of ambiguous diegetic motivation. The final documentary image of the opening sequence, a skeleton half-embedded in the mud, dissolves into a compositionally similar shot of Corporal Hamp (Tom Courtenay), the film's fictional protagonist who is awaiting trial for desertion: a shot transition which unambiguously signals Hamp's eventual fate.

Critics have observed that the mood of *King and Country* is 'reminiscent of the poignance and passion of the war poems' (Palmer and Riley 1993: 23). In its recourse to distressing historic photographs, the film makes a further connection with a particular war poet, Wilfred Owen. Pat Barker, from whose novel the film *Regeneration* was adapted, has declared herself fascinated by allegations that Owen procured photographs of the horrors of the trenches, kept these in his tunic pocket, and showed them to acquaintances (quoted in Sinker 1997: 24). For both Owen and Losey, the fiction film and poetry were perhaps inadequate forms in themselves to express the true character of the Great War. Both, therefore, in different ways, invoked the photographic documentary image to bring consciousness – their own, and that of those confronted by the images – into a more direct contact with the awfulness of the war.

The centrepiece of *King and Country* is the military trial and execution of Hamp, a volunteer soldier who has been on the Western Front for three years and, in desperation and confusion, 'decides to walk home'. His defence is conducted by Major Hargreaves (Dirk Bogarde), a typically Loseyan character who is forced to confront a complex moral crisis. Initially, Hargreaves concedes that the accused lacked backbone: 'And what does one do with a dog that has broken its back? Shoot it.' However, he comes to form a more complex appreciation of duty, one that embraces a responsibility to traumatised soldiers like Hamp, who have had close colleagues blown up over them and been dragged, near-drowned, out of the all-enveloping mud of the trenches. Hamp simply tells the defending officer that the experience of combat is 'worse than anything'.

At the conclusion of the trial, the articulate Hargreaves attempts to find justification for the war, arguing to the officers of the Court Martial that the fight is on behalf of humanity, and that it is their moral duty to express justice if not to pronounce the law in the case. The Colonel presiding (Peter Copley) casually dismisses this reasoning as a 'matter of opinion'. For the officers of the Court Martial, the trial is nothing more than a technical legal procedure in which Hargreaves's moral and humanitarian concerns have no place, and the prosecuting officer Captain Midgely (James Villiers) later rebukes Hargreaves for what he considers an unprofessional defence. During all of this Hamp says very little, and

Figure 3.1 Issues of class and conflicting notions of duty: Major Hargreaves (Dirk Bogarde) defends Corporal Hamp (Tom Courtenay), on trial for desertion, in the tense Court Martial at the centre of *King and Country* (1964).

Source: British Cinema and Television Research Group archive, De Montfort University (BHE).

when he does his naïveté tends to incriminate him further. He is effectively outside the dialogue taking place over him and around him, a near-silent bystander in the elaborate charade that will inexorably bring his execution as a tonic to stiffen the resolve of his fellow infantrymen. The Colonel then arrogantly details Hamp's own junior officer, Lieutenant Webb (Barry Foster) to oversee the execution: 'His man, his platoon, his mistake . . . teach him a lesson'.

By the final scene of Hamp's execution by firing squad, the film has brought into question the too-simplistic notion of duty embodied in the exhortation: 'For King and Country'. Crucially, in his plea for justice, Hargreaves argues for the State's responsibility for the enlisted soldier who, like numerous real-life Britons, has volunteered his life for the national cause in response to the patriotic call of 1914. In return, Hamp is shown to have been treated with contempt by a powerful class who show little regard for the ordinary soldier's horrific experience of the front line but are prepared to dispense with those who 'fail' in their duty in the belief that this will improve general morale. Hargreaves in effect questions this evacuation of responsibility by the officer class, arguing that one of their duties is to show compassion towards men such as Hamp who served loyally until fatigue or terror overcame them.

Several members of the firing squad, made up of Hamp's own platoon, shoot wide, and Webb cannot bring himself to deliver the *coup de grâce*. Ironically, it is left to Hargreaves to bring an end to the travesty. From a military perspective, Hamp's failure to die in the manner and at the time prescribed by the Court Martial is yet another instance of failing to do his duty, and so he limply apologises to the senior officer. The camera pans along the soldier's body to rest on his feet in a parody of the war-memorial image of the opening sequence. However, in place of a monument to the heroic fallen of the Great War, Losey's film offers instead an anti-monument to the hypocrisy and injustices dispensed by a class and a system that exercised privilege without responsibility or compassion.

Richard Attenborough's directorial debut, *Oh! What a Lovely War*, won considerable praise and success with audiences on its release in 1969. It is a very different film from *King and Country* – in particular, it trades the earlier film's intimacy for a much broader canvas – but it shares a similar narrational complexity, and with 'impressive dexterity' (French 1969: 93) mixes fantasy and reality, sometimes within the same shot. The film's unconventional stylisation was explained by critic Philip French in terms of the exhaustion of traditional modes of representation for dealing with the Great War. In the mid-1960s, the BBC had broadcast the astonishingly successful 26-part documentary series *The Great War*, and, in French's words, 'every reminiscence seemed to have been tapped, all the news-reels exposed, the archives ransacked, the paths of glory and the long, long trail trodden flat' (French 1969: 93).

The dramatic mode of *Oh! What a Lovely War* is mocking and the film is concerned with perspective and reality. To a considerable extent, its tone and dramatic approach were determined by its origins in a one-hour BBC radio programme[5] broadcast at Christmas 1961. This had two narrators, one representing official history, the other the viewpoint of the ordinary soldier. It then evolved into a television version and, most famously, into Joan Littlewood's stage production which opened at the Theatre Royal, Stratford East, London, in March 1963. The dual narration, presenting two perspectives on the conflict, remained central to the film's realisation, although it also drew much inspiration from the stage play. Thus, for the Home Front – fittingly played out in the film on Brighton Pier, which also houses the headquarters of the General Staff – the war is shown to be a lively entertainment, while the reality of the trenches is portrayed as inescapable and altogether different. The structuring of the film's narrative maintains this separation, with the contrast 'continually re-emphasised' (Bolas 1969: 87).

One technically audacious shot illustrates perfectly the dramatic and stylistic project of the film. The aim was to transpose a character, dressed in civvies, from a shooting gallery on the pier to a front-line trench where he then appears in uniform. The transition, anchored around the shooting weapon, enacts a shift in perspective from carefree amusement to deadly earnest combat. Attenborough has explained the motivation:

> The normal way to achieve this effect would have been simply to cut away or dissolve. But, by staying with the shot, we took the audience with us, persuading them unconsciously to swallow the fantasy. They then readily accepted that the style of the film was going to take them seamlessly from fantasy to reality and reality to fantasy.
>
> (quoted in Robinson 1992: 47)

Oh! What a Lovely War also subverts the meaning of some of the most enduring symbols of the conflict. The red poppy recurs as a motif in the film, but the flower's symbolic reference to the war dead is altered from that of a memorialising tribute to a sign of anticipation and expectation of death. Thus, poppies litter the film's trenches, but are absent from the vast war cemetery shown towards the end of the film. Instead, they return in the hall where the Armistice is signed, standing as a forewarning of future carnages (Bolas 1969: 87).

That other memorial, the two-minute silence observed on the anniversary of the Armistice, is similarly interrogated for its failure to produce an adequate critical perspective on the Great War. Here, the two-minute silence fails to unite the living with the dead.[6] Rather, it confirms and consolidates their separation, further suggesting the complete inability of the Home Front, both historically and in the present, to imagine the circumstances of the Fighting Front. In a silent montage sequence the working-class Smith brothers, slaughtered in the war, are unable to connect with their living womenfolk. Only the mother fleetingly senses the presence of Jack Smith, who stands behind her on a hillside. The silence is punctuated by the young daughter's question: 'What did Daddy do in the war?' As the women, now all dressed in white, wander among a sea of white crosses, the men answer with the song 'They'll Never Believe Us'. 'And we are left', in Philip French's summation, 'with a sense of wasted lives, a feeling of impenetrable sadness, of unassuageable grief' (French 1969: 94).

Oh! What a Lovely War ends simply and inconclusively with a fade to black, and denies the audience the formal culmination of a conventional end title. The war, the loss, and its remembrance are thus constituted as permanent connections between past and present, between recorded history and lived reality; and how we make sense of them and imagine them are the central issues with which the film self-reflexively engages.

The absence of combat scenes in the two films so far discussed makes them untypical of Great War fictional cinema. Such classics of American-made First World War cinema as *All Quiet on the Western Front* and Stanley Kubrick's *Paths of Glory* (1957) had established the visual and narrative conventions of the realistic depiction of trench warfare, and such scenes were integral to those films' evocations of brutality and futility. Thematically, the US films accord closely with the post-1960 British First World War cinema. But, in contrast with their US counterparts – and partly as a consequence of budget – all four of the British films considered here eschew prolonged or detailed combat scenes and locate their emotional drama in the periods before and after actual combat.

The 1990s films *Regeneration* and *The Trench*, while presenting some scenes of bloody fighting, concern themselves more with other conflicts, stresses and psychological traumas associated with the war. *The Trench*, author and screenwriter William Boyd's directorial debut, plays its opening titles over a series of historical photographs of the trenches, but with an effect that is quite different from Losey's use of still photographic images in *King and Country*. Where Losey's intention was to position the viewer at a critical distance from the narrative events, Boyd's purpose is to affirm by association the realism of his presentation. This is achieved through the final still image coming to life as the film, thus cementing the representational present of the film to the veracity of the historical photograph. Tellingly, wartime photographs also acted as the cinematographer's aesthetic references for the combat scenes in *Regeneration* (Thompson 1997: 113).

The Trench seeks to bring the viewer into the lives and dramas of the characters in a British front-line trench in the forty-eight hours leading up to the first day of the Somme offensive. Reviewers tended to judge the film as 'absurdly inadequate' (Tunney 1999: 57) in its depiction of the Front, although these inadequacies were more a reflection of its low-budget logistics than its artistry. The narrative focuses on a platoon of working-class Tommies with the aim of capturing the routine, boredom, procedures and vocabulary of trench life: the mornings standing to, trench raids, Blighty wounds (wounds severe enough to warrant hospitalisation or convalescence in Britain) and rum rations. The men do not embody the romantic ideal of front-line comradeship; instead the stress brings out their regional distinctions and emotional divisions, and the daily round lurches between confrontations and petty squabbles. Their officer, Lieutenant Harte (Julian Rhind-Tutt), a clichéd shadow of *Journey's End*'s Stanhope, has taken to drink, for, as he says, it 'keeps me sane'. In the final moment before the 'Big Push', the men too have to be bolstered with hard drink to get them 'over the top'.

The focus on the ordinary Tommy distinguishes *The Trench* from the other three Great War films considered in detail in this chapter.[7] Despite critically engaging with class, *King and Country*, *Oh! What a Lovely War* and *Regeneration* filter the sensitive and controversial issues of duty, service, responsibility, justice and humanity through the officer class and display little actual engagement with the other ranks. This post-1960 First World War cinema draws at least in part on the view of the war articulated by the literate, educated elite.

This is most evident in *Regeneration*, which features three of the distinguished war poets – Sassoon, Owen and Robert Graves – in its story of mental rehabilitation. Across all these films, language functions as a crucial mechanism for marking class distinctions, and its deployment as such needs to be made sense of in relation to the influential and privileged means of expressing the experience of the war available to the war poets. In *King and Country*, the inarticulate Private Hamp nominates Captain Hargreaves to speak for him at the trial because of his inability to express himself adequately. In *Regeneration*, proletarian officer Billy Prior (Jonny Lee Miller) discovers that his mutism is a symptom of trauma specific to the working class;[8] among the higher-class officers, trauma manifests itself in stuttering.

The class distinction is savagely underlined by the contrasting treatment meted out to *Regeneration*'s various patients. The officers are tended by the 'gentle miracles' of Dr Rivers (Jonathan Pryce) at Craiglockhart, a Scottish country estate; the lower ranks, seemingly under guard in an austere metropolitan hospital, are brutally subjected to electric shocks in order to forcibly have their 'silence taken away from them'. The class-conscious Prior angrily remonstrates about the inequalities between officers and men, and expresses guilt that he had to censor his men's letters home while he and his fellow officers were treated as beyond reproach.

By contrast, *The Trench* directly gives cinematic voice to the working-class experience of the First World War, and opts to do this in terms of a conventional notion of realism. On only a single, but significant, occasion does the film foreground the process of representation. This occurs in an important scene in which the platoon is filmed by the 'flickers' in a staged set-up for a patriotic documentary. It is made clear here that the front-line soldiers' enthusiasm and patriotism are manufactured for the camera: a private is furnished with a Union Jack and another with a banner bearing the slogan 'For King, Country and Empire' to wave during the scene. As the film crew and senior officer depart, a disrespectful comment is aimed after them – but of course, such dissent will remain outside the 'official' representation of the war.[9]

The film establishes emphatically that the rankers have little respect for the officer class: they dismiss their platoon leader, Lieutenant Harte, as 'a bit of a fucking idiot . . . They're bred that way'. The officer's pistol is a significant motif in the film. When Harte feels incapable of leading a trench raid he loans the weapon to his sergeant, and in the hands of the latter it is used in aggression against the enemy. However, at the moment of the 'Big Push', Harte reveals the true purpose of the pistol: to threaten the British Tommies out of the trenches and over the top.

An entirely different relationship between the officers and ordinary ranks is posited in *Regeneration*. Here, the loyalty and affection of officers like Sassoon and Prior for the men – a historically documented phenomenon – are central to an understanding of their desire to return to the trenches; to an experience described by Prior as both 'exciting and ridiculous'. *The Trench* adapts an alternative strand in the myth, one that critiques the military leadership and is most powerfully evoked in the suggestion that the men were led by 'donkeys'. *Oh! What a Lovely War*'s biting criticism of General Haig and the General Staff was the classic articulation of this idea; however, *The Trench* extends the portrayal of incompetence considerably further down the military hierarchy.

The Trench, for the reasons already cited, is perhaps unfair in its blanket condemnation of the officer class. Its prejudiced approach is revealed in a seemingly innocuous scene, derived from a real incident, towards the end of the film. Shortly before the men are to go over the top, they are issued with a football and directed to kick it over with them to the German lines. This, it is stated, will be good for morale. The film presents the order as pathetic and as showing outrageous disregard for what the men are about to confront. In fact, the real-life instigator of the idea, Captain Wilfred Nevill, went over the top himself with one of the footballs and died gallantly leading the assault in ferocious conditions. This action quickly established itself as legend, and attracted varied interpretations at the time. It was honoured in a poem, *The Game*, published in the *Daily Mail* and written in the heroic style of Sir Henry Newbolt:

> And now at last is ended
> The task so well begun;
> Though savagely defended
> The lines of death are won.
> In this, their hour of glory,
> A deathless place they claim
> In England's splendid story,
> The men who played the game![10]

The *Illustrated London News* commemorated the event with a drawing by its most famous artist, R. Caton Woodville: 'The Surreys play the game! Kicking footballs towards the German trenches under a hail of shells'. In Britain, the action, fully reported in the newspapers, was presented and understood as a 'shining example of bravery and *sangfroid*' (quoted in Brown 1978: pages 170–1). Intriguingly, the Germans used the action to point to the idiocy of the British. It is this interpretation that is replicated in *The Trench*, although with specific reference to the officer class.

The most interesting aspect of *Regeneration* with a bearing on this discussion is its meditation on the nature of duty, and in this respect the film is as complex as *King and Country*. The nature of duty, loyalty and the responsibilities of officers are debated by Sassoon and Dr Rivers. Sassoon, like Owen, is explicit in his non-pacifism, and his objection is to the aims of the war, not its conduct. Rivers, by contrast, is the one major character in any of the four films under discussion to give serious voice to a pro-war position. Rivers seeks to reinvest Sassoon with a sense of duty; but he increasingly comes to question his own role in returning men to the slaughter, particularly once he has witnessed the brutal electrotherapy treatment being meted out to the lower ranks. Rivers questions Sassoon as to whether his protest has made things any better for his men, 'those he claims to represent'. Meanwhile, Prior suggests provocatively to Rivers: 'Maybe you're the one that's ill?'

Prior's observation has a double meaning: Rivers has developed a speech impediment due to the stress of his work – he has become 'shell-shocked by his patients' – but Prior is also expressing disgust at Rivers's compliance in returning men to the front. Sassoon eventually decides to return to active duty, but not out of a change of heart. He tells Rivers that his motivation is expressed in some lines of Owen's poetry, and these connect eloquently with the film's concern with articulacy and language:

> I heard the sighs of men,
> That have no skill to speak of their distress.
> No, nor the will.
> A voice I know,
> And this time I must go.

It might seem from the preceding discussion that the dominant myth of the Great War given expression by the war poets has been substantially absorbed into the British cultural consciousness and that alternative ways of imagining the war enjoy little credibility. Indeed, one critique of this dominant interpretation has conceded that there has been a singular failure by revisionist historians to communicate their viewpoint to the wider public (Sheffield 1996). However, the third significant historical approach, that which gives central consideration to the testimony of front-line servicemen, has had a more positive impact. This can be seen in the common interest in articulacy across the post-1960 war films considered here. I wish to conclude, though, with a brief consideration of two recent controversies that have surfaced in Britain surrounding the Great War concerning its representation and its remembrance.

In 1987, at the height of Thatcherism, a storm of press criticism met the broadcast of the BBC's television drama series *The Monocled Mutineer* (directed by Jim O'Brien). The producers were accused in some quarters of a wilful failure in their duty as purveyors of public history. The Conservative mid-market tabloid the *Daily Mail* accused the BBC of being 'engaged in a long-term operation to rewrite history because of its hatred of our Imperial past' (quoted in Petley 1987: 126). Conservative MPs, who since the early 1980s had been waging a campaign against what they perceived as a leftist bias in the Corporation, added their voice to the backlash.

The series, which drew a large audience, 'reconstructed' the politically sensitive incident of the mutiny at Etaples in 1917 at a time when the documents relating to the event remained protected and therefore inaccessible under the Official Secrets Act.[11] Its writer, Alan Bleasdale, recognised the attack as part of a broader, sinister reaction against popular culture's imagining of the national past in anything but positive terms, commenting 'But of course it *is* a sign of our bleak times that anyone who expresses any concern for cannon fodder and humankind is castigated as some sort of dangerous revolutionary' (quoted in Petley 1987: 131).

A further controversy emerged in the 1990s, following a campaign to exonerate servicemen of the Great War who had been executed for failing to do their duty. During the war, more than 300 British and Empire servicemen had been executed for a variety of charges, some as trivial as falling asleep on duty. This matter had long troubled some consciences, and in addition to *King and Country*, with its central focus on the trial of a deserter, references are made to such incidents in *Regeneration*, *The Trench* and *The Monocled Mutineer*.

However, despite the greater psychological awareness of the present, a Private Member's Bill to the British Parliament, an ongoing Posthumous Pardons Campaign and the support of the Royal British Legion, the Ministry of Defence and government remained unwilling to exonerate those executed (HMSO 1994; Thornton 1997; Shrimsley 1998). The controversy spilled over into many local parishes, where campaigns were mounted to include the names of those executed on village war memorials, although usually without success. In one significant reversal, a compassionate art student, Andy DeComyn, produced a statue of a blindfolded soldier awaiting execution for erection at the National Memorial Arboretum in Staffordshire (Anon. 2000).

It seems, then, that despite the potency of the myth of the Great War as hopelessly tragic, wasteful and futile, this myth remains insufficient to challenge or displace the traditions of memorialising established directly after the conflict and annually perpetuated in the ritual of Remembrance Sunday. As for British films from the early 1960s onwards, these increasingly came to adopt the ideals of the myth and, through their ability to vividly present the sights and sounds of trench warfare, perpetuated and enhanced it. But this unequivocal interpretation gathered force at a time when cinema was declining as a popular medium, and this, it might be argued, allowed for a rejection of the more ambiguous approach found in the earlier British First World War films from the 1930s. As cinema's mass audience and influence declined, it was allowed a latitude of expression previously reserved for elite forms.

In this context, it is significant that none of the post-1945 films considered here generated the storm of protest that attended *The Monocled Mutineer*, myth-making that was delivered directly into people's homes through television – which, still a genuinely popular medium, continued to attract scrutiny from patriotic watchdogs. A similar vigilance ensures that Britain's annual ritual of remembrance still stubbornly refuses to be sullied by the incorporation of cowards and shirkers into the celebration of the heroic war dead, and the national failure to understand or forgive remains a significant legacy of the Great War. More than eighty years after the cessation of hostilities, and after several decades of a deepening cultural myth expounding the tragedy of the war, the British state refuses to shift its position on war in general. When called upon, men must do their duty, make the ultimate sacrifice if necessary, and in heroic death shall find honour and glory.

Notes

1 Sweeny used the term with reference to his continued participation in what he dreaded most, the long drawn-out battle of Passchendaele in 1917.
2 The scale of this shared loss can be further measured in the temendous public support for war memorials: see Hynes 1990: 269–82.
3 'War films: 58,000 wives and mothers protest', *Co-operative News*, 3 March, 1928: 12. The Women's Co-operative Guild was at the forefront of the British Peace Movement in the 1920s and 1930s, and in 1933 introduced the controversial 'peace poppy', which was manufactured by the Co-operative Wholesale Society as the British Legion refused to have anything to do with it (Morrison 1996: 92).
4 A later British film, *Aces High* (Jack Gold, UK/France, 1976), in effect relocates *Journey's End*'s narrative and concerns to the Royal Flying Corps.
5 'The Long, Long Trail – Soldiers' Songs of the First World War.'
6 For a discussion of the problems and issues faced by the first filmmaker to attempt the representation of the two-minute silence on film, George Pearson in *Reveille* (1924), see Peet 2001.
7 Writing before the release of *The Trench*, Andrew Kelly had observed, 'for British cinema the War is always an officers' war' (Kelly 1997b: 25).
8 This neurotic mutism has been interpreted by some as a war protest equivalent to that of the war poets (Sinker 1997: 12).
9 A real-life equivalent was the official film *The Battle of the Somme* (1916), which had a tremendous popular and emotional impact when it was screened to Home Front audiences. See Reeves 1993: 181–201.
10 All details of this incident, and its contemporary reception, cited here are taken from 'The Surreys play the game – the story of Captain Wilfred Nevill, killed 1 July 1916' in Brown 1978: 170–1.
11 *The Trench* contains a brief reference to Etaples: a wounded private is sent to the base hospital there.

Bibliography

Note: Page numbers were not always available for articles and reviews accessed via library archives and websites.

Anon. (2000) 'New tribute to servicemen', *The Times*, 29 May 2000.
Bolas, T. (1969) '*Oh! What a Lovely War*' [review], *Screen*, May/June 1969: 84–8.
Brown, M. (1978) *Tommy Goes To War*, London: J. M. Dent.
French, P. (1969) '*Oh! What a Lovely War*' [review], *Sight and Sound*, Spring 1969: 93–4.
Fussell, P. (1975) *The Great War and Modern Memory*, Oxford: Oxford University Press.
Her Majesty's Stationery Office (1994) *Pardon for Soldiers of the Great War*, London: HMSO.
Hynes, S. (1990) *A War Imagined: The First World War and English Culture*, London: Bodley Head.
Kelly, A. (1997a) *Cinema and the Great War*, London: Routledge.

Kelly, A. (1997b) 'Trench footnotes', *Sight and Sound*, December 1997: 25.

Marwick, A. (1965) *The Deluge: British Society and the First World War*, London: Bodley Head.

Morrison, C. (1996) 'The Women's Co-operative Guild: campaigns for peace, 1918–1939' in B. Lancaster and P. Maguire (eds) *Towards the Co-operative Commonwealth: Essays in the History of Co-operation*, Manchester: Co-operative College and History Workshop Trust: 89–93.

Palmer, J. and Riley, M. (1993) *The Films of Joseph Losey*, Cambridge: Cambridge University Press.

Paris, M. (1999) 'Enduring heroes: British feature films and the First World War, 1919–1997' in M. Paris (ed.) *The First World War and Popular Cinema: 1914 to the Present*, Edinburgh: Edinburgh University Press.

Peet, S. (2001) 'George Pearson and his "two minutes silence"' in A. Burton and L. Porter (eds) *The Showman, The Spectacle and the Two-minute Silence: Performing British Cinema Before 1930*, Trowbridge: Flicks Books: 73–5.

Petley, J. (1987) 'Over the top', *Sight and Sound*, Spring 1987: 126–31.

Reeves, N. (1993) 'The power of film propaganda – myth or reality?', *Historical Journal of Film, Radio and Television*, 13, 2: 181–201.

—— (1999) 'Official British film propaganda' in M. Paris (ed.), 27–50.

Robertson, J. C. (1984) '*Dawn* (1928): Edith Cavell and Anglo-German relations', *Historical Journal of Film, Radio and Television*, 4, 1: 15–28.

Robinson, D. (1992) *Richard Attenborough* (NFT Dossier 9), London: National Film Theatre.

Routt, W. D. (1994) 'Some early British films considered in the light of early Australian production', *Metro*, Summer 1994: 65–9.

Sheffield, G. D. (1996) '"Oh! What a futile war": representations of the Western Front in modern British media and popular culture' in I. Stewart and L. Carruthers (eds) *War, Culture and the Media: Representations of the Military in 20th Century Britain*, Trowbridge: Flicks Books: 54–74.

Shrimsley, R. (1998) 'No pardon for deserters shot in Great War', *Daily Telegraph*, 30 April 1998: page unknown.

Sinker, M. (1997) 'Temporary gentlemen', *Sight and Sound*, December 1997: 22–4.

Smith, M. (1995) 'The war and British culture' in S. Constantine *et al.* (eds) *The First World War in British History*, London: Edward Arnold: 168–83.

Thompson, A. O. (1997) 'A cosmopolitan celebration of cinema', *American Cinematographer*, December 1997: 113–16.

Thornton, J. (1997) 'Defender of war's forgotten victims arrested', *Daily Telegraph*, 9 November 1997: page unknown.

Tunney, T. (1999) '*The Trench*' [review], *Sight and Sound*, October 1999: 57.

Ward, C. (1997) 'Impressions of the Somme: an experiment', *Rethinking History*, 1, 3.

Warner, M. (1979) *The Crack in the Teacup: Britain in the 20th Century*, London: Andre Deutsch.

Winter, D. (1979) *Death's Men: Soldiers of the Great War*, London: Penguin.

4 Secrets and lies

Black histories and British historical films

Stephen Bourne

In the 1960s a new generation of African-Caribbean children were growing up in racially-mixed communities all over Britain: the offspring of parents who had come to Britain as part of the large-scale post-Second World War migration of Commonwealth citizens from Africa and the Caribbean. On council estates and in school playgrounds, these black children were often subjected to name-calling, very often originating from a popular film or television programme (Bourne 2000: 62–3). After the UK release of the film *Zulu* (Cy Endfield) in 1964, the film's title spread as a term of racist abuse for children of African descent. White British children were captivated by the film, which told the story of 105[1] soldiers from a Welsh regiment defending Rorke's Drift against 4,000 Zulus in 1879. For them, it was like watching a Hollywood western in which the 'savage' plains of Africa stood in for America's Wild West. Stanley Baker took the place of John Wayne, and Africans stood in for Native Americans, brandishing spears instead of toma-hawks.

Zulu was released at a time when black children in Britain were being exposed to BBC television's popular variety series *The Black and White Minstrel Show*, and Helen Bannerman's 1899 book *Little Black Sambo* was still being reprinted and used in schools and libraries. Perhaps unintentionally, *Zulu* added to this pool of racist propaganda. Black children who lived in isolation, in areas without a black com-munity, were particularly vulnerable.

Sadly, what British children of all cultural backgrounds were *not* made aware of – in schools, by the media, or by popular film – was that there had been a black presence in Britain since at least the mid-sixteenth century. Perhaps if this situa-tion had been different, Britain's first large-scale generation of black children might have felt better equipped to deal with the racism generated by films like *Zulu*. Perhaps white children, and their parents, might have been less disposed towards racism if they had been adequately informed about the longstanding black pres-ence within Britain's national story.

The invisibility of, and silence around, Britain's black history (or, on a more personal level, black British histories) is, of course, a problem permeating British

Figure 4.1 A rare acknowledgement of the historical black presence in Britain: an uncredited
          black extra appears in the dock with Magwitch (Finlay Currie) in David Lean's
          Great Expectations (1946).
Source: BFI Stills, Posters and Designs, courtesy of Rank/Cineguild.

society and culture, not a phenomenon confined to British films. My concern in
this chapter is the near-total exclusion of this history from British cinema – particularly, but not exclusively, from British popular cinema. However, this absence
cannot be illuminated in isolation from the wider workings of racism, representation, racial politics and policy in Britain over recent decades, and so these
will inevitably inform my discussion. Because of my own personal background
and expertise, my focus will be on British cinema's excision – or, more rarely,
acknowledgement – of the historical presence in Britain of people of African
or Caribbean descent (typically referred to as African-Caribbeans in Britain or
African-Americans in the USA). However, clearly there are equivalent points to
be made about the denial of the historical presence of Britain's Indian, Bangla-
deshi, Chinese and other immigrant communities in British films.

   Over more than a century of cinema, the black historical presence in Britain has
been all but invisible in British popular films. In this entire period, black appearances in films with British historical settings have been limited to a few fleeting
appearances by extras, most notably in David Lean's *Great Expectations* (1946) and
Oliver Twist (1948); one supporting role in a Gainsborough costume melodrama,
The Man in Grey (1943); and – in an exception that proves the rule – the interna-

tionally acclaimed literary adaptation *The Sailor's Return* (Jack Gold, 1978), which featured a central black female protagonist and was denied a theatrical release. A more recent effort, *The Tichborne Claimant* (David Yates, 1998), based on an eccentric real-life Victorian case, relied on unconventional sources of finance and was barely released in British cinemas.[2]

British-based black filmmakers in the independent sector which has emerged since the 1980s have on occasion acknowledged the black presence in Britain's past. However, their films have typically been set in the very recent past rather than the pre-Second World War or pre-twentieth-century era. Examples include Martina Attille, whose award-winning short *Dreaming Rivers* (1988) was an evocative exploration of the displacement of post-war Caribbean settlers; Isaac Julien's *Young Soul Rebels* (1991), set during Queen Elizabeth II's Silver Jubilee celebrations of 1977; and *Who Needs a Heart?* (1991), in which writer/director John Akomfrah looked at 'Black Power' in 1960s and 1970s Britain by investigating the life of the Trinidad-born Black Muslim leader Michael X, also known as Michael Abdul Malik. In other cases, black British independent filmmakers have engaged on a more abstracted, self-reflexive level with the *act* of articulating black British histories: see, for example, Julien's *Territories* (1984). Furthermore, black British filmmakers have tended to produce work which asserts an international – rather than 'British' – black cultural and political identity (on this diasporic identification, see Gilroy 1987: 154): see, for example, Julien's *Looking for Langston* (1988) and *Frantz Fanon: Black Skin, White Mask* (UK/France, 1996). Combined with other factors such as the conditions of UK film production and the smallness of the black British audience compared to the African-American market, these tendencies have contributed to the lack of any British equivalent to US mainstream black historical films such as *Amistad* (Steven Spielberg, USA, 1997).

Shockingly, the increasing awareness of Britain as a multicultural society in the present has had little impact on British cinema's acknowledgement of our multicultural past: as I will show, there was more of a black presence in some British historical films of the 1910s than in recent high-profile British period successes of the 1990s. Reflecting in 1996 on her 40-year career in Britain, the African-Caribbean actress Carmen Munroe said: 'I feel disheartened every time I look at the screen and see something like *Pride and Prejudice* [the 1995 BBC television production which attracted record audiences for British television period drama] or *Sense and Sensibility* [Ang Lee, USA/UK, 1996] that will exclude . . . minority ethnic artists' (interviewed in Bourne 1998: 172). The perspectives of black British commentators and performers quoted throughout my chapter will make it clear that there is ample ammunition for regarding 'whiteness' as a specific generic trait of British period films, even if it is one that their audiences unthinkingly take for granted.

There is, of course, one substantial body of British historical films in which black performers have always been visible in volume (although typically nameless and speechless): the British imperial adventure or epic.[3] However, in defining black Africans or Caribbeans exclusively as colonised, conquered or insurrection-ary 'foreign' subjects, these films further reinforce the false image of Britain's domestic past as exclusively 'white'. Given the number of British imperial films made over the decades and their popularity with white audiences, it is unsurprising that most existing academic work which addresses black African or Caribbean representation in British historical films has done so with reference to those set within the British Empire.[4] As these films have already been substantially analysed – notably in the important work of Jeffrey Richards (1973 and 1997) – I will not discuss them further here.

It is important to understand that British cinema's erasure of the historical black presence in Britain is not confined to films set in the past; indeed, it cannot be understood in isolation from the equivalent erasure of black communities from British films set in the present. *Notting Hill* (Roger Michell, 1999), one of the most profitable and popular British films of all time, is one of the most obvious examples of an entire black British community, and thus its history, being success-fully erased from its – present-day – setting. In the film's opening sequence, bookseller William Thacker (Hugh Grant) lists the reasons why Notting Hill has become his 'favourite bit of London'. There is, however, one important attraction Grant does not include in his 'list' – the event for which Notting Hill has been most famous since the early 1960s, the two days in August when the predom-inantly African-Caribbean neighbourhood celebrates Carnival. Indeed, the only two black actors in *Notting Hill* were bit-players: Clarke Peters as Julia Roberts's co-star in the film-within-a-film *Helix*, and Tony Armatrading as a film-set security man. Neither featured in the sequences in Notting Hill itself. Unsurprisingly, *Notting Hill* angered a number of black British actors (such as Lennie James 2000: 66). It was denounced as an 'insult' by the journalist Yasmin Alibhai-Brown, who accused its makers, including screenwriter Richard Curtis, of

> [whitening the] most famously Black area in London . . . It is not that they don't see us, but that film-makers don't want us to litter up their olde worlde landscape. In this country 99 per cent of films are written by white, middle-class people . . . We have no Spike Lee yet or Denzel Washington because the much applauded British film industry has done nothing to make them happen.
>
> (Alibhai-Brown 2000: 259)

Notting Hill is by no means the first British film to erase an entire black community and its history and culture from the screen. Four decades earlier, director J. Lee Thompson had filmed the murder and kidnap melodrama *Tiger Bay* (1959) on location in Bute Town – known as 'Tiger Bay' – situated close to the Cardiff docks in South Wales. The area had been well known for its racially mixed community for over seventy years, starting with the arrival of a Barbadian settler in 1885 (Little 1948: 54), and including, famously, the internationally acclaimed singer Shirley Bassey. In Thompson's film – which was a considerable box-office success – Tiger Bay became little more than an exotic backdrop for a thriller that told the story of a displaced white child from London, who witnesses the murder of Anya (Yvonne Mitchell) by Korchinsky (Horst Buchholz), her Polish seaman lover. The child then befriends the killer. In spite of Tiger Bay's real-life racial mix, no black residents are shown to live in the tenement building where the child shares a home with her aunt and uncle. The film was nevertheless important to the local African-Welsh community: some residents welcomed it as a filmed record of their neigh-bourhood, particularly the main location, Loudoun Square, before redevelopment razed it to the ground (Sinclair 1993: 46–50). However, other black residents expressed concerns about Thompson's portrayal of Tiger Bay during the filming. One, quoted in the *Spectator* of 31 October 1958, complained: 'When people see the story of this film, they are going to think that [Tiger Bay] is where a man can pick up a girl easily. They'll think all coloured people have loose morals. Think we play dice down here all day.'

Over the past thirty years the presence of black settlers in Britain since at least the mid-sixteenth century has been documented by a substantial number of historians (Scobie 1972, Walvin 1973, Shyllon 1977, File and Power 1981, Fryer 1984, Dabydeen 1985, Bygott 1992, Adi 1995, Bourne and Bruce 1996, Green 1998, Okokon 1998). However, this work has tended to be marginalised by the mainstream. Too often, book editors on the broadsheet newspapers ignore such histories (Bourne 2000: 63). It appears that, in Britain, the white-dominated media prefers to maintain the silence around the history of our nation's black people. The same criticism can be made of British historical films that also constantly overlook the black presence.

Writing in *IC3: The Penguin Book of New Black Writing in Britain*, London-based black community activist Linda Bellos observed:

> I have noticed with increasing irritation that there is hardly any reference to Black people that draws upon history. Or if it is, it's a history framed and referenced by Europeans. What I mean by this is that it is not often that a historical context is provided for events and achievements by Black people. Newspapers and broadcast journalists are particularly keen on reporting stories about Black people which emphasize our being the first to have done something . . . It was even more evident when in 1998 BBC television and subsequently the rest of the media went overboard with the celebration of the arrival of *Empire Windrush*[5] fifty years earlier. Commentators not only referred to Black people as having first arrived in Britain in 1948 but, more worry-ingly, many people of African origin who had lived, worked and struggled in Britain throughout the previous centuries were excluded. The implication of

this omission was that, prior to their arrival in Britain, those 500 'immigrants' had no history.

(Bellos 2000: 120)

In 1998, the fiftieth anniversary celebrations of the arrival in Britain of the *Empire Windrush* coincided with the release of the film *Shakespeare in Love* (John Madden), which was to win both the American Academy Award and the British Academy Award (Bafta) for Best Film. *Shakespeare in Love* is historically inaccurate insofar as it features no black characters or extras. This omission prompted a reader of the UK black newspaper *The Voice* to complain:

> With many cases of racial discrimination and attacks being reported, I am concerned about why the media is promoting a British film which promotes segregation. For some unknown reason, there are no Black actors in the critically acclaimed new film about the Bard, *Shakespeare in Love*. History shows that Black people were contributing to the social and cultural growth of Britain during Shakespeare's time . . . I see this particular film as promoting segregation.
>
> (Hart 1999: 8)

Some historians may argue that the black presence in Elizabethan England was too small and insignificant to be worth acknowledging. However, by 1601, the black population was large enough for Queen Elizabeth I to have made two attempts to repatriate her black citizens. She failed on both occasions. As for Shakespeare, in the 1590s he befriended Luce Morgan – also known as Lucy Negro – a beautiful and famous African courtesan who ran a brothel in Clerkenwell, London. Some authorities on Shakespeare believe that he fell in love with her, and at least one, Dr George Bagshawe Harrison, has identified her as Shakespeare's Dark Lady of the Sonnets (Harrison 1933: 310–11).

Although recent British historical films like *Shakespeare in Love* exclude black characters, this has not always been the case – particularly in the silent era (Bourne 1998: 1–12). For instance, Ernest Trimmingham (1879–1942), who came to Edwardian Britain from Bermuda, was successful in finding work in the performing arts as an actor and dramatist, and can be regarded as Britain's first black film actor until others of African descent are identified. So far several appearances by Trimmingham have been identified in silent films, including a few films with historical settings. Released in 1912, *The Adventures of Dick Turpin: The King of Highwaymen* featured Trimmingham as a character called Beetles alongside Percy Moran's Turpin. With no known print of the film surviving and little documentation, it is not clear who or what 'Beetles' is, but it is unusual to find a black character given prominence in a story about the famous English highwayman who was hanged in 1739. Produced by the British and Colonial Kinematograph Company, the Dick

Turpin series was popular, and this first entry received an enthusiastic review in *The Bioscope* (Anon. 1912). However, there is no mention of Trimmingham in the review.

A black seaman can be seen fighting at Admiral Horatio Nelson's side on the deck of HMS *Victory* in a painting by Denis Dighton (1792–1827). C. W. Sharpe's painting *Death of Nelson* from 1805 also features a black seaman. The inclusion of a black sailor in the silent film *Nelson* (Maurice Elvey, 1919) is perhaps due to the influence of these paintings. But we do not know the names of the black sailors depicted in Dighton and Sharpe's paintings or Elvey's film – nor in Daniel Maclise's 1860s mural *The Death of Nelson* in the Houses of Parliament and at the base of Nelson's Column in Trafalgar Square (Green 2000: 32).

A more substantial acknowledgement of the history of black Britons is found in the opening sequence of *Song of Freedom* (J. Elder Wills, 1936), an exceptional star vehicle for the African-American singer, actor and political activist Paul Robeson. When Robeson became a star in British films in the mid-1930s, he attempted to use his star power to break away from the traditional stereotypes. Although his roles in his British films were generally more believable than those he was offered by US producers, Robeson often found himself in conflict with an industry that glorified the British Empire and colonialism (Bourne 1998: 15–20). This was certainly the case with his first commercial film, *Sanders of the River* (Zoltan Korda, 1935) – one of the 1930s cycle of imperial adventures produced by Alexander Korda at London Films. The film not only featured the embarrassing spectacle of Robeson as the half-naked 'native' Bosambo, but required him to sing, not insincerely, a 'hymn' to the white colonial administrator, Sanders: 'Sandy the strong/ Sandy the wise/Righter of wrongs/Hater of lies'. It is little wonder Robeson hated and disowned it – and it led Marcus Garvey, the outspoken Jamaican nationalist leader credited with inspiring black consciousness internationally, to denounce him for 'pleasing England by the gross slander and libel of the Negro' (Garvey 1935).[6]

Despite this experience, Robeson believed that the British film industry had something positive to offer, and he continued acting in British films for several years. Before starting work on his next film, *Song of Freedom*, he insisted on a clause in his contract which would give him the right to approve the final edit.

In *Song of Freedom* Robeson played John Zinga, a London-born docker who acknowledges Africa as his ancestral home – which he dreams of visiting – and possesses a 'natural', untrained but powerful, singing voice. In a highly improbable and melodramatic plot, Zinga is discovered by an impresario who successfully transforms him into an internationally acclaimed concert singer. From an anthropologist, he learns that the medallion he wears around his neck has been inherited from the King of Casanga, an island off the coast of West Africa which is still inhabited by the King's descendants. In the words of Robeson's biographer, Martin Bauml Duberman:

Abandoning his concert career to return to his people, [Zinga] is met with scorn and abuse from them until he bursts into sacred song, thus persuading him of his royal heritage. The film ends with Zinga resuming a part-time concert career in order to raise needed revenue for his people. Though inane as narrative, [the film] showed blacks coping within the context of ordinary life – a welcome switch from the previous stereotypes of shuffling idiot, faithful retainer, happy-go-lucky hedonist, or menacing con-man. Zinga himself is portrayed in the film as a natural aristocrat, a man of charm and intelligence.

(Bauml Duberman 1989: 204)

In spite of its shortcomings, the film was important to Robeson because he felt that it was

[the first] to give a true picture of many aspects of the life of the coloured man in the west. Hitherto, on the screen, he has been caricatured or presented only as a comedy character. This film shows him as a real man, with problems to be solved, difficulties to be overcome.

(Robeson 1936: 17)

The historical prologue of *Song of Freedom* is extraordinarily moving. A montage of striking images depicts the historical process by which people of African descent came to settle in Britain. The horrors of the eighteenth-century slave trade are exposed – an extreme rarity in a British film, even today – and the film recounts its abolition in 1838. Throughout this sequence, the King of Casanga's song and medallion are passed down from generation to generation, from Zinga's African ancestors on Casanga – who are then captured by slavers and shown chained together in a slave ship – to John Zinga, shown working on the docks near Tower Bridge in London in the 1930s 'present' where the remainder of the film is set.

Robeson's performance beautifully expresses Zinga's feeling of social displacement, his desire to visit his ancestral home, and his need to find his people. Zinga is shown to have integrated into the multicultural dockland community, together with his wife Ruth (Elisabeth Welch), although some critics have found the couple's portrayal bourgeois and unrealistic (Bogle 1973: 137 and Young 1996: 71–9). Zinga acknowledges his African ancestry by wearing the Casanga medallion and singing fragments of the King's song he had been taught as a child: 'It's been at the back of my head since I was a little fella,' he explains. In an early sequence in the local pub he meets Harry, a sailor who is about to depart to the West African coast. 'What part do you come from?' he asks Zinga, who replies: 'I don't know. Wish I did.'

For a British film of the 1930s, all of this is revolutionary – especially when we remember that *Song of Freedom* was released within a year of *Sanders of the River*. *Song of Freedom* is a landmark film within the history of British cinema for two reasons: it acknowledges the black presence in 1930s England, and it shows that it was possible for a black man to be born in Britain. It is the only film in which Robeson played a British-born character rather than Africans or African-Americans. It is a radical departure from previous representations of black people in British films, but sadly one that has never been fully appreciated. Only a handful of writers have recognised the film's strengths and emotional power. One of them, Kenneth M. Cameron, argued:

> [*Song of Freedom*] exploited stereotypes as part of a strategy to dramatize Robeson's myth. It acknowledged 'savagery' but did not use it as a stick with which to beat Africans, suggesting rather that problems could be corrected without white presence. It sees a high place for returned blacks in Africa. It asserts that the real triumph is not the fame and wealth to be found in white culture, but the productive life to be found in black culture: 'Tomorrow, he goes back again.' It takes the African stereotypes of commercial motion pictures and stands them on their heads.
>
> (Cameron 1994: 102)

In the 1940s the British director David Lean used black extras in his renowned screen versions of Charles Dickens's novels *Great Expectations* (1946) and *Oliver Twist* (1948). This must have been a deliberate choice on Lean's part, since few other directors before or since have acknowledged Britain's black presence in this way. In fact, today, it is almost impossible to find a black extra or actor cast in an adaptation of a novel by Dickens: see, for example, BBC television's acclaimed April 1999 two-part adaptation of *Great Expectations*. Admittedly Dickens did not include black characters in his novels, unlike William Shakespeare in his plays (for example, the Prince of Morocco in *The Merchant of Venice* or Othello), but this does not mean that black actors could not plausibly be cast as some of his characters. By the time *Great Expectations* was published in 1861, many thousands of people of African descent were living and working in London, and there is no reason why this should not have been reflected in the 1999 BBC adaptation.

One of the most memorable images in Lean's *Great Expectations* of fifty years earlier is the tracking shot showing Magwitch (Finlay Currie) and other prisoners in the dock as they are about to be sentenced by the judge. Prominent in this scene is an unidentified black extra who appears in chains, looking defiant. Two years later Lean used two black extras, including the veteran bit player Napoleon Florent (c.1870–1959), in his version of *Oliver Twist*. They are clearly visible among the patrons of the Three Cripples pub. At least one other adaptation of Dickens from this period of British filmmaking featured a black extra: in *The Pickwick Papers* (Noel Langley, 1952), set in 1830, a black inmate can be seen in the workhouse. A year later, Peter Brook's 1953 film of *The Beggar's Opera*, based on John Gay's ballad opera of 1728 and starring Laurence Olivier as MacHeath the Highwayman, featured two black pages in Mrs Trapes's gambling house. They are exotically dressed in turbans and gold earrings, and one speaks with a cockney accent.

However, no speaking roles have ever been given to black actors in adaptations from Dickens, although a breakthrough was almost made by the director Carol Reed in 1968 when he filmed Lionel Bart's musical *Oliver!*, based on *Oliver Twist*. Robert F. Moss reports that when casting Nancy, 'Reed's first choice for this part was Shirley Bassey, but Columbia [Studios] vetoed her because it was felt that a black Nancy would alienate filmgoers in the American South' (Moss 1987: 251).

One of the most glaring omissions from British historical films has been the erasure of the contribution made by people of African and Caribbean descent to the First and Second World Wars. Britain's post-Second World War African-Caribbean film actors, notably Earl Cameron, Errol John and Cy Grant – who joined the RAF as a Bomber Command navigator in 1941 and was a prisoner of war in Germany for two years – are noticeably absent from the heroic Second World War films of the 1950s such as *The Cruel Sea* (Charles Frend, 1953), *The Colditz Story* (Guy Hamilton, 1954), *Reach for the Sky* (Lewis Gilbert, 1956) and *Dunkirk* (Leslie Norman, 1958). Nor do these films feature a single black extra. In his book *Censored*, Tom Dewe Mathews observes drily:

> Probably the nearest thing to a cinematic representation of blacks was in *The Dam Busters* [Michael Anderson, 1954], and this did not show the British film industry's racial attitudes in a favourable light. At the end of a bombing mission the squadron leader (Richard Todd) climbs out of his plane, crouches down, holds out his arms and then shouts, 'Nigger, Nigger,' as his black labrador runs towards him.
>
> (Dewe Mathews 1994: 151)

The word nigger is used fourteen times in the script of *The Dam Busters*; but to this date British cinema has yet to acknowledge the contribution to the war effort by people of African descent, either in the Armed Forces or on the Home Front. However, Sikh airmen are visible – though silent – in *A Matter of Life and Death* (Michael Powell and Emeric Pressburger, 1946) and *633 Squadron* (Walter E. Grauman, 1964).

Only two commercial British films set in Britain's past, *The Man in Grey* (Leslie Arliss, 1943) and *The Sailor's Return* (Jack Gold, 1978), have featured important black characters. *The Man in Grey*, set during the Regency period (1811–20), was one of Gainsborough Studios's costume melodramas, renowned for their commercial success with working-class, mainly female, audiences but excoriated by 1940s critics. Like many of the Gainsborough melodramas it was based on twentieth-century popular romantic fiction – here, by Lady Eleanor Smith. In a narrative of infidelity and female bad behaviour told in flashback from the Second World

War present – a device typical of the Gainsborough costume cycle – it portrayed Regency England as a place as dark and dangerous as the war-torn present. Most unusual for the time is the appearance of a young black page called Toby, played by Harry Scott,[7] who offers a rare glimpse of black servant life in early nineteenth-century Britain. It has been estimated that at that time there were around 20,000 people of African descent in London alone, out of a total London population of 750,000 (Alexander and Dewjee 1981: 3). The majority had originally been slaves brought to this country by captains of sea vessels and plantation owners from the Caribbean. In Britain, black servants, especially children, became a popular fashion accessory for the rich. Sue Harper notes that Toby's role in the film is 'greatly expanded' from his role in the source novel, and that this is consistent with wider trends in the Gainsborough costume films, which 'accord more utterance' to lower-class characters and those from marginalised social groups (notably gypsies) while punishing male aristocratic excess (Harper 1994: 125).

Toby is the devoted servant of Clarissa (Phyllis Calvert), a 'lovely and amiable' young woman who treats him with kindness. In return, Toby buys his mistress a fan as a wedding present, and tries to protect her from the erotically appealing villain Peter Rokeby (Stewart Granger) when he holds up their coach. Clarissa's life is complicated by her friendship with Hesther (Margaret Lockwood), a scheming, ambitious adventuress who is unimpressed by Clarissa's 'goodness': 'I don't care for sugary things,' she says when offered a sweet by Clarissa at their first encounter. Hester shows nothing but contempt for Toby, calling him an 'urchin' and 'a slave's brat'. However, in contrast with the portrayals of black servants in Hollywood films of the period, which often lapsed into cartoonish, one-dimensional racial stereotypes, Toby is portrayed with some respect and sympathy. Although we are not told anything about his background, he is not seen in total isolation from other black characters. In the Barnes Fair sequence he encounters a black wrestler (Sam Blake), described as the 'Nubian Hercules'. Clarissa is neither a condescending nor cruel mistress, treating Toby as a friend and equal. In return, at the end of the film, Toby avenges Clarissa's death at the hands of Hester by exposing the 'bad' woman's guilt.

The Sailor's Return was adapted from the novella by David Garnett, a member of the celebrated Bloomsbury Group of writers that also included E. M. Forster and Virginia Woolf. First published in 1924, Garnett's book belonged to a very English tradition of doomed love stories (epitomised by the novels of Thomas Hardy). Set in the mid-Victorian era, it tells the story of the love between a sailor, Targett (Tom Bell), and his wife Tulip, an African princess (Shope Shodeinde). Targett brings Tulip home to England, where they settle in Dorset in the West Country as the tenant landlords of a village inn. At first they are happy. The villagers show curiosity, but not hostility. However, the couple are soon confronted by bigotry and violence, mostly stirred up by Targett's sister Lucy (Paola Dionisotti), who objects to the relationship. The story is told primarily from Tulip's viewpoint,

Figure 4.2 Targett (Tom Bell) and his African bride Tulip (Shope Shodeinde) settle in
1850s Wessex in *The Sailor's Return* (1978).
Source: BFI Stills, Posters and Designs, courtesy of Euston Films.

revealing differences between the attitudes, culture and traditions of African tribal
society and those of nineteenth-century rural England. 'I am black and I love my
black baby. I shall never love him the same after he is washed white,' Tulip tells
her husband when he attempts to have their son baptised (Garnett 1978: 52).

By 1858, the year of Targett and Tulip's arrival in the West Country, women
of African descent had been living and working in Britain since at least the early
sixteenth century. It is known that the court of King James IV of Scotland (who
died in 1513) included two African maidservants to his Queen, Margaret Tudor
(1489–1541). From the seventeenth century black women found employment as
domestic servants, seamstresses, laundry maids, children's nurses, cooks and street
and fairground performers. In Victorian times, the most famous black woman
living in Britain was Jamaican-born Mary Seacole (1805–81). An experienced
'doctress', she travelled at her own expense to the battlefields of the Crimean
War in order to tend the wounded. In 1857, one year before *The Sailor's Return*'s
narrative begins, she published a best-selling autobiography. She was awarded the

Crimean Medal and gained the admiration and affection of Queen Victoria (Bourne and Bruce 1996: 1–2).[8]

Earlier attempts had been made to adapt *The Sailor's Return* for the screen. In the 1930s, the British-based Austrian director Berthold Viertel (*The Passing of the Third Floor Back* [1935]; *Rhodes of Africa* [1936]) had tried persistently, without success, to raise finance for a film of the novel. In 1953, the year he made *Roman Holiday* with Audrey Hepburn, the US director William Wyler acquired the rights only to find that, even at the height of his Hollywood career, he was unable to interest a studio in the project. One Hollywood financier asked Wyler: 'If you have to have a black woman in it, couldn't it be played by a white woman [in blackface]?' (Euston Films 1979: 2). In 1955 the BBC adapted the novella for radio, with Nadia Cattouse as Tulip.

In 1971 the film rights were acquired from Wyler by Otto Plaschkes, the producer of *Georgy Girl* (1966), with financial backing from the National Film Finance Corporation. In 1977, following the success of Thames Television's *The Naked Civil Servant* (1975) – a drama based on the life of the homosexual Quentin Crisp, who confronted virulent homophobia on the streets of London in the 1930s, which became a landmark in British television history – its director, Jack Gold, signed a three-film contract with Thames Television. Plaschkes had worked with Gold in the past, and *The Sailor's Return* became one of the projects they offered to Thames's location drama offshoot Euston Films.[9] Garnett's novel was adapted by screenwriter James Saunders.

Gold decided to treat *The Sailor's Return* as

> a romantic story [but with] a gritty edge to it. It's also a beautiful love story although it's a very potent subject dealing with the colour problem and how it is accepted by outsiders. The theme will always be with us of a stranger in the community . . . People mistrust the things they don't know and understand.
> (Gold, interviewed by McAsh 1978: 182–3)

The Sailor's Return was made with loving care and meticulous attention to detail, from Brian Tufano's cinematography to Carl Davis's original music score, which deservedly won a Bafta. John Wyver, reviewing the film in *Time Out* magazine, commented: 'Every frame looks like a movie, with detail and composition in depth only possible in 35mm' (Wyver 1989: 516). The performances of Tom Bell and newcomer Shope Shodeinde – London-born of Nigerian parents – were outstanding: they played together with such naturalism that they seemed to have forgotten the presence of the camera, as did the viewer. At times the idyllic beauty of the rural locations – *The Sailor's Return* was filmed mainly in the Cotswold village of Upper Slaughter, a renowned tourist destination – threatens to upstage the actors. Yet Gold is never quite taken in by this conventionally 'English' spectacle, allowing us to see that behind it lie deep-rooted ignorance and hypocrisy.

In an interview with Sheila Whitaker in *Framework*, Gold explained why making a film about a black character in a historical setting was important to him:

> One of the advantages of the film in setting it in a period and a place like that is that it might clarify the situation of a black person for the first time. In other words, although one is aware of all the various implications, the intention was that maybe we would see it more clearly or purely in this way. This wasn't the first thought, but that was what arose out of the book and one of the reasons why I was intrigued by it, but if you did it as a contemporary film, which I have done on TV about a black girl and a white boy,[10] it is immediately loaded with all the contemporary knowledge of the situation . . . but by setting it in a period one has to try and clarify the situation. Every prejudice is openly stated but in a non-malicious way because there hasn't been time for malice to grow – it is the strangeness, the 'otherness' you were talking about – and what I am really hoping is that one would go back and cleanse one's mind of all the edifice of sociology, politics, crime etc. and actually try and see a black person as for the first time and what it is like to be a black person. I think that those are the parameters of the film.
>
> (interviewed by Whitaker 1978/9: 41)

Tulip's 'failure' to find acceptance in – in effect – the society of Thomas Hardy's nineteenth-century Wessex lies at the centre of the drama. The welcome and empathy she might have hoped for from the villagers has been destroyed by the teachings of the Church of England, which has filled their heads with false beliefs. At first the acts of racism are small, even comical, and the couple manage to overcome them. Then Targett is informed by the owner of the inn that unless he marries Tulip in a Christian ceremony they will have to go. Gradually the acts of bigotry lead to a bloody crescendo, and Targett is killed in a fight with a boxer. Tulip, once a princess who had servants of her own, lives out the rest of her days washing pots in the very inn she once presided over with the husband she adored.

Although *The Sailor's Return* was selected for and screened at the 1978 Cannes, Karlovy Vary and London Film Festivals, it was not theatrically released. Consequently

> Euston Films found itself . . . making its third feature film for the cinema for which . . . it couldn't obtain theatrical release. [Executive Producer] Verity Lambert still thinks it was a very good film . . . which, had it been made six years later, would have worked in a cinema when placed in the context of films like *The Ploughman's Lunch*. The time just wasn't right in 1977 and so it ended up being transmitted on television.
>
> (Alvarado and Stewart 1985: 77)

The Sailor's Return was eventually screened on ITV in December 1980, followed by one repeat in 1985. Said Otto Plaschkes:

> Films that deal with 'problems', that have no conventional star values, that have no conventional up-beat ending, whose main financier is more interested in a television than a theatrical sale, have an extremely difficult life. We were caught between a financier who wanted the film shown on television, and a distributor who wanted the film purely for prestige rather than for commercial purposes. The history of *The Sailor's Return* is a classic illustration of the power of television, the arrogance of the duopoly and the confusion between nurturing a so-called difficult film and the instant 'bonanza'.
>
> (Plaschkes 1982)

In 1980, two years after *The Sailor's Return* was denied a theatrical release, Polish art-cinema auteur Roman Polanski enjoyed international critical acclaim and commercial success with *Tess*, his version of Thomas Hardy's novel *Tess of the D'Urbervilles*, thus proving there was an audience for such films at that time.

In recent years, several British period television drama series – usually literary adaptations – have featured important black characters. *A Respectable Trade* (BBC1, 1998) was an impressive four-part drama serial about the trading of African slaves through the port of Bristol in the late eighteenth century. Based on the novel of the same title by Philippa Gregory – a writer known for her careful historical research – it focused on the complex relationships between its wealthy white slave-owning family, the Coles, and the slaves in their household – in particular, the close relationship between Frances Cole (Emma Fielding) and Mehuru (Ariyon Bakare), the slave of her husband Josiah (Warren Clarke). Later that year, BBC1's six-part adaptation of William Makepeace Thackeray's *Vanity Fair* (first published in 1847–8) included an hilarious performance by Felix Dexter as the servant Samuel. In Dexter's hands, Samuel was no stereotype but a figure who exposed the shallowness of his materialistic employers by asserting his superiority. *Colour Blind* (Festival Film and Television for Carlton, also 1998) was a three-part adaptation of one of the late Catherine Cookson's period bestsellers, an inter-racial romance exposing racism in Cookson's native working-class Tyneside between the First and Second World Wars. It is a pity that contemporary British filmmakers are not following these examples.

It seems that the more information historians uncover about the lives of Britain's black population since the sixteenth century, the more British cinema ignores it. Admittedly, detailed historical knowledge of the lives of people of African descent in Britain before the 1948 arrival of the *Empire Windrush* remains limited. But this is no excuse for black people to be omitted altogether from historical films such as *Shakespeare in Love* – particularly in the current climate, in which British period films such as *Elizabeth* (Shekhar Kapur, 1998) are happy to interpret historical material creatively in almost every other respect. In a recent exception, the Canadian director Patricia Rozema's bold version of Jane Austen's *Mansfield Park* (USA/ UK, 1999) explicitly foregrounded the issue of slavery (only briefly alluded to in Austen's novel), showing that the genteel lifestyle of Sir Thomas Bertram (Harold Pinter) and his family was founded upon plantation ownership in Antigua and the terrible abuse of slaves. However, it did so without any depiction of black characters.

The black absence from recent British period films may be a symptom of the 'colour-blind' discourse around race and racism which is prevalent in much of white Britain today. As Ann Widdecombe, the right-wing Conservative Shadow Home Secretary, explained recently in the Commission for Racial Equality's journal *Connections*:

> My idea of good race relations is when you don't even consciously notice if the person you are speaking to is black, white, brown or anything else. The real test of racism is terribly simple; it's whether you notice the person you're talking to.
>
> (interviewed by Younge 2000: 18)

Unfortunately, this is a view shared by many white Britons of all political persuasions – including filmmakers. They believe that by refusing to 'notice' a person's colour they are being non-racist. Nothing could be further from the truth: for to refuse to 'notice' the colour of a person's skin is to deny their history, culture and identity. In 1996, the white director Mike Leigh – regarded by many as one of British cinema's most socially and politically committed auteurs – had written and directed *Secrets and Lies*. In this highly acclaimed comedy-drama, Hortense (Marianne Jean-Baptiste), a young black woman who has been fostered, discovers she has a white mother. Whether Leigh took the 'colour-blind' approach is a matter for debate. But despite Marianne Jean-Baptiste's terrific performance, which earned her American Academy Award and Bafta nominations for Best Supporting Actress, and the memorable comedy and complexity of the scenes in which she confronts her white mother (Brenda Blethyn), Hortense remains a white liberal's creation. In a perceptive review, *The Voice*'s critic Onyekachi Wambu commented:

> The film has been widely praised because the unspoken understanding is that, through a powerful metaphor, director Mike Leigh has achieved something of a breakthrough in exorcising part of the guilt and shame that accompanied Britain's relations with Black people since slavery and empire. In this film he finally offers us the possibility of a clan bloodlink – a sort of emotional equality.
>
> But despite generally liking the film, I nevertheless had huge problems with how far the exorcism had gone. When most Black people arrived in Britain, we did not arrive as strangers. Some of us were coming 'home' to the

'mother country', drawing on a 400-year relationship with the British which was mainly painful and brutal. The ignorance, hostility and fear which confronted us on our arrival, despite the centuries-old relationship, was one of the most astonishing things to hit the 'Windrush generation'.

This fear and ignorance continues to haunt Britain still, and one catches hints of it, even in *Secrets and Lies*. Hortense goes forward to meet her White family – but in order to do this she has to go alone. We see no pictures of her Black foster parents, her two brothers are seen once arguing with each other but never talk to her. But it is not just her Black foster family (read Black culture here) who must remain 'strangers' – the Black man remains somewhere on the edge of the abyss, a dark shadowy figure who in this movie cannot be brought in from the cold.

(Wambu 1996: 10)

Notes

1 The figure 105 is reported by most sources (e.g. Richards 1973: 210) but disputed by some historians: see Sheldon Hall's chapter in this volume (Chapter 8).
2 *The Tichborne Claimant* gave a central role to the eminent black South African actor John Kani. However, it is predominantly a white man's story narrated and interpreted by his black servant (Kani), and – in a familiar tradition of British period films – functions centrally as a showcase for white British character acting (the cast included Stephen Fry, Robert Hardy and Sir John Gielgud). In view of these limitations, it will not be discussed in detail in this chapter.
3 *Editors' note:* See also Sheldon Hall's chapter on *Zulu* (Chapter 8). On representations of India and Indians in the 1980s cycle of films set in the British Raj, see T. Muraleedharan's chapter (Chapter 10).
4 The work of Lola Young (1996) is a notable exception to this tendency.
5 The arrival of the ship the *Empire Windrush* at Tilbury Docks on 21 June 1948 marked the beginning of post-war settlement in Britain of people from Guyana and the Caribbean. *Windrush* carried the first wave of settlers who were seeking a new life on the land they called the 'Mother Country'.
6 Writing in 1935 in his radical American journal *Black Man*, Garvey complained: 'The promoters are skilful in putting over their propaganda. The wonder is that Paul Robeson cannot see that he is being used to the dishonor and discredit of his race' (Garvey 1935).
7 Harry Scott was the son of the African-American music hall and radio comedian Harry Scott (1879–1947) who, with his partner Eddie Whaley, came to Britain in 1909. Scott and Whaley were so successful that they never returned to the USA, and they became the first black performers to star in a British film, *Kentucky Minstrels* (John Baxter, 1934), inspired by the popularity of their BBC radio show.
8 Other black women who made an impact in Britain during the Victorian era included Ellen Craft (1826–90), an African-American who escaped from slavery in the United States and arrived in England in the 1850s, and Elizabeth Taylor Greenfield (1809–76), known as The Black Swan, an African-American concert singer who was popular in Europe in the 1850s and gave a command performance for Queen Victoria.

9 For an overview of the origins of Euston Films as a company and its relationship with Thames Television (itself now defunct), see Alvarado and Stewart 1985: 30–2.

10 Gold is referring to *Saturday Night Theatre: Faith and Henry*, produced by London Weekend Television and screened on 6 December 1969.

Bibliography

Note: Page numbers were not always available for articles accessed via library archives.

Anon. (1912) '——' [review of *The Adventures of Dick Turpin*], *The Bioscope*, 16 May 1912.

Adi, H. (1995) *The History of the African and Caribbean Communities in Britain*, Hove, East Sussex: Wayland.

Alexander, Z. and Dewjee, A. (1981) *Roots in Britain: Black and Asian Citizens from Elizabeth I to Elizabeth II*, London: Brent Library Service pamphlet.

Alibhai-Brown, Y. (2000) *Who Do We Think We Are? Imagining the New Britain*, London: Allen Lane/The Penguin Press.

Alvarado, M. and Stewart, J. (eds) (1985) *Made for Television: Euston Films Limited*, London: BFI/Thames Television/Methuen.

Bauml Duberman, M. (1989) *Paul Robeson*, London: Bodley Head.

Bellos, L. (2000) 'History' in C. Newland and K. Sesay (eds), *IC3: The Penguin Book of New Black Writing in Britain*, London: Hamish Hamilton.

Bogle, D. (1973) *Toms, Coons, Mulattoes, Mammies and Bucks: An Interpretive History of Blacks in American Films*, New York: Viking.

Bourne, S. (1998) *Black in the British Frame: Black People in British Film and Television 1896–1996*, London: Cassell.

—— (2000) 'Point of departure', *History Today*, 50, 2, February 2000: 62–3.

Bourne, S. and Bruce, E. (1996) *Aunt Esther's Story*, London: Hammersmith and Fulham Ethnic Communities Oral History Project.

Bygott, D. (1992) *Black and British*, Oxford: Oxford University Press.

Cameron, K. M. (1994) *Africa on Film: Beyond Black and White*, New York: Continuum.

Dabydeen, D. (1985) *Hogarth's Blacks: Images of Blacks in Eighteenth Century English Art*, Kingston-upon-Thames, Surrey: Dangaroo Press.

Dewe Mathews, T. (1994) *Censored*, London: Chatto and Windus.

Euston Films (1979) *The Sailor's Return*: Production Notes, March 1979 (in the BFI Library microfiche collection on *The Sailor's Return*).

File, N. and Power, C. (1981) *Black Settlers in Britain 1555–1958*, London: Heinemann.

Fryer, P. (1984) *Staying Power: The History of Black People in Britain*, London: Pluto.

Garnett, D. (1924) *The Sailor's Return*, London: Chatto and Windus. Page numbers refer to the 1978 edition, London: Penguin.

Garvey, M. (1935) '——' [article title unknown], *Black Man*, 1, 7, June 1935.

Gilroy, P. (1987) *'There Ain't No Black in the Union Jack': The Cultural Politics of Race and Nation*, London: Hutchinson.

Green, J. (1998) *Black Edwardians: Black People in Britain 1901–1914*, London: Frank Cass.

—— (2000) 'Before the *Windrush*', *History Today*, 50, 10, October 2000: 29–35.

Harper, S. (1994) *Picturing the Past: The Rise and Fall of the British Costume Film*, London: BFI.

Harrison, G. B. (1933) *Shakespeare at Work 1592–1603*, London: Routledge.

Hart, M. (1999) '——' [reader's letter], *The Voice*, 15 February 1999: 8.

James, L. (2000) 'Wot a double act', *Pride*, September 2000: 66.

Little, K. (1948) *Negroes in Britain: A Study of Racial Relations in English Society*, London: Kegan Paul.

McAsh, I. F. (1978) '*The Sailor's Return/The Medusa Touch*' [interview with Jack Gold], *Films Illustrated*, January 1978: 182–3.

Moss, R. F. (1987) *The Films of Carol Reed*, New York: Columbia University Press.

Okokon, S. (1998) *Black Londoners 1880–1990*, Stroud, Gloucestershire: Sutton.

Plaschkes, O. (1982) Letter to Stephen Bourne, 15 November 1982.

Richards, J. (1973) *Visions of Yesterday*, London: Routledge and Kegan Paul.

—— (1997), *Films and British National Identity: From Dickens to Dad's Army*, Manchester: Manchester University Press.

Robeson, P. (1936) 'Paul Robeson introduces *Song of Freedom*', *Film Weekly*, 23 May 1936: 17.

Scobie, E. (1972) *Black Britannia: A History of Blacks in Britain*, Chicago: Johnson.

Shyllon, F. (1977) *Black People in Britain 1555–1833*, Oxford: Oxford University Press.

Sinclair, N. (1993) *The Tiger Bay Story*, Butetown: Butetown History and Arts Project.

Walvin, J. (1973) *Black and White: The Negro and English Society 1555–1945*, London: Allen Lane/The Penguin Press.

Wambu, O. (1996) 'Stranger in the house', *The Voice*, 11 June 1996: 10.

Whitaker, S. (1978/9) 'Jack Gold: an interview', *Framework*, 9, Winter 1978/79: 38–42.

Wyver, J. (1989) '——' [review of *The Sailor's Return*], reprinted in T. Milne (ed.) *The Time Out Film Guide*, London: Penguin.

Young, L. (1996) *Fear of the Dark: 'Race', Gender and Sexuality in the Cinema*, London/New York: Routledge.

Younge, G. (2000) 'A shadow without a doubt' [interview with Ann Widdecombe], *Connections* (journal of the Commission for Racial Equality), Spring 2000: 18.

5   'If the world does not please you, you can change it'

The History of Mr Polly (1949) and
The Card (1952)

Tim O'Sullivan

Introduction

From its earliest times, British cinema has provided various kinds of cinematic peephole into the imagined communities and spectacles of the recent or more distant past. For modern generations, film has played a significant part in the construction and mediation of a sense of British history and heritage. As Michael Chanan has suggested:

> The modern world almost seems to have begun with the birth of film, at any rate in retrospect. Because we're used to seeing film images of the First World War, the First World War seems to be part of the modern period. But anything more than twenty years earlier than that belongs to an era which we easily feel to be lost.
>
> (Chanan 1980: 16)

In another vein, British cinema has played a significant part in bringing this premodern past to life. In her valuable research on the subject, Sue Harper identifies a series of cycles of British historical films from the late 1920s to the 1950s which drew upon historical myth, incident and personality as raw materials for 'picturing the past' and mobilising popular cinema audiences in the period:

> Historical film[1] played a particularly crucial part in the composition of film culture in Britain in the period 1933–50; indeed I would argue that it played an important part in cultural life as a whole. It permitted notions of national consciousness to be perceived in a new and vital way. It reassessed certain historical periods and recuperated them for new purposes, and it captured the past as the site of fantasy in a period when other 'fantastic' modes were not markedly successful. It never reflected history, but produced symbolic readings of it which were always, as it were, at a tangent from reality.
>
> (Harper 1994: 188)

This chapter focuses upon two British period films of the immediate post-Second World War years which have received little attention within critical studies of popular British cinema: *The History of Mr Polly*, directed by Anthony Pelissier, first screened in British cinemas early in February 1949, and *The Card*, directed by Ronald Neame, released in March 1952.

Neither film was especially successful in its box-office performance nor in the tenor of its critical reception.[2] Both were produced, promoted and released into a depressed, austere and turbulent post-war environment in which British cinema attendance had already embarked on its inexorable decline (see Docherty *et al.* 1987) and British cinema itself seemed to be moving into what one film critic was to characterise as 'the battleship grey decade of the 50s' (Anon. 1983: 1). The films are of interest precisely because they date from a phase in the production of British period films which has been little analysed. To a great extent this has been because by the 1950s the British historical film was, in Harper's judgement, declining 'in a minor key' (Harper 1994: 188). Both films nevertheless constitute telling appropriations of works of popular Edwardian fiction for contemporary purposes which attempt to capitalise both on literary adaptation and on the box-office popularity of their stars – John Mills and Alec Guinness – within the modes of British popular historical cinema of the immediate post-war decade. Both are comic melodramas concerning the interwoven public and private masculine career stories of their heroes, set within their respective romantic and nostalgic versions of the Edwardian world.[3]

Both films translate the episodic formats of their source novels – both minor works by popular Edwardian writers – fairly directly to the screen. *The History of Mr Polly*, written by H. G. Wells, was published in 1910; *The Card*, written by Arnold Bennett early in 1909, was eventually published in novel format in 1911. In his article tracing the importance of literary adaptations to British cinema, Brian McFarlane observes that cinematic reworkings of the literary heritage reached a low ebb during the Second World War years but that a post-war boom followed, beginning with the success of David Lean's *Great Expectations* in 1946. In the four years from 1947, 115 of the 315 British feature films produced were based on British novels. Furthermore, McFarlane notes that the British tradition of film adaptation:

> has not often been a radical approach to the original material but, rather, a characteristic tendency to be awed by or to trade on the prestige and popularity of the source novels, and the result has often been to contribute another unadventurous element to the British cinema at large.
>
> (McFarlane 1986: 120)

McFarlane's criticism certainly applies to *The History of Mr Polly* and *The Card*. In their speculative whimsicality, they are, as one commentator has suggested of the former, 'very English and rather appealingly done' (Halliwell 1979: 402).

While the two films are united in several important respects, there are also significant differences between them, not least in their central discourses on trade, commerce and class and in their contrasting positions regarding the nature of 'everyman', his relations with 'everywoman', and their heroes' respective possibilities for advancement within modern society.

In one of the few analytically informed academic references to either film, Marcia Landy has identified *The History of Mr Polly* as one of a number of British post-war film melodramas which dealt with the themes of masculinity and the sudden insecurities of patriarchial power in a peacetime, and hence unstable, world. She argues that the film is a 'conversion drama' (Landy 1991: 260); and indeed this notion can be used fruitfully to illuminate and focus analysis of both films. Alfred Polly may more easily be understood as a social misfit – who in Landy's terms is converted – than Denry Machin, the eponymous 'card'. However, both films – like their source novels – work through a sequence of biographical 'snapshots' and episodes: short segments which reveal the protagonists' principal trials in their respective quests for self-improvement, self-realisation and self-discovery.

The films are of interest in part because they do not neatly fit the established critical frameworks and discourses which have evolved around either British period genres or the British cinema of the 1950s. On the one hand, Polly and Denry are clearly not known or 'real' historical figures. Their personal tales of the unknown and unexpected – quite distinctive among the films of that time – are not even loosely based on recognised historical events or myths, thus excluding them from consideration within one dominant body of literature around the 'historical' film. On the other hand, although the two films are fantastical in the wish-fulfilment they offer their male protagonists, they do not construct the past as an exotic, spectacular 'site of fantasy' (Harper 1994: 188) marked by its distance from the everyday, as do the Gainsborough melodramas such as *The Wicked Lady* (Leslie Arliss, 1945), of central interest to Harper and Pam Cook (Cook 1996 and 1997). Yet, like films belonging to more easily identifiable and widely-analysed period genres, their uses of a particular past perform particular functions in the context of their time. Within their refracted versions of the Edwardian world, they narrate the life fortunes of central male characters who act as popular screen typifications for 'everyday' people. In this narrative, those who begin as anonymous individuals – 'just like us' – end up making their mark by romantically asserting themselves and their 'difference' against the pressures of conformist society and, more broadly, the weight of their/'our' history.

In this, the films can be read as masculine fantasies with some intriguing parallels to the feminine fantasy of the Gainsborough melodramas – which have been read as appealing to the desire for self-determination of 'ordinary', working-class women (Harper 1994: 135, 185). *Because* of their initial ordinariness, Polly and Denry become the bearers of significant social values: in terms of how they are 'trapped' and by what; the strategies they subsequently adopt; and the stages they go through in order to break out and achieve their final 'conversion'. Two contrasting kinds of career management are on display in the films, however. One hero retreats from modernity, to a settled rural community and to idyllic peace, where he can live on his own terms, unfettered by the chains of social convention, commerce or bureacracy. The other is driven by ambition and entrepreneurial opportunism to achieve success and social endorsement beyond the constraints of birth, embodying class mobility and meritocracy – and thus prefiguring the dominant myths of the subsequent post-war decades.

The History of Mr Polly (1949)

> I think it is the very greatest art, with the possibility of becoming the greatest art form that has ever existed. What I think is so extraordinary in the last four or five years is the way in which voice production has reached a point of perfection and the photographing of the face for dramatic effect – so that you can have more drama on the film than you can have on the stage. I don't know how it seems to you, but it seems to me that the film is likely to oust both the opera and the stage in the long run.
>
> H. G. Wells on film and cinema[4]

By the time H. G. Wells died in 1946, he had enjoyed a productive relationship with both film and broadcasting – the new media of the twentieth century. Orson Welles's controversial radio production of *War of the Worlds*, broadcast in America in 1938, had given a new twist to Wells's reputation as one of the foremost prophets of the 'new age', capable of juxtaposing utopian vision and dystopian critique. Other, domestic and class-related, issues had been broached in *Kipps* (filmed by Harold M. Shaw in 1921 and Carol Reed, 1941), *The Passionate Friends* (filmed by Maurice Elvey in 1922 and by David Lean in 1948) and the golfing sequence based on a Wells story in the compendium film *Dead of Night* (Alberto Cavalcanti/Charles Crichton/Basil Dearden/Robert Hamer, 1945). By the time Wells published his autobiography in 1934, ten films had already been made from his novels and short stories, including *The Island of Lost Souls* (Erle C. Kenton, USA, 1932, based on *The Island of Dr Moreau*) and *The Invisible Man* (James Whale, USA, 1933). To follow were *Things to Come* (William Cameron Menzies, 1936), *War of the Worlds* (Byron Haskin, USA, 1953) and a number of other notable film and television productions, remakes and spin-offs.

Anthony Pelissier, *The History of Mr Polly*'s director, also adapted the novel for the screen. His script deviates little from the narrative sequence established by Wells. However, some critics judged that the film compressed too much the novel's early stages dealing with the drudgery of Polly's life as an outfitters' shop assistant, especially given the sequence's autobiographical origins in Wells's own experience as a draper's assistant. The film was made under the Rank umbrella for Two Cities Films at Denham Studios. John Mills, who starred in the title role, was also credited, on the first of only two occasions in his career (the second being Pelissier's *The Rocking Horse Winner* in the same year) as producer. Reflecting nearly fifty years later on this never-to-be-repeated experience, Mills noted: 'Now, I'm rather proud of them . . . I'm not ashamed of doing either of them, but they weren't hits with the public. Anthony Pelissier was a great friend of mine . . . I gave him his start with those two films' (McFarlane 1997: 415).

Contemporary critics generally approved of Mills's performance; however, there is evidence that audiences resented his switch away from heroic wartime roles, epitomised by those in Anthony Asquith's *We Dive at Dawn* (1943) and *The Way to the Stars* (1945). Indeed, *The History of Mr Polly* made an uneasy successor to Mills's preceding role as *Scott of the Antarctic* (Charles Frend, 1948) and was followed by his return to type in *Morning Departure* (Roy Baker, 1950). Mills later hinted that this factor may have compromised the film's box-office success: 'At the time, Mr Polly didn't succeed because I was then a blue-eyed hero and the audiences hated seeing me as a little, wizened chap with smarmed hair and a moustache, being a henpecked husband' (McFarlane 1997: 415).

The film's opening introduces the young, fresh-faced Mr Polly, who much prefers reading romantic tales of chivalry and derring-do to the mindless and demeaning work he performs as a counter assistant in the gentlemen's outfitters' department of a large Edwardian emporium in south-east England. The monotony, imposed humility and pecking order of such a service-class position are rapidly established. This opening ushers in the first of the film's three principal phases, each coterminous with a key stage in Polly's life/career.

The first phase outlines the dilemmas and conditions of Mr Polly's social entrapment as well as his romantic nature. Polly is rapidly and summarily dismissed from his position, and experiences the anxieties of unemployment. 'A social misfit, that's what I am', he muses in response to this change of circumstances. The sudden illness and death of his father further develop the theme of Polly as a figure who is not yet in control of his destiny. His subsequent involvement in the arcane conventions and rites of his father's funeral, and the cacophony of the funeral meal – which overwhelms him – allow for considerable character development and reinforce this view. Polly's network of relations are first encountered in the funeral setting, notably including his raucous cousins, the Larkins – Annie (Diana Churchill), Minnie (Shelagh Fraser) and Miriam (Betty Ann Davis) – their redoubtable mother Ma Larkins (Gladys Henson) and the bad-tempered Uncle Penstemon (Moore Marriott). After the funeral, Polly learns from his cousin Johnson (Edward Chapman, also cast as Mr Duncalf in *The Card*) that he has inherited £500. He disregards prudent family advice to invest this in a 'little shop', and instead buys a bicycle. This purchase facilitates a release from the claustrophobic social relations of both 'trade' and the parlour and enables Polly – and the film –

to begin a relationship with the countryside and the rural, a motif that is continued and developed later. The bicycle also provides him with the means to visit the Larkins – en route to whom he experiences his initial romantic encounter with the schoolgirl Christabel (Sally Anne Howes).

On his first, unannounced, visit to the Larkins's home, the film presents Mr Polly as the centre of attention, and as he enters into the banter of the female household he is clearly earmarked by Ma Larkins as the potential husband for any one of her three daughters. His prospects for a secure future – defined in terms of 'the shop' and 'marriage' – but also the tensions surrounding this new security are important motifs in this first phase of the film and Polly's life. But, significantly and ironically, it is his subsequent encounter with Christabel that delivers him into the arms of Miriam and the matriarch Larkins. In a scene on top of a school boundary wall, he confesses his love to this haughty schoolgirl, only to find that his dream of chivalrous romance is shattered – turned into a sham, a performance, as he is eavesdropped upon by Christabel's younger schoolfriends. This rebuff leads directly to his marriage on the rebound to Miriam Larkins and the rather grim honeymoon train journey to his new shop in provincial Fishbourne. This first phase of the film ends with Polly, in his mid-twenties, embarking upon a new – and, we presume from our knowledge so far, unstable – phase in his career as a married man and owner of his own outfitters' shop.

The film's second phase opens with a cut to a point some fifteen years later, and invites assessment of the achievements and state of Mr Polly as he approaches his fortieth year.[5] Neither Polly's marriage to Miriam nor the shop – which is piling up bills – have flourished, and the film documents a relationship of unremitting grind, lacking in either affection or fulfilment. Continuing to find solace and escape in his books and the romantic dreams they inspire, Polly is shown to be at loggerheads both with Miriam and with his neighbouring shopkeepers. At this juncture, the film paraphrases what is in fact the opening passage of the book. Seated on a stile in the countryside overlooking Fishbourne, Polly confesses himself to be in 'a beastly, silly wheeze of a hole' – with a 'beastly home – beastly life' – and the thought of killing himself seems to make perfect sense and offers a solution to everything.

As at other significant moments of crisis for Polly in the film, the whimsical comedy of historical manners and knowing observation here gives way to a slapstick-based comic mode redolent of the silent era. Polly's incompetence leads to a bungled 'suicide arsonical' as he accidentally sets fire to the shop before he is ready and finds himself unable to cut his own throat. In the ensuing blaze, he saves a frail old woman (Edie Martin) from the roof, and as a result is fêted by his erstwhile enemies in the local community. Polly finds temporary accommodation after the fire at Fishbourne's Temperance Hotel. Despite Polly's newly conferred heroic reputation, this middle section of the film concludes with his realisation that 'One thing's clear: if you don't like your life – you can change it':[6] a theme that is

equally crucial to *The Card*. From this point onwards, Polly embarks upon a rede-
fined personal romantic mission.

The final section of the film is focused around a compelling place of rural idyll,
The Potwell Inn. A less dyspeptic and altogether healthier Mr Polly is shown,
tramping through the countryside, at ease with himself and with life in general.
He happens upon the inn, its food and its landlady 'The Plump Woman' (Megs
Jenkins), and feels at home. The inn and its inhabitants are, however, under threat
from her deceased sister's husband, Uncle Jim (Finlay Currie) a drunken bully
who views the pub as his own territory. After initially retreating from Uncle Jim,
Polly is tested – in a highly theatrical sequence – by conscience and destiny,
leading the 'little man' to return to the inn to stand his ground and claim his place.
Finally, after further slapstick sequences, Polly despatches Uncle Jim into the weir
downstream of the inn. Thereafter, Polly appears established in his new identity
and in circumstances that are conducive to his happiness. A state of harmonious
utopia has been gained.

The film ends with a small but significant coda, set some three years later.
While fishing, and pondering life in the relaxed rural environs of The Potwell Inn,
Polly finds himself thinking of Miriam and Fishbourne and, out of conscience and
curiosity, resolves to revisit his old world. In place of his old shop, destroyed by
the fire, he encounters a tearoom under the sign of 'Polly & Larkins'. Entering
incognito, he discovers that he has been assumed dead since Uncle Jim's watery
demise, which due to an error was in fact recorded as his own death. Polly leaves
the tearoom confident that Miriam is well, not in want or need; and as he passes
her on the stairs, a flicker of mutual recognition occurs as he leaves behind his old
life – and wife – forever. The film's final scene finds Polly restored to The Potwell
Inn, witnessing with 'The Plump Woman' an idyllic sunset. Mr Polly is settled
finally in his place. He has encountered and triumphed over the strictures of un-
successful trade and marriage and the life-threatening challenges of the fire and of
Uncle Jim. He – and we – find ourselves finally 'at peace with the world'.

The Card (1952)

> And he knew of a surety that he was that most admired type in the bustling,
> industrial provinces – a card.[7]
>
> (Bennett 1975: 34)

> A charmingly anachronistic work set in an Edwardian era seemingly devoid of
> hardship or real poverty.
>
> (Von Gunden 1987: 56)

Just as *The History of Mr Polly* had been a vehicle for its established star John Mills
(by then a veteran of more than thirty films), *The Card* was a vehicle for the comic

talents of the rising Alec Guinness: his credits already included his key roles as Fagin in *Oliver Twist* (David Lean, 1948) and in the Ealing comedies *Kind Hearts and Coronets* (Robert Hamer, 1949), *The Lavender Hill Mob* (Charles Crichton, 1951) and *The Man in the White Suit* (Alexander Mackendrick, 1951). Its director Ronald Neame had already worked with both Mills and Guinness as one of the screenwriters of Lean's *Great Expectations* (1946) – in which Mills had played Pip and Guinness Herbert Pocket – and as producer of *Oliver Twist*, and would later direct Guinness in three further films.[8] *The Card* was made by British Film Makers for Rank at Pinewood Studios; its producer was John Bryan, Academy Award-winning art director of *Great Expectations*. The popular British novelist Eric Ambler adapted Bennett's novel for the screen.

Bennett had died in 1931, and by the 1950s remained known first and foremost as a popular Edwardian novelist. Although, intriguingly, he had scripted E. A. Dupont's expressionistic melodrama *Piccadilly* (1929), starring Anna Mae Wong, in contrast with Wells his books remained largely unmined by the film industry. Bennett's novel *Buried Alive* (1908) had been filmed as *Holy Matrimony* (John Stahl, USA, 1943), and a film version of *Mr Prohack* (1922) had been released as *Dear Mr Prohack* (Thornton Freeland, 1949), but neither met with great acclaim. An earlier version of *The Card* (A. V. Bramble, 1922) had been filmed in the silent era.

The Card (1911), like most of Bennett's work (including, most famously, the *Clayhanger* novels)[9] is set in the northern Midlands of the 'Five Towns' – Bennett's term for the towns that today form the borough of Stoke-on-Trent in Stafford-shire, a conurbation also known in Britain as 'The Potteries' in acknowledgement of its traditional main industry. Contemporary and more recent literary critics' assessments of *The Card* make clear its status as a popular, rather than prestige, literary source: it has been compared adversely to Bennett's other works and was condemned on its publication as 'too appealing to a magazine public' (Lucas 1974: 124), although 'less heavy-handed than Wells's *Kipps*' (Barker 1966: 158).

The Card tells the story of Denry (Edward Henry) Machin (played in the film by Guinness), a washerwoman's son who is determined to make his way in the world. The early stages of the film show Denry (played as a child by Guinness's son Matthew) growing up in Bursley, the most prominent of the Five Towns – a provincial confederation hailed by the novel and film as an epicentre of *fin-de-siècle* progress and civilisation. Whereas *Mr Polly* is represented as a social misfit who retreats from work and imposed social obligations in search of romantic ideals, Denry achieves his best 'against the grain', confounding his humble origins through a mixture of luck, opportunism, entrepreneurship and canny ambition. Alec Guinness's performance builds a portrait of Denry as a benign 'rogue trader' of his age. Despite the apparent brio of his performance and the generally positive reviews he received, Guinness later expressed ambivalence about the role: 'I never felt I was the right actor to play Denry in *The Card*. They should have had someone more obviously tougher. I think I treated it too lightly' (McFarlane 1997: 262).

As a film, *The Card*, like *The History of Mr Polly*, is firmly episodic and chrono-logical and is structured into three principal segments or life stages, telling the story of Denry's life through separate but neatly linked incidents. The first seg-ment establishes the humble circumstances of Denry's birth and childhood, but also sows the seeds of his potential 'conversion' – here, defined by upward mobility. Denry is shown altering his examination results at primary school, but this willing-ness to give providence a helping hand is rewarded with a scholarship to a Gram-mar school – although here he is taunted as 'washerwoman' due to his mother's (Veronica Turleigh) occupation. On leaving, further opportunism leads him to a job as articled clerk to solicitor Mr Duncalf (Edward Chapman). Denry uses this position to accelerate his destiny by exploiting his control of the invitations to the Countess of Chell's (Valerie Hobson) Grand Civic Ball. He has already encoun-tered a dancing teacher, Ruth Earp (Glynis Johns), and her tuition pays off when, on the evening of the ball, he accepts a wager to dance with the Countess. For the duration of this waltz, he becomes the centre of attention among Bursley's high society – for the first time, but not the last. This social visibility, however, rebounds on Denry when, the following morning, he is dismissed by Duncalf for inviting himself and his friends of similar social origin to the ball, thus transgressing his place in the social hierarchy: 'A washerwoman's son . . . dancing with your betters'.

However, Denry almost instantaneously encounters a new opportunity as rent collector for a landlady, Mrs Codleyn (Joan Hickson). He takes this role in his stride, acquiring a small donkey-cart with his name on the side and even lending money to some of the deserving tenants in arrears. Although resistant to the feminine wiles of Ruth Earp, who hopes to evade paying her overdue rent, Denry nevertheless come to her aid when her rent-avoidance culminates in a 'moonlight flit', rescuing her when her escape vehicle, a furniture wagon, runs headlong into the canal. As another landlord (George Devine) who commissions him to collect rents wryly observes, Denry is by now 'getting to be quite a card'.

The film's second phase sees Denry progress from an opportunistic, youthful wide-boy to an established and promising entrepreneur. This phase establishes both romantic and fiscal possibilities, but these do not combine in initial harmony. The segment begins with an innocent holiday trip to Llandudno with Ruth, now Denry's fiancée, and her friend Nellie Cotterill (Petula Clark) as companion and chaperone. Denry's patience is sorely tested during this jaunt by Ruth's ability to spend his money without limits. These tensions are brought to a head during a storm and a ship rescue when Denry encounters final evidence of Ruth's pro-fligacy. Ruth breaks off their engagement – but Denry has already identified the germ of his next money-making venture, and he sets in motion what proves to be a very profitable enterprise: tourist boat trips to the wrecked ship. After a short summer season's work, Denry returns home to his mother with a hatbox full of sovereigns. This second phase of the film closes with the cash – over £1,000 – spread out on his shocked mother's floor.

The film's final phase deals with Denry's continuing rise to affluence and re-spectability. In particular, it constitutes Denry as a 'new' kind of entrepreneur: one whose personal rise is a justifiable reward for his public works and philan-thropy. He puts his money to work by founding the Universal Thrift Club, a co-operative organisation which offers credit and discounts for subscribers. The scheme rapidly absorbs all of Denry's capital and he needs to borrow more in order to see the venture through to its fruition. His bank manager (Michael Hordern) suggests that he needs a suitable patron to guarantee success. Denry devises an inventive plot which results in the Countess of Chell agreeing to become his patron, and this ensures his future prosperity and success. Denry exchanges his donkey cart for a motor car and buys his mother an expensive fur stole. 'Some folk have got so grand,' she observes when Denry becomes a local councillor. Ruth Earp resur-faces briefly. She is now the wealthy, recently widowed Lady Capron-Smith, and Denry's ambitions have rekindled her interest in him – he aims to become the youngest-ever Mayor of Bursley.

In the mayoral campaign, Denry again crosses swords with his old employer Duncalf, who is also standing for Mayor. Duncalf is no match, however, for Denry's ability to capture the popular vote.[10] The fortunes of the local football club be-come the key to Denry's electoral victory. At a meeting convened to close down the team due to their lacklustre sporting and commercial performance, Denry takes the stage and introduces to the crowd the 'greatest centre-forward in Eng-land', Callear (actor uncredited), who came from Bursley before moving on to greater things. Denry has bought Callear back 'as a present for the club'; this generosity not only transforms the performance of the team, but also precipitates Denry's electoral success.

At this point, however, news arrives of Nellie's father's bankruptcy and of her family's imminent departure from Liverpool to Canada – travelling steerage – and Denry and Ruth Earp set out on a mercy mission. They buy Nellie's parents out of the ignominy of the lower deck; but, at the moment of departure, Denry realises that he cannot live without Nellie. He escapes the boat with her, evading Ruth – whose own happy ending is assured when she attracts the attentions of an anony-mous wealthy lord (Wilfred Hyde-White) on the quayside. Nellie and Denry's marriage coincides with his election as the youngest Mayor of Bursley. At the celebratory civic parade, where Denry and Nellie appear in his little donkey cart, Duncalf mockingly asks the Countess, what 'great cause' Denry has ever been associated with. She unhesitatingly answers: 'Cheering us all up'.

Two kinds of conversion

In her discussion of the British costume film, Sue Harper (1994) draws upon a number of geological analogies to characterise the field of British historical cin-ema. Borrowing from Gramsci, she suggests that popular culture and memory carry many 'fossils' – or residual deposits and traces – from the past, originally formed in response to specific historical force fields of dynamics and pressures. The two films discussed here are both usefully understood as such 'fossils', produced by and embedded in the strata of the British film industry, cinematic culture and wider society of the late 1940s and early 1950s.

As whimsical comic melodramas, both *The History of Mr Polly* and *The Card* embody and trace historically situated versions of 'a dream world inhabited by dream people . . . An idealisation and simplification of the world of reality . . . in fact the world the audiences want but cannot get' (Booth 1965: 14). In their simplified typifications of Edwardian life, both films activate and appeal to a rather comfortable and reassuring form of nostalgia for a mythic turn-of-the-century era, imagined in these films as pre-modern, and for simple romantic stories of individual achievement against social – rather than wartime or military – odds. As such, both films offer a momentary escape into what has become one of the intensified elements of post-war experience and culture: 'a perpetual staple of nostalgic yearning . . . the search for a simple and stable past as a refuge from the turbulent and chaotic present' (Lowental 1989: 21).

However, the films also start to explore – albeit obliquely and within a historical setting – some emergent contemporary concerns: in particular, around class mobility in a new era of promised meritocratic possibility and around the place of men and the nature of masculinity in a post-war, peacetime Britain. They consequently provide some evidence in support of Neil Rattigan's suggestion that: '[British film in] the period 1946–59 deserves more attention than it has received, notably for the very way in which it is precisely a bridge between wartime films and those of the socially realist 1960s' (Rattigan 1994: 143).

At the heart of each of the two films lies a set of issues concerning the determining power of history, social structure and circumstance of birth versus the possibilities of autonomous agency and social mobility in a society preoccupied with class and status. The forces of acquiescence, unquestioning conformity, conservatism and deference confront both Polly and Denry, seeking to regulate or stifle them. In response, Polly and Denry employ differing tactics; but both can be interpreted as early harbingers of agents of change who would emerge in more radical and outspoken form – in British cinema and the wider culture – as the 1950s changed gear into the 1960s.[11] Both protagonists function as historically displaced metaphors for the voyage from austerity to affluence that conventionally has been claimed to characterise the quantum shift – and shifting tensions – within British society and film culture in the post-war period (as documented by, for example, Durgnat, 1970).

Mr Polly is a hopeless romantic idealist whose inclination is to retreat from the demands of the modern age, or at least to let them drift around him. He rails against the routine and subservience of his work and the shackles of petit-bourgeois/trade sensibilities and respectability. He is equally unable to reconcile

Figure 5.1 At ease with the world: *The History of Mr Polly* (1949) reaches its close as Polly (John Mills) finds rural peace and harmony with 'The Plump Woman' (Megs Jenkins) at The Potwell Inn – but at the price of a retreat from sexuality and marriage.
Source: Courtesy of Two Cities Films.

the realities of his relationships with women with his romantic ideals. Once he finally stands his ground when he finds something worth fighting for, he is rewarded with an existence of peaceful, rural harmony – but this reward is the result of a retreat from women and marriage, which are equated with his entrapment. He fights for the inn, its bucolic surroundings and his idyllic way of life there more than for 'The Plump Woman'. 'The Plump Woman', by her own admission, needs 'a man about the place', and Mr Polly enters into a ready-made family; but her attractions are represented in the film as more maternal and gastronomic than sexual. There is a curious contradiction in this ending – a romantic conclusion that leaves Mr Polly ultimately unfulfilled.

By contrast, Denry Machin – 'the card', with whom the film assumes we will all identify – stands for a new kind of modern entrepreneur as salient to the nascent 1950s as to the Edwardian age. Unconstrained by the class or economic circumstances of his birth, he fights – with wit and opportunism as his weapons – for self-advancement and hence to usher in the new, meritocratic, modern era; through his commercial energy, he is able to short-circuit the rigidities of the old regime. Significantly, however, Denry's seamless translation of his *nouveau-riche/*

Figure 5.2 An optimistic lesson in self-advancement: washerwoman's son Denry (Alec
Guinness), newly wed to Nellie (Petula Clark), is elected youngest-ever Mayor
of the Five Towns in *The Card* (1952) – a seamless rise that anticipated Britain's
post-war voyage from austerity to affluence.
Source: Courtesy of Rank/British Film Makers/Carlton International.

commercial success into electoral and social advancement is achieved through the
support of old money and the old aristocracy in the form of the Countess of Chell.
The film – and specifically Guinness's performance – contrive to present an amusing, innocent version of capitalist entrepreneurship, fully consonant with the emerging political mood of individualism which had returned the Conservative government
to power in 1951, and anticipating the rhetoric of democratised affluence which
would typify the 'never had it so good' era of the later 1950s.[12] *The Card* is unique
as a British film which offers a positive depiction of a rent-collector and his rise to
commercial and civic success. Far from hinting that any of Denry's activities might
deserve criticism or condemnation, the film presents his career as an exemplary
model of self-propulsion, an optimistic lesson in how to 'get on'.

The prominence of discourses of progress, self-advancement and confident
modernity throughout *The Card* place it in clear contrast with *The History of Mr
Polly*. Both films nevertheless recommend for their male heroes the importance of
coming to terms with change, whether by moving with the times or by finding an
appropriate – whether ascendant or regressive – niche for oneself in a changing
world. But, importantly, both also suggested to their post-Second World War
viewers that they/we – or, at least, the films' male protagonists – were not totally

pre-determined, not trapped in the cage of history: that their/our destinies depended principally upon what they/we made of them.

These reassurances are, however, addressed to the male viewer. A less positive picture emerges if we ask what meanings the films mobilise for women. 'Conversion' for men in these narratives is conditional upon accommodation by women. After the active roles permitted to women in at least some 1940s British cinema – from the period adventures of Lady Barbara Skelton (Margaret Lockwood) in *The Wicked Lady* to the Second World War factory workers of *Millions Like Us* (Frank Launder and Sidney Gilliat, 1943) – female characters here are decisively returned to supporting roles. They either inhabit the traditional domestic sphere – to which officialdom was anxious to return women after the war – or function as objects of male idealisation and adoration. Women who exceed these roles – Miriam in *The History of Mr Polly* and Ruth in *The Card* – are portrayed as shrews or gold diggers and accordingly eliminated from the male narrative and its positive ending. The one exception to this pattern is the Countess of Chell, seemingly exempted by class from the strictures imposed on 'ordinary' women (intriguingly, there is no Lord Chell). The message to post-war women viewers seems to be that they must resume their 'natural' feminine, caring role – defined as one of offering sympathy and career support to the male population engaged in their own post-war readjustment or 'conversion' – if they are not to risk a similar fate.

Both films hark back to imagined historical communities of the strangely potent Edwardian age – which, significantly, was revisited and appropriated in a number of other British films of the period, notably *Kind Hearts and Coronets* and *Genevieve* (Henry Cornelius, 1953). For the British generations born into the mid-twentieth century, the Edwardian era was *the* golden age: poised just before modernity, living memory and the onset of industrialised, total warfare. In their respective appropriations of this era, *The History of Mr Polly* and *The Card* epitomise and betray some of the tensions of the post-Second World War culture: to retreat or to progress, to eulogise romantically or to assess realistically, to hold on to the past or to march forward with the new. It can validly be argued that these same oppositions and dilemmas have continued to confront British culture and society, and British filmmakers and their audiences, ever since the 1950s. However, in the nature of their particular 'happy endings', and in their oblique engagements with the realities of contemporary conditions, the two films remain very specifically fixed in – and very telling about – the juncture of the late 1940s/early 1950s. Like many other films of their time, they look now 'as if they come from another world' (Geraghty 2000: 37).

Acknowledgements

My thanks to Robert Murphy, Claire Monk, Steve Chibnall, and Alan Burton for their comments on earlier drafts of this chapter.

Notes

1 *Editors' note:* As will be clear from the quoted passage, Harper uses the term 'historical film' as a broad, inclusive category encompassing a variety of period genres and modes of representing the past. By contrast, some contributors in this volume use the term 'historical film' to indicate a specific period film genre with distinct conventions: see in particular Quinn and Kingsley-Smith.

2 Reviewers were on the whole kind to the two films, applauding especially the performances of their popular stars. For representative reviews of *The History of Mr Polly*, see Anon. 1949 (*Monthly Film Bulletin*) and 'C.A.W.' 1949. For reviews of *The Card*, see 'P.H.' 1952, 'J.G.W.' 1952, Anon. 1952 (*Kinematograph Weekly*) and Herbstman 1952. For pre-production features on *The Card*, see Samson 1951 and 1952.

3 *The Card* was made in the year of my birth. I first encountered each film on television, I suspect in the early/mid-1960s. There may be a double nostalgia at work here: that of the post-war era looking back to the Edwardian age in the films, and from the perspective of the early 2000s looking back to the 1950s in this discussion. Interesting issues of a generational nature are raised by much current historical analysis of film.

4 From a 1935 interview Wells gave to the US publication *The Era* (quoted in Wykes 1977: 14).

5 In his introduction to *The History of Mr Polly*, Frank Wells highlights the centrality of mid-life crisis as a theme of the novel (and hence film): 'Reaching the age of forty is a natural process that causes us much mental pain and gives us the opportunity to disturb our minds. Forty seems to be the ridge; behind us is prehistory and youth; before us is nothing but old age and death' (Wells 1953: 9).

6 Here, the script paraphrases Wells's precise words in the book (which provide the title for this chapter): 'But when a man has once broken through the paper walls of everyday circumstance, those unsubstantial walls that hold so many of us securely prisoned from the cradle to the grave, he has made a discovery. If the world does not please you, you can change it. Determine to alter it at any price, and you can change it altogether' (Wells 1953: 193).

7 *Editors' note:* 'Card' is an English slang expression – today little used – for 'a person' (the nuance is loosely similar to the Jewish colloquial use of the German *mensch*) – particularly 'an odd or amusing person'. (Definitions taken from Oxford 1991: 222.)

8 The most successful was *The Horse's Mouth* (1958); the others were *Tunes of Glory* (1960) and the musical *Scrooge* (1970).

9 Which were dramatised by BBC-TV in the 1970s.

10 In this connection, it is interesting that the film omits a significant episode in the novel in which Denry becomes a newspaper proprietor and engages in a circulation war.

11 For instance, Denry Machin stands in an interesting relationship to Joe Lampton in *Room at the Top* (novel: John Braine, 1957; film: Jack Clayton, 1958). However, the latter notably refuses to configure its central character as a populist local hero: his scheming and self-advancement are presented as individualistic, ruthless, amoral and hence socially suspect. The successors of Polly are less easy to identify: perhaps his traces reappear much later, in 1970s British television, in the tragi-comic Reginald Perrin (*The Fall and Rise of Reginald Perrin*) and *The Good Life*'s suburban sitcom utopian Tom Good (both BBC-TV).

12 The famous phrase was coined by the newly elected Conservative Prime Minister Harold Macmillan in a speech in Bradford on 20 July 1957, where he declared that 'Most of our people have never had it so good'.

Bibliography

Anon. (1949) '——' [review of *The History of Mr Polly*], *Monthly Film Bulletin*, March 1949: 40.

Anon. (1952) '——' [review of *The Card*], *Kinematograph Weekly*, 28 February 1952: 22.

Anon. (1983) 'Pat Jackson', *Film Dope*, 27, July 1983: 1.

Barker, D. (1966) *Writer by Trade: A View of Arnold Bennett*, London: Allen & Unwin.

Bennett, A. (1975) *The Card: A Story of Adventure in the Five Towns* [1911], London: Penguin.

Booth, M. R. (1965) *English Melodrama*, London: Herbert Jenkins.

Chanan, M. (1980) *The Dream that Kicks: The Prehistory and Early Years of Cinema in Britain*, London: Routledge and Kegan Paul.

Cook, P. (1996) *Fashioning the Nation: Costume and Identity in British Cinema*, London: BFI.

—— (ed.) (1997) *Gainsborough Pictures*, London: Cassell.

Docherty, D., Morrison, D. and Tracey, M. (1987) *The Last Picture Show? Britain's Changing Film Audiences*, London: BFI.

Durgnat, R. (1970) *A Mirror for England*, London: Faber and Faber.

Geraghty, C. (2000) *British Cinema in the Fifties: Gender, Genre and The 'New Look'*, London: Routledge.

'P.H.' (1952) '——' [review of *The Card*], *Monthly Film Bulletin*, April 1952: 44.

Halliwell, L. (1979) *Halliwell's Film Guide*, London: Paladin.

Harper, S. (1994) *Picturing the Past: The Rise and Fall of the British Costume Film*, London: BFI.

Herbstman, M. (1952) '——' [review of *The Card*], *Motion Picture Herald*, 25 October 1952: 1581.

Landy, M. (1991) *British Genres: Cinema and Society 1930–1960*, Princeton, NJ: Princeton University Press.

Lowental, D. (1989) 'Nostalgia tells it like it wasn't' in C. Shaw and M. Chase (eds) *The Imagined Past: History and Nostalgia*, Manchester: Manchester University Press.

Lucas, J. (1974) *Arnold Bennett: A Study of His Fiction*, London: Methuen.

McFarlane, B. (1986) 'A literary cinema? British films and British novels' in C. Barr (ed.) *All Our Yesterdays: 90 Years of British Cinema*, London: BFI.

—— (1997) *An Autobiography of British Cinema*, London: Methuen.

Oxford University Press (1991) *The Oxford Encyclopaedic English Dictionary*, Oxford: Oxford University Press.

Rattigan, N. (1994) 'The last gasp of the middle class: British war films of the 1950s' in W. Wheeler Dixon (ed.) *Re-Viewing British Cinema*, New York: SUNY Press.

Samson, H. (1951) 'After the Card Mayor's Show', *Picturegoer*, 20 October 1951: 8–9.

—— (1952) 'The Card – Guinness's ace?', *Picturegoer*, 23 February 1952: 10–11.

Von Gunden, K. (1987) *Alec Guinness: The Films*, Jefferson, NC and London: McFarland.

'C.A.W.' (1949) '——' [review of *The History of Mr Polly*], *Today's Cinema*, 9 February 1949: 12.

'J.G.W.' (1952) '——' [review of *The Card*], *Today's Cinema*, 26 February 1952: 27.

Wells, H. G. (1934) *Experiment in Autobiography: Discoveries and Conclusions of a Very Ordinary Brain* (*since 1866*), two vols. London: Gollancz and Cresset Press.

—— (1953) *The History of Mr Polly* [1910], with an introduction by Frank Wells, London: Collins.

Wykes, A. (1977) *H. G. Wells in the Cinema*, London: Jupiter.

6 Cinema, monarchy and the making of heritage

A Queen Is Crowned (1953)

James Chapman

A Queen Is Crowned (Castleton Knight, 1953) occupies a unique place in British cinema history. A Technicolor documentary celebrating the coronation of Queen Elizabeth II, it was the year's most successful film at the British box-office – the only occasion upon which a non-fiction film has achieved that distinction.[1] It was also a popular attraction throughout the British Commonwealth and became a surprise success in the United States where it was voted the best foreign film of 1953 by the National Board of Review of Motion Pictures.[2] It was received by some critics in tones of the highest reverence, while even those who were less awestruck by the colour spectacle of the coronation recognised the historical importance of the film as a record and were impressed by its level of technical achievement.[3] There is no question that, in 1953, the film was a major popular success, being a 'must see' attraction for many cinemagoers.

For all its undoubted popularity, however, *A Queen Is Crowned* is now virtually forgotten, a curio item that rarely merits even a footnote in standard histories of British cinema. There are several likely reasons for the film having been overlooked by historians. In the first place, although it is a documentary film, it does not fit into the 'documentary-realist' tradition which privileges films which show the lives of 'ordinary' people and which foreground issues such as living conditions and other social problems. Indeed, the pageantry and splendour of *A Queen Is Crowned* are as far removed from the Griersonian ethos of 'the creative treatment of actuality' as can be imagined. Furthermore, the film has not found any champions among the revisionist scholars who have reclaimed *popular* British cinema as a subject worthy of historical investigation and critical analysis. The visual and emotional pleasures which recent commentators have identified in cycles such as the Gainsborough costume melodramas, the Hammer horror films and the James Bond series are of a very different order from the stately and reverential style of *A Queen Is Crowned*. Perhaps more than any other reason, however, *A Queen Is Crowned* has been overlooked because it is essentially a record of an event – an event which had much greater historical significance for British society than the film ever did for British film culture.

Yet there are good reasons for looking afresh at *A Queen Is Crowned* and its place in British cinema history. These have to do both with the nature of the film itself and with the wider implications of its popularity at the time. *A Queen Is Crowned* is neither a traditional documentary in the British realist style, nor is it a historical narrative in any accepted sense, but it does nevertheless present certain images and articulate certain discourses which offer significant insights into the ways in which British heritage and culture have been constructed in the cinema. Marcia Landy, who stands alone as the only commentator to have offered any discussion of the film at all, considers that it 'was indicative of many attempts in the 1950s cinema to recover images of national identity through the evocation of history' (Landy 1991: 94–5). The style of the film, while certainly very far removed from 'the creative treatment of actuality' that had characterised the Griersonian tradition, does have its precedents in British cinema, suggesting that *A Queen Is Crowned* might be located in a wider lineage of cultural and historical representation. Furthermore, the very popularity of the film is suggestive of wider social and political values in the early 1950s. At the very least the box-office success of *A Queen Is Crowned* provides evidence about popular attitudes towards monarchy during a period which has variously been characterised as an age of 'social consensus' (Marwick 1996: 11) and 'the last age of chivalry' (Richards 1997: 170).

Insofar as the immediate context of *A Queen Is Crowned* was the coronation itself, then it is necessary to consider the importance (both symbolic and actual) of this event for British society. The symbolic importance is effectively described by David Cannadine, who suggests that the coronation was 'a retrospectively unconvincing reaffirmation of Britain's continued great-power status' (Cannadine 1979: 46). Although it was not especially apparent to contemporaries, the Second World War is now generally seen as marking the end of Britain as a world power. In fact, the consequences of the war for Britain were mixed. On the one hand, the election of the Labour government in 1945 on a groundswell of opinion in favour of social reform and welfare state policies had seemed to promise the arrival of the 'New Jerusalem' in which poverty, unemployment, ill-health and slums would all be things of the past. On the other hand, the crippling cost of six years of total war had left Britain exhausted, her cities bomb-damaged, her economic resources depleted, and dependent upon the 'American life-support machine' that was Marshall Aid (Barnett 1996: 85).

Both the Labour government and the Conservative government which replaced it in 1951 clung to the idea that Britain was still the third world power alongside the United States of America and the Soviet Union, even as the bipolar geopolitical system which developed with the onset of the Cold War in the late 1940s squeezed Britain into the role of an ally of the USA rather than an equal. Furthermore, the granting of independence to India in 1947, for so long the 'jewel in the crown' of the British Empire, signalled the beginning of the end of Britain's imperial power, a process that would be hastened by the débâcle of Suez in 1956.

With the benefit of hindsight, the fact of Britain's decline in world power status and prestige is strikingly obvious. Yet this was not a perspective available to politicians or social commentators in the early 1950s. Indeed, by the early 1950s there was a general feeling that the storm had been weathered and that Britain stood on the verge of recovery and renewal. Political consensus had returned as both the Labour and Conservative parties accepted the welfare state, while the term 'Butskellism' was coined to describe the continuity of economic policy between the outgoing Labour Chancellor of the Exchequer Hugh Gaitskell and the incoming Conservative one, R. A. Butler. The Festival of Britain in 1951 'made a spectacular showpiece for the inventiveness and genius of British scientists and technologists' (Morgan 1990: 110). National pride was reasserted through events such as the escape of the frigate HMS *Amethyst* (July 1949) from the Yangtze River during the Chinese revolution, the valiant defence of the 'Glorious Gloucesters' during the Battle of the Imjin River (April 1951) in the Korean War, and the ascent of Mount Everest by Edmund Hillary and Sherpa Tensing (May 1953), all of which were greeted with great jubilation in Britain.[4] The youth and, not least, the name of the new Queen drew obvious comparisons to the past, and there was much talk in the press of a 'new Elizabethan age' in British culture and achievement.

It is evident from opinion polls that 'one central feature of British values was a strong loyalty to the institution of monarchy' (Marwick 1996: 104). The underlying monarchical sentiments of the country were most evident at times of major events, principally royal weddings and funerals. The wedding of Princess Elizabeth to the Greek-born Prince Philip in November 1947 revealed the extent of popular support for the monarchy (potential criticisms of the lavish wedding during the years of austerity were partly offset by royal couturier Norman Hartnell being allowed only a hundred clothing coupons to make the wedding dress) as did the genuine grief felt when King George VI died unexpectedly in his sleep on the night of 5–6 February 1952. The King's death at the age of only 56 came as a shock to a public which held him in the highest esteem for the sense of duty and service he had displayed during the war (the royal family had refused Churchill's suggestion that they should leave Britain for Canada in 1940) and for his own personal courage in overcoming a severe speech impediment when he unexpectedly succeeded his elder brother, Edward VIII, following the Abdication Crisis of 1936. The death of one monarch, however, meant the coronation of another. Freed from the worst of the austerity regime, there was greater scope for spectacle and displays of pageantry at the coronation, which, like the Festival of Britain, was regarded as an opportunity to promote national unity and cultural renewal in the aftermath of war: 'The Coronation was planned as a major national event – the Elizabethan age was to dawn with pomp and ceremony, in affirmation of a monarchy that had grown popular through the steadfastness of the King and Queen in sharing the people's war' (Gardiner 1999: 97). The historical significance of the coronation as evidence of the public attitude towards the monarchy is summarised thus by Arthur Marwick:

> The nearer the coronation of Queen Elizabeth II came, the more public opinion polls showed enthusiasm for, and interest in, that event. At least two million people turned out in the streets to watch the coronation procession; but the new twist was that almost twenty-and-a-half million people, 56 per cent of the adult population, could watch, and did watch, the entire proceedings on television; a further 32 per cent, 11.7 million, listened on radio. From survey material, it does seem that the coronation was associated in many people's minds, however vaguely, with the idea of a new Elizabethan age in which, through the Commonwealth if not through the Empire, Britain would still retain a glorious place in the world.
>
> (Marwick 1996: 105–6)

Yet the coronation not only reflects popular attitudes towards the monarchy in 1953; it also provides an example of how the spectacle and pageantry associated with the public face of royalty has been used to promote the institution of monarchy in the modern era. In the age of mass democracy the institutions of constitutional government need to appeal to a much wider constituency than just the political elites. 'In the past royal ceremonies had been heavy with symbolism intended to impress the participants, who were the most important people in the country,' writes T. O. Lloyd. 'By the twentieth century these ceremonies had to be designed for the entire country to watch' (Lloyd 1993: 488).

It is only in the twentieth century, moreover, that the general public has been able to witness royal ceremonial due to the mass media. Film, radio and television have all played their part in disseminating images of the monarchy to the population at large. Film cameramen were present to record scenes of Queen Victoria's Diamond Jubilee in 1897 and of her funeral in 1901. Cecil Hepworth recalled that the silence of the funeral procession was 'shattered' when he turned on his camera and that the noise 'caught the attention, as it must certainly have done, of the new King, Edward VII' who temporarily halted the procession 'so that posterity might have the advantage of the cinematograph record' (Hepworth 1951: 56). The BBC had broadcast radio commentary of the coronation of George VI in 1937, and its television cameras had been present at Hyde Park Corner to record scenes of the royal procession. For the 1953 coronation, television cameras were allowed inside Westminster Abbey itself. The BBC's own audience research found that of the approximately 20 million people in Britain who watched the coronation on television, 7,800,000 did so in their own homes, 10,400,000 did so in friends' homes, and 1,500,000 did so in public places such as cinemas and public halls which were equipped with television screens (Briggs 1979: 429). The BBC received great plaudits for its coverage of the event, even from its rivals in the film industry. 'For once, I think, quite fairly we have to give the BBC best,' remarked one trade commentator writing in the *Daily Film Renter*. 'The television service rose to the occasion magnificently, and in many respects their presentation of the entire Coronation ceremony and other events of the day was something the trade could not hope to surpass' (Anon. 1953: 4). Certainly the importance of the BBC's coverage in making the coronation a national event cannot be overstated.

What the cinema could provide which television could not, of course, was colour. There were, in fact, two feature-length films and one short colour film of the coronation. *A Queen Is Crowned*, made in Technicolor, was produced by Castleton Knight for the Rank Organisation with music by Guy Warrack and a commentary written by playwright Christopher Fry and spoken by Sir Laurence Olivier. *Elizabeth Is Queen*, made in Warnercolor, was produced by Howard Thomas for Associated British-Pathé with music by Sir Adrian Boult and commentary written by poet John Pudney and spoken by Leo Genn. Both films were released to cinemas within days of the coronation and, according to Leslie Halliwell, 'it quickly became clear to press and public alike that *A Queen Is Crowned* was the one to see, mainly because it was longer' (Halliwell 1985: 178). The short film, *Coronation Day*, made in a process called Gevacolor, was produced by British Movietonews with a commentary spoken by James McKechnie.

The extra length of *A Queen Is Crowned* is due to the fact that it is more than just a film record of the coronation. Although the coronation procession and ceremony takes up most of its 89-minute running time, the film also deploys an array of cultural and historical motifs to locate the coronation itself within a wider national context. As with most cultural constructions of nationhood, these motifs are as interesting for what they exclude as for what they include. It can be argued, indeed, that *A Queen Is Crowned* is the visual representation of just one of the three Englands identified by J. B. Priestley in his famous *English Journey* of the 1930s. For, while the film itself is at pains to mention all parts of the United Kingdom, its representation of Britain is essentially the same as the 'Old England' described by Priestley as 'the country of the cathedrals and minsters and manor houses and inns, of parson and squire; guidebook and quaint highways and byways of England' (Priestley 1997: 321).

The film begins with a montage of images which foreground the rural and the pastoral. There are shots of green countryside, rolling hillsides, lakes and mountains, rows of thatched cottages surrounded by spring blossoms, a herd of cattle in a meadow next to a country church, a village green and inn, a squire and his children on horseback, and long shots of the royal castles of Windsor and Balmoral. Priestley's other two Englands – 'the nineteenth-century England,' the industrial England of coal, iron, steel, cotton, wool, railways' and the modern England, 'the England of arterial and bypass roads, of filling stations and factories that look like exhibition buildings, of giant cinemas and dance halls and cafés' (Ibid: 322–5) – are conspicuously absent from this sequence. The only urban image in the montage, indeed, is a long shot of Edinburgh Castle, and even that is centred on the castle as a historic monument rather than on the streets and slums of the city. The use of Hubert Parry's hymn 'Jerusalem' on the soundtrack iron-ically draws attention to the fact that the film visualises only 'England's green and pleasant land' and not 'those dark satanic mills' envisaged by William Blake.

This opening montage, moreover, is accompanied by the sonorous tones of Olivier reciting John of Gaunt's deathbed speech from Shakespeare's *Richard II* ('This royal throne of kings, this sceptred isle/This earth of majesty, this seat of Mars . . . This blessed plot, this earth, this realm, this England') which places the film within a specific lineage of cultural representations. During the Second World War, the John of Gaunt speech had been used frequently in anthologies of patri-otic verse and in recitals on the radio, as well as providing the resonant titles for three wartime films: *This England* (1941), *The Demi-Paradise* (1943) and *This Happy Breed* (1944). Olivier's narration further recalls Humphrey Jennings's *Words for Battle* (1941) which had set the words of Milton, Camden, Blake, Browning and Kipling alongside those of Lincoln and Churchill, all spoken by Olivier (Chapman 1998: 239–40). But whereas Jennings's film had also used visual imagery to marry the words of the past with the iconography of war (shots of Spitfires and civil defence workers, for example), the images used in *A Queen Is Crowned* could almost have been taken at any time in the last five hundred years, such is the absence of any signs of the present (there are no cars or trains or industrial landscapes, for instance).

The films which *A Queen Is Crowned* most closely resembles, however, are the wartime 'cultural propaganda' films sponsored by the British Council. The British Council had been set up in 1934 to promote positive images of British life and British institutions to overseas countries. During the war it had sponsored docu-mentary films on aspects of British life and culture which had drawn scathing criticism for their old-fashioned outlook and for not engaging with the many social changes that occurred during the war. The Ministry of Information, which had overall responsibility for official propaganda policy, had castigated the British Council for producing films on such subjects as Kew Gardens, the Western Isles of Scot-land, and English inns and waterways, because '[t]o audiences in neutral countries they will seem to be living proof of Goebbels's statements that the British have lost the intellectual, moral and industrial lead which they once held . . . A film on the Clyde which does not show a single warship, a single sailor or even a convoy, will come as a shock to every neutral'. The British Council, for its part, defended its films on the grounds that it wanted to show 'that our country has a living past and is in continual development rather than sudden change'.[5] The bitter argu-ments which raged between the Ministry of Information and the British Council over the projection of Britain illustrate how the subject of British culture can become a site of contestation and struggle during times of national crisis (Harper 1994: 81–4).

After 1945, however, it was no longer necessary to project images of the British war effort for overseas consumption. What was necessary, though, was to reassure those at home that while British society may have been changed by the experience of war, it was still underpinned by traditional and historic British values. The images of British culture presented in the much-derided wartime films of the British Council were reasserted through the 'official' discourses of culture apparent at the Festival of Britain. The 'Lion and Unicorn Pavilion' (a name that directly recalls George Orwell's famous wartime celebration of Englishness), in the words of one historian, 'served to celebrate past glories, age-old institutions, and hallowed and cherished folkways. The British monarchy, British sports, British pub life, London's red buses, and the village "bobby" were on display, almost preserved in aspic' (Morgan 1990: 110).

A Queen Is Crowned similarly preserves the monarchy in a kind of Technicolor aspic. 'Verbally and visually,' Landy remarks, 'the film calls attention to the monumental nature of the historical moment, stressing symbols from the past through images of architecture, clothing, and ritual' (Landy 1991: 95). The camera lingers on objects, particularly the crown, the five swords of state, and the banners of chivalry inside Westminster Abbey. Continuity between past and present is emphasised through the proclamation of the coronation by heralds and the lengthy sequence of the coronation ceremony and oath. Amidst all the pomp and tradition, however, there are also reminders of the recent past, with the narration drawing attention especially to the stained glass window in the abbey commemorating 'the Few'.

Yet for all its foregrounding of symbols of the past, *A Queen Is Crowned* is still very much a film of and for its time. The displays of pomp and pageantry are more than a mere showcase for tradition, but serve an ideological purpose in the context of early 1950s Britain. For one thing, the visual opulence of the film draws attention to the end of post-war austerity: the Conservative government had removed most rationing controls by 1954 and by the second half of the decade there were visible signs of greater wealth and affluence across most social classes. On another level, the film is also very much at pains to represent Britain as a world power, the centre of a vast Commonwealth of Nations. The narration remarks that the coronation was proclaimed throughout 'all the realms and territories of the Queen', while the procession of heads of state and government from all over the world to attend the coronation once again asserts British prestige and influence. The emphasis on the Commonwealth anticipates one of the features of Elizabeth II's reign, which has seen great changes in the relationship between the Crown and the former British Empire. As head of the Commonwealth, the Queen has sought to maintain political and cultural links between Britain and her former colonies after they gained their independence in the 1950s and 1960s.

A Queen Is Crowned, then, deserves to be regarded as more than a mere curio. More than just a record of the coronation, the film clearly sets out to present the monarchy in the most favourable light. The foregrounding of tradition, heraldry and the institutions of constitutional government legitimates the monarchy by locating it in a historical context. The film's essentially pastoral representation of Britain, moreover, places it in the same lineage of political and cultural conservatism that was later to find expression in the policies of organisations such as English Heritage. At the same time, however, the popularity of the film is evidence of widespread support for the values and institutions which it promotes. Contemporary reviews of the film provide unwitting testimony of the genuine affection in which the monarchy was held. 'Time and again at the preview yesterday the audience was roused to bursts of applause by things great and small' reported Campbell Dixon (Dixon 1953).

This sort of reaction is indicative of the time when the film was made, before the royal family had been discredited by scandals and divorces. One reason the film is so little known today, undoubtedly, is that the same reverential attitude towards the monarchy no longer exists. '*A Queen Is Crowned*, put out now, can't expect the same innocent, wholehearted reaction,' one critic remarked when the film was shown on television over thirty years later. 'Somewhere, in Bolton, there's an old grannie who still takes it seriously. What she made of this overwrought presentation I know not' (Eveling 1986). In the last analysis, the fascination of *A Queen Is Crowned* is that it is a time capsule that speaks of and for its moment.

Notes

1 Precise details regarding box-office statistics were not made widely available at this time, so film historians have generally had to rely upon the annual listings compiled by the trade press. *A Queen Is Crowned* was rated top British box-office attraction in 1953 by both the British trade paper *Kinematograph Weekly* and the US trade paper *Motion Picture Herald*. '*A Queen Is Crowned* was unquestionably the film of this, or for that matter any, year,' declared the veteran British trade commentator R. H. 'Josh' Billings. 'Every exhibitor who played the film, and most did, makes it his top' (Billings 1953: 10). The box-office runners-up that year were the Bob Hope–Bing Crosby–Dorothy Lamour comedy *Road to Bali* (1952), the British war film *The Cruel Sea* (1953) and the British comedy *Genevieve* (1953). Further testimony to the popularity of *A Queen Is Crowned* was provided by Leslie Halliwell, then assistant manager of the Rex Cinema in Cambridge, who recalled that the film smashed the house record by taking £3,000 in its first week and a further £1,200 in its second (the yardstick of a 'very good' week at the cinema being £900). Halliwell estimated that 'in those seven days nearly half the population of Cambridge must have visited the Rex' (Halliwell 1985: 178). For discussion of popular cinema-going in Britain at this time see the articles by Harper and Porter (1999) and Thumim (1991).

2 The BFI Library's microfiche on the film includes press reports about its reception in the United States. *Time* (22 June 1953) reported that 'in its first week of US showings *A Queen Is Crowned* began making unheard-of box-office records. In Manhattan the little (450 seats) Guild Theater opened with six shows a day, hastily raised it to nine when

waiting lines strung out around the block. In five days with the film, Boston's Exeter Theater drew in twice as many patrons as usual. In Richmond, the Capitol's business was four times bigger than normal in one day; the Pix in White Plains, NY, did three times its average business.' According to *Variety* (23 December 1953), however, the film's box-office performance in the United States was 'completely irregular . . . It did very well in some spots and died in others only a few miles away.' In common with other British films in America, *A Queen Is Crowned* was shown mostly in smaller cinemas in locations where there was an audience for foreign films. Vincent Porter notes that, according to the Odeon Theatre's Annual Report of June 1953, '*A Queen Is Crowned* was successful everywhere except the USA' (Porter 1997: 129).

3   The critical reception of *A Queen Is Crowned* can be discerned from the reviews collected on the BFI microfiche. It was equally well received by the quality and popular press: '*A Queen Is Crowned* is the richest and most profoundly stirring film I have ever seen. I trust it will go all over the world and that a copy will be preserved, as an historic document, for as long as celluloid will last' (Dixon 1953). '*A Queen Is Crowned*, the eagerly-awaited, full-length film of the coronation, in Technicolor, is the screen spectacle of the century' (Whitley 1953). 'Now I must pay tribute to a film that is not only historical in character but in itself makes history. If *A Queen Is Crowned* had cost a hundred millions to make the sum would be trifling compared with the good will that it will earn for this country throughout the world' (Baxter 1953). Some of the middlebrow critics, such as the *New Statesman*'s William Whitebait and the *News Chronicle*'s Richard Winnington, were slightly less impressed, arguing that both *A Queen Is Crowned* and the other 'coronation film', *Elizabeth Is Queen*, were too reverent: 'The sentimental cliché in both cases has got just a bit too thick' (Whitebait 1953). 'Both, alas, wallow in an inflated commentary supposed to denote the highest pitch of reverence . . . This pretentiousness is a mistake which seriously impairs the great technical progress and devoted teamwork that is obvious in these films. And it gives to the occasion an air of vulgar snobbery that was not to be detected in the BBC approach' (Winnington 1953).

4   The Everest expedition, led by Colonel John Hunt, had pressed ahead in order that news of the ascent, which was made on Friday 29 May 1953, would reach Britain before the coronation on 2 June. Hillary, a New Zealander, was immediately knighted.

5   Public Record Office: BW 4/64, MOI report entitled 'Four British Council Films' undated; BW 4/17, 'Recommendations on the British Council Film Production Programme' by Oliver Bell, Director of the British Film Institute, March 1942.

Bibliography

Anon. (1953) '———' [commentary on BBC-TV's coronation coverage], *Daily Film Renter*, 4 June 1953: 4.

Barnett, C. (1996) *The Lost Victory: British Dreams, British Realities 1945–1950*, London: Pan.

Baxter, B. (1953) 'Envoy in colour . . . ', *Sunday Express*, 7 June 1953.

Billings, R. H. 'J.', (1953) 'Gold Spinners of 1953', *Kinematograph Weekly*, 17 December 1953: 10.

Briggs, A. (1979) *The History of Broadcasting in the United Kingdom* IV: *Sound and Vision 1945–55*, Oxford: Oxford University Press.

Cannadine, D. (1979) 'James Bond and the decline of England', *Encounter*, 53, 3, November 1979: 46–55.

Chapman, J. (1998) *The British at War: Cinema, State and Propaganda, 1939–1945*, London: I. B. Tauris.

Dixon, C. (1953) 'Coronation film gives finest view' [review of *A Queen Is Crowned*], *Daily Telegraph*, 6 June 1953.

Eveling, S. (1986) '——' [review of television broadcast of *A Queen Is Crowned*], *Scotsman*, 7 June 1986.

Gardiner, J. (1999) *From the Bomb to the Beatles: The Changing Face of Postwar Britain 1945–1965*, London: Collins & Brown.

Halliwell, L. (1985) *Seats in All Parts: Half a Lifetime at the Movies*, London: Granada.

Harper, S. (1994) *Picturing the Past: The Rise and Fall of the British Costume Film*, London: BFI.

Harper, S. and Porter, V. (1999) 'Cinema audience tastes in 1950s Britain', *Journal of Popular British Cinema* 2: 66–82.

Hepworth, C. (1951) *Came the Dawn: Memories of a Film Pioneer*, London: Phoenix House.

Landy, M. (1991) *British Genres: Cinema and Society, 1930–1960*, Princeton, NJ: Princeton University Press.

Lloyd, T. O. (1993) *Empire, Welfare State, Europe: English History 1906–1992*, fourth edition, Oxford: Oxford University Press.

Marwick, A. (1996) *British Society Since 1945*, third edition, Harmondsworth: Penguin.

Morgan, K. O. (1990) *The People's Peace: Britain 1945–1990*, Oxford: Oxford University Press.

Porter, V. (1997) 'Methodism versus the market-place: The Rank Organisation and British cinema', in Robert Murphy (ed.) *The British Cinema Book*, London: BFI: 122–32.

Priestley, J. B. (1997) *English Journey*, London: The Folio Society (first published by William Heinemann in association with Victor Gollancz, 1934).

Richards, J. (1997) *Films and British National Identity: From Dickens to Dad's Army*, Manchester: Manchester University Press.

Thumim, J. (1991) 'The "popular", cash and culture in the postwar British cinema industry', *Screen*, 32, 3: 245–71.

Whitebait, W. (1953) '——' [review of *A Queen Is Crowned*], *New Statesman*, 13 June 1953.

Whitley, R. (1953) 'The film spectacle of the century', *Daily Mirror*, 6 June 1953.

Winnington, R. (1953) 'The big message on a small screen', *News Chronicle*, 6 June 1953.

7 Camping on the borders

History, identity and Britishness in the *Carry On* costume parodies, 1963–74

Nicholas J. Cull

In the 1968 comedy *Carry On Up the Khyber* the frontier between the British Empire and Afghanistan is represented by a wooden farm gate in a mountain pass, guarded by a lone member of the Third Foot and Mouth Highland regiment. This border is central to the action of the film, as British and Indian characters slip to and fro across it in a comic struggle for domination of the North-West Frontier in the 1890s. Yet the frontier of *Carry On Up the Khyber* is only the most visible of the many borders that feature in the *Carry On* films based on historical themes or costume genre parody. Borders of gender and sexuality were always moot in the world of *Carry On* comedy, but the historical *Carry On* films also played with borders of time and place: the border between the historical past and the present, and the border between Britain and the rest of the world.

This attention to borders opens one central issue: Britishness. To engage with the costume drama is to engage with a genre closely identified with the representation of Britain. Moreover, just as *Carry On Up the Khyber* is resolved with a grand assertion of British identity – the staff of the provincial governor's residency eat dinner unperturbed as 'native' siege guns bring plaster crashing down on their heads – so the action of the historical *Carry Ons* consistently returns to representation of Britishness.

The *Carry On* series was well established before developing historical subject matter. The cycle began in 1958 with the unexpectedly successful army comedy: *Carry On Sergeant*. Producer, Peter Rogers, director Gerald Thomas and writer Norman Hudis followed up with a series of comedies tackling work-related situations: a hospital, a school, the police, an employment agency and a cruise liner.[1] In 1963, Hudis accepted a job in Hollywood. The experienced comic writer Talbot Rothwell took his place.

Rothwell's first success had been the 1948 stage play whose title referred to the contemporary exploitation of heritage, *Queen Elizabeth Slept Here*. He had since written widely for stage, radio and screen, and was best known for *Carry On Sergeant*'s television spin-off *The Army Game*. While Rothwell and his collaborator Sid Colin worked on the script of *Carry On Cabby* (1963), Rothwell's agent Kevin

Kavanagh approached Peter Rogers with a suggestion for a further comedy written by Rothwell alone. The story would be set in the Royal Navy at the time of Nelson, and hence ride on the coat tails of the recent Columbia film *HMS Defiant* (Lewis Gilbert, 1962). In a letter of 25 June 1962, Kavanagh suggested:

> With the thought that perhaps the props of *HMS Defiant* may still be lying about Talbot Rothwell has written the enclosed story line for a screen comedy. It strikes me that this could be a completely new look for the 'Carry On' gang, and I hope it will amuse you.[2]

Rogers responded well to Rothwell's outline and a full screenplay followed in October 1962. The film promised to be a rousing swipe at swashbuckling and the sort of before-the-mast adventure typified by C. S. Forester's *Hornblower* adventure novels. As the project developed the title changed from *Steady, Boys, Steady* to *Poopdecker RN*, but soon after submission Rogers began experimenting with *Carry On* titles. Early possibilities were *Up the Armada* (which was rejected for being too like 'up the arse'), *Carry On Sailor* (too similar to *Carry On Cruising*) and *Carry On Mate*. The final choice – *Carry On Jack* – had appropriate historical resonance. The film opened in November 1963. Historical *Carry On* had arrived.[3]

Rogers and the team followed up with a spoof thriller: *Carry On Spying* (1964). The rationale for the series by the early 1960s was genre parody, and given the importance of the costume drama and literary adaptation within British and Hollywood filmmaking it was to be expected that a significant proportion of these parodies would engage with historical themes. Moreover, *Jack* had earned an 'A' certificate rather than a 'U'. This adult certification gave Rothwell ample room to develop the bawdy streak in his humour. The early historically located films in the series parodied two Hollywood genres – the Roman epic in *Carry On Cleo* (1964) and the Western in *Carry On Cowboy* (1965) – and Britain's own Hammer Horror series in *Carry On Screaming* (1966).

In 1966 the Rank Organisation bought the *Carry On* series. Rogers temporarily abandoned the *Carry On* title, but costume comedy remained prominent in what he saw as a 'more visual' style.[4] He produced *Don't Lose Your Head* (1966), a parody of films set during the French Revolution (especially Alexander Korda's 1934 *The Scarlet Pimpernel*), and *Follow that Camel* (1966), which spoofed the French Foreign Legion film and especially *Beau Geste* (William A. Wellman, USA, 1939). Then came the satire of Kipling and the British Empire film: *Carry On Up the Khyber* (1968) and Tarzan and the Safari movie in *Carry On Up the Jungle* (1970). Following numerous 'straight' film treatments of the reign of Henry VIII, the team delivered *Carry On Henry* (1971).

With the turn of the decade the series returned to contemporary settings and coarsened its style. Costumed sketches figured prominently in the *Carry On* team's television specials, and Rogers had registered the title *Carry On Charlie* to treat

Bonnie Prince Charlie.[5] The only historical film actually made was Rothwell's final script: a reworking of a tawdry treatment of the exploits of the highwayman Dick Turpin, *Carry On Dick* (1974).[6] The film required substantial cuts to obtain the usual 'A' certificate.[7] A coarse Second World War home-front comedy titled *Carry On England* followed in 1976. The series foundered in 1978, yet it was a testament to the significance of costume drama within the series that Rogers and Thomas should choose a historical subject for their reunion for a final film: *Carry On Columbus* in 1992.

From the early days, the *Carry On* films had a special connection to Britishness. The comedy evoked a cosy tradition of the cheeky seaside postcards, Christmas pantomimes and music-hall humour. At their core the *Carry On* films drew on a rich British heritage of camp humour. In the world of camp, the signs of identity are rendered ridiculous by exaggeration and repetition. In its original gay context these signs were specifically the markers of sexual identity. *Carry On* performers like Kenneth Williams and Charles Hawtrey maintained this tradition.[8] However, the historical *Carry On* films applied the same approach to markers of national identity in both the past and the present. One such marker was the genre that had for many decades been held to dominate cinematic representations of Britain: the costume drama.

The targets: camping from the outside

Just as historical plays, paintings and pageants had been central to Victorian culture, so the costume film has always been an important part of British filmmaking. The international success of Alexander Korda's irreverent *The Private Life of Henry VIII* (1933) gave the genre a new centrality. But not all Korda's successors and imitators took his light-hearted approach to the past. By the 1960s, elaborate and serious adaptations of British history and literature were familiar territory for Hollywood, and staples of British television, and especially the BBC, where 'Classic Serials' adaptations of Dickens and other canonical authors – on occasion, continental European as well as British – became a regular feature.

Carry On history set out to invade the territory that had been dominated by the forces of high British culture and million-dollar Hollywood budgets, and reassert lowbrow British humour. Merely casting the familiar *Carry On* stars in historical roles undermined the pretence of historical filmmaking to re-create the past. The stock types – the lovable, lecherous Cockney rogue played by the South African-born comic, Sid James; the pretentious, effete Kenneth Williams; the puny, camp and bespectacled Charles Hawtrey; the strident and sexually assertive Joan Sims; the buffoon, Kenneth Connor or Peter Butterworth – were always more recognisable as themselves and, collectively, as the 'Carry On gang' than as the historical people they purported to portray. Each film unfolded with a cascade of sight gags, slapstick and punning dialogue with numerous sexual *double entendres*, and dis-

King Henry VIII (Richard Burton) and his courtiers arrive at Hever Castle where he sees Anne Boleyn (Genevieve Bujold) for the first time

Figure 7.1 The grandeur, pomp and solemnity of the lavish historical films of the 1960s and 1970s proved an irresistible target for the *Carry On* team. *Anne of the Thousand Days* (1969), above – starring Richard Burton as Henry VIII – was one of several sources of topical inspiration for *Carry On Henry* (1971).

Source: British Cinema and Television Research Group archive, De Montfort University (Universal).

rupted the lavish settings, grandeur and solemnity that had become the hallmark of costume genre. In some films this disruption is quite literal: at the climax of *Don't Lose Your Head* the team demolish an elaborately re-created interior of a French château stuffed with antiques. The bottom line for the writer Talbot Rothwell was just that: he believed that the essence of British humour was the lavatory, and accordingly the *Carry On* version of the past was studded with chamber pots and privies.[9] British low comedy had invaded the inner sanctum of national self-image.

The chosen targets for *Carry On* history were typically among the best-known pictures of the day. Twentieth Century-Fox's *Cleopatra* (Joseph L. Mankiewicz and others, USA, 1963), spoofed in *Carry On Cleo*, was seldom out of the headlines in the early 1960s. *Carry On Henry* took aim at films including Fred Zinnemann's *A Man for All Seasons*, which had scooped multiple Academy Awards at the 1966 Oscars, though more topical inspiration came from the coincidence of Universal's *Anne of the Thousand Days* (Charles Jarrott, 1969) and BBC-TV's *Six Wives of Henry VIII* (1970). The flogging of Bernard Cribbins in *Carry On Jack* was fresh thanks to the 1962 remake of the legendary 1935 MGM version of *Mutiny on the Bounty* (Frank Lloyd, USA). Elizabeth Taylor's bath and arrival in Caesar's bedroom rolled up in a carpet from *Cleopatra* both figure in *Carry On Cleo*. The summary marriage improvised by Sid James's Henry VIII and sudden arrival of the King of France in *Carry On Henry* both echo scenes in the life of an earlier Henry, Peter O'Toole's Henry II in the acclaimed *The Lion in Winter* (Anthony Harvey, 1968).

Where the source films were embedded in screen history, the expected material could be blended with allusions to recent box office hits. Bernard Bresslaw's sheikh in *Follow that Camel* draws on Anthony Quinn's performance in David Lean's *Lawrence of Arabia* (1962). Peter Butterworth's missionary, Belcher, in *Carry On Up the Khyber* owes much to Jack Hawkins in Cy Endfield's *Zulu* (1964). The *Carry Ons* also made fun of the dialogue clichés of costume film. In *Carry On Jack*, Captain Fearless (Kenneth Williams) hears the Bo'sun threaten 'a taste of the cat' and believes it might refer to his pet cat. *Carry On Henry* makes much play with the historical English usage of the words 'issue' and 'chaste', as with the question and answer: 'Has she been chaste?' 'All over Normandy'. In *Follow that Camel*, the aristocratic English Legionnaire B. O. West (Jim Dale) protests grandly: 'I must remember the family name'. His comically devoted Butler, Simpson (Peter Butterworth), replies with the helpful prompt: 'West'. When the Highlanders make their stand against the charging Burpar tribesmen in *Khyber*, the command familiar from *Zulu* and numerous other Empire films is heard: 'Fire at will' – only to be followed by the quip from Butterworth: 'Poor old Will, why do they always fire at him?'

There are plenty of nods to the heritage of the British period film. *Don't Lose Your Head* could draw on audience memories of three British screen versions of *The Scarlet Pimpernel* (and at least five adaptations of *A Tale of Two Cities*), though because the Pimpernel novels were still in copyright Rogers officially insisted that the film was: 'not in any way based on *The Scarlet Pimpernel*.'[10] *Carry On Henry* borrowed most from Korda's *The Private Life of Henry VIII*. In both films Henry is repulsed by his foreign wife's love of garlic and declares 'the things I do for England'. In the Korda film Anne of Cleves (Elsa Lanchester) delays consummation of her marriage by playing cards with the King (Charles Laughton). In the *Carry On* version, the King (Sid James) teaches the French Queen (Joan Sims) tiddlywinks to the same end. Korda's 1941 film *That Hamilton Woman* is briefly implicated in *Carry On Jack*. When Bernard Cribbins appears in a bar dazed and wearing only a frock, a member of the press gang quips: 'Lady Hamilton, I presume!' As Robert Ross has noted, Sid James's character in *Carry On Up the Jungle* is a nod to Humphrey Bogart in John Huston's *The African Queen* (USA, 1951) (Ross 1996: 85).

Carry On Up the Khyber harked back to the glory days of Hollywood's love affair with the British Empire and Kipling adaptations, not least George Stevens's *Gunga Din* (USA, 1939). As the leader of the Afghans is called Bunghit Din, the chief villain Kenneth Williams has the chance to intone a variation on Kipling's famous refrain: 'You're a better man than I am, Gunga Din'.[11] *Carry On Dick* had numerous sources, dating back ultimately to the eighteenth century's own celebration of Dick Turpin. Joking about the era had vague topicality thanks to the success of Tony Richardson's *Tom Jones* (1963), but the subject material was standard fare of British costume fantasy. The scenario of Turpin living a double life as a vicar was borrowed from the historical romance by Russell Thorndyke, *Christopher Syn*, a tale of a country parson who lives a double life as a pirate and smuggler, which had been filmed by three of the great players in the depiction of Britain in historical fantasy: Gaumont, Hammer and Disney.[12]

The films made fun of the stylistic devices used by mainstream historical film to establish their authenticity. *Carry On Dick* uses prints of eighteenth-century London in its opening. In *Carry On Jack*, a historical painting fades into life and comic action much as the reconstructed Roman wall paintings come alive at the opening of Twentieth Century-Fox's *Cleopatra*. The most widely used device, however, is the all-knowing 'voice-of-god' narrator, setting the scene for the audiences. *Carry On* had no difficulty mocking this cliché of the historical genre: examples of the period included Orson Welles's narration at the opening of Richard Fleischer's *The Vikings* (USA, 1958) or Richard Burton's scene-setting for *Zulu*. The opening description of the French Revolution in *Don't Lose Your Head* (spoken by Patrick Allen) refers to 'men and women of both sexes'. *Carry On Henry* followed *A Man for All Seasons* (Fred Zinnemann, 1966) quite literally. Key locations such as Windsor Castle and the Tower of London, which had been used to establish the authenticity of the earlier film, were revisited for comic effect in the *Carry Ons*.[13] Stock footage from 'serious' historical films was used in establishing shots, and the Eric Rogers's music generally mocked the grand themes of costume drama. In *Carry On Henry* this involved a parody of 'Greensleeves'.

Carry On Henry also takes aim at those historical films purporting to be based on historically substantiated narratives or documents. An opening title claims:

> This film is based on a recently discovered manuscript by one William Cobbler, which reveals the fact that Henry VIII did in fact have two more wives. Although it was first thought that Cromwell originated the story, it is now known to be definitely all Cobbler's . . . from beginning to end.

The films also played with the anachronisms that infest historical filmmaking. Charles Hawtrey's ubiquitous spectacles were merely the most obvious liberty. The audience could be expected to realise that Guy Fawkes (who was not born till 1570) had no business plotting against Henry VIII in the 1530s. Here the anachronisms were all part of the fun.[14]

The *Carry On* trawl through the dominant representations of Britain was an exercise in reclaiming and humanising the past. *Cleo* and *Cowboy* could be seen as specifically aimed at Hollywood, but the rest had targets closer to home. The insertion of low Cockney characters into aristocratic roles, such as the Governor of the North-West Frontier province in colonial India in 1895 or the Crown of England, was a gesture against the strictures of the class system. Comedy in and about historical representation drew attention to the stories that underpinned the social order in 1960s Britain. To question them raised the possibility of living differently in the future.

The tradition: camping from the inside

For all their subversive qualities, the *Carry On* histories also maintained an element of respect for their target genre. The films certainly joked with elements of the costume genre, but ultimately they joked within the genre. Unlike Mel Brooks's 1974 treatment of the Western, *Blazing Saddles*, the costume film ultimately survives intact. The films are resolved as appropriate to their originating genre. There are unions at the end of the romances *Don't Lose Your Head* and *Carry on Dick*; the flag flies at the end of *Khyber*; honour is restored at the end of *Follow that Camel*; the family is reunited at the end of *Jungle*; and the gender switch is corrected at the end of *Jack*. *Cleo* and *Henry* return their narratives to something close to the true course of history with Caesar dead in the former and Henry VIII pursuing his next historical wife, Catherine Howard, in the latter.

The *Carry On* histories strained but never broke the boundaries of their chosen genre(s). Indeed, by subverting the stuffier screen versions of the past, they maintained an alternative tradition of British historical filmmaking. Just like the classic historical romances of Gaumont-British and Gainsborough Studios analysed by Sue Harper (Harper 1994), the *Carry On* films used the past as a zone of escape in which rich costumes added a level of pleasure. In *Carry On* the past became once again an exotic territory in which fantasy could be indulged.

The *Carry On* version of history consistently sought out and exaggerated the sensational – and the foremost sensation was sex. At the most basic level, the costumes worn by women in *Carry On* emphasised cleavage and the plots dwelt on sexual license. Women in *Carry On* history desire sex and are prepared to chase men to get it. Each film has its scene with buxom bargirls (*Cowboy*, *Camel* and *Dick*), scantily clad courtesans (*Cleo*, *Camel* and *Khyber*) or women eager to marry for advancement (*Don't Lose Your Head*). The bargirls in *Jack* are explicitly prostitutes (though unrecognised as such by the protagonist). In *Henry* a young woman demands money for having granted the King a sexual favour. In such scenes the past becomes a place for repressed British male audiences to explore fantasies of sexual freedom.

The other extreme feature of the past sought out by *Carry On* was sensational death. At one level the films undermined the fetish of death as presented in grand narrative history. The very first joke in the costume *Carry On* cycle spoofed the

Victorian cult of the noble death. At the opening of *Carry On Jack*, Arthur William Devis's 1806 painting of the death of Nelson dissolves into live action. Crewmen bend over the dying Nelson, as he lies stricken below decks. As the camera moves gently into the scene, we hear him instructing his friend Captain Hardy: 'We must have more men Hardy . . . More men . . . ' Hardy urges him to rest. So far it is the scene familiar from school lessons and Laurence Olivier's performance in Alexander Korda's *That Hamilton Woman* (USA, 1941). Nelson (Jimmy Thompson) turns to his friend and captain, Hardy (Anton Rodgers). He utters his most famous line and the *Carry On* unfolds:

Nelson: Kiss me, Hardy . . .
Hardy: (perturbed) I beg your pardon Sir!
Nelson: Kiss me, Hardy.
Hardy: Are you mad? What will they say at the Admiralty, Sir?
Nelson: They'll only be jealous.
Hardy: I don't know. You're very weak, Sir. It may not be good for you.
(Hardy kisses Nelson's temple gently.)
Nelson: Eugh. (He dies.)
Hardy: I told you so.

In *Carry On Up the Khyber* Private Widdle (Charles Hawtrey) finds his regiment massacred with Indian lances still protruding from their bodies: 'look at them lying around like a lot of unwanted cocktail snacks' he says. His friend Ginger (Peter Gilmore) is still alive. The scene proceeds to satirise the melodramatic soldier's death on the field. As Widdle cradles the dying Ginger in his arms, Ginger murmurs: 'Am I going to be all right?' Widdle replies: 'Course not, Ginge mate.' After objecting to Widdle's frankness, Ginger fades, revives and then expires as a result of the heavy coat which his comrades sentimentally drape over him.

Yet the historical *Carry Ons* dwell on an even more theatrical form of death: the execution. Their preoccupation with it is such that the final line of *Carry On Henry* – 'Carry on executioner! Carry on!' – is appropriate for the cycle as a whole. Characters are threatened with walking the plank; being fed to the lions; mutilation by angry tribesmen; 'the death of a thousand cuts' in Afghanistan; being eaten in Africa; and the noose of British justice in *Carry On Dick*. The guillotine is implicit in the title and poster-art for *Don't Lose Your Head*, and the poster for *Carry On Henry* both pictured the King with a giant axe and carried the *double entendre*-heavy tag line: 'a great guy with his chopper'.

Associated jokes turn on the theatre of execution, fixing on such things as the need for famous last words, the reaction of the crowd and even the similarity of executions to contemporary sporting events. In *Carry On Henry*, as Cardinal Wolsey (Terry Scott) follows the condemned Queen as she walks to the block, he delivers a running commentary like a modern-day broadcaster covering a sporting or state occasion. Often characters don't understand that they are to be executed: Lady Ruff-Diamond (Joan Sims) in *Khyber* believes the evil Khasi (Kenneth Williams) is promising her sex, and the slave Hengist Podd (Kenneth Connor) in *Cleo* thinks 'the lions' are the family he is going to work for. In *Don't Lose Your Head* the condemned Duc de Pommfrit (Charles Hawtrey) refuses to read a letter on the steps of the scaffold, but suggests it be placed in the basket at the foot of the guillotine, so that he can read it later.

Perhaps in a late-1950s and early-1960s Britain newly free from the death penalty, the practice of execution marked a convenient borderline between a civilised present and a barbarous past – but for the purposes of *Carry On*, it was all part of the fun and frisson of a foreign world. The fixation on execution was also a testament to Rothwell's black sense of humour. His scripts were frequently darker than the final film. The first draft of *Carry On Jack* ends with Arthur and Walter (Bernard Cribbins and Charles Hawtrey) press-ganged again into the Navy on the eve of Arthur's wedding. They find that the evil first officer, Howlett (Donald Houston) has been promoted to Captain and changed his name to Bligh and the ship is the Bounty, bound for the Pacific. The first draft of *Cleo* leaves Hengist (Kenneth Connor) a cuckold raising another man's children. It was a testament to the changing times that by the later 1960s Rothwell's downbeat endings could be used. *Cleo*'s cuckold ending appears in *Follow that Camel* with the additional twist of the hero being blown up on the cricket field by a vengeful sheikh.[15]

The films observed the conventional internal logic of their respective genres. The characters seek historically appropriate goals. Henry VIII wants revenue and an heir; the slaves of *Cleo* want their freedom; Citizen Bidet in *Don't Lose Your Head* actually believes in the principles of Liberty, Egality and Fraternity (although his master, Citizen Camembert, is bent on personal profit). On occasions the *Carry On* version reflects genuine issues that had been neglected in film and academic history. Recent research by the American historian Suzanne J. Stark has found numerous cases of women impersonating men in order to serve in the British fleet as in *Carry On Jack* (Stark 1998). Finally, the presentation of the body of the coloniser as a key element in colonial control – so dramatically demonstrated by *Carry On Up the Khyber*'s final scene of 'natives' running from the sight of naked British genitals – strikes a chord with many of the more sensitive accounts of colonialism. In his essay 'Shooting an Elephant' George Orwell presents an oddly parallel portrait of colonial power in which the body of the coloniser – in this case Orwell himself suppressing fear and shooting a rogue elephant – holds the 'natives' in thrall (Orwell 1961). Similarly, Franz Fanon's *The Wretched of the Earth* stressed the way in which the body of the coloniser became an icon of imperial domination, which, in Fanon's view, explained the extreme violence seen in colonial rebellion (Fanon 1967).[16]

By creating a double perspective, both looking at the past from the outside and creating a coherent world within which the characters are able to comment on the values of the past, the films joked about both the ways in which people behaved in the past and the ways in which history had been represented. A gentle example of this humour occurs early in *Carry On Jack*, with a comically prolonged ritual of bowing between a sedan chair porter (Jim Dale) and his passenger (Bernard Cribbins) on the doorstep of the tavern. The exchange of bows is broken only when the porter warns: 'I'd get in if I were you . . . they'll be shut'. In *Khyber* there is a comic collision between the historical niceties of hospitality and etiquette and the tradition of saving a bullet for suicide when in a tight spot. During the Burpar attack Sir Sidney Ruff-Diamond (Sid James) instructs his wife to 'try and save the last bullet for Mr Belcher – after all, he is our guest'. Such comic representation of manners becomes especially significant when explicitly tied to the ideas of British identity, which the real life 'Sir Sidneys' of the British elite had promoted among the masses embodied by the comic persona of Sid James.

Carry On and British identity

The subjects selected by the *Carry On* team sat at the heart of the received version of British history. As scholars like Linda Colley have pointed out, the stories at the core of British identity establish the nation as a bourgeois, Protestant naval power with an Empire, defined in contrast to Catholic Spain and (the great Other and source of all ills in *Carry On* and elsewhere in English culture) the alternately Catholic/Republican/Napoleonic France (Colley 1992). Within Britain itself, there is a story of values of fair play and law and order. For the purposes of *Carry On* ideological differences between Britain and the rest of the world are represented culturally. In *Carry On Henry* food stands in for Catholicism; Queen Marie of Normandy (Joan Sims) seeks to persuade Henry to 'renounce all other seasonings and convert to garlic'. But otherwise the historical milestones are the same. *Carry On* makes fun at the expense of the ideological jugular of Britishness. In some cases the jokes are subversive: in *Carry On Henry* the King creates the Church of England on a whim as he leaps onto the bed of his new mistress Bettina (Barbara Windsor). The prototype for the modern British police force – the Bow Street Runners – are shown as incompetent bunglers; naval heroes prevail only by chance.

The historical stories developed in *Carry On* typically turn on international border crossing; only *Henry*, *Dick* and the best-forgotten *England* take place wholly in Britain. In *Jack*, British sailors find themselves behind enemy lines in Napoleonic Spain. In *Cleo* the Romans are in Britain and then the British are slaves in Rome. In *Cowboy* Jim Dale plays a lone Englishman abroad in the Wild West. In *Don't Lose Your Head* the British venture into France to rescue aristocrats from the guillotine and French spies circulate in British high society. In *Follow that Camel* the British are doubly alien, being strangers both to the French Foreign Legion and to the desert to which they are posted, which is of course the southernmost border of European 'Civilisation'. The British legionnaires are contrasted against Rif tribesmen, an American sergeant (Phil Silvers) and an Austrian Commandant in the Erich von Stroheim mould (Kenneth Williams). In *Khyber* the British hold the border in India, and cross into Afghanistan. In *Jungle* the team are lost in the Congo. In *Henry* the British meet the French through the intricacies of marriage diplomacy. *Carry On Dick* is resolved by the escape of Turpin and his lover across the border into Scotland and includes a character posing as a Frenchwoman (Joan Sims). With such plots the films could not but discuss Britishness.

British behaviour is written large in the films. It is loudly asserted in *Jungle* when Professor Tinkle (Frankie Howerd) protests against being eaten by cannibals crying: 'They can't possibly do this to us, after all we are British subjects!' Sid James replies: 'They've got no taste, these people. They'll eat anything!' Britishness typically involves an over-emphasis on matters of honour. The plot of *Camel* turns on a young Englishman named B. O. West (Jim Dale) joining the French Foreign Legion in 1906 to escape the shame of having been accused (wrongly) of cheating in cricket. One character quips: 'His life wouldn't have been worth living here . . . no cricket club would have had him.' The most sustained discussion of British manners is in *Carry On Up the Khyber*. When cornered in an Afghan jail the young officer Captain Keene (Roy Castle) urges his fellow prisoners: 'Remember we are British . . . keep a stiff upper lip.' The sceptical civilian missionary (Peter Butterworth) replies: 'I'm not going to wait around for mine to stiffen.' The dinner party at the climax of the film, during which guests carry on eating and stoically refuse to acknowledge that the residency is being demolished about their ears, is not so much a satire of the 'stiff upper lip' as a celebration of it.

At its most basic level, the behaviour of the British drives outsiders to pronounce them insane. The final line of *Khyber* is: 'Of course, they're all raving mad you know.'[17] In *Camel*, the Rif sheikh (Bernard Bresslaw) observes of Europeans in general: 'The behaviour of the white infidels is like blood coming from a stone . . . a bleeding mystery.' Foreign manners are also exaggerated by way of contrast. In *Don't Lose Your Head*, Citizen Bidet (Peter Butterworth) despairs of the English and asks: 'Why don't they eat frogs' legs and snails like normal people do?' The Afghans of *Khyber* are constructed as opposites of the British to such an extent that they nod their heads for 'no', shake their heads for 'yes' and open fire on a speaker to indicate their pleasure. The 'other' in *Carry On Up the Jungle* is also represented as an opposite familiar from ancient time: a tribe of women warriors.

Just as the geographical border between Britain and the rest of the world is explored by being crossed in the films, so the trappings of the foreign are explored through changes of costume. Like so many characters in British historical fact and fiction, from the explorer Richard Burton through Sherlock Holmes, Kipling's Kim and Lawrence of Arabia, to the resourceful escapees in British prisoner-of-war movies, the characters in historical *Carry On* have the ability to disguise them-

Figure 7.2 Camping across the borders of time and gender: Sid James – as the eighteenth-century highwayman Dick Turpin disguised as a woman – threatens Kenneth Williams – as the police captain Desmond Fancy – in *Carry On Dick* (1974).
Source: Courtesy of Carlton International.

selves as the other and pass undetected in enemy territory. In *Carry On* this central conceit in the British historical imagination is at least camped by ludicrously obvious disguises: the crew of HMS *Venus* are no more convincing as Spaniards in *Jack* than the troops of *Khyber* are as Afghans. The only convincing master of disguise is the mysterious Black Fingernail of *Don't Lose Your Head*, whose skills drive Citizen Camembert to give 'orders to hold anyone disguised as anyone'. Both the Finger-nail and Dick Turpin (in *Carry On Dick*) have secret identities (as a fop and a clergyman respectively).

The fascination with costume and identity extends into the realm of gender. In most of the historical *Carry On*s characters are called upon to cross-dress. In *Cleo*, *Camel* and *Khyber*, the male characters cross-dress as women (specifically vestal virgins and courtesans); and, in the tradition of such films as Gainsborough Studios' *The Wicked Lady* (Leslie Arliss, 1945), women in *Jack*, *Dick* and (briefly) *Don't Lose Your Head* disguise themselves as men. Unlike the cross-dressing in films like *A Funny Thing Happened on the Way to the Forum* (Richard Lester, 1966) the characters are never allowed to explore trans-gendered *alter egos* while in their costumes, but rather retain their original character underneath the costume. The only play with identity is in the mind of third parties watching within the frame of the film, as in *Carry On Jack* when the Captain (Kenneth Williams), unaware that his Midshipman (Juliet Mills) is a woman in disguise, is shocked to see her kiss a fellow sailor: 'I may like to run a happy ship' he says 'but this is ridiculous.' The message of *Carry On* cross-dressing appears to be that identity is more than a quality of clothing, and that the British are uniquely able to manipulate this to their advantage. Rather than blurring the line between men and women, the humour seems to firm up the distinction, which was doubtless reassuring in the shifting world of gender relations in the 1960s.

If *Carry On* questioned some of the historical elements in British identity, it did at least furnish an alternative: an imagined community of humour. The films relied on nationally specific slang. *Carry On Up the Khyber* manages to throw in words like the army term for the lavatory, the khasi (used as the title of the Indian prince); the nursery term for urination, jimmy widdle (a soldier's name); and a London slang term for the anus, jacksey (a frontier town). The film's title itself plays on the Cockney rhyming-slang use of Khyber Pass for arse.[18] Puns are used throughout the scripts. In *Jack* the officer in charge of the press gang (Donald Houston) asks the hapless Walter (Charles Hawtrey) 'wouldn't you like to go to sea, friend?' 'Go to see what?' Walter replies. In *Camel*, when Sergeant Nocker finds crates of laxative at the legion fort, he muses: 'I guess they weren't regular soldiers.' The scripts return repeatedly to *double entendres* as a means to joke about sexual subjects. The moment in *Don't Lose Your Head* when a lady tells her host Sir Rodney Ffing (Sid James) 'You've always had magnificent balls' is typical of the *Carry On* approach.[19]

Camping the present: *Carry On* history as history

Beyond their use of current national slang, the historical *Carry On*s frequently remind the audience that they are located in the present and viewing the past with the advantages of hindsight. This perspective allows humour at the expense of the self-satisfied Policeman Captain (Kenneth Williams) in *Carry On Dick*, who launches a carrier pigeon with the words: 'I often wonder what chance crime has against the modern scientific methods at our disposal . . . It seems incredible to me that that message will actually be in London this time tomorrow morning.' The pigeon proceeds to drop mess on his head.

Yet the present is also fair game, and the *Carry On* histories make frequent references to the contemporary events of their time. These include comments at the decline of contemporary Britain, particularly with reference to the industrial decline, union activism and economic crises of the late 1960s and early 1970s. In *Cleo* a Roman slave-merchant bemoans the quality of British slaves as though they were consumer durables: 'Can't use this British stuff, they don't make it like they used to.' Similarly in *Khyber* the beleaguered staff of the residency agree 'What will we do?' 'We are British, we won't do anything . . .' The missionary (Peter Butterworth) interjects: '. . . until it's too late.' Kenneth Williams usually delivered the political jokes. In *Cleo*, his speech as Caesar includes impersonations of both Winston Churchill and the Conservative Prime Minister of 1957–63 Harold Macmillan. In *Don't Lose Your Head*, when told as Citizen Camembert that the English have 'struck again' he quips: 'It's the one thing the English are good at . . . striking.' When the villainous Burpar chief Bunghit Din (Bernard Bresslaw) declares that the British 'will die the death of a thousand cuts', he replies: 'The British are used to cuts.' Much of *Henry* concerns the King's attempts to raise money through taxation. Thomas Cromwell (Williams) proposes a SET (sex enjoyment tax), an obvious stand-in for the new scourge of the era, VAT (value-added tax). Later, Henry (Sid James) responds to the news: 'the Queen is in labour' with a quip about the fortunes of the British Labour Party: 'Don't worry, they'll never get back in.'

The historical *Carry On*s also made regular comments on the social developments of their times. The storeroom in the desert fort in *Camel* contains a pile of crates labelled 'The Pill'. The dialogue runs: 'The Pill! What do you suppose they used that for?' 'I can't conceive.' The opening narration of *Dick* delivers a catalogue of the crime and disorder prevalent in the England of 1750 and adds 'hasn't changed much, has it?' There are jokes about the declining value of money. At the end of *Carry On Jack* the heroes are delighted to be awarded an annual pension of seven shillings and sixpence each. In *Carry On Henry*, a peasant girl demands money for a sexual favour from the King. He protests that he only has two shillings, whereupon the girl apologises for her inability to give him any change. There is a swipe at Beatlemania in *Cleo* and a spoof of the Beatles song 'She Loves You' in *Don't Lose Your Head*. Modern 'GB' car-plates, familiar from the British cars then venturing for the first time *en masse* into continental Europe, appear on the rump of the Governor's elephant in *Khyber*. Finally, current British social tensions over immigration are noted. In *Khyber*, the Burpar chief fires a cannon at the British, remarking: 'That will teach them to ban turbans on the buses.'[20]

Viewed today, the presence of contemporary comment in the historical *Carry On*s is a potent reminder that the films were themselves products of their time. They served the particular needs of the generation that had lived through the middle years of the century. Their use of armed-services slang and army concert-party comedy drew on the shared heritage of Second World War and National Service in the military. Kenneth Williams had entertained the troops in Malaya and Burma. Pilot Officer Talbot Rothwell of 244 Coastal Command Squadron,

Leuchars, had entered showbusiness while a prisoner-of-war in the German camp featured in *The Great Escape* (John Sturges, US, 1963), Stalag Luft Three. He and *Carry On* regular Peter Butterworth were part of a troupe that wrote and performed comic shows to entertain fellow inmates and distract the guards from escape bids.[21] His later presentation of the military in *Carry On* had a knowing edge that would have been appreciated at the time, as when the gruff Sergeant Major MacNutt (Terry Scott), encourages Widdle (Hawtrey) to recount his story to an officer by yelling: 'story . . . from the beginning . . . begin'.

The *Carry On* films were products of a frontier: the border between the culturally repressed Britain of the 1950s and the uncensored Britain of the 1970s. Their humour turned on the need to discuss such things as sex and bodily functions through euphemism. When, in the 1970s, the films were willing and able to dispose of euphemism the films lost money and the series died. When wordplay was replaced by explicit crudity, the humour just seemed puerile. Moreover, reactionary attempts at topicality began to alienate sections of the films' audience. *Carry On at Your Convenience* (1971) was a rabidly anti-trade union piece set in a toilet factory. Originally planned as *Carry On Comrade* and released with the subtitle *Up the Workers*, the film became the first *Carry On* flop. *Carry On Girls* (1973) attempted to play to the gallery by attacking women's liberation. The problem was compounded by the generational nature of the comedy. The stars and the jokes aged but the British filmgoing audience became disproportionately younger. *Carry On* seemed like something out of the past. The *Carry On* films with contemporary settings sometimes contributed to this sense, as in *Carry On Camping* (1969), in which the 'gang' disguised themselves as hippies in order to sabotage a rock festival. There were some borders that the *Carry On* team just could not cross. Yet despite the disappearance of the series from the cinema, the *Carry On*s became a staple of television schedules, and an inspiration to a new generation of comedians. In many ways, BBC-TV's *Blackadder* series, which began in 1983, picked up costume genre comedy where the *Carry On* series left off.

In some ways the border crossing of the *Carry On*s betrayed a hidden awareness of the nation's limitations. The plots suggested that Britain was not internally self-sufficient but required contact with the outside world to move into the future. Characters have to prove themselves overseas and often marry foreign girls at the end of their adventures.[22] In *Cleo* the Ancient Briton, Hengist (Kenneth Connor) returns cured of his impotence by an Egyptian 'love philtre'. But so much else in the films affirmed national identity. Even though the films made fun of many things traditionally identified with Britishness the *Carry On* histories asserted a heritage of British comedy, language and historical situations, and played to national concerns. The shooting script for *Carry On Up the Khyber* described the final shot as: 'CS Union Jack flying proudly. Across the middle the words: "I'm Backing Britain."' Like that flag, the historical *Carry On*s could always be read as 'backing Britain'.

Notes

1 Interview: Peter Rogers, 21 July 1998 (by telephone). The essential introduction to the *Carry On* series is Ross 1996. See also Hibbin and Hibbin 1988 and the author's own study of *Carry On Cleo* (Cull 2001).

2 British Film Institute, Gerald Thomas papers (source abbreviated hereafter as 'BFI: Thomas'), *Carry On Jack*, Box 2, Kavanagh to Rodgers, 25 June 1962.

3 BFI: Thomas: *Carry On Jack*, Boxes 1 and 2.

4 BFI: Thomas: *Don't Lose Your Head*, Box 2. Minutes of a pre-publicity meeting at Pinewood Studios, 1 September 1966, note: 'Mr Rogers wondered whether the words "Carry On" need be used in the picture. He thought that, as the film was more visual than previous "Carry On" productions, it could stand on its own without any reference to "Carry On".' The first two Rank films were re-released with the *Carry On* prefix in 1968.

5 On television *Carry On* productions, see Ross 1996: 138–60. Ross notes that the 1973 Christmas show included treatments of Robin Hood and the First World War. In 1975 two series of television comedy specials were produced for ATV under the general title *Carry On Laughing*. These dealt exclusively with historical comedy, including treatments of King Arthur, the Battle of Hastings and Oliver Cromwell, and satires of the British television period drama series *Upstairs, Downstairs* and *Lord Peter Wimsey* and *The Prisoner of Zenda* (filmed by John Cromwell, USA, 1937; Richard Thorpe, USA, 1952; and again by Richard Quine, USA, 1979, this time from a script by British television comedy writers Dick Clement and Ian La Frenais). *Charlie* is noted in BFI: Thomas, *Carry On Henry*, Box 2, registration documentation of 8 May 1970.

6 BFI: Thomas: *Carry On Dick*, Box 1. The first script was by Laurie Wyman and George Evans. Turpin and his henchman Tom King became Twirpin and the 'very camp' Tom Queen who wants to 'rape the men'. Jokes included a pun on auspices and horse pisses. The only element that remained in Rothwell's version was the basic device of pitting Turpin against the Bow Street Runners and naming one of them Jock Strapp.

7 BFI: Thomas: *Carry On Dick*, Box 2, Gerald Thomas to Stephen Murphy (British Board of Film Censors), 3 June 1974. Thomas agreed to cut fifteen *risqué* lines, including dialogue between Turpin and the impresario of a tavern show: 'My girls will fight for their honour.' 'Whores de combat, eh?' The previous film *Carry On Girls* (1973) had suffered from a British AA certificate, restricting its audience to those aged fourteen or over.

8 In the world of camp (from the French verb *se camper*: to posture or flaunt) the signs of sexual identities are repeated with a twist, exaggerated until they can be recognised to be not facets of nature but the constructs of culture. Received identity is revealed as artificial and transformed into a mask of performance. A space for existence is created behind that mask and a means of expression is established through the medium of the performance. When one has acknowledged that all life is theatre, one can both enjoy the performance and, perhaps, begin to change the script. For an introduction to camp see Core 1984: 115. Indispensable discussions may be found in Bubuscio 1980 and Sontag 1961: 275–92. For a discussion of the role of the camp character in the *Carry Ons*, see Anderson 1998.

9 Rothwell's views on the importance of the toilet in English humour are quoted in his obituary, *The Times*, 2 March 1981.

10 BFI: Thomas: *Don't Lose Your Head*, Box 2, Rogers to Michael Harriman of A. P. Watt & Son, 20 June 1966.

11 On Gunga Din and Kipling adaptations, see Cull 1996.

12 *Dr Syn* (Roy William Neill, Gaumont-British, 1937); *Captain Clegg* (Peter Graham, Hammer, 1962); *Dr Syn Alias the Scarecrow* (James Nielson, Disney, 1962).

13 BFI: Thomas: *Carry On Henry*, Box 2, includes permission to film on location in Windsor Great Park, and a bill for £4.10.0 for permission to use British Movietone News shots of the Tower of London.

14 *Carry On* history is also happy to speak of Prince Albert (dead in 1861) as alive in 1895; to have Dick Turpin (dead in 1739) alive in 1750, and show Caesar and Mark Antony courting *Cleopatra* simultaneously.

15 BFI: Thomas: *Carry On Jack*, Box 1, script: *Poopdecker RN*; *Carry On Cleo*, Box 1.

16 Rothwell had had personal experience of Empire as an officer in the Palestine police. In an autobiographical note for the publicity for *Don't Lose Your Head* he wrote that he went to Palestine in 1936 'in search of adventure' and 'despite being ambushed, shot-up, stabbed in a dark alley, fleeced by post card sellers' he 'stayed there for 18 months at the end of which time pausing only to shake the sand out of things' he 'fled home' (BFI: Thomas: Information Folder: *Don't Lose Your Head*: 43). For a post-Orwell, post-Fanon examination of the body in British India, see Sinha 1995.

17 In the case of *Khyber* the outsider is the British missionary Belcher (Peter Butterworth) who doesn't share the ethics of the stiff upper lip.

18 For the origins and definitions of these terms see Partridge 1996 and Thorne 1997. Both authorities tie kharsi/carsey to the army, where it has also had the meaning of anus. Thorne speculates on an Indian origin. Partridge suggests that it is a variation on the Italian *casa* for house, adapted in London slang from the 1880s (following Italian migration) as both 'case' and 'carsey' for low taverns, brothels and toilets.

19 There is an interesting reversed use of the *double entendre* in *Dick*. The policeman Fancey (Kenneth Williams) attempts to convey details of the anatomy of Dick Turpin to the Reverend Flasher (Sid James). Fancey's lines are whispered, but euphemisms for the penis can be deduced from Flasher's uncomprehending replies.

20 In its transition from script to screen *Khyber* at least lost some of its racially offensive elements, such as the subtitle 'a Sikh-making saga' and a line in which Lady Ruff-Diamond refers to the Khasi as a 'brown job'. The screenplay also included a scene in which Keene (Roy Castle) fantasises about his marriage to Jelhi. On the honeymoon night she is revealed to have extra arms like an Indian idol, a detail as likely to have been dropped to keep the film to its very tight budget as for reasons of taste (BFI: Thomas: *Carry On Up the Khyber*, Box 1, final script).

21 BFI: Thomas: Information Folder: *Don't Lose Your Head*: 29, 45–6. Their first performance together, a cross-talk routine and song called 'The letter edged in black', covered an escape by two prisoners-of-war, later recaptured in a boat on the Baltic.

22 This theme is developed in the first contemporary *Carry On* to deal with the world outside Britain, the treatment of the package holiday: *Carry On Abroad* (1972). Rogers was reluctant to take contemporary *Carry On* overseas. He had earlier rejected the first draft of *Carry On Camping* because he didn't like the foreign setting (BFI: Thomas: *Carry On Up the Khyber*, Box 2, Rothwell to Rogers, 13 June 1968).

Bibliography

Anderson, M. (1998) ' "Stop messing about!" The gay fool in the *Carry On* films', *Journal of Popular British Cinema* 1: 37–47.

Bubuscio, J. (1980) 'Camp and the gay sensibility' in R. Dyer (ed.) *Gays and Film*, London: BFI: 40–58.

Colley, L. (1992) *Britons: Forging the Nation, 1707–1837*, London: Pimlico.

Core, P. (1984) *Camp: The Lie that Tells the Truth*, London: Plexus.

Cull, N. J. (1996) 'America's Raj: Kipling, masculinity and Empire' in C. E. Gittings (ed.) *Imperialism and Gender: Constructions of Masculinity*, Hebden Bridge, West Yorkshire: Dangaroo: 85–7.

—— (2001) ' "Infamy, Infamy, They've all got it in for me": *Carry On Cleo* and British camp comedies of Ancient Rome' in S. R. Joshel, M. Malamud and D. T. McGuire Jr. (eds) (2001) *Imperial Projections*, Baltimore, MD: Johns Hopkins University Press: 162–90.

Fanon, F. (1967) *The Wretched of the Earth*, Harmondsworth: Penguin.

Harper, S. (1994) *Picturing the Past: The Rise and Fall of the British Costume Film*, London: BFI.

Hibbin, H. and Hibbin, N. (1988) *What a Carry On: The Official Story of the Carry On Film Series*, London: Hamlyn.

Orwell, G. (1961) *Collected Essays*, London: Secker and Warburg.

Partridge, E. (1996) *A Dictionary of Slang and Unconventional English*, eighth edition, London: Routledge and Kegan Paul.

Ross, R. (1996) *The Carry On Companion*, London: Batsford.

Sinha, M. (1995) *Colonial Masculinity: The 'Manly Englishman' and the 'Effeminate Bengali' in the Late Nineteenth Century*, Manchester: Manchester University Press.

Sontag, S. (1961) *Against Interpretation and Other Essays*, New York: Farrar, Straus and Giroux.

Stark, S. J. (1988) *Female Tars: Women Aboard Ship in the Age of Sail*, London: Pimlico.

Thorne, T. (1997) *Dictionary of Contemporary Slang*, London: Bloomsbury.

8 Monkey feathers
Defending *Zulu* (1964)

Sheldon Hall

When films as antiracist as Cy Endfield's *Zulu* (1964), Herbert Biberman's *Slaves* (1969), and Richard Fleischer's *Mandingo* (1975) were first released in the States, they were all generally ignored in the press . . . or treated as if they were shameless pieces of racist exploitation. The diverse methods by which films of social protest become neutralized in mainstream discourse, through either misreadings or lack of attention, are too numerous and complex to be explored in detail here, but it is a problem that needs to be acknowledged at the outset.

(Jonathan Rosenbaum 1995: 281–2)[1]

This chapter is concerned with various critical perceptions and, I will argue, misperceptions of the British imperial epic *Zulu* (directed by Cy Endfield, filmed and copyrighted in 1963, first released in 1964). It is not a study of *Zulu*'s 'reception' as such, though it draws upon primary and secondary sources that express a range of opinion on the film. Rather, it is intended as an intervention in a notional debate about the range of legitimate critical responses to a work of historical drama on film.

Like all forms of discourse, this chapter is written from a particular position. Though I am loath to accept that critical positions are determined by an individual's biographical history or background, it is perhaps appropriate, given the film's subject matter, to state at the outset that I am a white English male born in the year of *Zulu*'s initial release. I first saw the film on its 1972 theatrical reissue (three times); and more than a dozen subsequent viewings have not reduced my enthusiasm or admiration for it.

A positive valuation of *Zulu* – or any film – is not, for me, conditional upon a convincing demonstration of its 'progressiveness', however that might be interpreted. Such qualities as intelligence, complexity and formal skill are, in my view, more signi-ficant for evaluative *criticism* than questions of political affiliation or ideological effectivity – though the latter factors remain highly relevant to any study of a film's relationship to its social and historical context. This is not a call for a rejection of politics as a legitimate subject for critical attention – merely an assertion that there are other values at stake in films than ideological ones. This chapter seeks to offer a critical account of *Zulu* that resists being caught up in a sterile and simplistic opposition between 'progressive' (and therefore good) texts and 'conservative' or 'reactionary' (and therefore bad) ones. It is part of the great interest of *Zulu* that it resists such easy pigeonholing.

Zulu reconstructs the Battle of Rorke's Drift, which took place on 22 and 23 January 1879 during the Anglo-Zulu War. A small garrison of British troops, assigned to protect the army stores and field hospital at a mission station near the Buffalo River in Natal, South Africa – where at least thirty men were already sick or injured – held off for twelve hours an attack from a force of around 4,000 Zulu warriors. Only seventeen Britons out of the 153 defenders (Knight 1993: 162) were killed in action or died later of wounds, compared to at least 500 Zulus. The successful defence was hailed as a triumph by the Victorian establishment, and eleven of the British survivors were recognised with Victoria Crosses, still the largest number awarded for any single military action. This contrasted with the disaster of the Battle of Isandhlwana, also on 22 January 1879, in which 20,000 Zulus massacred a British column of around 1,700 men: perhaps the greatest single military defeat in British colonial history, and still remembered by the Zulus as a triumph, though it has largely been forgotten in Britain.[2]

The film was developed (initially under the working title *The Battle of Rorke's Drift*) from a magazine article by the historian John Prebble, which came to the attention of the US-born director Cy Endfield and the Welsh actor Stanley Baker, with whom Endfield had made four previous films.[3] The story's focus on a mainly Welsh regiment appealed to Baker, and he and Endfield co-produced the project for their company Diamond Films. The screenplay, written by Endfield and Prebble, largely follows the two official accounts of the battle given by the British commanding officer, Lieutenant John Chard, played in the film by Baker.[4] Location shooting took place in the Natal National Park, South Africa, about 100 miles from the site of the actual battle, with the British cast and crew supplemented by white South African National Servicemen and Zulus drawn from local tribes. Chief Mangosuthu G. Buthelezi (now Chief Minister of KwaZulu) played his own great-grandfather, King Cetewayo, and – according to the film's production notes – advised Endfield and his crew on Zulu battle tactics, as did other local chiefs.

Zulu received its world premiere at London's Plaza cinema on 22 January 1964, the 85th anniversary of the battle. It was a considerable box-office success: in the first three months of its UK release the film's distributor recorded 3,268,056 admissions at 224 theatres, from an anticipated total of around 1,500 playdates in the UK market, setting a record for a general release on the ABC circuit.[5] The film was claimed by both *Kinematograph Weekly* (Altria 1964: 9) and *Films and Filming* (Anon. 1965: 39) to be the third most successful UK general release of 1964, after the James Bond film *Goldfinger* (Guy Hamilton, 1964) and The Beatles's vehicle *A*

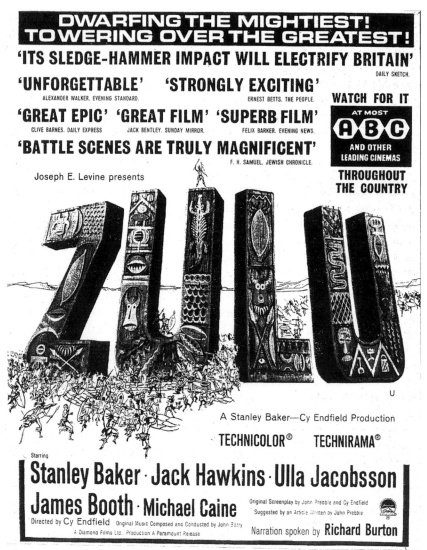

Figure 8.1 The third most successful UK general release of 1964: advertisement artwork
from *Zulu* 's initial release testifies to critics' enthusiasm – in the UK, at least –
while the ambiguous catch-line accommodates diverse readings of the film.
Source: *Films and Filming*, courtesy of Paramount/Diamond Films.

Hard Day's Night (Richard Lester, 1964), and was subsequently reissued in 1967,
1972 and 1976. *Zulu* had a negative cost of $3.5 million – above average for a
British film of the time, but still modest in view of its large scale – and, according
to Stanley Baker's obituaries, it had earned worldwide rentals of $12 million by
1976 (cited in Berry 1994: 266).

The film's high standing in British popular memory can be gauged by its appearance in several film polls conducted for the advent of the millennium. It achieved thirty-first place in the British Film Institute's BFI 100 list of favourite 'culturally British movies', as voted for by invited film-industry figures, critics, journalists and academics. In the Sky Premier satellite television channel's Millennium Movies poll, drawn from the votes of an estimated 60,000 Sky Premier subscribers, *Zulu* was ranked eighteenth favourite – the second-highest place, after *The Full Monty* (Peter Cattaneo, 1997), achieved by any British film. In a breakdown of votes by UK region, *Zulu* achieved seventh and eighth position in Wales/West and the South-West respectively, beating *The Full Monty* in these regions.

However, the film's British success was not replicated in the USA, where *Zulu* failed to achieve the minimum rental figure of $1 million needed to gain a place in *Variety*'s 1964 year-end chart of box-office hits (although the film has since acquired 'cult' status through exposure on US television). While other British Empire-themed movies of the decade also failed to find a large audience in the US, *Zulu*'s failure may be partly attributable to its release there by an independent company, Embassy, whose chief executive, Joseph E. Levine, had provided production finance. (In the rest of the world, *Zulu* was released by Paramount, the Hollywood major with which Levine had an extensive distribution deal.) However, *Zulu* may also have encountered a degree of political opposition in the US – then in the throes of the civil-rights debate – not matched in Britain. American reviewers certainly tended to be more conscious than British ones of ethical and political issues arising from the film, as illustrated by the comments of the *New York Times*'s Bosley Crowther:

> [T]he question is whether such a picture, coming at this time, with tensions and discords so prevalent, is discreet or desirable. Is it a contribution to the cause of harmony to show so much vicious acrimony between black men and white, to wallow in blood-spurting slaughter, to make an exciting thing of firing rifles into the faces of charging warriors and sticking bayonets into them?
>
> And is the ideal of the white man's burden, which this picture tacitly presents (for all its terminal disgust with the slaughter), in the contemporary spirit? You decide.
>
> (Crowther 1964: 38)

It is precisely the success of *Zulu* in Britain that has led hostile critics to identify an ideological role for the film in its own time comparable with that of Rorke's Drift itself for the Victorians. Following Indian independence in 1947, the 1950s and early 1960s bore witness to the crumbling of Britain's colonial power, as one subject nation after another declared its independence. Between 1956 and 1968, more than thirty former dependencies, mainly in Africa, achieved self-rule – seventeen in 1960 alone, the year of Harold Macmillan's famous 'wind of change' speech before the South African parliament.[6] Popular support for a film which represented the victory of a beleaguered white minority over an insurgent racial Other could thus easily be read as an expression of white British feelings of loss and resentment regarding the changing post-colonial landscape. The film's highly organised, fiercely belligerent native forces could be seen as an objective correlative for the ascendant or newly independent African nations, and their defeat as appealing to reactionary nostalgia for imperial power and dominance over subject races. The fact that *Zulu* was exhibited to whites-only audiences in apartheid South Africa, after being declared 'unfit for black consumption' by the country's Publications Control Board (Mann 1969), may not help the case for its critical defence. It is, of course, intriguing to speculate on *why* it was judged unfit – perhaps the example of their forefathers' militancy was feared likely to provoke black African viewers to revolutionary violence.

It is no surprise, then, that for many present-day observers in the fields of both film studies and history, *Zulu* is a pernicious misrepresentation: a film which, in selecting an atypical incident as the basis for an heroic epic, inverts historical reality, portraying the victims of imperialist aggression as themselves the aggressors, and the white imperialist forces as an oppressed minority. From this perspective, the film is at best 'anachronistic – a last desperate bid to mount an old-style imperial epic' (Auty 1981: 1392), or 'spectacular but mostly mindless' (Cameron 1994: 141). At worst, it is 'an epic step backwards [which] only reveals the racial conservatism of much liberal-inclined English movie-making' (Pines 1975: 78). Jim Pines, the author of this last comment, later expanded on this judgement in a programme note produced to accompany a screening of *Zulu* as part of a 1986 National Film Theatre season entitled Images of Empire:

> In the context of Images of Empire, this colonial war adventure can only be seen as exploitative pulp – although in general most reviewers have shown an ambivalence towards the film's sheer force and impact . . . What seems to be in play here is some notion of historical authenticity, which not only heightens the film's unquestioned glorification of British heroism, but also disguises its more unsavoury aspects, of which there are many. The tendency in colonial narratives to collapse African characters into a (typically menacing) mass is grandly exhibited here. And despite the film's apparently 'liberal' gesture, in acknowledging the magnificence of the Zulu warriors – in a romanticised way – the main thrust is clearly toward emphasising the militaristic and, more importantly, spiritual superiority of the hugely outnumbered British. Not surprisingly, the political issues surrounding the historical events, particularly the African point of view, is [sic] of little concern in the film. In the end, 'the whites and Zulus go their separate ways,' as Raymond Durgnat wryly puts it. 'Real understanding is attained through – apartheid, might one say?'[7]
>
> (Pines 1986)

More recently, Christopher Sharrett has published a substantial article on *Zulu* that professes to acknowledge its virtues, yet constitutes the most sustained critical attack on it to date. Sharrett argues that the film's 'liberal ideological veneer cloaks a reliance on a surprising number of generic conventions as well as some key historical distortions and omissions in order to perpetuate its own colonialist political agenda' (Sharrett 2000: 29). Though a detailed refutation of his account will have to await another occasion – there is something to dispute in virtually every sentence – it is important to address here the unexamined assumptions on which it is built.[8] These are that the genre conventions deployed – principally those of the Western and war film, though Sharrett also finds horror-film imagery in *Zulu* – are inherently conservative and repressive; that the use of these conventions necessarily conflicts with any attempt at a 'truthful' representation of historical actuality and perhaps with 'realism' in general; and that historical truth, insofar as it can be determined, should be the primary concern of any film which dramatises an event from history. All three points seem to me highly arguable, and at times are even contradicted by Sharrett himself: for example, he demands historical accuracy from *Zulu* but wants to be spared even its token depiction of nineteenth-century attitudes and language ('fuzzies') uncongenial to a modern liberal sensibility.

On the matter of historical reconstruction, I would contend that filmmakers, like other artists, are entitled to as much latitude as they care to take in adapting the raw material of history to the demands of dramatic narrative. Their interests and responsibilities are those of dramatists, not historians, and critics in turn have a responsibility to attend to their work with these priorities in mind. Historians, of course, have their priorities too; but I would argue that historical fictions, whatever their basis in fact, should be treated as such and not as works of history proper. Historians should not expect the popular cinema to do their work for them, nor should audiences expect a visit to the movies to provide a short-cut history lesson – no matter how inviting either prospect might seem.

My polemic may, of course, be wishful thinking given the widespread determination to see things otherwise. On 28 November 1999 (47–9), as part of a Millennial series entitled 'Make a date with history', the *News of the World* reprinted its front page of 23 February 1879, which included Chard's report on the Battle of Rorke's Drift to Lord Chelmsford, commander-in-chief of British forces in South Africa. The reprint was preceded by a short article (Jones 1999), headlined 'Zulu' in large lettering and featuring a still from the film alongside a contemporary sketch of the battle: ample testimony to the popular 'reading' of history through cinema.

Critical analysis does not, of course, rule out a consideration of moral, ethical or political issues, which cannot easily be disentangled from aesthetic ones. But any such discussion must begin by acknowledging what kind of thing a film is, and what evaluative terms it is appropriate to bring to one. A central assumption underpinning my argument is that criticism should be concerned with what the film is *doing* with its source material – the film's position in relation to it – and the consequences of this for our response to it *as drama* or, more precisely, as cinema, rather than as history.

The related, but comparatively minor, objection that *Zulu* is simply inaccurate in the detail of its historical reconstruction I shall not discuss here at length. The analysis of a film's 'distortions' of documented historical truth can indeed reveal the existence of an ideological agenda, or simply broader thematic interests, as I shall discuss later. There is plentiful evidence to support claims that *Zulu* 'gets it wrong' – often consciously – in areas ranging from the appearance and characterisation of the main protagonists and the order of events in the battle, to details of uniforms, equipment and physical locations and the twentieth-century fillings visible in the teeth of Michael Caine (playing Chard's second-in-command Lieutenant Bromhead). None of this need overly concern the film critic, much as it may distress serious military historians and amateur buffs. Ironically, the fact that *Zulu* characterises the British participants at Rorke's Drift – often unflatteringly – in greater depth than the Zulus left it particularly susceptible to objections from the descendants of the former, some of whom certainly made public their sense of grievance. Lieutenant-Colonel Sir Benjamin Bromhead, who had been a senior military guest of honour at the film's London premiere, wrote to the *Daily Telegraph* in protest at Caine's portrayal of his great-uncle (Bromhead 1964).[9] Chief Buthelezi may have had the advantage in being on hand to play his own ancestor.

Within the sphere of historical reconstruction in the fiction film, it is necessary to distinguish between *accuracy* of detail and *authenticity* of impression. The latter is less a matter of strict fidelity to the recorded historical facts than of the achievement of dramatic verisimilitude – that is, a convincing illusion. This verisimilitude may depend upon one or more of the following: the fulfilment of viewers' expectations through adherence to established representational conventions; the reinvigoration of conventions which had appeared to be exhausted; or seeming to break through 'convention' to a more direct apprehension of (what we imagine to be) 'the truth', which may in itself lead to the establishment of a new set of conventions. *Zulu* works largely within the second of these three modes, drawing upon established generic conventions while adapting them to the emerging values of the 1960s.

One example to clarify the point being made: the British reviews of *Zulu* at the time of its release were of the kind usually described as 'mixed'. However, virtually all of those I consulted singled out for praise the 'astonishingly fine' performance (Barker 1964), 'right in character *and period*' (Walker 1964: reviewer's italics) of Nigel Green as Colour-Sergeant Bourne: 'every tough but tender-hearted colour-sergeant compressed into one ramrod' (Wilson 1964), 'whose mutton-chop whiskers, bright blue eyes and rough but understanding attitude seem so absolutely right that one feels he has stepped out of the history books'

(Pacey 1964). Even Nina Hibbin of the Communist Party of Great Britain's newspaper the *Daily Worker* remarked that Green 'almost persuades you to believe in this quaint invention of British Army fiction' (Hibbin 1964). Green was 39 when the film was made, and his manner is accurately and approvingly described by more than one reviewer as 'paternal'. The real Frank Bourne was 25 at the time of the battle (which earned him a Distinguished Conduct Medal) and was known to his comrades as 'the kid' (Brown 1994). No matter: the critics were right; it is sufficient that Green's performance is 'true' to the relevant conventions.

One of the main criticisms made by Sharrett and others is that *Zulu* offers little or no historical contextualisation which would enable the uninformed spectator to understand the place of Rorke's Drift in the Zulu War or that of the war in British imperial policy. Whether one is disposed to defend this or not, it is certainly the case. The film presents only the barest historical context for the action at Rorke's Drift. An omniscient narrator, employed at the outset of a movie to induct us into an unfamiliar historical world and explain its narrative 'backstory', is a common enough device in the epic film – see, for example, *The Fall of the Roman Empire* (Anthony Mann, 1964, USA) – and one which could have been used more fully here. However, *Zulu*'s introductory voiceover narration (spoken by Richard Burton) is brief, consisting only of the opening paragraphs of a letter reporting the massacre at Isandhlwana, and fading out before the reading is completed as sound and image dissolve into the flames of the devastated battlefield. At the film's end, the same voiceover reads the roll-call of the honorees awarded the Victoria Cross for their role in the defence of Rorke's Drift. All other immediately relevant data (such as the number and ranks of the defenders) is disclosed via action and dialogue between the – highly fictionalised – characters, and then only selectively. The film suggests, for example, that the British casualty rate was higher than it was in reality, even though a body count reveals no more than fifteen British deaths actually depicted on screen. Beyond this, historical 'analysis' is scant. Even the – disputable – strategic importance of the post at Rorke's Drift, which was seen at the time as the last line of defence protecting Natal Colony from Zulu invasion, is not made explicit.

This sparsity of historical contextualisation can, however, be viewed as a symptom of *Zulu*'s equivocal character as an 'epic'. The battle it describes was relatively minor in national or global impact; its principal value to Britain was as a much-needed diversion from the disaster at Isandhlwana. It did not announce the imminent rise or fall of a civilisation, although it anticipated the Zulus' ultimate defeat by the British at the Battle of Ulundi some months later. Nor does the film's narrative sweep over a broad geographical or historical span, as do those of most epics; indeed, the story is notable for its compactness, unfolding over less than two days. Its visual spectacle aside, *Zulu*'s epic qualities are largely of the folkloric kind, in that it recounts great heroic deeds of the past for the admiration and moral inspiration of present generations. It constitutes material for an epic primarily because of the fantastically disproportionate military odds involved, and the extremes of courage and fortitude required of both the defenders and attackers.

In view of this, it is appropriate to examine the film's relationships with other major genres. While Sharrett is right to invoke the conventions of the Western and war film in his discussion, he draws the wrong conclusions from them. It is no more than a commonplace to observe that the American Western and the British imperial adventure resemble one another in many respects. Hollywood has produced any number of films in both genres sharing the same landscapes, themes, plots and personnel. John Ford directed several British imperial adventures in the 1920s and 1930s in addition to his more customary Westerns; and 1962 even saw *Gunga Din* (George Stevens, 1939, USA), inspired by Rudyard Kipling's poem, remade as a Western, John Sturges's *Sergeants Three*.

In the mid-1960s, both the Western and the British imperial adventure were undergoing crucial transformations in response to a changing cultural and political climate, transformations of which *Zulu* is clearly symptomatic. The decade saw the appearance in America of the 'revisionist' Western, expressing an increasingly disillusioned view of the relations between white America and its native peoples. Two key examples, released within a few months of *Zulu*, were John Ford's final Western, the bitter, pro-Native-American *Cheyenne Autumn* (1964); and Raoul Walsh's last film, *A Distant Trumpet* (1964), the first sound Western to include subtitled translations of Native-American dialogue. In Britain, *Northwest Frontier* (J. Lee Thompson, 1959) was perhaps the last major production that could endorse unambiguously the virtues of colonial rule – although even here, the British were shown to be embattled by the forces of Indian nationalism. The 1960s brought a cycle of 'post-imperial' British period films – like *Zulu*, American-financed prestige productions – which conveyed a sense of the impending end of Empire or a more complex and ambivalent attitude towards it. These included *Lawrence of Arabia* (David Lean, 1962), *Khartoum* (Basil Dearden, 1966) and *The Charge of the Light Brigade* (Tony Richardson, 1968). Emerging alongside, and in some cases anticipating, them was a less distinguished, mostly low-budget series of colonial swashbucklers with native rebels as heroes: *Zarak* (Terence Young, 1956), *The Bandit of Zhobe* (John Gilling, 1959), *The Brigand of Kandahar* (John Gilling, 1965) and *The Long Duel* (Ken Annakin, 1967).

The kinship between the Western and the British imperial adventure is matched by that between British and American examples of the war film. Jeanine Basinger has listed sixteen distinctive 'generic requirements' of the World War Two combat film, as established in such pictures as *Wake Island* (John Farrow, USA, 1942) and *Bataan* (Tay Garnett, USA, 1943) and maintained or developed in the majority of subsequent US and British war films (Basinger 1986: 61–2). All but one of these requirements are met directly or indirectly by *Zulu*. For example: Chard in *Zulu* performs the role of 'a hero who is part of the group, but is forced to separate himself from it because of the demands of leadership'. The film features 'internal group conflicts' (between Chard and Bromhead, between the private soldiers, and between Chard and the pacifist missionaries the Witts); a 'faceless enemy' (the Zulus are seen mostly from a distance and not characterised in detail); and 'the need to remember and discuss home' (here, the Welsh privates' nostalgia for the valleys).

Significantly, however, the one generic element missing from *Zulu* is 'propaganda, the discussion of why we fight and how justified it is' (Basinger 1986: 62). At no point in the film do officers or other ranks discuss the political justification or strategic objectives of the war and the battle in which they are engaged. The remoteness of the Zulu War, and the Victorian military-colonialist ethos, for 1960s audiences is one explanation for this omission. Another is that the film, following a common convention of the combat genre, presents battle from the point of view of the foot soldier – here, ranks no higher than lieutenant – rather than from that of generals, strategists and politicians. The loss of overview is compensated for in dramatic terms by a close identification with the ground-level participants.

The duty of lower-ranking officers and men was and is to follow orders, not to question them or determine the reasons for obeying them. Lieutenants Chard and Bromhead have received orders to hold their ground at Rorke's Drift, and most of their own discussions and disagreements relate to the most effective ways of achieving that objective. The film's one clear reference to the larger context of colonial politics beyond the characters' immediate situation comes in a brief, good-natured but suggestive exchange between Bromhead and the Boer officer Adendorff (Gert Van Den Bergh):

> Adendorff: I'm a Boer, the Zulus are the enemy of my blood. What are you doing here?
> Bromhead: You don't object to our help, I hope?
> Adendorff: It all depends on what you damned English want for it, afterwards.

While barely commenting on colonial politics, the film does, however, repeatedly give expression to the subordinate ranks' sense of frustration and bewilderment at their very presence in Africa. Ordered to prepare defences in the hospital where he is confined, Private Hook (James Booth) wants to know: 'What for? Did I see a Zulu walk down the City Road? No – so why am I here?' As the soldiers wait expectantly for the first Zulu attack, the nervous, sweating Private Cole (Gary Bond) asks Bourne: 'Why is it us, eh? Why us?' and receives the stoical reply: 'Because we're here, lad – nobody else. Just us.' Later, mortally wounded, Cole repeatedly asks a similar question of the surgeon attending him and is told, 'I'm damned if I can tell you why'. The precise object of the question 'Why?' is left deliberately vague. It may refer to Cole's own imminent death, the specific action of defending Rorke's Drift, the purpose of the war in Africa, or the European colonial presence in Africa; exact interpretation is left to the spectator.

Zulu's ambivalence concerning the British presence in Africa is further suggested by the soldiers' continuous visual prominence in the African *mise-en-scène*, where they frequently appear displaced and ill at ease. Much of the film's pleasure as spectacle derives from the contrasting splendours of spruce military uniforms, traditional Zulu (un)dress and massive, stark landscapes. Private Thomas (Neil McCarthy) comments on the contrast between the parched grasslands of South Africa and the greenery of his native Wales. In doing so, he draws the viewer's attention to the highly visible incongruity of red-clad white men in a geographical terrain in which they clearly do not belong and to which they are ill-suited. Frequent long shots take advantage of the towering mountain scenery surrounding Rorke's Drift (or rather the film's reconstruction of it), emphasising the smallness and vulnerability of the European outpost. In the film's early sequence in Cetewayo's royal *kraal* (homestead), the camera tracks along a row of warriors in feathered costume to halt before the anachronistic sight of the Swedish missionary, the Reverend Otto Witt (Jack Hawkins), and his daughter Margareta (Ulla Jacobsson) ensconced among them.

The Zulus, by contrast – heard before they are seen with the eerie sound of *assegais* rattling against war shields, 'like a train in the distance' – seem to emerge from the land itself. They are first glimpsed arrayed on the crest of a hill overlooking the garrison, gradually appearing from behind it to fill and dominate the horizon. Throughout their assaults, the Zulus are able to take cover in gullies and dips in the land, seeming to blend in to the landscape as if part of it: 'I can't see a bloody one now.' 'They've gone to ground.' 'Oh.' (See Knight 1993: 156 for similar observations.)

A further key war-movie convention listed by Basinger is that 'the attitudes that an audience should take to the war are taught through events, conversations, and actions' (Basinger 1986: 62). It is the tenor of the attitudes dramatised in *Zulu* that defines its ambivalent position with regard to the imperialist project. Some of the film's reviewers and contemporary commentators have lamented that these attitudes are those of the 1960s, not the 1870s, and there is some validity in this objection. Again, the issue here is questionable dramatic verisimilitude, not infidelity to the known or assumed views of actual historical figures. The film's protagonists display none of the unashamed jingoism and (despite Sharrett's insistence to the contrary) 'casual racism' which one might expect to find among nineteenth-century soldiery (and which is evident in the testimonies of actual survivors of the battle, such as those collected in Knight and Castle 1993). Indeed, most of the white characters speak well of the Zulus. The Swiss Corporal Schiess (Dickie Owen) swiftly quashes a Welsh soldier's assumption that their foe is a 'bunch of savages, isn't it?' by praising the Zulus' physical capabilities. The Welsh are equally impressed by the Zulus' courage and stamina in the battle, remarking: 'They've got more guts than we have, boyo'.[10] Sharrett suggests that this is merely a form of imperialist self-aggrandisement: 'The emphasis on the superhuman skills of the

Other makes all the more grand the white victory' (Sharrett 2000: 30). It seems that for him the film is damned whatever it does.

The most derogatory comment we hear made about the Zulus, uttered by Bromhead about the native auxiliaries who died with the column at Isandhlwana ('Damn the levies man – more cowardly blacks'), is forcefully denounced by, of all characters, the Boer Adendorff. The white viewer is never encouraged to take a simplistically racist attitude towards 'the enemy' – at least insofar as such attitudes are not directly dramatised on screen. Viewers determined to read the film in racist terms can, of course, still do so: filmmakers may attempt to guide spectators' responses, but cannot hope to determine them. Thus a further correspondent to the *Daily Telegraph* of 28 February 1964, one Major F. A. I. de Gruchy, asserted that Rorke's Drift (the battle itself, not the film's re-creation) demonstrated 'the eternal story of the British Empire, won often in the fields at odds of 100 to one . . . the victory of quality against mere quantity.' The writer gives no indication of actually having seen *Zulu*.

Another common criticism of the film (see Pines 1986, Sharrett 2000, and Knight and Castle 1993) is that it fails to offer any Zulu or African perspective on the events depicted, since its drama is narrated solely from the point of view, in the broadest sense, of the British soldiers. Subjective shots from white characters' *literal* points of view are in fact given only, and then very briefly, to Chard during the battle and, in the *kraal* sequence mentioned earlier, to Margareta Witt; contrary to Sharrett's claim, the latter do not '[anchor] audience point of view and [embody] its sensibility' (Sharrett 2000: 31). A number of shots in the film do show the British encampment from the Zulus' position in the hills surrounding the mission. We see, for example, Zulus training rifles they have recovered from the Isandhlwana battlefield on the British soldiers, and being ordered by their commanders not to attack the departing Witts. These are, however, brief inserts, insufficient to disrupt the spectator's predominant engagement with the British.

It is true also that King Cetewayo is the film's sole clearly individuated Zulu character. Though three other Zulu actors are credited in addition to Chief Buthelezi, the few words of dialogue spoken by him and these others are not subtitled, but are translated by the Swedish colonial missionary Reverend Witt. One possible rationale for this absence – although one which is open to debate – is suggested by the historians Ian Knight and Ian Castle:

> The use of the single word Zulu as the [film's] title is intended to conjure up the potent myth, which dates back to the war itself, that the Zulus were the epitome of African savagery. To provide a Zulu voice within the film would have served only to dilute this objective, but it does reveal how inherently limited such a mythology is.
>
> (Knight and Castle 1993: 255–6)

In the film's original screenplay, however, a young Zulu boy whom Witt has taught English and named Jacob (seen standing between Witt and Cetewayo in the *kraal* scene, and played by a credited actor, Daniel Tshabalala) *was* given a brief speech which would have supplied both historical information and a Zulu view-point: 'The great Nkosi Cetewayo is angry. He says the red-coated soldiers are already upon his land and wish to take all the hills between the Blood River and the Buffalo' (Prebble and Endfield 1963: 28). When news of the Isandhlwana massacre is received, Jacob renounces his designated Christian name and grins in triumph at his people's victory. These speeches are deleted in the finished film.

While *Zulu*'s adoption of a predominantly white British perspective will con-tinue to attract criticism, this restricted point of view can be defended insofar as it strengthens the film's dramatic effectiveness. It enables the viewer to share with-out distraction the British soldiers' feelings of terror and entrapment at finding themselves in a situation not of their own making and beyond their control. *Zulu* can be compared in this respect to another, contemporaneous transatlantic group of films concerned with siege, or 'last stand', situations: *The Alamo* (John Wayne, USA, 1960), *55 Days at Peking* (Nicholas Ray/Andrew Marton/Guy Green, USA, 1963) and, again, *Khartoum*. The effectiveness of siege narratives depends heavily upon the viewer siding with one set of protagonists over another, even if the antagonists are characterised in some depth (as is the case in *Peking* and *Khartoum*). The sense of isolation experienced by the soldiers at Rorke's Drift, and the con-struction of empathy with their fears – not in themselves racist – of an unknown, overwhelming and intimidating enemy, logically demand a concentration upon the besieged faction.

The pitfalls of more dispersed patterns of identification are well enough demonstrated by *Zulu*'s belated 'prequel', written by Cy Endfield: *Zulu Dawn* (Douglas Hickox, USA/Holland, 1979). A critical and commercial failure, the later film re-enacts the Zulu massacre of British forces at Isandhlwana on the same day as Rorke's Drift in the manner of the epic battle reconstructions which were also a feature of the 1960s international cinema. Examples include *The Longest Day* (Ken Annakin/Andrew Marton/Gerd Oswald/Bernhard Wicki/Darryl F. Zanuck, USA, 1962), *Battle of Britain* (Guy Hamilton, UK, 1969), *Tora! Tora! Tora!* (Richard Fleischer, USA/Japan, 1970) and *Waterloo* (Sergei Bondarchuk, Italy/USSR, 1970). Peter Watkins's 1964 docu-drama 'reconstruction' *Culloden* for BBC-TV, written by *Zulu* screenwriter John Prebble, should also be located in relation to this cycle.

The greater scale of the Isandhlwana engagement and its more sprawling nature – as well as the fact of the Zulus' victory – demanded a different treatment from that of the Battle of Rorke's Drift in *Zulu*. Accordingly, *Zulu Dawn* intercuts be-tween a large number of parallel plotlines, including the kind of contextualising material on British colonial policy and the military aims of the war missing from *Zulu*. There are also scenes set in the Zulus' encampment without white characters present to 'mediate' for a presumed white Anglophone audience; Zulu dialogue is given subtitled translation; and the film features several sympathetically individuated Zulu characters. (Here, Cetewayo is played by Simon Sabela, who also appeared as a dance leader in *Zulu*.) Yet the result is diffuse and unwieldy, confused rather than enlightening, and almost wholly lacking in dramatic tension. *Zulu Dawn* is more explicit than *Zulu* about the egregiousness of European empire-building and the chastisement of imperialist presumption which the massive defeat of British forces at Isandhlwana represented. By contrast, *Zulu*'s relative inexplicitness – in diffusing any commentary on imperialism into a more generalised, but also more resonant, sense of the British soldiers' displacement and disorientation – can be seen to work greatly in its favour.

It is doubtful that any unambiguously anti-imperial film could have been made of the Battle of Rorke's Drift. Filmmakers wishing to make such a statement would surely instead have chosen the battles of Isandhlwana (as was apparently the case with *Zulu Dawn*) or Ulundi, where the Zulu nation was finally routed. *Zulu* is neither straightforwardly pro- nor anti-imperialist; it is, rather, *unconvinced* by the imperialist project. The opportunities for death-or-glory romanticism which its subject offers are for the most part emphatically refused, or admitted in only the most equivocal terms. The exchange of impressions between Bromhead and Chard, as they take stock when the fight appears to be won, presents not triumphant self-congratulation, nor the jocular banter of relieved survivors, but the officers' weariness and revulsion at their first direct experience of mass bloodshed and their discovery of their own capacity for violence:

> Chard: Well, you've fought your first action.
> Bromhead: Does everyone feel like this, afterwards?
> Chard: How *do* you feel?
> Bromhead: Sick.
> Chard: Well, you have to be alive to feel sick.
> Bromhead: You asked me, I told you. (pause) There's something else. I feel ashamed. Was that how it was for you – the first time?
> Chard: The first time? Do you think I could stand this butcher's yard more than once?[11]

Displays of fighting tactics are nonetheless a crucial element in the film's generic vocabulary. Like any combat film, 'anti-war' or otherwise, *Zulu* entertains its audience with the spectacular depiction of violent death. However, it seems to me that the film negotiates with success the unavoidable contradiction of offering pleasure based on violence, without seeming to endorse the violence itself or ignoring its terrible human consequences. This is apparent in sequences such as the final Zulu assault, after which the camera moves slowly across a field littered with black bodies to close in on the small group of white soldiers staring out at the carnage with a mixture of disbelief, horror and sheer exhaustion.

This merging of Western and Zulu musical traditions in the *Zulu* score further symbolises the spiritual equality the film accords to the two cultures. Of course, the film's critics might argue that this is a further instance of its suppression of an authentic Zulu viewpoint: perhaps even a literal form of cultural imperialism, with a Western orchestra 'colonising' Zulu music. But a reverse interpretation – that Zulu rhythms are infiltrating the European symphonic tradition – is equally feasible. We are dealing here with meaning at the *non*-representational level, where interpretation is especially conjectural. But it is precisely such ambiguities and resonances that give *Zulu* its unusual distinction. It cannot be reduced to a simplistic 'positive' or 'negative' message or statement, nor can its values be read off unproblematically from a synopsis of its plot. As a product of white, First-World culture, *Zulu* could not possibly be expected to 'speak for' the Zulus; nor could its makers ever validly have claimed to represent the Zulus' viewpoint authentically. It accomplishes instead an impressive gesture of respect, much like that offered by Chard in its closing shot.[13] As the end titles play out over the image of a single Zulu war shield, erected by Chard as a kind of makeshift gravestone or memorial to the Zulu dead, a choral reprise of 'Men of Harlech' ultimately gives way to an emphatic orchestral restatement of the Zulu-influenced main theme.

Acknowledgements

I should like to express thanks to my colleague Sylvia Harvey and to students at Sheffield Hallam University – especially Lawrence Sutcliffe and Jenny Hirst – with whom I have discussed *Zulu* in seminars. My grateful thanks also to George Smith of the Anglo-Zulu War Historical Research Association, formerly of National Screen Service, and to *Zulu*'s associate producer Basil Keys, for sharing their knowledge with me.

Notes

1 This epigraph is offered with apologies to Jonathan Rosenbaum, who might not wish to be associated with the critical position developed in this chapter.

2 The spellings of African names used here are those used in the film itself and its documentation. Note, however, the more modern spellings of Isandhlwana (Isandlwana) and Cetewayo (Cetshwayo). For historical accounts of the Battles of Rorke's Drift and Isandhlwana, and the context of the Anglo-Zulu War, see Glover 1975, Knight 1993 and Knight and Castle 1993.

3 Endfield had been based in Britain since 1951, having fled the HUAC's anti-Communist persecution in Hollywood, and died in 1995. He is sometimes mistakenly reported as having been born in South Africa. For details of his career and excerpts from an interview, see Rosenbaum 1995 and 1997. For further information on the making of *Zulu*, see Smith 1994 and the film's production notes held on microfiche in the British Film Institute (BFI) Library.

4 For the lengthier of Chard's reports and other eyewitness accounts from survivors of Rorke's Drift, see Knight and Castle 1993: 47–71.

5 Source: letter from Paramount International Films, Inc. to Joseph E. Levine, dated 25 May 1964; reproduced in a trade advertisement in *Motion Picture Herald*, 10 June 1964: 15–16.

6 In this speech Macmillan declared: 'The wind of change is blowing through this continent [Africa], and whether we like it or not, this growth of national consciousness is a political fact.'

7 Source: Durgnat 1970: 82. Durgnat's criticism depends on sophistry for its effect: if 'separatism' is substituted for 'apartheid' – the Zulus do, after all, *choose* to leave the battlefield – the connotation becomes significantly different. For more favourable academic accounts of *Zulu*, see Taves 1993 and Richards 1973, 1981 and 1997. Knight 1993 is also broadly sympathetic towards the film, though critical of its historical omissions and inaccuracies.

8 For letters responding to Sharrett's article, and Sharrett's reply, see Ivens 2001 and Nicholson 2001.

9 For John Prebble's response to criticism of the film's (deliberate) historical inaccuracies, see Prebble 1964.

10 The accounts of Zulu War veterans collected in Knight and Castle include similar tributes.

11 Endfield and Prebble's unpublished screenplay includes even more explicitly anti-military dialogue.

12 There is uncertainty over the precise number of Zulu extras in *Zulu*. According to Rosenbaum (1997: 335), the film used no more than 250 at any one time, rather than the thousands claimed in some sources.

13 The phrase 'gesture of respect' is used in the screenplay to describe this shot (Prebble and Endfield 1963: 123).

Bibliography

Note: Page numbers were not available for articles and reviews accessed via the BFI Library microfiche collection on *Zulu*.

Anon. (1965) 'Bond – Beatles – Zulus: what would you pick?' *Films and Filming*, February 1965: 39.

Altria, B. (1964) 'British films romp home – fill first five places', *Kinematograph Weekly*, 17 December 1964: 8–9, 140–1.

Auty, M. (1981) 'Revolting natives', *The Movie*, 70: 1390–2.

Barker, F. (1964) 'I'd like to give *Zulu* a V.C. of its own', *Evening News*, 23 January 1964.

Basinger, J. (1986) *The World War II Combat Film: Anatomy of a Genre*, New York: Columbia University Press.

Berry, D. (1994) *Wales and Cinema: The First Hundred Years*, Cardiff: University of Wales Press.

Bromhead, B. (1964) 'Rorke's Drift' [letter], *Daily Telegraph*, 28 February 1964.

Brown, T. (1994) '——' [letter], *Movie Collector*, 1, 5, April 1994: 74.

Cameron, K. M. (1994) *Africa on Film: Beyond Black and White*, New York: Continuum.

Crowther, B. (1964) '——' [review of *Zulu*], *New York Times*, 8 July 1964: 38.

Drew, W. (1985) 'Views of the Valleys: images of Welsh culture and history', National Film Theatre (NFT) programme note, 17 March 1985.

Durgnat, R. (1970) *A Mirror for England: British Movies from Austerity to Affluence*, London: Faber and Faber.

Glover, M. (1975) *Rorke's Drift: A Victorian Epic*, London: Leo Cooper.

Hibbin, N. (1964) 'A lovely war!' *Daily Worker*, 25 January 1964.

Ivens, P. (2001), 'Debating the politics of *Zulu*' [letter], *Cineaste*, 26, 2: 59.

Jones, M. (1999) '*Zulu*', *News of the World*, 28 November 1999: 47.

Knight, I. (1993) *Nothing Remains But to Fight: The Defence of Rorke's Drift, 1879*, London: Greenhill Books.

Knight, I. and Castle, I. (1993) *The Zulu War: Then and Now*, London: Battle of Britain Prints International Ltd.

Mann, R. (1969) 'Banned', *Daily Express*, 14 December 1969.

Nicholson, K. (2001), 'Misinterpreting *Zulu*' [letter], *Cineaste*, 26, 2: 59–60.

Pacey, A. (1964) 'Zulus Deserved a Medal, Too', *Daily Herald*, 24 January 1964.

Pines, J. (1975) *Blacks in Films: A Survey of Racial Themes and Images in the American Film*, London: Studio Vista.

—— (1986) 'Images of Empire: colonial surveillance', NFT programme note, 7 June 1986 (in BFI Library microfiche on *Zulu*).

Prebble, J. (1964) 'Two Clergymen at Rorke's Drift' [letter], *Daily Telegraph*, 17 February 1964.

Prebble, J. and Endfield, C. (1963) *Zulu (The Battle of Rorke's Drift)* [unpublished screenplay], Diamond Films Limited (in BFI Library Special Collections).

Richards, J. (1973) *Visions of Yesterday*, London: Routledge and Kegan Paul.

—— (1981) 'The last heroes', in *The Movie* 62: 1221–4.

—— (1997) *Films and British National Identity: From Dickens to* Dad's Army, Manchester: Manchester University Press.

Rosenbaum, J. (1995) *Placing Movies: The Practice of Film Criticism*, Berkeley, CA: University of California Press.

—— (1997) *Movies as Politics*, Berkeley, CA: University of California Press.

Sharrett, C. (2000) '*Zulu*, or the limits of liberalism', *Cineaste*, 25, 4: 28–33.

Smith, G. (1994) '*Zulu* – behind the scenes', *Movie Collector*, 1, 4, March 1994: 11–15.

Taves, B. (1993) *The Romance of Adventure: The Genre of Historical Adventure Movies*, Jackson, MS: University Press of Mississippi.

Walker, A. (1964) 'Blood and spectacle – but I wanted history, too', *Evening Standard*, 23 January 1964.

Wilson, C. (1964) 'A savage tale of Errol Flynnery', *Daily Mail*, 21 January 1964.

9 Ireland, the past and British cinema

Ryan's Daughter (1970)

Fidelma Farley

The Irish in British cinema

In British cinema's representation of Irish history, there is an important sense in which Ireland is always already 'the past'. By this I mean that Ireland and the Irish are consistently placed by British films in an atemporal, essentially pre-social realm, one which lacks the social, political and economic structures of modern, advanced civilisation. Britain's colonial relationship with Ireland shaped its construction of the Irish as a people who were less advanced and less civilised and therefore in need of the benefits of colonisation. Anne McClintock describes this imperial mobilisation and narration of time and history to underline the superiority of the white race and European civilisation as one which reached its apogee in the late Victorian era, and emerged from the Western belief in evolutionary progress. A paradox emerges, however, in that the colonised are seen to inhabit a parallel space which is outside of history, and therefore not subject to the forces of change, evolution and progress.[1] Calling this parallel space 'anachronistic space', McClintock argues that

> The agency of women, the colonized and the industrial working class are disavowed and projected onto anachronistic space: prehistoric, atavistic and irrational, inherently out of place in the historical time of modernity . . . Imperial progress across the space of empire is figured as a journey backward in time to an anachronistic moment of prehistory . . . Geographical difference across space is figured as a historical difference across time.
>
> (McClintock 1995: 40)

These constructions of history and race linger on into the twentieth century in films dealing with Anglo-Irish history and encounters between the English and the Irish, and are frequently mobilised to contrast the rationality of the English to the irrationality of the Irish. As John Hill has argued in relation to British films addressing Anglo-Irish politics, the repeated instances of violent resistance of the

Irish to British rule are decontextualised, unmoored from historical and political explanations and attributed either to fate or to a national proclivity towards violence (Hill 1988).[2] Irish violence is thus construed as irrational and atavistic, operating outside the constraining framework of reason.[3]

The presentation of the Irish landscape as a spectacle of wild beauty is a common feature of films set in Ireland (see Gibbons 1988 and Meaney 1993[4]). The wild, natural landscape underlines the perception of Ireland as a pre-social space, dominated by nature rather than culture, its inhabitants as passionate and unpredictable as their natural environment. Encountering this landscape can provide regeneration and a retrieval of 'authentic', that is anti-materialist, values for the protagonist, as in *Hear My Song* (Peter Chelsom, 1991), for example. However, given that the land itself has been the source of conflict between Britain and Ireland, the landscape also carries political meanings and functions as a site of danger and violence. In films such as *Captain Boycott* (Frank Launder, 1946), *The Gentle Gunman* (Basil Dearden, 1952), *Shake Hands with the Devil* (Michael Anderson, Ireland, 1959) and *The Crying Game* (Neil Jordan, 1992), remote rural areas facilitate IRA hideouts, and at the beginning of *A Prayer for the Dying* (Mike Hodges, 1988), a panoramic view of a winding country road is overlooked by IRA operatives waiting to blow up a school bus. In *Hungry Hill* (Brian Desmond Hurst, 1947), the hill of the title is imbued with colonial guilt and desire. The lovers commence their courtship and consummate their relationship on the hill, but the hill is also deadly, devouring and killing the Anglo-Irish who 'rape' her by sinking a copper-mine and seeking to profit from her.

However, although many British films about Ireland do continue to be shaped by colonialist attitudes, there is often an ambiguity surrounding national identity and national allegiance in the representation of Irish characters. Ironically, this is satirised in *The Gentle Gunman*, where an English landlady, unaware that her tenants are IRA men, comments gratefully to them after they have contributed to the Spitfire fund, 'I knew you were all English at heart!' *I See a Dark Stranger* (Frank Launder, 1945), also set during the Second World War, traces its Irish protagonist's shift in allegiance from an anti-English nationalism which leads her to spy for the Nazis, to active support for the Allied cause.[5] *Black Narcissus* (Michael Powell and Emeric Pressburger, 1947) is a particularly good example of this ambiguity, as it locates 'Englishness' and 'Irishness' in a single character, Sister Clodagh (Deborah Kerr). In keeping, however, with the discussion above on the teleology of imperialism, Clodagh's 'Irishness', which emerges, significantly, in flashback sequences, is associated with youth, spontaneity, desire and the past, and 'Englishness' with adulthood, sexual repression and the present.

This film is also useful in comparing the treatment of the Irish landscape with that of another former British colony, India. The Indian landscape is exotic and threatening, endangering colonial dominance, producing anxiety around British

Figure 9.1 Cross-national romance as erotic allegory: David Lean on location filming Sarah
    Miles as Rosy and Christopher Jones as Major Doryan in *Ryan's Daughter* (1970)
Source: Irish Film Archive of the Film Institute of Ireland

national identity and unleashing uncontrolled and excessive desire. While the Irish
landscape is also sensual, and the site of unfulfilled desire, it is benign and familiar
(the first scene set in Ireland is of a fox hunt crossing rolling green fields) and thus
less threatening than the mysterious exoticism of India. Ireland's proximity to
Britain and the whiteness of its inhabitants make it, ultimately, less 'othered' than
the landscapes and people of Britain's other former colonies.[6]

The King's mistress: *Ryan's Daughter*

Ryan's Daughter (David Lean, 1970) is a useful film through which to explore the
issues briefly discussed above. As a filmmaker, Lean is known for his penchant for
simultaneously romanticising and critiquing Empire. *Ryan's Daughter* exhibits a
nostalgia for Empire or, more accurately, a nostalgia for a secure British identity,
one which is not challenged by belligerent natives, peasants or the working classes.
It nonetheless acknowledges that the future belongs to these 'others', revealing
towards them a mixture of fear and admiration.

In his discussion of the heritage film and its treatment of the past, John Hill
draws attention to the 'special problems' (1999: 117) presented by the cinematic
treatment of Irish history:

It is, of course, the case that heritage films . . . do often chart the beginnings of the end of Empire, and thus the demise of the settled social order which British rule supposedly provided. However, the past which they represent does, it has been suggested, appear to be sealed off from the present . . . In the case of Ireland, however, this separation from the past is much more problematic given the continuation of the 'troubles' into a much later era and, thus, the unresolved character of the conflicts with which they deal.

(Hill 1999: 118)

Thus the events portrayed by *A Passage to India* (David Lean, 1984) for example, are, to the contemporary audience, over and done with, but to the audiences of *Ryan's Daughter*, the events portrayed had, at the time of the film's release, contemporary resonances.

Ryan's Daughter is set in 1916 and was released in 1970, both times of nationalist resistance to British occupation of Ireland. By 1970, violent unrest had broken out in Northern Ireland and the Provisional IRA had been formed. Events in the film invite comparison with the developing situation in Northern Ireland: conflict between civilians and British soldiers; armed attacks on barracks; the attack on Rosy (Sarah Miles), which recalls the tarring and feathering of Catholic women in Northern Ireland who were suspected of having liaisons with British soldiers. *Ryan's Daughter*, then, focuses on the rise in nationalist sentiment that led to British withdrawal from Southern Ireland and was filmed at a time when Britain was coming under international criticism for its methods of dealing with the unrest in Northern Ireland. In both periods, Britain's imperial role was being questioned and undermined and this doubt and uncertainty over Britain's waning power pervades the film.

However, despite these suggestive parallels, 'history' in *Ryan's Daughter* is not a dynamic, open-ended force which interacts productively and critically with the present. Although the events portrayed in the film may indeed resonate closely with events occurring at the time of the film's release,[7] because nationalist/republican violence has consistently been framed as atavistic and 'primitive', the political violence in the film, and by implication the contemporary political violence which it echoes, is still cast in the anachronistic space to which McClintock refers. The spectacular landscape scenes of huge, brooding skies, miles of golden beach, sunny forest glades and wild, stormy seas which dominate the film visually (and, for many critics, overwhelm the narrative and character development) construct Ireland and its people as primitive, passionate and unpredictable. According to Terry Eagleton:

Ireland [in the aftermath of the Great Famine] . . . comes to figure as the monstrous unconscious of the metropolitan society; it incarnates . . . the Tennysonian nightmare of a Nature red in tooth and claw, stubbornly resistant to ideological refinement. (Though the unconscious, of course, is the site of ambivalence: if Ireland is raw, turbulent, destructive, it is also a place of pleasure, fantasy, eroticism, a blessed release from the reality principle.)

(Eagleton 1995: 110)

Thus in *Ryan's Daughter*, the villagers' cruel antipathy to the British soldiers in their midst, their indifference to the death-toll in the trenches in Europe, their ecstatic support of the nationalist leader, Tim O'Leary (Barry Foster) and their sadistic attack on Rosy can all be explained in terms of their 'primitive' nature, shaped by the raw, natural, elemental forces which surround them. This conflation of political passion with nature reaches its climax in the storm scene, where the entire village, with the exception of Rosy and her husband, risks life and limb to rescue from the sea arms sent from Germany to aid the nationalist cause. Here, the population of the village is framed against, and at times immersed in, the raging sea and crashing waves.

The pessimism of *Ryan's Daughter* can be explained by the fact that it clearly sees that the future of Ireland is in the hands of the peasants and their nationalist leaders. Throughout the film, a fear of nationalism's perceived potential for un-ruly, uncontrolled violence is evident, culminating in the mob's attack on Rosy. Nonetheless, there is also an ambivalence about nationalism and its adherents. Produced when the rectitude of Britain's political dealings in relation to Ireland was being seriously questioned, the film seems envious of the moral conviction and the certainty of national identity that committed nationalism appears to pro-vide. The general lack of patriotism and national fervour of the British soldiers contrasts with the nationalist commitment of the villagers, who risk drowning to rescue arms from the sea. The English are, for the most part, characterised by apathy and alienation in contrast to the passion of the Irish. The doomed vulner-ability of Major Doryan (Christopher Jones) and the cultured apathy of the Irish middle classes are ultimately eclipsed by the vitality and dynamism of the villagers and the popular, nationalist leader, Tim O'Leary.

It is O'Leary's character which expresses the film's ambivalence about nation-alism. In the first scene in which he appears, he shoots in the back a portly police-man who has recognised him and he later exhibits a similar ruthlessness when he offers Ryan (Leo McKern) the opportunity of killing the village policeman. How-ever, in his direction of the rescue of the arms from the sea and the popular support he receives from the villagers, he takes on the qualities of masculine authority and leadership which Major Doryan patently lacks. When the arms have been loaded onto a truck, O'Leary gives a hearty kiss to Maureen (one of the village women), in an unabashed and uncomplicated display of spontaneous sexu-ality which neither Charles, Rosy's husband (Robert Mitchum), nor Major Doryan is capable of. Britain, site of reason and restraint, no longer possesses the will and authority to impose order, leaving the way clear for a descent into unchecked, atavistic violence. The film exhibits both a nostalgia for the waning of Empire and a recognition of the inevitability of national independence. It also, however, expresses a profound doubt as to the ability of the natives to rule themselves without resorting to violence.

Class and nationality

Lean tends to offset the restraint of his middle-class characters against a group which is portrayed as uninhibited and unrestrained, both sexually and in terms of social interaction. In his earlier films set in Britain, the English working class fulfils this function, as, for example, in the scene in the railway station café in *Brief Encounter* (1945), where Laura's and Alex's awkward, tentative, guilty conversation takes place alongside the easy banter of the working-class clientele, or the comparison in *Great Expectations* (1946) between Pip as a 'gentleman' and Joe. In the later films, natives occupy the role of embodying a sensuality and lack of inhibition which is at once attractive and frightening.

In *Ryan's Daughter*, the Irish middle classes function in much the same way as the British middle classes do in Lean's other films, that is, as a commentary on oppressive social codes which constrain sensuality and spontaneity. Although Rosy Ryan is one in a long line of feisty Irish heroines who are strongly associated with nature and sensuality,[8] she is nonetheless like many of Lean's English characters in her yearning for sexual and emotional release. Like Laura of *Brief Encounter*, Rosy has romantic fantasies of escaping a dull and safe marriage and she too chooses to return to the safety of that marriage after her adventure with romance and passion. Thus, Rosy, though Irish, also functions to explore the longing of the English middle and upper classes to break free from unspoken codes of restraint and sexual propriety.

Similarly, Charles is hampered by middle-class apathy, though he shows none of Rosy's desire to inject passion into his life. A telling, if rather heavy-handed, scene early in their marriage shows Charles pressing flowers, while Rosy claims that she prefers the flowers growing, nature signifying the contrast between their attitudes to life and love. Charles is a cultured, educated schoolmaster, who goes to Dublin for teachers' conventions and to attend concerts. He is uninterested in nationalism, and the men in the pub are amazed that he has been to Dublin and has not gone to see the places where the Easter Rising took place. He comments to Rosy that all governments are essentially the same, that an Irish government will be as good or as bad as a British one. His lack of physical passion is in keeping with his lack of political passion: the sex on their wedding night is brief and perfunctory, and when he discovers that Rosy and Doryan are having an affair, he decides not to intervene. In failing to intervene to curb his wife's sexuality and assert his authority over her, he unwittingly contributes to the violent climax of her punishment. One shot in particular emphasises the 'feminine' passivity of this position:

Rosy, knowing that Charles knows about her affair, leaves their bed in the night to join the Major. We see Charles looking out of the rain-soaked window, a classic shot evoking feminine passivity, helplessness and entrapment within the domestic realm, and one that occurs with frequency in melodramas and women's films, particularly (Doane 1987). In Charles's case, the domestic realm includes the schoolhouse – he is contained and restrained by his class, education and culture, which have sapped his sexual vitality.

The aforementioned wedding-night scene explicitly contrasts middle-class re-straint with the lack of inhibition of the peasants, cutting between the agonising awkwardness of Charles and Rosy in their bedroom and the raucous drunkenness and licentiousness of the villagers downstairs. Indeed, in its depiction of the Irish peasant villagers, *Ryan's Daughter* almost reaches the extremes of nineteenth-century imagery of wily, unpredictable and potentially savage peasants. E. Butler Cullingford, for example, observes that Michael (John Mills), the village idiot, who functions as Doryan's grotesque doppelgänger, is reminiscent of the simian 'Fenians' who appeared in satirical cartoons in nineteenth-century publications such as *Punch*, *Judy* and *Fun* (Butler Cullingford 1997).[9]

Gender, romance and Empire

In his discussion of the fourteen-part British Raj television drama serial *The Jewel in the Crown* (Granada Television, 1984), Richard Dyer observes in relation to Empire films that

> when a text is one of celebration, it is the manly white qualities of expansive-ness, enterprise, courage and control (of self and others) that are in the fore-ground; but when doubt and uncertainty creep in, women begin to take centre stage. The white male spirit achieves and maintains empire; the white female soul is associated with its demise.
>
> (Dyer 1997: 184)

While this comment is true for films set in other ex-colonies of Europe – such as *Chocolat* (Claire Denis, France, 1988), *Indochine* (Régis Warnier, France, 1991), *Out of Africa* (Sydney Pollack, USA/UK, 1985) and *Heat and Dust* (James Ivory, UK, 1982) – *Ryan's Daughter* is unusual in figuring the demise of Empire princi-pally through a male character, Major Doryan. Although Rosy is white, she is also one of the colonised, so while her illicit desire contributes to the demise of the Empire, she cannot carry the same meanings as these other heroines. It is instead the vulnerable, wounded male figure who represents the instability and decline of British imperial identity and the film's evident nostalgia for the loss of a secure British identity.

According to Kaja Silverman, the 'dominant fiction', composed of a culture's narratives and images which establish consensus and a belief in phallic masculinity, undergoes a crisis at certain moments in history.

> Not only does a loss of belief in the dominant fiction generally lead to a loss of belief in male adequacy, but the spectacle of male castration may very well result in a destructive questioning of the dominant fiction. Male subjectivity is a kind of stress point, the juncture at which social crisis and turmoil frequently find most dramatic expression. Major rifts between the dominant fiction and the larger social formation can almost always be detected within a classic narrative film through the breakdown of sexual difference – through the disclosure of male lack or impotence.
>
> (Silverman 1990: 114)

At both the time in which *Ryan's Daughter* is set, and the time of its release, the dominant fiction of Empire and of the English masculine authority, which is integral to both the idea and maintenance of Empire, was being undermined. The First World War produced doubts about upper-class male authority and indeed produced eroticised images of male vulnerability in poetry and painting; 1916 saw the Easter Rising, the event which led to the War of Independence and the establishment of the Irish Free State; in the intervening years, Britain's other colonies demanded and acquired independence and the Empire was gradually dismantled; finally, the outbreak of the troubles in Northern Ireland yet again raised questions about Britain's role in Ireland.

In *Ryan's Daughter*, the regretful acknowledgement that the Empire is no longer tenable is figured through the spectacle of male lack, principally manifested in Major Doryan, whose physical and psychic vulnerability is repeatedly underlined by the film, and serves to emphasise the instability of the Empire he represents. He is modeled on the hero of romantic fiction, dark, brooding, handsome and full of repressed anguish. Several shots show him, Heathcliff-like, silhouetted against the evening sky, standing on a hill beside a rock. Given the implication at the very beginning of the film that Rosy applies the romantic vision of the books she reads to real life, it is logical that the object of her desire should appear as a character from romantic fiction, but it does also have implications for the representation of English masculinity. In *Ryan's Daughter* we see that the 'stiff upper lip' which is so characteristic of representations of English upper-class masculinity 'hides a shattered psyche', in the words of E. Butler Cullingford, who sees Major Doryan's character as evidence of a faltering English identity, which 'maintains a fragile equilibrium with a history that is no longer unequivocally on his side' (Butler Cullingford 1997: 168).

Englishness and masculinity are sites of anxiety in *Ryan's Daughter*, the representation of each conveying a nostalgia for lost national/imperial and masculine authority.

In a paper titled 'David Lean: Home and the Concept of Englishness', Neil Sinyard remarks that the notion of 'home', in the sense of both the domestic space and the nation, is frequently problematised in Lean's films: '"Home" is a key motif in Lean . . . and it is somehow connected to . . . Englishness. Lean's later characters will bestride the world but still carry Englishness as their emotional baggage' (Sinyard 1998). 'Home' is clearly problematic in *Ryan's Daughter* for the English characters, as their English nationality requires that they leave their country to participate in war and colonial duties. The soldiers' barracks are drab and uninviting, with the throb of the generator serving as a constant reminder of war for the Major. It is strongly hinted at that the Major's marriage is broken, even though he keeps a photograph of his wife by his bed. 'Home', in the domestic and national sense, conventionally represented by a woman, particularly in times of war, is no longer a stable, taken-for-granted place or concept. Britain, demanding that her sons fight and die for her in wars which have no clear moral purpose, can no longer provide a coherent, unproblematic national identity.

The clearest indications of this in the film are, firstly, the broken marriage of the Major: the private, domestic sphere has failed to fulfil its social purpose as the site of respite from the labours and demands of the public sphere and its symbolic purpose as microcosm of the nation. The second indication is the treatment of the Major's 'heroism'. Earlier British imperial and war films fashion their male protagonists in the conventional heroic mode of masculinity, implying an unquestioning confidence in the rectitude of the hero's actions against the enemy and/or natives. While earlier British war/imperial heroes are inviolate, the Major has not escaped unscathed from the war: his limp is prominent, a visible sign of his viability and the vulnerability of the male body. He has also suffered psychological damage, which manifests itself physically when he hears sounds which remind him of the war. Even though his fellow soldiers admire him and call him a hero, the Major himself rejects this title.

What is at issue here is a loss of moral authority underpinning English masculinity. The Major is wounded, physically and psychologically, but apparently without purpose. Nightmare visions of the war still assail him, we learn that the British are suffering huge casualties at the front, and the Major quite clearly does not relish his duties as a colonial agent in a country whose inhabitants are actively hostile to him and to what he represents. His fragile mental state, induced by war, and the suffering that doing his duty as an Englishman imposes on him, all question the construction of English masculine identity as patriotic, authoritative and controlling, but the eroticisation of his trauma betrays a nostalgia for the stability of that very identity.

For Silverman, the eroticisation of male lack is a potentially radical challenge to patriarchal definitions of masculinity as controlling and authoritative. However, it is difficult to see the portrayal of Major Doryan as one which presents a challenge to patriarchal definitions of masculinity, or to the fictions of Empire. First, as already stated, his eroticisation betrays a nostalgia for the days when English masculinity was implicitly underpinned by social and moral authority, an interpretation which is underlined by his suicide at the end of the film – his wounded state may be erotic, but it is doomed, associated with death, not life. Second, it has no place in a world populated by virile, passionate, politically committed men such as the nationalist leader Tim O'Leary. O'Leary too is wounded, but he is wounded while fighting for the cause he believes in and for which he has widespread, popular support. Finally, Doryan's portrayal undermines his involvement in colonialism by casting him as a doomed, romantic figure, radically uncertain of his place in the world, weighed down and finally crushed by the burden of duty to nation.

The film's disavowal of Doryan's status as colonial agent is clear in the scene where he shoots O'Leary. Doryan and his men have stopped the truck containing the recuperated arms and when O'Leary escapes through the crowd, Major Doryan stands on top of the truck and shoots O'Leary in the back. As he watches the wounded O'Leary struggle in the mud, Doryan has a memory, shown in flashback, of himself at the front, having been shot in the leg, and he begins to shake uncontrollably, almost collapsing. His violent act is thus instantly mitigated by his vulnerability. In addition, the linking of the British presence in Ireland with the First World War through the flashback of the trenches which is prompted by the sight of O'Leary, obscures the very different contexts and motivations behind each in a liberal 'isn't war terrible' manner.

If the British nation does not function as 'home' to its men, neither do its colonies, the former extended family of Empire. The soldiers are treated with unrelenting contempt by the villagers who jeer at them as they walk by. The local women, according to one of the soldiers, are sexually unresponsive. The Major finds a temporary home in the solace of Rosy's arms, however, and several of the love scenes between them are filmed in such a way as to position Rosy in a maternal role, offering comfort to the suffering Major. In their first encounter, the banging of the village idiot's feet against wooden benches induces a collapse in the Major and he hallucinates he is back in the trenches. Rosy's concerned face appears to him, drawing him out of the trenches into her arms. Similarly, after they make love in the forest, Major Doryan lies on Rosy's breast. Nature, lush and beautiful, appears initially to provide a safe, private place for the lovers to meet (the cliffs, the beach, the forest), but their privacy is illusory, as they are spied on by Michael, the village idiot, and Charles knows of their affair after seeing their footsteps on the beach and finding sand in Rosy's riding hat. Ultimately, Rosy rejects the Major, and so neither nature nor woman give him shelter and stability away from the demands of English masculinity. Rootless and homeless, the Major finally commits suicide, using the remnants of the arms from Germany to blow himself up, a prefiguring of British withdrawal from Ireland (Butler Cullingford 1997).

Ryan's Daughter can usefully be compared to Lean's later film, *A Passage to India*, another post-Empire heritage film. The heroine of *A Passage to India*, Adela Quested (Judy Davis), is, like Rosy Ryan, a romanticist, who yearns, like Rosy, to break free of social constraint and convention, and in both films, the landscape functions as a metaphor for the heroines' desires. Both characters, attached to unsatisfying men of their own nationality, channel their desires into exotic foreigners and again in both films, female desire, coded as excessive, has disastrous consequences for the female characters and for the community at large. Finally, in both films cross-national desires inflame political tensions and bring forth strong nationalist sentiments on the part of the colonised people.

There are, however, significant differences between the films, which are not simply a consequence of the gap of fifteen years which separates them. Because the cross-national desire in *A Passage to India* is also cross-racial, it not only is never consummated but is revealed to be entirely in the mind and overheated imagination of the Englishwoman, Adela Quested. In *Ryan's Daughter*, however, no such racial taboo arises: in cinema, Irish women and British men – and occasionally Irish men and British women, as in *Beloved Enemy* (H. C. Potter, USA, 1936) or *A Prayer for the Dying* – are eligible sexual partners. Racial similarity underlines the desirability of romantic union, even if the differences arising from national identity and the colonial relationship frequently prevent it.[10]

According to John Hill, the romance narrative is a device used by *Ryan's Daughter* to avoid political explanations.

> Like *I See a Dark Stranger*, there is also a traversal of the Anglo–Irish divide via 'Romance'. But whereas love triumphs in *I See a Dark Stranger*, it is destined to failure in *Ryan's Daughter*. The collapse of politics is, however, similar . . . the political conflicts are robbed of any substance and simply provide the back-drop against which doomed passion must work itself out. If they have any meaning at all, it is only as a barrier to love and a common humanity.
>
> (Hill 1988: 176)

But 'love and a common humanity' are not apolitical, even if they are presented as such. Writing of the political function and ideological significance of Latin-American popular novels in encouraging allegiance to new nation-states, Doris Sommer argues that by intertwining romance and politics, the novels mobilise the reader's desire for the successful formation of the couple – and thus hostility towards the political factors which keep them apart.

> The unrequited passion of the love story produces a surplus of energy directed against the political interference between the lovers . . . every obstacle that the lovers encounter heightens more than their mutual desire to (be a) couple, more than our voyeuristic but keenly felt passion; it also

heightens their/our love for the possible nation in which the affair could be consummated.

(Sommer 1993: 40–1)

The majority of films about Northern Ireland function in this fashion, mobilising the viewer's hostility against (usually) the IRA for preventing romantic resolution and thus the formation of the family, which represents the possibility of a stable society/nation. The many examples include *Captain Boycott*, *Shake Hands with the Devil*, *A Terrible Beauty* (Tay Garnett, 1960), *The Violent Enemy* (Don Sharp, 1969), *Cal* (Pat O'Connor, 1984), *A Prayer for the Dying*, *Michael Collins* (Neil Jordan, USA, 1996) and *The Boxer* (Jim Sheridan, Ireland/UK/USA, 1997).

The romance between Major Doryan and Rosy also functions in this way, as an 'erotic allegory', to use the term adopted by Shohat and Stam to describe the ways in which mainstream films figure politics through narratives of romance (1994: 230–1). In an early scene, the priest meets Rosy on the beach and asks her what she does all day. Rosy defiantly shows him the paperback novel she is reading, *The King's Mistress*. The title of the novel, a lurid romance, neatly encapsulates the colonial and sexual aspects of *Ryan's Daughter*. It is reminiscent of the colonial metaphor of sexual possession for colonial possession, but the 'mistress' of the title indicates the illicit nature of the liaison. Shortly after the meeting with the priest, Rosy throws the book away and becomes, if not the King's mistress, then the mistress of one of the King's representatives, in the form of Major Doryan.

That this cross-national romance is doomed from the start is indicative of the impossibility of an Anglo-Irish union. Whereas the films mentioned above use their romance narratives to gesture towards the kind of social stability that could be achieved if political violence were to end, the doomed romance between Rosy and the Major betrays a nostalgia for the (imaginary) days when the Anglo-Irish union was uncontested. Rosy, oscillating between Charles and Doryan, signifies the uncertain 'ownership' of Ireland at this period. The violent and hostile reaction of the villagers to Rosy and Doryan's liaison, Doryan's suicide and Rosy's return to her Irish husband narrate the end of Britain's possession of Ireland and the violence which brought it about. Nevertheless, *Ryan's Daughter* offers little hope either for the future of Ireland after British withdrawal nor for a Britain which has lost its pre-eminence on the world stage.

Conclusion

In *Ryan's Daughter*, the suggestive parallels between the events depicted by the film and the events occurring in Northern Ireland at the time of the film's release do not, as may initially appear to be the case, imply an open-endedness to the history of Anglo–Irish relations. Rather, the construction of nationalism as an unrestrained and irrational force places it and those who practice it in a pre-social realm, free from the restraining framework of reason and rationality. In the many British films, and, indeed, several Irish ones too, which address Anglo-Irish relations, Irish history is similarly construed as an endless cycle of violence, outside the linear narrative of historical progress.[11]

There have been, however, a number of recent films by Irish directors concerning Anglo-Irish politics which demonstrate a more productive relationship with the shared past of Britain and Ireland and which attempt to explore, to greater or lesser degrees, nationalist politics. *Some Mother's Son* (Terry George, Ireland/USA, 1996), for example, follows the dilemma of a woman whose son takes part in the hunger-strikes of 1980–1; *In the Name of the Father* (Jim Sheridan, Ireland/UK/USA, 1993) tells the story of the wrongfully imprisoned Guildford Four, although several critics have noted that its depiction of IRA leader Joe McAndrew (Don Baker) as a ruthless fanatic is in keeping with similar depictions of IRA activists in countless other films about Northern Ireland (Kirkland forthcoming; McLoone 2000).

The most notable of these recent films is *Michael Collins*, where, in marked contrast to the reception of *Ryan's Daughter*, the parallels between the events depicted in the film and those that were occurring in Anglo-Irish politics at the time of its production and release were discussed at length in the British and Irish press.[12] The negotiation between the Irish and British governments which led to the Treaty of 1921 echoed the peace talks; de Valera's refusal to accept the Treaty and declaration of war echoed Sinn Féin's removal from the talks in June 1995 and the breaking of the IRA ceasefire with the bomb in Canary Wharf in February 1996; the parallels between Michael Collins and Gerry Adams, leader of Sinn Féin, were noted, in that both moved from advocating resistance through armed force to adopting constitutional politics. *Michael Collins*'s refusal to cast nationalism as an unruly, atavistic force was one of the factors which contributed towards its active engagement with history, and its varied reception in Britain and Ireland underlined the contingency of historical interpretation. The film and its reception demonstrated clearly that the past is never sealed off from the present and that British and Irish cinema have a duty to explore the history of their relations in a way which illuminates rather than obscures present relations between the two countries.

Notes

1 See also Homi Bhabha's 'Of mimicry and man', where he argues that the Enlightenment ideal to bring education and progress to all of mankind is undone in the colonial context, for if the natives are shaped in the image of the European, the justification for colonialism is no longer valid (Bhabha 1994).

2 David Lloyd's analysis of *The Crying Game* draws on Hill's argument to maintain that the film constructs a contrast between the progressive space of metropolitan London and the atavistic space of Northern Ireland (Lloyd 1999).

3 The contrast between English rationality and Irish irrationality is not always perceived unfavourably, however. In two relatively recent television drama series, for example, *The Irish RM* (1983–5, Channel Four/RTE/UTV) and *Ballykissangel* (1996 onwards, BBC-TV), the English characters' adherence to rules and logic is inhibiting, and acts as a contrast to the natural spontaneity and liberating disregard for rules and conventions that characterise the Irish. The anachronistic space occupied by the Irish functions here as a fantasy of escape from the tyranny of the rationality exercised by modernity.

4 See Gibbons (1988) and Meaney (1993).

5 See Antonia Lant's analysis of the operation of discourses of gender and national identity in *I See a Dark Stranger* (Lant 1990).

6 See John Hill's comparison between *Fools of Fortune* (Pat O'Connor, 1990) and Lean's *A Passage to India* (Hill 1999). See also Gibbons (1996) and McClintock (1995) for discussions of the significance of the whiteness of the Irish.

7 However, according to Pettitt, recognition of these parallels was limited to Irish audiences, and he surmises that for British audiences, the film did indeed effectively seal off the past: 'According to the evidence of Lean's biography and a survey of just about all the English-based press, British cinema-goers seemed blinkered to the contemporary resonance of political violence in the film, convinced that the past puts the problems of Anglo–Irish history safely at a distance' (Pettitt 2000: 99–100). Roy Greenslade's interpretation of the lack of recognition of historical parallels with the present in the British press's reception of *Ryan's Daughter* is that it was released before the first Provisional IRA killing of a British Army soldier and before the press adopted the censorious and condemnatory tone against the IRA that rapidly emerged once the Troubles escalated (Greenslade 2000).

8 For example, Mary Kate in *The Quiet Man* (John Ford, USA, 1952), Fanny Rosa in *Hungry Hill* and Bridie Quilty in *I See a Dark Stranger*.

9 See Perry Curtis (1997) for an analysis of these images, and Curtis (1984) on the recurrence of racist images of the Irish from the eleventh century to the present.

10 See Lant's analysis of *I See a Dark Stranger*, where an Irishwoman, Bridie (Deborah Kerr), overcomes her hatred of the English to marry an Englishman, David Baines (Trevor Howard). However, the final scene shows Bridie walking away from the hotel they are to spend their wedding night in, having discovered that it is called The Cromwell Arms. As Lant comments, Bridie's threatening status as a single woman has been resolved by her marriage to Baines, but her Irish nationality (and nationalism) are less easily contained (Lant 1990).

11 See Hill (1988) and McLoone (2000) for analyses of Irish films along these lines.

12 See Dodd (1996), Greenslade (2000), Hopper (1997) and McIlroy (1999) for discussions of the reception of *Michael Collins* in the British and Irish press.

Bibliography

Bhabha, H. (1994) *The Location of Culture*, London/New York: Routledge.

Butler Cullingford, E. (1997) 'Gender, sexuality and Englishness in modern Irish drama and film', in A. Bradley and M. Gialanella Valiulis (eds) *Gender and Sexuality in Modern Ireland*, Amherst, MA: University of Massachusetts Press: 159–86.

Curtis, L. (1984) *Nothing But the Same Old Story: The Roots of Anti-Irish Racism*, London: Information on Ireland.

Doane, M. A. (1987) *The Desire to Desire: The Woman's Film of the 1940s*, London: Macmillan.

Dodd, P. (1996) 'Ghosts from the Civil War', *Sight and Sound*, 6, 12: 30–2.

Dyer, R. (1997) *White*, London/New York: Routledge.

Eagleton, T. (1995) *Heathcliff and the Great Hunger*, London: Verso.

Gibbons, L. (1988) 'Romanticism, realism and Irish cinema', in Rockett, Gibbons and Hill: 194–257.

—— (1996) 'Race against time: racial discourse and Irish history' in L. Gibbons *Transformations in Irish Culture*, Cork: Cork University Press: 149–64.

Greenslade, R. (2000) 'Editors as censors: The British press and films about Ireland', *Journal of Popular British Cinema*, 3: 77–92.

Hill, J. (1988) 'Images of violence' in Rockett, Gibbons and Hill: 147–93.

—— (1999) *British Cinema in the 1980s*, Oxford: Oxford University Press.

Hopper, K. (1997) '"Cat-calls from the cheap seats": the third meaning of Neil Jordan's *Michael Collins*', *The Irish Review* 21: 1–28.

Kirkland, R. (forthcoming) *Identity Parades: Northern Irish Culture and Dissident Subjects*, Liverpool: Liverpool University Press.

Lant, A. (1990) 'The female spy: gender, nationality and war in *I See a Dark Stranger*' in R. Sklar and C. Musser (eds) *Resisting Images: Essays in Cinema and History*, Philadelphia, PA: Temple University Press: 173–99.

Lloyd, D. (1999) *Ireland After History*, Cork: Cork University Press.

McClintock, A. (1995) *Imperial Leather: Race, Gender and Sexuality in the Colonial Context*, New York/London: Routledge.

McIlroy, B. (1999) 'History without borders: *Michael Collins*' in J. MacKillop (ed.) *Contemporary Irish Cinema: From* The Quiet Man *to* Dancing at Lughnasa, Syracuse, NY: Syracuse University Press: 22–8.

McLoone, M. (2000) *Irish Film: The Emergence of a Contemporary Cinema*, London: BFI.

Meaney, G. (1993) 'Landscapes of desire: women and Ireland on film', *Women: A Cultural Review*, 9, 3: 237–51.

Perry Curtis Jr., L. (1997) *Apes and Angels: The Irishman in Victorian Caricature*, revised edition, Washington, DC, and London: Smithsonian Institution Press.

Pettitt, L. (2000) *Screening Ireland: Film and Television Representation*, Manchester: Manchester University Press.

Rockett, K., Gibbons, L. and Hill, J. (1988) *Cinema and Ireland*, Syracuse, NY: Syracuse University Press.

Shohat, E. and Stam, R. (1994) *Unthinking Eurocentrism: Multiculturalism and the Media*, New York/London: Routledge.

Silverman, K. (1990) 'Historical trauma and male subjectivity' in E. A. Kaplan (ed.) *Psychoanalysis and Cinema*, New York/London: Routledge: 110–27.

Sinyard, N. (1998) 'David Lean: home and the concept of Englishness', unpublished paper.

Sommer, D. (1993) 'Love and country in Latin America: an allegorical speculation' in M. Ringrose and A. J. Lerner (eds) *Reimagining the Nation*, Buckingham/Philadelphia: Open University Press: 29–45.

10 Imperial migrations

Reading the Raj cinema of the 1980s

T. Muraleedharan

Being a narrative account of the past, history is now understood as a structuring of the temporal which negotiates with the anxieties and desires of the present. This functional potential of the past becomes more potent when historiography acquires the fictional licence of artistic creations. In this paper I shall attempt a critical reading of one such narrativising of the past, that which appears in Raj cinema – a genre of films which attained considerable popularity in Britain during the 1980s, and in many cases also critical acclaim and commercial success in many export markets.

The term 'Raj cinema' is commonly used to refer to a cycle of films (and television dramas) about India made in Britain during the early 1980s, which provide the most overt evidence of a nostalgia for the days of the British Raj being invoked in the UK at that time. Prominent among the films were *Gandhi* (Richard Attenborough, 1982), *Heat and Dust* (James Ivory, 1982) based on the 1975 novel by Ivory's regular screenwriter Ruth Prawer Jhabwala, *A Passage to India* (David Lean, 1984), based on E. M. Forster's famous 1924 novel, and a new film version of Kipling's *Kim* (John Davies, 1984). The most prominent of the Raj television dramas were two serials *The Far Pavilions* (1984) and *The Jewel in the Crown* (1984), based on M. M. Kaye's 1978 novel and Paul Scott's *Raj Quartet* of novels (1966–75) respectively. *The Jewel in the Crown* had already been preceded by a one-off television film, *Staying On* (Silvio Narizzano, 1979), based on Scott's 1977 Booker-prize-winning sequel to the quartet, which takes up the story of two of its minor white characters (played by Trevor Howard and Celia Johnson) who attempt to 'stay on' in post-Independence India. British television documentaries about India produced during the 1980s included *The Courtesans of Bombay* (Ismail Merchant, 1982, Merchant Ivory Productions for Channel 4 Television), *The Anglo-Indians* (David Malony, 1986), *The Kind of Beasts* (Timothy Forder, 1988) and a series, *The End of the Empire*, made during 1985–6 by Granada Television.

This resurgence of British interest in India, which surfaced almost forty years after Britain had lost political domination over the Orient, deserves to be seen as something more than the continuing interest of the coloniser in a former colony;

especially since these films differ significantly in content and approach from the propagandist literature and films produced under the sponsorship – or with the blessing – of the Empire Marketing Board during the British Raj.[1] As a genre, the 1980s Raj films dealt retrospectively with a period in the history of the two nations – Britain and India – when they were bonded in a relationship of domination and subordination. More than three decades after the official uncoupling of that bond, these films attempted a backward glance at that relationship. What is of interest to this study is not merely the apparent nostalgia for the Raj that these films and television fictions seem to activate at a specific historical conjuncture in Britain, but also the architectural contours of the subsequent historical imagination that finds expression in these films. In other words, what is attempted here is an examination of the ways in which imperialism migrates to new historical contexts and constructs convenient patterns of identification.

Ever since the emergence of post-colonial studies as a significant academic force, the representations of non-white and subordinated races appearing in cultural artefacts of the First World have frequently been subjected to critical analyses which revealed their racist/imperialist foundations. My project in this paper is slightly different: as I try to read these British films about India, my purpose is not merely to call attention to the representation of South Asians in them. The focus of my critical gaze is on the images of the 'white' man and woman, embedded as they are within the frames that capture the 'coloured' people. Thus my intention is not only to intercept the cinematic gaze directed towards the non-white races but also to return it towards the whites.

Moreover, with the exception of Attenborough's celebrated *Gandhi*, most of the 1980s Raj films received scant critical attention when they were exhibited in India. Some of them were exhibited only in a few metropolitan cities and hence were not seen by a major section of India's film enthusiasts. Subsequently in this chapter, as I read Raj cinema in terms of the rearticulation of racist and imperialist perspectives they seem to undertake, my intention is certainly not to suggest any conscious involvement on the part of the filmmakers in the neo-racist discourse. Instead, my attempt is to present a reading of these films from the perspective of a post-colonial subject who cannot wipe away the experience of colonial domination from his/her history and identity.

Due to limitations of space and time, I shall confine my discussion to two important films belonging to the genre of Raj cinema: James Ivory's *Heat and Dust* (1982) and David Lean's *A Passage to India* (1984). I have chosen to discuss these films together because of certain very obvious thematic similarities. Prominent among these is a 'reverse' migration which, significantly, is from the West to the East. The trope of young white women coming to India occupies the central space in both these texts, though the pattern of their representation varies considerably.

Thanks to the hegemonic Eurocentric imagination, the dominant use of the term migration designates the movement of fortune-seekers from the primitive and underdeveloped hinterlands of civilisation, also known as the Third World, towards the economic allure and immense capitalist possibilities of the normative Western world. Coded into this definition are the discomfort and unease experienced by the so-called First World at this uninvited encroachment into its cultural and political integrity. In the second half of the twentieth century, overt or covert expressions of anxiety or disapproval at the swelling of migrant populations from African, Caribbean, Asian and (recently) Balkan countries have surfaced in most of the European nations. British discourses around immigration have passed through various waves since the large-scale post-colonial migrations of the 1950s, although official policies and public attitudes have not always been in perfect concordance. Observers have pointed out how the conservative discourse on immigration during the 1960s was coloured by an overt and unabashed racism, but was recast in the garb of nationalism and cultural belonging during the Thatcher regime of the 1980s.

I consider it interesting to note that these two important British films made in the early 1980s portray an apparent reversal of the situation and present a movement in the opposite direction, i.e. from imperial Britain to colonised or post-colonial India. This central trope in these films also makes me curious to locate them in their socio-political context before speculating on their significance. Both these films were made at a time when middle-class white Western liberalism had, in certain ways, evolved what appeared to be a counter-discourse to the conventional racist attitudes towards immigration. Moreover the East had once again become a favoured destination for young travellers from the West, motivated by the post-Woodstock spirit and the subsequent hippie trail, and this evidently constitutes part of the background to *Heat and Dust*, one of the two films chosen for discussion here.

The Birmingham School of Cultural Studies, as well as journals like *Marxism Today* and the *New Left Review*, have paid considerable attention to what commentators on the Left identified as an 'organic crisis' that developed in British society during the 1960s and 1970s (Nairn 1977 and 1982; Anderson 1992). Analysing the prominent economic factors that constituted the crisis, these commentators pointed out that the social basis of the post-World War Two settlement had become fragile by the late 1960s. By the 1970s, burgeoning inflation and a growth in unemployment – following the 'full' employment of the earlier 1960s – began to cause much anxiety; combined with the rise of a wider set of dissatisfactions and demands among the organised industrial working class, this led to widespread unrest and occasional violence. Dominating this unease was the continuing trauma of the loss of the Empire, which had precipitated a crisis in British identity as well as being held responsible for economic problems.

The early 1970s saw racial attacks and demonstrations by white racists and the rise of the National Front as a political force in the UK. The decade was notable also for strikes and industrial unrest. Observers point out that the onset of the Thatcherite regime following the election of Margaret Thatcher's Conservative government in 1979 marked a radical break from the consensus politics of the post-war settlement and a concerted attack on organised labour. By 1981, unemployment was reported to have clambered towards three million. The early 1980s also brought a series of riots, which erupted in inner-city areas with large immigrant communities in response to racist policing and to poverty and unemployment divided along racial lines.

Britain during the 1960s and 1970s had already been going through important social transitions. Continuing empowerment of the working class was manifested in the strengthening and spread of trade union activities. The 'second wave' of the feminist movement had started to question the gendered foundations of the patriarchal society, and the period also saw the beginnings of the gay liberation movement. Increasing involvement of women in trade union activities, and the emergence (or, at least, increased and unapologetic visibility) of single-parent families, heterosexual co-habitation outside marriage and gay pairings were developments that seriously troubled the conservative society. At the same time, the deteriorating self-image of the nation was further disturbed by the proliferation of critiques of imperialism and neo-colonialism from the recently liberated colonies as well as from radical sections within Britain itself.

One of the significant socio-political developments in Britain from the late 1970s was the emergence of a radical right wing which became known as the New Right, whose ideologies and favoured policies – centred around a near-religious faith in *laissez-faire* free-market economics – were zealously embraced by the new Thatcher government. As well as marking a decisive break from post-war consensus politics and Keynesian economics, this movement can be seen as a deliberate backlash, constituted during the Thatcher period, against the permissive 1960s and its supposed aftermath. The discourses of the New Right were distinguished by the tactfulness and subtlety with which they handled the issue of race – or, more specifically, their disavowal of any racism in their own discourse – often obscuring the fundamental fascist underpinnings of their position. Anyway, racism in the modern context cannot be studied merely as the overt manifestation of ethnic fundamentalism. As David Lloyd has pointed out, 'racism of culture is not a question of certain contingent racist observations by its major theoreticians nor of the still incomplete dissemination of its goods but an ineradicable effect of its fundamental structures' (Lloyd 1991: 63). Moreover, racism also has to be understood as historically specific, whatever common features it may appear to share with other social prejudices. Though it may draw on the cultural and ideological traces which are deposited in a society by previous historical phases, it invariably assumes specific forms, which arise out of the present conditions and organisation of society.

Thus, the redeployment of racism in Britain during the 1970s and 1980s can be seen to be particularly responsive towards the question of immigration. The emergence of Asian and Black Caribbean communities as significant social forces in Britain had already made race an important issue in social discourses. The 1980s were notable for increased political consciousness and resistance among the immigrant populations (often second- or third-generation), and for organised anti-racist and pro-multiculturalist activity which achieved some success in beating the National Front (subsequently renamed the British National Party) into retreat. Discourses around 'difference' and identity were also gaining increasing currency during this period.[2]

Subsequently and consequently the strategies of the neo-racist discourse became more cautious and diffused, a shift manifested over a wide range of cultural artefacts from newspaper stories to popular cinema. However, the motif of an alien cultural aggression that was posing a fatal threat to the British civilisation and at the same time destroying the country economically continued to feature in some of these debates. This is exemplified by, for example, an article by Alfred Sherman in the *Daily Telegraph*, which chose to describe the toleration of mass immigration as a symptom of a national death wish (Sherman 1979a: 3). On the other hand the neo-racist ideologues were discreet enough to avoid a direct pre-occupation with notions such as racial superiority. The attempt was mainly to re-work the whole meaning of 'Britishness' in terms of powerful images of purity of the nation, family and ways of life, now jeopardised by the alien, external wedge.

Commonsense images of the 'normal' family and 'natural' gender/sex roles were widely deployed in these discourses so as to pose 'race' as a 'problem'. This strategy assigned responsibility for the many 'problems' faced by the present – the financial crisis, the break-up of the conventional family system, the emergence of non-traditional gender roles and alternative sexualities – to the immigrant Asian and Afro-Caribbean populations. Citing various examples from newspaper stories and articles in contemporary journals, Errol Lawrence argues that the central ideology of the neo-racist discourses was the suggestion that 'blacks' brought 'problems' with them (Lawrence 1982: 5). They were imagined as the enemies within, the main culprits undermining the structure of the civil society. This, in turn, also became an attempt to redefine the national identity in a manner that defined as outside it a whole range of 'others', including non-white immigrant populations. According to another of Alfred Sherman's articles for the *Daily Telegraph*:

> The United Kingdom is the national homeland of the English, Scots, Welsh, Ulstermen . . . They wish to survive as an identifiable national entity . . . they have been willing to work, suffer and die for it. By contrast, for the jet-age migrants, Britain is simply a haven of convenience where they acquire rights without national obligation.
>
> (Sherman 1979b: 8)

The 1980s production and release of the films *Heat and Dust* and *A Passage to India* have interesting implications when analysed in the context of this widespread deployment of neo-racism. My attempt here is to go beyond a mere structural analysis of the film texts and to investigate their participation in the hegemonic social discourses of the time. I have already discussed in detail the rearticulation of race attempted by 1980s Raj cinema in another paper (Muraleedharan 1997); in this discussion I shall therefore pay more attention to the redefining of gender that these films appear to undertake in tandem with their discourse on race.

The film of *A Passage to India* begins with the arrival of Adela Quested (Judy Davis) in colonised India with the intention of marrying and settling down with Ronny Heaslop (Nigel Havers), the District Judge of Chandrapore. The film subsequently explores how she befriends Mr Fielding (James Fox) and his Indian friend Dr Aziz (Victor Banerjee), decides against marrying Ronny, and undertakes an excursion to the Marabar caves in the company of Aziz and Ronny's mother, Mrs Moore (Peggy Ashcroft). Inside the cave Adela is assaulted and almost raped. This is followed by the trial of the accused, Dr Aziz, which aggravates the existing conflict between the British and the locals and merges with the concurrent struggles of the Indian national movement. Events reach an unexpected conclusion when Adela withdraws her accusation in a dramatic manner. Nevertheless she becomes instrumental in breaking the Fielding–Aziz friendship. She eventually returns to England to lead a lonely life. The film ends showing Fielding returning to 'independent' post-1947 India with his wife Stella (Sandy Hotz) and reviving his friendship with Aziz.

In *Heat and Dust*, there are two migrant women. Anne (Julie Christie), a young BBC correspondent from England, comes to India during the 1980s in search of her past, prompted by the preserved letters and diary of her great-aunt, Olivia (Greta Scacchi), who lived in colonised India during the 1920s as the wife of Douglas (Christopher Cazenove), the District Collector (a junior colonial official) on the Civil Lines at Satipur. In the 1920s narrative, Olivia is seduced by the lustful local Nawab (Shashi Kapoor), becomes pregnant, and has to undergo a gory, unscientific abortion; later, cast out by the scandalised British imperial community, she elopes with the Nawab. In the film's parallel story set in the present, Anne also becomes pregnant by her Indian lover, Inder Lal (Zakir Hussain), who has an epileptic wife, Rita (Ratna Pathak). But she escapes a fate parallel to Olivia's by deciding to keep the baby but leave Inder and become a single mother.

Both films seem to be drawing an analytical contrast between the white women in colonised India (Olivia in *Heat and Dust*, Adela in *A Passage to India*) and those who come to 'independent' India (Anne in *Heat and Dust* and Stella in *A Passage to India*). This contrast is merely suggested in *A Passage to India*, but becomes the central concern in *Heat and Dust*.

Imagining India

Representation of the colonised as the cultural other of the coloniser has been a prominent feature of colonial discourses, and this has already merited sufficient

Figure 10.1 The white community as helpless victims: as Adela (Judy Davis) and Mrs
Moore (Peggy Ashcroft) disembark in Bombay in *A Passage to India* (1984), the
India that encircles them is immediately characterised by an aggressive, sensual — and male — physicality which the captivated Adela is powerless to
resist.

Source: BFI Stills, Posters and Designs (EMI).

critical attention. Yet old and much-repeated stereotypes, such as the lustful or
effeminate oriental male and castrating oriental female, can be seen to reappear in
the Raj films of the post-colonial 1980s. The most significant feature of the rewriting of history attempted by *A Passage to India* and *Heat and Dust* is the films' neat
reversal of the oppressor/victim dichotomy. Colonised India — a victim of political and economic oppression and exploitation — ends up appearing in these films
as a mysterious and evil force that disrupts the middle-class domesticity of England. Simultaneously it also functions as a source of violence.

An obvious example is the portrayal of the Nawab in *Heat and Dust*, who is seen
entertaining his guests at a dinner party with the stories of ruthless violence performed by his ancestors. His association is with gun-wielding criminals. Even in
love he is aggressive and violent. There is an obvious contrast suggested in the
tender, sensuous love-making of Douglas and Olivia to the violently passionate
union of the Nawab with Olivia. In the source novel, Douglas is sexually impo-
tent; hence the film's decision to change this detail — presenting the Englishman as
merely mild and gentle, in direct contrast to the violent and powerful Nawab — is
a significant one.

The Nawab and his royal lifestyle also provide a striking contrast with the existence of the British civil authorities in colonised India. The film presents Indian royalty, represented prominently by the Nawab and his family, as always engaged in entertainment and decadent indulgence – rich food, idleness, and wasteful games such as gambling. By contrast, the British civil authorities are always seen engaged in hard labour. Douglas scales the rough, rocky countryside every day to serve the poor Indians and Dr Saunders (Patrick Godfrey) is forever briskly walking along the narrow corridors of the humble hospital building, while the Nawab inhabits the resplendent interiors of the palace and moves around in a leisurely fashion. Thus, in spite of Britain's imperial dominance over India, *Heat and Dust* transfers the guilt of imperial luxury entirely to the Indian royalty. The spaces occupied and inhabited by the representatives of the British Raj are defined as respectably middle-class and presented as starkly simple when compared to the glitter and exoticism that define the habitats of the Indian royalty.

Apart from inverting real colonial power relations, this representational strategy also assists the narrative in condemning Olivia's fascination for the Nawab for which she is promptly punished. Olivia is presented as a victim of her misguided fascination. Though the narrative states that she eventually eloped with the Nawab, the final frames of the 1920s flashback segment of the film show a forlorn Olivia, weak after the abortion, fleeing the Civil Lines. Her elopement with the Nawab thus becomes an act of desperation rather than a radical choice. In his analysis of *Heat and Dust*, John Hill describes Olivia as both a rebel and a victim (Hill 1999: 114). But, on my reading, she is a victim *of* her own rebellion – and thus functions as a warning to all women who feel tempted to rebel. Even her life with the Nawab in the remote Himalayan hill station, after her elopement, is like an exile rather than a fulfilling existence.

Another prominent figure of violence is the Nawab's mother, the Begum (Madhur Jaffrey), marked out by her fixed, cold stares. This image of India as a captivating and hostile force is retained even in the film's episodes depicting the post-independence era. The uncontrollable crowds, oppressive sunshine and overwhelming superstitions that leave Anne disgusted repeat a stereotype of India that used to recur in colonial writings, and contrast impressively with the film's portrayal of the white community in the colonial era, which appears far more civilised and gentle. This powerful contrast also solicits the viewer to dismiss the 'minor' negative qualities of the whites – the mildly suggested racial hatred and occasional gossiping.

Imperial ideology functions in these films predominantly by means of a narrative seduction of the viewer. Sharon Willis points out that

> To analyze cinema as a social machine entails understanding seduction in general, not as a privatized exchange, but as part of social, libidinal channelling and mapping . . . seduction does not just lead towards; it always leads away

from something as well. I am interested in those moments and details that we
may be seduced into not seeing.

(Willis 1989: 9)

In these two examples of 1980s Raj cinema, the narrative seduction functions
to wean the viewer's imagination away from the British Raj as a politically and
economically exploitative phenomenon. *Heat and Dust* accomplishes a complete
rewriting of Britain's imperial mission in India by translating the imperial civil
authorities into the terms of the English middle class of the 1980s and their values.
Thus Olivia and Douglas live in a modest cottage in which the accent is not on
luxury but on middle-class comfort, the only sign of colonial glory being the tiger
skin on the wall. The two prominent male characters who inhabit the Civil Lines
– Douglas and Dr Saunders – are honest men, decent, duty-conscious and genuinely concerned with the welfare of the natives. Both of them end up making
sacrifices in their enthusiasm to fulfil their duties. The stay in India costs Dr Saunders
his child and also his wife's mental balance, as the death of her child leaves Mrs
Saunders (Jennifer Kendal) hysterical and hyper-reactive. Douglas too is shown to
lose his wife because of his dedication to duty. Thus the film re-creates imperial
domination as basically a civilising mission and an act of sacrifice.

Moreover, both *Heat and Dust* and *A Passage to India* also translate the self-
acknowledged 'negative aspects' of colonialism into other motifs, such as irrational racial paranoia or distrust, thus trivialising the oppressive dimensions of the
colonial encounter. Most of the whites who express overt racist sentiments in the
two films are peripheral characters marked by 'grotesquely comic' mannerisms.
Even Ronny in *A Passage to India*, who is one of the few main characters to voice
racist sentiments, appears more of a victim than an oppressor, for his attitude
towards India appears to be more a product of fear than of hatred. His resentment
towards the eagerness of the two white women, Mrs Moore and Adela, to mix too
much with the natives is prompted by his protective concern for them and also
fear of the unforeseen dangers that await them – a sentiment amply justified by the
narrative's later developments. Ronny seems a prisoner of circumstances – one
who inhabits closed spaces most of the time and is trapped in a world of bureau-
cratic decorum and official rituals. His official engagements leave him with no
time to give a proper welcome to his mother and fiancée, and his relationship with
Adela is affected by his devotion to his duties as the District Magistrate – a fate
similar to that of Douglas in *Heat and Dust*.

The image of the white community in colonised India as a set of helpless victims, trapped in a seductive and at the same time oppressive environment of heat
and dust and perpetually yearning to go back home, recurs in both these films.[3]
Nostalgia and the desire to go back are sentiments repeatedly expressed in various
ways by most of the whites in *Heat and Dust*. Prominent among these is Harry
(Nickolas Grace), the young white man who lives in the palace of the Nawab. A

Figure 10.2 Punished for her misguided fascination: in *Heat and Dust* (1982), the affair
between Olivia (Greta Scacchi), wife of a British official in 1920s colonial
India, and the violent and decadent Nawab (Shashi Kapoor), results in her
pregnancy, abortion, and expulsion from the British imperial community.
Source: BFI Stills, Posters and Designs, courtesy of Merchant Ivory Productions.

glimpse of the homeland of his dreams is presented in a few fleeting shots which
appear in the form of Harry's reverie as he listens to Olivia's piano recital. It is an
England of meadows, groves, streams and a church steeple – the England of pastoral poetry. Apart from constructing a romantic picture of England, these shots
also emphasise the otherness of India, constructed in the film in terms of dry
barren plains, crowded dusty bazaars and garishly exotic palaces. Such an India is
further shown as entrapping and victimising the white men and women. Given
that most of these white characters are directly or indirectly involved in the colonial project, such a presentation achieves a twin purpose: redefining colonialism as
the 'white man's burden' while at the same time reactivating the myth of India as
a dangerous mystery, at once alluring and – literally – captivating.

The India that encircles Adela in *A Passage to India* is similarly aggressive, and
marked by a sensual physicality. Surrounded by this mysterious power, Adela is
like a trapped victim, not capable of resisting its ominous strength. Departing
from Forster's novel significantly, Lean introduces several tropes to elaborate this
new interpretation of Indo-British relations. One of the recurring images of India
in the film is that of the 'crowds', which are predominantly male. The aggression
towards and victimisation of Adela begin almost as soon as she reaches India in the

scene where she is pushed and jostled by the crowd on the Bombay docks. The motif of naked brown bodies, which will later reappear several times in the film, is introduced in this scene. The crowd appears again inside the Marabar caves, where the nakedness of the brown bodies is more prominently stated. These bodies encircle Adela and Mrs Moore, frightening them both. Later when Aziz helps Adela to climb the rocks, a close-up of their hands holding each other emphasises the difference in their skin colours – a white hand clasped in a brown one. This shot becomes a forewarning of Adela's subsequent assault, since the mysteriously dangerous and evil nature of brownness has already been established. The crowd appears again during the trial sequence – now all-male and more aggressive. They preside over the humiliation of Adela in the court, which is also a spiritual rape.

The motif of brown-skinned crowds is interconnected in the film with that of monkeys. The monkey makes several appearances in the film. When Adela reaches Chandrapore, the monkey extends an arresting glance from the roof of the railway station. The object of this glance is readable as either Adela or the splendour of the British Raj, the latter enacted in the form of a reception for the local British Governor taking place at the station; both later undergo symbolic castration. Lean's most significant innovation and departure from Forster's novel is his addition of the episode in the ruined temple.[4] It has tremendous significance in the narrative construction of Adela as a victim. The erotic statues that capture Adela's sensual fascination are also images of violence. They loom large in recurring close-ups as oppressive structures, their gaze fixed and aggressive. In the close-ups their static gaze is directed straight at the camera, persuading the viewer to internalise Adela's helplessness. Thus the so-called sensual awakening of Adela is explained as an inevitable response, the entire responsibility being shifted to the statues and subsequently to India. This is followed by the monkey sequence: dozens of monkeys suddenly appear and scramble down, almost like an evil power emerging from the statues. They frighten and chase Adela. It is obviously a prelude to the attempted rape. The monkey later appears again, to frighten Adela as she goes to the court; it has now acquired human stature – it is a semi-nude Indian youth disguised as a monkey. The motifs of brown bodies and of the monkeys are here merged. The movement of the demonstrating Indian crowd during the trial sequence is quite often exactly like the movement of the monkeys in the temple sequence as they chase Adela.

But the danger that India poses for British sensibility is much more than monkey mischief. The fear India evokes is enhanced by the mystery that surrounds it. Thus India is also portrayed in Lean's *A Passage to India* as the waters of the Ganges – with crocodiles hiding in it, as Aziz explains. India is also the cave, dark and with mysterious echoes, which frightens Mrs Moore and inside which the assault of Adela takes place. Hence Adela is evidently a victim of violence. Her appearance after the alleged rape strengthens this impression: she is bruised and bleeding, pierced all over by cactus thorns – a female Christ figure.

Thus two important patterns emerge in the re-imagining of India that these films seem to undertake. The most prominent of these is the reassertion of a colonial perspective that viewed the Orient as exotic, mysterious and potentially dangerous. Moreover, the 'threat' posed by India is further designated in terms of a 'primitive' sensual aggression capable of endangering the purity of middle-class English domesticity. Adela decides not to marry Ronny after she meets Aziz, and Olivia elopes with the Nawab despite having a protective and loving husband, Douglas. These narrative developments could be interpreted as further evidence that the films invert (and so disavow) 'real' colonial power relations: in both cases, the white man cannot win out over the 'force' of India.

Yet a significant shift is evident in these post-colonial cinematic re-imaginings of the colonial encounter. A hard-line colonial perspective would, surely, reject the possibility of British–Indian (hetero)sexual relationships. Hence the seemingly liberal representation of such relations in these films might appear like a disavowal of the conventional colonial perspective. However, it is also evident that these relations are not shown in either of the films as healthy or lasting. Instead, they are depicted as the outcome of the fascination of the white British woman towards the exoticism and mystery of India, which presumably makes middle-class English domesticity seem by contrast dull and unappealing. By promptly punishing the women who give in to this fascination, the films reinstate the desirability of English domesticity. Yet it is important here also to mention the differing ways in which the two films re-imagine English domesticity. In *A Passage to India*, it is defined in terms of Stella's 'ideal marriage' to Fielding. In *Heat and Dust*, by contrast, it is represented by Anne's single motherhood, which fits more conveniently with the redefining of family norms taking place in the context of contemporary liberal thought, as well as with the film's assumption of a somewhat highbrow perspective. Either way, India appears in both these films as a mysterious force that seduces and assaults English women and, at the same time, causes the breakdown of the normative English family. By such a representation, these films could also be seen to be turning their backs on contemporary 1980s debates on multiculturalism and identity and harking back to the discourse on race and immigration prevalent in Britain from the 1950s to the 1970s.

Rewriting gender

The narrative construction of subjectivity is a topic of crucial importance in contemporary film studies. Cinematic representations are no longer studied as reflections of 'real worlds' or 'real people' but more often as a mapping of the social vision into subjectivity. Teresa de Lauretis has pointed out that

> cinema's binding of fantasy to significant images affects the spectator as a
> subjective production, and so the movement of the film actually inscribes and

orients desire. In this manner, cinema powerfully participates in the production of forms of subjectivity that are individually shaped yet unequivocally social.

(de Lauretis 1984: 8)

What de Lauretis as well as many others have underscored is the inevitable social moorings of the orienting and reorienting of the viewer into subject positions undertaken by films. This further emphasises the need to read films with reference to the socio-historical contexts in which they are made and viewed. In the rest of this paper, I shall try to examine the patterns of gendered representations in the two films under discussion and shall speculate on their signification in the context of the broader redefining of identities taking place in 1980s Britain.

Women, especially young women, are represented in both films mainly as shallow and ridiculous, and their prominent characteristics are idleness, racism and at times a simplistic fascination with the 'exotic' in India. This is most striking in the case of the peripheral female characters. The representations of Olivia and Adela are characterised by a certain amount of ambivalence: they are presented within their respective films as both frivolous and vulnerable, and simultaneously ridiculous and pathetic.[5] In the process both texts appear to shift the responsibility of colonial oppression to the 'feminine', which is then differentiated from the 'masculine' or 'real' British culture. Moreover, by equating colonial oppression with the words and actions of a few women who either appear as peripheral to the films' central themes or are portrayed as frail and ridiculous, these films manage to disavow the oppressive dimension of colonial domination. At the same time, by projecting these 'guilty' women as simultaneously helpless and vulnerable, dazed by the overwhelming mystery of India, the narratives shift the blame back to India.

In both films, the most overt racist sentiments are invariably expressed by minor female characters – typically, the wives of British colonial civil servants. In the 1920s strand of *Heat and Dust*, the white community in India is divided into two neat groups. The men, represented prominently but not only by Douglas and other colonial officials such as Dr Saunders and Mr Crawford (Julian Glover), are hardworking and sincerely engaged in the civilising mission. The women, on the other hand, are openly contemptuous of Indians and their culture. Particularly interesting in *Heat and Dust* is the character of Mrs Saunders, played by Jennifer Kendal. She is portrayed as both negative and ridiculous. She is bitchy and at the same time paranoiac about the uncontrollable lust of Indians. Her agitation at the sight of a young Indian waiter is portrayed in the film with evident sarcasm. Yet, at the same time, the narrative assigns the responsibility for these reactions back to the environment in which she is trapped – that is, India. Thus, almost immediately after presenting Mrs Saunders as bitchy and ridiculous, the narrative solicits the viewer's sympathy by calling attention to her trauma at the death of her baby, presumably caused by the hot and humid Indian weather.

Similarly, in *A Passage to India*, the car which hits Aziz's cycle at the start of the film is pictured from one side, so that right at the centre of the frame is Mrs Turton, who waves and smiles at the crowds around her in a manner that is almost grotesque. The two white women who emerge from Major Calendar's house to snatch away Aziz's *tonga* (a horse-drawn carriage, common in India during the British period) are also remarkable for their exaggerated mannerisms. Even the legal persecution of Aziz, which is the central issue in the film, is explained as the result of Adela's sexual frustration and her subsequent erotic hallucination. Thus the entire responsibility of causing the break-up of the Aziz–Fielding friendship – which in the films functions as a metonym for the Indo-British relationship – is placed on Adela's shoulders.

Yet Adela appears in the film more as a victim than an oppressor, and she is finally elevated to the status of a martyr. From the choice of actor to play the role to the type of make-up, costume and lighting used, everything reveals a conscious attempt to portray Adela as fragile and vulnerable. Forster's Adela was plain, but Lean's Adela, as played by Judy Davis, is definitely attractive, despite the other characters describing her as ugly. In the film she appears like a wax statue, the pale translucence of her skin heightened by the flat, soft lighting given to her in the close ups, once again suggesting a quaint, fragile vulnerability.[6] The controversial rape attempt in Forster's novel takes place in a gap between two chapters, which assigns the event an evident ambiguity. Forster takes pains not to give any indication as to whether the attempt has actually taken place, whereas in Lean's film the rape attempt has certainly taken place. The bloodied appearance of Adela after the cave episode presents her as an obvious victim of violence. The ambiguity is only regarding the identity of the assailant.[7]

Though both the films discussed here seem to define the 'feminine in British culture' as shallow and frivolous, their respective concepts of 'the feminine' appear to be strikingly different. In *A Passage to India*, 'the feminine' is represented entirely by women; but in *Heat and Dust*, it is represented not only by the biologically female but also by a male 'lacking in masculinity'. This seems to be the narrative function of Harry, who is the only English man in the film seen indulging in sensual pleasures and gossip 'like women' [*sic*]. The narrative differentiates him from the other male representatives of the British Raj by making him a guest of the Nawab. The possibility of a homosexual affair between him and the Nawab is suggested only in muted terms, yet his lack of masculinity is emphasised by showing him frequently in the company of women, underscoring his lack of any erotic interest in them. Later he is shown also as ill and remaining in bed. Thus, if the ever-active Douglas and the film's other white men represent the 'masculine', Harry stands for the lack of it.

Harry is also a tool in the hands of the Nawab in the Nawab's power struggle with Douglas – a factor that gives him a narrative function similar to that of Olivia. Both end up betraying the British 'masculine' (Douglas) in their fascination for the exotic India (the Nawab). Douglas desperately tries to pull Harry away from the Nawab's influence and send him back to Britain; but the cool and confident Nawab inevitably wins, and Harry decides to go with him. The narrative punishes Harry for this crime in a curious manner: he is left behind, alone, when the Nawab elopes with Olivia. At the start of the film, he appears like Tiresias, punished with endless life and destined to tell the future generations about the past. His fate is to live on to tell Anne – a representative of the present – about the bygone days as well as the mystery of India.[8]

Thus both films can be seen as assigning to the 'feminine' the responsibility of betraying the 'masculine' and thereby accomplishing the decline of the Empire. Yet they can also be seen to celebrate another version of the feminine, defined as maternal and asexual. This is the function of the character of Mrs Moore in *A Passage to India*. She is the antithesis of the castrating mother, as represented by the Begum in *Heat and Dust*: the benign Christian mother. She is the only character who does not go through any significant transformation during the course of the film. She is appreciative of Indian culture, friendly with the Indians and extremely critical of her son's distrust of them.[9] She instinctively knows that Adela and Ronny may not make a compatible pair, yet is affectionate and friendly towards Adela. After the alleged rape attempt, Mrs Moore remains concerned about Adela's health yet refuses to believe that Aziz is guilty. Thus she represents the values of humanism, the very same values that presided over the so-called civilising mission of the British. In the film she is also constantly associated with the spiritual and the divine. What fascinates her in India is the grandeur of a ruined mosque in which she discovers the presence of God, and the mysterious waters of the Ganges resplendent in the moonlight. Thus her asexuality is garnished with a strain of 'spirituality'. Aziz comments that hers is the kindest face he had ever seen. The saintliness of Mrs Moore is emphasised in the scene in which she leaves India: through the window of the train, her hooded figure is framed like the portrait of a saint, the golden light playing on her white hair, heightening the effect of an aura round her head.

The film also elevates Mrs Moore to the status of the patron saint of the imperial mission. It is her absence that triggers the separation of the two cultures. Thus the assault on Adela takes place when Mrs Moore is absent. Later, during the court case, Adela and the entire British community are put to shame because Mrs Moore is not present. The agitated Indians repeatedly ask for Mrs Moore; in a chorus, they chant: 'We want Mrs Moore'. When the British fail to produce her, the Indians walk out of the court.

The narrative resolution of the central crisis in *A Passage to India* is finally accomplished by the re-creation of Mrs Moore. This is done in two different ways. On the one hand, Fielding comes back to India after marrying Stella, Mrs Moore's daughter, who manages to restore the lost friendship between the two men. Meanwhile, Adela, who had been a fragile, sensuous woman fascinated by the exotic

India, has been transformed into an asexual, saintly figure who could replace Mrs Moore. Adela's transition from a sensuous fascination with India to the Christian virtue of sacrifice and expiation of sin through suffering is clearly indicated in the court scene in which she withdraws her allegations. The final shots of Adela which appear while Aziz reads her letter resemble the shots of Mrs Moore on the train: standing near a window, she is framed in the centre of a shot which presents her in the pattern of the portrait of a saint.

There are remarkable equivalences in the representation of the female characters in *Heat and Dust*. Though much younger, the film's present-day protagonist Anne represents the same values of humanism and tolerance personified by Mrs Moore. Unlike her aunt Olivia, Anne is not fascinated by the exotic Orient and is capable of leaving her Indian friend, Inder. Where Olivia had been punished for her fascination for India by a gory abortion and exile from the British community in the Nawab's hill station, *Heat and Dust* ends by showing Anne scaling the Himalayan heights, seeking a spiritual location in which to give birth to her child. In doing so, she re-defines herself singularly in terms of the maternal. In other words, *Heat and Dust* too resolves its narrative by the re-creation of a Mrs Moore — that is, by re-creation of the 'feminine', defined as spiritual and maternal.

John Hill observes that the significance of Anne's retreat to the mountains, away from the 'heat and dust' below, is not wholly clear. But I read it as an obvious indication of her breaking all the ties with the exotic India that seduced her aunt. The snowscapes of the mountain present a spectacle that contrasts visually with the hot and dusty India hitherto emphasised for most of the film — an iconography that further distances Anne's maternity from signifying an inter-racial union.

The patterns that emerge in these two films can be found in the other British Raj films and television dramas/drama series of the 1980s as well. The colonial encounter is imagined in most of these films and dramas as essentially a male friendship. A sensual woman's fascination for the exotic Orient is assigned the responsibility for breaking up that friendship. Yet these women are also portrayed as weak and vulnerable, seduced and assaulted by a mysterious and potentially dangerous force named India. They are nevertheless punished by the narratives through physical assaults or violence — Adela is almost raped and Olivia has to undergo a violent and unscientific abortion. Finally, the films suggest that order can be restored only through a redefining of the feminine as asexual, maternal and spiritual.

And all three 'new Mrs Moores' — Stella, the reformed Adela and Anne — live in the post-colonial context. It is these women who are shown to redeem British womanhood from the past mistakes assigned to it — mistakes which led to a series of catastrophes including the loss of the Empire.

It is obvious that *Heat and Dust* and *A Passage to India* do not seek to project identical messages. Neither can either film be considered as a mere vehicle for propaganda. A more complex narrative and a seemingly more complex perspective (and the prestige signified by Merchant Ivory Productions as a 'brand') provide *Heat and Dust* with the trappings of a more highbrow artistic endeavour than *A Passage to India*. Yet, as Hill rightly points out, even the limited optimism of resolving differences expressed in the final shot of *A Passage to India* is absent from *Heat and Dust*, which instead reinforces the irreconcilable differences between the two cultures.

Film texts signify only in the contexts in which they are viewed, and hence it is important to examine and acknowledge the various readings the Raj films permit or produce – from a post-colonial Indian perspective as well as in the context of contemporary British discourses around race, migration and nation. As I read these films from a perspective that is non-western, my intention is certainly that which Salman Rushdie prominently stated in his well-known critique of the 'Raj revival' literature and films of the 1980s:

> When we cry, we cry partly for the safety we have lost; but we also cry to affirm ourselves, to say, here I am, I matter, too – you're going to have to reckon with me.
>
> (Rushdie 1984: 136)

For these films are dealing with a history that is mine as well – and I consider it important to make known my reading of, and my feelings about, the rewriting of such a history which these films seem to undertake.

Notes

1 The 1930s was the peak decade for British Empire propaganda films, and these fell into two categories: the documentaries produced by the EMB Film Unit (formed in 1929 under the directorship of John Grierson), and studio-produced imperial fiction feature films. Prominent examples of the latter include *Sanders of the River* (Zoltan Korda, 1935), *Elephant Boy* (Robert Flaherty/Korda, 1936), *The Drum* (Zoltan Korda, 1938), *The Four Feathers* (Zoltan Korda, 1939), *Lives of a Bengal Lancer* (Henry Hathaway, USA, 1934) and *Gunga Din* (George Stevens, USA, 1939). One of the two leading British producers of the period, Alexander Korda at London Films, notably specialised in films about the Empire, including India.

2 For a detailed discussion, see Ali 1991.

3 In this connection, Richard Dyer suggests that the butterfly net in *The Jewel in the Crown* metaphorically represents the predicament of the British in colonised India – they are like butterflies caught in a net (Dyer 1997: 204). Readers are referred also to the title of the chapter (expanded from an earlier article) in which Dyer presents this argument: 'There's nothing I can do! Nothing!'

4 *Editors' note*: For an account of Lean's stated rationale for introducing this episode, see Brownlow 1996: 651–3. Brownlow's account of the film's production (Chapters 44–7) is also revealing regarding Lean's attitudes to the former colonial relationship and his fraught relations during filming with Victor Banerjee (Aziz) and Judy Davis (Adela) –

who (according to Lean) 'thought I despised her because she was a colonial [i.e. Australian]' (Brownlow: 675).

5 Anne, the present-day female protagonist of *Heat and Dust*, is perhaps an exception in this regard and seems to have a definite narrative function, which I shall discuss later.

6 It would be reasonable to assume that Judy Davis's history of playing headstrong, supposedly plain women might have led Lean to cast her as Adela with the intention of activating these associations; however, accounts of Lean's conception of Adela strongly suggest otherwise (Brownlow 1996: 649–50, 653, 673). It should also be remembered that this image is a discursively constructed one which cannot structure the visual experience of viewers with limited exposure to Davis's past roles or the conventions of English-speaking cinema.

7 John Hill argues that the rape does not take place in the film either. He reads the rape charge as the result of Adela's sexual hysteria, caused by her lack of sexual fulfilment as well as her eroticised fascination with India (Hill 1999: 111).

8 John Hill comments on the potential homoeroticism of the male friendships between Harry and the Nawab and, in *A Passage to India*, between Fielding and Aziz (Hill 1999: 108). However, I feel that this aspect, evident in the source novels, is underplayed in both films, and I would read this as an attempt to keep away from the radical debates on sexuality that emerged after the Stonewall Riots in New York in 1969. Hill cites the scenes showing Fielding and Aziz sitting on each other's beds and walking holding hands as suggesting a homoerotic dimension to the relationship – but for male friends to sit on each other's beds or hold hands is considered perfectly 'normal' in the Indian context. Hill also notes that 'the camera lingers on Aziz applying make-up prior to Fielding's arrival after the trial', but this is a misreading: the scene shows Aziz applying *surma* (black, medicated eye make-up) to his eyes, which is common among traditional Muslim men in India. Thus this action is an assertion of Aziz's return to his (imagined) cultural roots rather than a sign of queerness – as well as almost the sole indication the film offers of Aziz's Muslim identity. (On the latter issue, see Brownlow 1996: 671.)

9 Hill (1999: 110) describes her as representing 'a more traditionally "feminine" and enquiring consciousness which refuses to accept all the conventions of colonial behaviour'.

Bibliography

Ali, Y. (1991) 'Echoes of empire: towards a politics of representation', in J. Corner and S. Harvey (eds), *Enterprise and Heritage: Crosscurrents of National Culture*, London: Routledge: 194–211.

Anderson P. (1992) *English Questions*, London: Verso.

Brownlow, K. (1996) *David Lean*, London: Faber and Faber.

Dyer, R. (1997) *White*, London: Routledge.

Hill, J. (1999) *British Cinema in the 1980s*, Oxford: Oxford University Press.

de Lauretis, T. (1984) *Alice Doesn't: Feminism, Semiotics, Cinema*, London: Macmillan.

Lawrence, E. (1982) 'Just plain commonsense: the "roots" of racism', in Centre for Contemporary Cultural Studies, University of Birmingham (eds), *The Empire Strikes Back: Race and Racism in 70s Britain*, London: Hutchinson: page numbers unavailable.

Lloyd, D. (1991) 'Race under representation', *Oxford Literary Review*, 18, 1–2: 62–94.

Muraleedharan, T. (1997) 'Re-reading *Gandhi*' in R. Frankenberg (ed.), *Displacing Whiteness: Essays in Social and Cultural Criticism*: Durham, NC: Duke University Press: 60–85.

Nairn, T. (1977) *The Break-Up of Britain*, London: Verso.

—— (1982) 'Britain's living legacy', *Marxism Today*, July 1982: 13–18.

Rushdie, S. (1984) 'Outside the whale', *Granta*, 2: 125–38.

Sherman, A. (1979a) 'Britain's urge to self-destruction', *Daily Telegraph*, 9 September 1979: 3–5.

—— (1979b) 'Britain is not Asia's financee', *Daily Telegraph*, 9 November 1979: 8.

Willis, S. (1989) 'Disputed territories: masculinity and social space', *Camera Obscura*, 19: 4–23.

Wollen, T. (1991) 'Over our shoulders: nostalgic screen fictions for the 1980s' in Corner and Harvey (eds) *Enterprise and Heritage*: 178–93.

11 Kenneth Branagh's *Henry V* (1989)

Genre and interpretation

James Quinn and Jane Kingsley-Smith

Producers, directors and studios, the publicity, distribution and exhibition sectors, critics and audiences have all recognised the British historical film as a separate, coherent category of cinema since the advent of sound. *Tudor Rose* (Robert Stevenson, 1936), *The Young Mr Pitt* (Carol Reed, 1942), *A Man for All Seasons* (Fred Zinnemann, 1966), and *Mary, Queen of Scots* (Charles Jarrott, 1971) have all been offered and received as members of this category, while costume dramas, such as *The Wicked Lady* (Leslie Arliss, 1945), and biopics such as *The Magic Box* (John Boulting, 1951) and *Prick Up Your Ears* (Stephen Frears, 1987) have not.

Texts popularly identified as 'historical films' have a number of features in common. These include the presence of title cards and voiceovers which establish a historical context for the narrative; the tendency of characters to understand themselves as being 'in history'; the overt 'quotation' of historical sources; the recurrence of particular stars; an often 'theatrical' *mise-en-scène* entailing spectacular long-shots; episodic and strictly chronological narratives; a concern with the nation and national identity; a pronounced interest in royalty and government; and a mythic-ritual propensity to explore questions of duty and sacrifice.[1]

The 1989 film of Shakespeare's *Henry V* directed by, scripted by and starring Kenneth Branagh, presents an interesting case study through which to explore the nature and constitution of historical genres in British cinema as articulated at a specific historical moment. Although it exhibits many of the characteristics of the historical film, Branagh's *Henry V* was not frequently or confidently identified as part of the historical film genre in the 1980s. As the wide range of popular and academic responses to the film suggests, it can be located within several alternative regions of the late-1980s generic landscape. This essay will explore this generic indeterminacy, and will discuss the possible impact of generic assumptions on readings of the film in light of the discourses and interpretations which surrounded it following its release.

Henry V as a 'Shakespeare film'

Shakespeare has sometimes been credited with the invention of the history play (Danson 2000: 87), but he may also be one of the progenitors of the British historical film. Shakespeare's history plays, based on Tudor chronicle history, focus on the private struggles of English kings against a backdrop of foreign and internecine warfare. The British historical film has been similarly concerned with the monarchy, with the private face behind the public mask, with threats to national sovereignty, and with questions of duty and self-sacrifice. In Nicholas Hytner's *The Madness of King George* (1995), adapted for the screen by Alan Bennett from his own play *The Madness of George III*, the eponymous King holds a play-reading in his garden. The play in question is *King Lear*, at the moment when Lear awakens from his delirium, with George (Nigel Hawthorne) taking the lead role and the courtiers as supporting cast. This extended reference to *King Lear* endows George with a certain tragic grandeur and the film also benefits from the cultural prestige attached to Shakespeare's name. But it is crucial that the play referred to is one of Shakespeare's histories,[2] for George implies that it is through Shakespeare's depiction of kingship that a king may know himself. As a result of playing Lear, George has 'remembered how to seem'. His idea of kingliness as a performance, but also the film's sense of the dignity, charisma and tragedy of a king, are explicitly associated with Shakespeare.

But if Shakespeare's history plays have partly shaped British historical cinema, the Shakespearean origins of a film like Kenneth Branagh's *Henry V* have also *prevented* its identification as a historical film. There is evidence that filmmakers adapting Shakespeare's history plays have translated them into the terms of historical film by adopting its characteristic codes and conventions. Laurence Olivier's *Richard III* (1955) opens with a shot of an illuminated manuscript. Orson Welles's *Chimes at Midnight* (Spain/Switzerland, 1965) includes passages from Holinshed's *Chronicles* in voiceover and was to have featured the death and funeral procession of Richard II. Branagh too considered incorporating some allusion to the earlier king into his *Henry V*. But these features may also be read as characteristic of the 'Shakespearean' film.[3] To the Shakespearean scholar (and the study of Shakespeare film adaptations has mainly been the domain of literary rather than film studies), any reference to Holinshed's *Chronicles* is chiefly significant for what it tells us of the dramatist's adaptation of his source. The interpolation into these films of scenes which contextualise the historical action – for example the death of Richard II in *Chimes at Midnight* or the Falstaff scenes in Branagh's *Henry V* – can be seen to lend more *Shakespeare* to the film rather than to historicise it further.

The majority of academic critics writing on Branagh's *Henry V* in the 1980s and early 1990s were Shakespearean scholars for whom the screen adaptation of Shakespeare's work could be seen as an extension of their own field, rather than a foray into the relatively unfamiliar territory of film studies. This was perhaps most obvious in their generally untroubled and unproblematising use of the term 'genre'. Thus, for example, Kenneth S. Rothwell described Branagh's *Henry V* as 'one of the outstanding Shakespeare movies of the century,' offering a 'bright prelude for the shapes that the genre may take in the twenty-first century' (Rothwell 1990:

173, 177). Shakespearean scholars like Rothwell made assumptions about genre without recourse to film genre theory, and in defiance of the fact that film criticism did not recognise the 'Shakespeare movie' as a generic category. Although in 1977, Jack J. Jorgens's *Shakespeare on Film* located a number of Shakespeare films within the generic landscape of contemporary cinema, there remains an air of novelty to Harry Keyishian's attempt in 2000 to locate three film versions of *Hamlet* within the genres of *film noir*, action-adventure and epic. Keyishian feels it necessary to remind us that 'we need to encounter Shakespeare films in the context of movie history and, in particular, film genre. We need to ask of any "Shakespeare film", "what kind of *movie* is this?"' (Keyishian 2000: 72).

However, film critics writing on *Henry V* for a range of contemporary newspapers were equally happy to locate the film within a 'venerable British tradition' of Shakespeare on film (Brown 1989; see also Lane 1989) and to foreground its relationship to its source text; Pauline McLeod, for example, described the film as a treatment of 'Shakespeare's classic *Henry V*' (McLeod 1989: 26). This Shakespeare-centred reading was one that the director, Kenneth Branagh, took pains to encourage. Branagh was repeatedly quoted in newspapers and popular film magazines describing *Henry V* as 'a popular Shakespeare film' (Branagh 1989a: 203; see also Renaissance Films 1989: 4–5). The souvenir brochure that accompanied *Henry V*'s release included an article on 'Shakespeare Films' by Russell Jackson, the Shakespearean academic with whom Branagh worked closely during the making of the film. Moreover, although Branagh suggested that he saw *Henry V* in terms of other film genres, referring to it as a 'political thriller' (Branagh 1989b: 10), he most consistently associated it with an earlier 'Shakespeare film', Laurence Olivier's *Henry V* (1945). Whether emulating this earlier film (as when Branagh's Henry makes his St Crispin's Day speech from a cart) or – more often – adopting strategies which would distance his work from Olivier's (Olivier's Elizabethan theatre is replaced by a film set), Branagh invited critics and audiences to compare his filming of *Henry V* with its illustrious precursor, both through explicit acknowledgement of his debt and through intertextual allusion.

By locating his film in this 'Shakespearean' context, Branagh suggested the terms on which it should be judged and valued. Branagh's film is 'Shakespearean' in various ways. It derives its plot, characterisation and all of its language from Shakespeare's *Henry V*. For many literary critics, the poetry is the key signifying feature, the essence of the 'Shakespearean', and it is primarily because they lack this element that silent and foreign film adaptations from Shakespeare have often been discounted as 'Shakespeare films'.[4] Branagh's *Henry V* made the most of the verse by placing it in the mouths of celebrated Shakespearean actors such as Paul Scofield, Judi Dench, and Robert Stephens; but the film also restored some of the morally ambiguous rhetoric excised from Olivier's film, a point which Branagh was keen to draw to the attention of audiences (Branagh 1989b: 12; see also Donaldson 1991 and Aitken 1991). Thus Branagh's Henry threatens rape and infanticide at the gates of Harfleur, and draws a moral lesson from the execution of a former friend. Such choices made this *Henry V* appear to be a radical departure from the Olivier film, 'updating' the play for the 1980s while simultaneously locating it within a conservative tradition of Shakespeare filmmaking which still regarded the source text in awe and argued that a film should have as much 'Shakespeare' in it as possible. Indeed, Branagh plundered other plays from the canon to enrich his film, placing *Henry V* within the cycle of Shakespeare's history plays by inserting scenes from *Henry IV Part One* and *Part Two*.[5]

Moreover, although the ambiguities Branagh discovered in the play might suggest a deconstructionist perspective at work, they were limited in their radical potential by Branagh's insistence (condoned by many of his critics) that Shakespeare's meaning was latent in the text, to be drawn out by the director. In his introduction to the screenplay, Branagh confesses that he has taken liberties with the play but hopes that 'they are Shakespearean in spirit – as I hope we have remained true to the spirit of the play' (Branagh 1989b: 12). The ensuing critical debate focused on whether this film really had captured the 'spirit' – or 'truth' – of the text, with some critics insisting that Branagh's 'liberties' had not gone far enough and others that he had betrayed the play. The literary scholar Curtis Breight offers an extreme example of this latter attitude. He condemned the film for failing to appreciate Shakespeare's bitter satire of Elizabethan militarism, arguing that Branagh's textual cuts and dramatic emphases amounted to the 'distortion of both text and history' (Breight 1991: 105). That Breight approached the film with a particular axe to grind is suggested by his publication of a 1996 monograph entitled *Surveillance and Militarism in the Elizabethan Era*. Here, all pretence that the literary critic understands *Henry V* to be a film, aimed at a popular audience, is forgotten in defence of literary (and historical) 'truth'.

Writing at the close of the 1990s, Neil Sinyard declared that there are now three ways of 'doing Shakespeare on film'. There is the conservative, spectacular, text-rich film in the tradition of Olivier; the adaptation which insists on the play's contemporary relevance by updating it to the twentieth century, such as Christine Edzard's *As You Like It* (1992) and Richard Loncraine's *Richard III* (1995); or the most radical form exemplified by Baz Luhrmann's *William Shakespeare's 'Romeo + Juliet'* (Australia, 1997), a 'reconceptualization of the play in the visual language and forms of today' (Sinyard 2000: 69). In Sinyard's terms, Branagh's *Henry V* appears conservative,[6] but to read *Henry V* in the terms of the 1980s – a decade in which there had been few Shakespeare films – was to be made more aware of its revisionist interpretation of the play and of the 'Shakespeare movie' itself.

Henry V as a heritage film

In *Big-Time Shakespeare*, Michael D. Bristol explores the complexity of the term 'Shakespeare' as a symbol of cultural value, and identifies a vernacular usage which signifies 'privilege, exclusion, and cultural pretension' (Bristol 1996: ix). The association of Shakespeare with these qualities aligns the Shakespearean film with the notion of 'heritage cinema'.

Branagh's *Henry V* exhibits many of the characteristics attributed to the 1980s heritage film by Andrew Higson in his seminal definition of the category.[7] It was independently produced (by Renaissance Films plc) on a low budget; filmed in an intimate style; emphasis was placed on Branagh's authorship; and it was 'valued for [its] cultural significance'. The film may be counted as one of a number of contemporary 'adaptations of culturally prestigious and canonic literary and theatrical properties', while 'the acting honours tend to be carried by almost a repertory company of key players, many of them drawing on the heritage of the English theatrical tradition' (Higson 1996: 232–3).

And yet, *Henry V* also differs in significant respects from the heritage film as conceived by Higson. For example, it does not present an unbroken spectacle of 'social deference' and upper-class ease (Higson 1996: 239–41). Branagh retains most of the statements of dissent articulated by the play's minor characters, and whereas Olivier's Henry is confident and consummate, tossing his crown over the back of his throne with Bond-like *brio* early in the 1945 film, Branagh's 1989 incarnation of the King is marked by effort rather than charisma. He wrestles the traitor, Scrope, as a dynamic camera moves with him. This Henry is introduced to us in silhouette through enormous doors, sweeping along like a medieval Darth Vader, and we assume his point of view as his councillors react with reverence and awe. But when the King is actually revealed, in the threatening shadows cast by a concealed fire, he looks pale and drawn, dwarfed by the magnificence of his throne.

Branagh himself was assiduous in distancing the film from the notion of heritage; as he told one interlocutor: 'I want this to be a popular film, not an art-house film or a museum piece' (Lewis 1989: 12). He was insistent that *Henry V* should be distributed through mainstream cinemas, rather than through the art-house circuit where – notwithstanding high-profile 'crossover' heritage successes such as *A Room with a View* (James Ivory, 1985) – heritage films found much of their audience during the 1980s. Nor was the term 'heritage', or anything suggesting or approximating to it, ever used to characterise *Henry V* in the public discourses surrounding it.

But for any viewer who did read *Henry V* within the interpretative framework of heritage cinema, it might have seemed something rather radical and innovative, a 'post-heritage' film ahead of its time.[8] The film's slow-motion combat scenes emphasise the fear and strenuousness of the battle, and the high-angle tracking shot which follows the haggard Henry through a muddy panorama strewn with bodies underlines the cost of victory. The contrast with 1980s texts commonly agreed to be 'heritage films', including *A Room with a View* and *A Handful of Dust* (Charles Sturridge, 1988) – films preoccupied with manners, morals and matters of personal and sexual fulfilment, and filmed in a graceful, unobtrusive style – would have been striking.

Furthermore, whereas Cairns Craig and others have attacked the heritage film's seemingly nostalgic and conservative view of the past (Craig 1991), Branagh was at pains to establish his project as the product of a progressive, pacifist conscience. In *Henry V*'s production notes he conceived of Shakespeare's play as something to be 'reclaimed from jingoism' and from the conservative, consensual associations it had acquired during the Second World War (Renaissance Films 1989: 2). One of Branagh's main strategies for achieving this would be to ensure that the film's realism did not stop short of depicting the true horror of the battlefield, designed in the film to evoke images of the First World War (Branagh 1989a: 220, 229). The majority of commentators subscribed to this view, casting the film as a work of pacific sensibility. Philip French, for example, argued:

> Olivier's magnificent film, glowing with patriotic pride, was made to stir a nation at war, connecting us to a heroic past . . . Branagh's pictorially low-key picture is made for a generation that has the Indo-China war and the Falklands campaign just behind it and is very wary of calls to arms.
>
> (French 1989)

Encouraged by such promptings and the publicity achieved by Branagh and the Renaissance Film Company, some viewers may have associated *Henry V* with the flurry of low-budget, bitter and oppositional British cinema which also appeared in the late 1980s – including *War Requiem* (Derek Jarman, 1988), *For Queen and Country* (Martin Stellman, 1988), *Resurrected* (Paul Greengrass, 1989) and, on British television, *Tumbledown* (Richard Eyre, BBC TV, 1988) – rather than with the perceived antithesis of these films, heritage cinema.

Henry V as a historical film

It has often been proposed that film is in various ways 'inadequate' to the task of representing Shakespeare and other literary texts. (See, for example, Miller 1986: 233, and Giddings *et al.* 1990: 20. In defence of film, see Béja 1976: 88.) However, it has similarly been asserted that film is too concerned with personalities and drama to do justice to *historical* processes and phenomena (Parenti 1992: 58). In some critical responses to Branagh's *Henry V*, this emphasis on an accurate representation of history was sometimes taken to absurd extremes. As we have seen, Curtis Breight expressed disdain for the film's lack of engagement with questions of Elizabethan militarism which he took to be central to Shakespeare's play (Breight 1991), while Ian Aitken argued that the film was disingenuous in its representation of medieval feudalism (Aitken 1991). These arguments disregard the populist criteria which Branagh had set himself, and also forget that Shakespeare himself showed little sense of reverence when it came to adapting his historical sources.

A clutch of non-academic writers went beyond mere allusion to history and the historical realities and significance of Henry's French campaigns, to describe *Henry V* actually as a historical film. Thus, *Film Monthly*'s reviewer described it as a 'historical saga', and opined that: '[h]istory, so long seen as the starched and exclusive province of culture-hogs, is coming clean out of the closet' (Riley 1989). *Empire* magazine, anticipating resistance from its young, mainstream readership, warned: 'Because it is Shakespeare and HISTORICAL [*sic*] it is clearly not every-one's cup of tea' (Errigo 1990). The same typology occurs in several alternative discursive contexts, encompassing such materials as the schools' pack assembled for the film by Film Education, a body funded by the British film industry to foster understanding and love of film. Alongside tasks and projects addressing questions of adaptation and character, the pack incorporated a section entitled 'The Genre of History', which suggested that students consider: 'When we watch the film of *Henry V*, how far does it relate to our ideas of what an historical film should be like? How has the director used our expectations of "history"?' (Film Education, 1989: 3).

There is insufficient space in this essay to consider *Henry V* in relation to all the characteristics of historical film enumerated in our introduction, so we have chosen to focus on three of the most important: a concern with the nation and national identity; a pronounced interest in royalty and government; and a mythic-ritual propensity to explore questions of duty and sacrifice. To borrow terms from Rick Altman (Altman 1987), these can be understood as 'syntactic' features of the historical film genre – that is, as themes, relationships and structures lying at the heart of the genre, and ordering its 'semantic' components. The semantic elements of a genre are not invariably genre-specific, and include, in the case of the historical film, particular stars and methods of presenting 'authentic' images of the past.

The nation and nationality have been widely understood as motifs fundamental to Shakespeare's play. But it was the context of national emergency in which Olivier's film of *Henry V* had been produced which created a heightened sensitivity to the patriotism of Branagh's version in 1989. Olivier recalled the inspiration behind his *Henry V* in distinctly patriotic terms, and the text is studded with images that appear likely to have had national and patriotic resonance for wartime audi-ences. His slow pans across a vibrant, Technicolor panorama of London, which bookend his film, and which form a stark contrast to the black-and-white, battle-scarred images of the capital familiar from newsreels, are a good example of this. We have seen that Branagh was keen to establish an anti-war frame of interpreta-tion for his *Henry V*, but the resulting film does not obscure the residual glamour of Shakespeare's text. Branagh's images may be uncompromising on the question of the suffering and loss engendered by war, but words and sounds seem to sug-gest or betray a different set of values. Henry's St Crispin's Day rhetoric is real-ised with full-bodied passion, and the soaring orchestral strains of Patrick Doyle's

Figure 11.1 'The loneliness and self-sacrifice entailed by royal duties': Charles, Prince of Wales visits director/star Kenneth Branagh – in costume as Henry – during the filming of *Henry V* (1989).
Source: BFI Stills, Posters and Designs, courtesy of Renaissance Films.

Non Nobis, though they can be viewed as ironic amid so much death, might very easily be interpreted as signifying triumph and divine sanction, as did William Walton's score for Olivier. It is thus possible to sustain an argument that Branagh's *Henry V* is favourably, and even enthusiastically, disposed towards the nation at the same time as it is profoundly sceptical about ideas of conquest and imperialism.

In place of the formality, ceremony and spectacle which have often helped to articulate the political and ideological perspectives of the historical film genre – by stressing the loneliness of the monarch and his/her devotion to duty, and showing the proper attitude to be taken by others towards the monarch as figurehead – Branagh favours a more intimate and prosaic style. He relies heavily on close-ups and deft, revealing reaction shots, and he develops his scenes in low-lit, close-packed interiors. One important effect of this is to intensify the discursive focus on leadership and the King.

Leadership and the issue of the ideal king are key motifs in the play; and it is arguable that Shakespeare's war is more a pretext for an examination of kingship than a subject in its own right. Branagh appeared to subscribe to this view, writing that the play 'seemed less like a historical pageant and more like a highly compli-

cated and ambiguous discourse on the nature of leadership' (Branagh 1989a: 139).
The film repeatedly emphasises the onerous responsibilities of kingship. There is
real menace in the King's initial warning to the prelates to take heed 'How you
awake our sleeping sword of war/. . . For never two such kingdoms did contend/
Without much fall of blood'. Moreover, this question of the King's justification of
and responsibility for bloodshed recurs throughout the film. On the night before
Agincourt, Henry watches over the sleeping bodies of his soldiers, tormented by
doubts. After the battle, when he learns of their victory over the French, he bursts
into tears of relief that 'God fought with us'.

And yet these moments in the film serve more to emphasise the heroic nature
of the King's self-sacrifice than to question his violent ambitions. Similarly, the
execution of Bardolph is described in the shooting script from Henry's point of
view. It is 'a public trial of strength', in which '[t]he cost to the King is enormous'
(Branagh 1989b: 71). In the film itself, Branagh selects long reaction shots of
Henry and includes few images of Bardolph. Thus the King is very much presented as the victim of the incident.

Overall, it seems that Branagh's Henry is eminently recognisable in terms
of the historical genre, as a committed, England-loving, self-sacrificing leader/
monarch. As is again often the case in historical film, Henry is also designated
and sanctioned as the hero by nature. In the stunned aftermath of the battle, we
find Henry with the sound of birdsong and the breeze around him, and it is notable
that he has been mainly outdoors since his first appearance. He thus seems more
vigorous and natural than the closeted King Charles (Paul Scofield).

A further interpretative context which seems likely to have impacted on contemporary readings of Branagh's film is the director's relationship with Prince
Charles. The Prince of Wales visited the *Henry V* set during filming. Some years
before, Branagh had also sought his advice when preparing for his performance as
Henry V for the Royal Shakespeare Company at Stratford. This initial contact later
led to the Prince becoming patron of Branagh's Renaissance Theatre Company,
which spawned the film (Branagh 1989a: 217). At their first meeting, in response
to Branagh's questions about the nature of royalty, he had been told by the Prince
of the loneliness and self-sacrifice entailed by royal duties (Branagh 1989a: 141–
4).

Moreover, at the time of the film's release, both in cinemas and on video, the
key themes of leadership and royalty, nationality and national heritage were lent
added prominence by the Prince of Wales's campaign for better English with
particular reference to Shakespeare, and by the British press's propensity for casting him as a battling Henry V. The *Independent*, for example, imagined him as a
Shakespearean monarch under the banner: 'Prince takes arms against bad English'
(Berwick 1989). Overall, in the absence of any overtly patriotic posturing, it is
through its sympathetic, positive and passionate portrayal of the royal figurehead,
and through such related extra-textual discourses as those pertaining to the Prince

of Wales, that Branagh's film seems to promote the idea of nation at the same time that it expresses reservations about jingoism and the notion of a national crusade.

That Branagh's *Henry V* has not frequently been identified in the discourses surrounding it as part of the historical film genre, despite exhibiting some of the genre's key traits and perspectives, is instructive in helping to establish where the boundaries of the historical film genre lay in the 1980s. The genre maintained a coherent enough identity for the label 'historical film' to be restricted in its application to films such as *Lady Jane* (Trevor Nunn, 1986), and – retrospectively, in the film and video guides that began to proliferate in the UK publishing market in the 1980s – to films including *Sixty Glorious Years* (Herbert Wilcox, 1938), *A Man For All Seasons* and *Alfred the Great* (Clive Donner, 1969). As in previous decades, the biopic (*Dance with A Stranger* [Mike Newell, 1985] and *My Left Foot* [Jim Sheridan, 1989]), and the costume drama (such as Michael Winner's 1983 remake of *The Wicked Lady*) were held by contemporary reviewers, interviewers and filmmaking interviewees to exist beyond the boundaries of the historical film. They were located alongside the heritage film, a new addition to the genre map.

Henry V lacks some elements characteristic of the historical film genre, including title cards and source quotations, a commitment to the notion of 'historical authenticity', and a detailed material re-creation of the historical setting. This was apparently enough to create doubt among both popular and academic commentators as to its membership of the historical film genre. In place of certainty about its historicality, we have seen that critics observed and construed other generic associations, with the film's much-written-about associations with Shakespeare and Olivier, and the multivalency of Kenneth Branagh's image, making for an especially complex interpretative landscape.

Henry V and its reception thus help to confirm that the term 'historical film', in British film culture, is a specific rather than general one, referring to a particular genre of film. Despite its frequent use as such by academic critics, it is not an umbrella term equally applicable to all films set in the near or distant past (see, for example, Landy 1991, Harper 1994 and Cook 1996). Secondly, our case study suggests how a film set in the past might have appeared to its original viewers to defy easy association with an established generic category, instead seeming to incorporate elements from a range of different genres, including the Shakespearean and the historical. Hence Branagh's *Henry V* also serves as a warning to critics of the problems entailed in applying a generic frame of interpretation on an unhistoricised, commonsense basis. It is difficult to access the opinions and preconceptions of film audiences on these matters, and academics often have enforced recourse to contemporary critics, whose views can be claimed to have some reflective or agenda-setting significance. But as a general principle, we would argue that textual readings – such as the ones we have tried to supply of *Henry V* as a Shakespeare, heritage and historical film – are only persuasive if allied to equivalent analyses of real readers, their recorded responses, and the historical circum-stances in which they encountered the film in question.

Notes

1 Our analysis of the historical film genre in this chapter is derived from James Quinn's PhD thesis, 'The British historical film, 1930–1990', Sheffield Hallam University, 2000 (as yet unpublished).
2 *King Lear* was first published in a version entitled *The Chronicle Historie of King Lear* and derived from the reign of King Leir as described in Holinshed's *Chronicles*.
3 Russell Jackson uses these examples to illustrate the ways in which Shakespeare's his-tory plays are adapted for the screen but he does not identify them as conventions of historical film (Jackson 2000: 28).
4 See, for example, Peter Brook's insistence that Akira Kurosawa's *Throne of Blood* is not a Shakespeare film, quoted in Reeves 1974.
5 It is notable that when Branagh applied the same principle in his 1997 film of *Hamlet*, a 'full-text' version which conflated two texts now thought to have their own individual integrity, the critical response was considerably less enthusiastic (see Murphy 2000: 11–13).
6 Sinyard cites Branagh's *Hamlet* (1997) as an example of the first category but makes no mention of his *Henry V*. To this list (though fitting none of the categories neatly) we might also add Branagh's *Love's Labour's Lost* (1999), a text-light filming of the play as a spectacular and escapist 1930s musical.
7 *Editors' note:* We argue elsewhere in this volume that the term 'heritage film' is applied by Higson and others to a set of films which cross a *range* of period genres. It follows from this that the 'heritage film' is not a genre *per se*, although it is often treated as one, in part for the sake of convenience (see, for example, Higson 1996: 234–5).
8 The term 'post-heritage' was first proposed by Claire Monk with reference to the films *Orlando* (Sally Potter, 1992) and *Carrington* (Christopher Hampton, 1995) (Monk 1995/ 2001). For a more extended discussion of 1990s transformations in heritage cinema, see Church Gibson 2000.

Bibliography

Note: Page numbers were not available for articles and reviews accessed via library micro-fiche archives.
Aitken, I. (1991) 'Formalism and realism: *Henry V*', *Critical Survey* 3, 3: 260–8.
Altman, R. (1987) *The American Film Musical*, Bloomington, IN: Indiana University Press.
Béja, M. (1976) *Film and Literature*, New York: Longman.
Berwick, S. (1989) 'Prince takes arms against bad English', *Independent*, 20 December 1989.
Branagh, K. (1989a) *Beginning*, London: Chatto and Windus.
—— (1989b) *Henry V: A Screenplay*, London: Chatto and Windus.
Breight, C. (1991) 'Branagh and the Prince, or a "royal fellowship of death"', in *Critical Quarterly* 33, 4: 95–111.
Bristol, M. D. (1996) *Big-Time Shakespeare*, London and New York: Routledge.

Brown, G. (1989) 'Larry's game is beyond our Ken', *The Times*, 2 October 1989.

Church Gibson, P. (2000) 'Fewer weddings and more funerals: changes in the heritage film', in R. Murphy (ed.), *British Cinema of the 90s*, London: BFI: 115–24.

Collick, J. (1989) *Shakespeare, Cinema, and Society*, Manchester: Manchester University Press.

Cook, P. (1996) *Fashioning the Nation: Costume and Identity in British Cinema*, London: BFI.

Craig, C. (1991) 'Rooms without a view', *Sight and Sound*, June 1991: 10–13.

Danson, L. (2000) *Shakespeare's Dramatic Genres*, Oxford: Oxford University Press.

Donaldson, P. S. (1991) 'Taking on Shakespeare: Kenneth Branagh's *Henry V*', *Shakespeare Quarterly*, 42: 60–71.

Errigo, A. (1990) *Henry V* [review], *Empire*, August 1990: 76.

Film Education (1989) *Henry V Study Guide*, London: Film Education (a copy is held in the BFI Library's Special Collection on *Henry V*).

French, P. (1989) *Henry V* [review], *Observer*, 8 October 1989: 42.

Giddings, R., Selby, K. and Wensley, G. (1990) *Screening the Novel: The Theory and Practice of Literary Dramatization*, London: Macmillan.

Harper, S. (1994) *Picturing the Past: The Rise and Fall of the British Costume Film*, London: BFI.

Higson, A. (1996) 'The heritage film and British cinema', in A. Higson (ed.) *Dissolving Views: Key Writings on British Cinema*, London: Cassell: 232–48.

Jackson, R. (2000) 'From play-script to screenplay', in R. Jackson (ed.), *The Cambridge Companion to Shakespeare on Film*, Cambridge: Cambridge University Press: 15–34.

Jorgens, J. (1977) *Shakespeare on Film*, Lanham, MD: University Press of America.

Keyishian, H. (2000) 'Shakespeare and movie genre: the case of *Hamlet*' in R. Jackson (ed.): 72–81.

Landy, M. (1991) *British Genres*, Princeton, NJ: Princeton University Press.

Lane, A. (1989) 'Insubstantial pageants', *Independent*, 30 September 1989.

Lewis, P. (1989) 'Hal and high water', *Sunday Telegraph Magazine*, 24 September 1989: 12–15.

McLeod, P. (1989) *Henry V* [review], *Daily Mirror*, 6 October 1989: 26.

Miller, J. (1986) *Subsequent Performances*, London: Faber and Faber.

Monk, C. (1995) 'Sexuality and the heritage', *Sight and Sound*, October 1995: 32–4. Reprinted in G. Vincendeau (ed.) (2001) *Film/Literature/Heritage: A Sight and Sound Reader*, London: BFI.

Murphy, A. (2000) 'The book on the screen: Shakespeare films and textual culture' in Thornton Burnett and Wray (eds): 10–25.

Parenti, M. (1992) *Make-Believe Media: The Politics of Entertainment*, New York: St Martin's Press.

Reeves, G. (1974) 'Finding Shakespeare on film: from an interview with Peter Brook' in G. Mast and M. Cohen (eds), *Film Theory and Criticism*, Oxford: Oxford University Press: 316–21.

Renaissance Films plc (1989): *Henry V* Production Notes, London: Renaissance Films.

Riley, W. (1989) *Henry V* [review], *Film Monthly*, October 1989.

Rothwell, K. S. (1990) 'Kenneth Branagh's *Henry V*: The gilt [guilt] in the crown re-examined', *Comparative Drama* 24, 2: 173, 177.

Sinyard, N. (2000) 'Shakespeare meets *The Godfather*: The postmodern populism of Al Pacino's *Looking for Richard*', in Thornton Burnett and Wray (eds): 58–72.

Thornton Burnett, M. and Wray, R. (eds) (2000) *Shakespeare, Film, Fin de Siècle*, London: Macmillan.

12 The British heritage-film debate revisited

Claire Monk

Introduction

Writing at the start of the twenty-first century, it can be stated uncontroversially that films and television dramatisations set in the past form an established, enduringly popular and reliably exportable strand of British moving-image culture. Indeed, period films and television dramas have come to be perceived by many – in the unavoidably globalised image market as much as in Britain itself – as *particularly* 'British', as *particularly* characteristic of British cinema and television.

The history of British period films and television dramas can of course legitimately be described in terms of cyclical trends, common characteristics and repetitions. However, it is also true that the many sub-categories implied by the shorthand 'British period screen fictions' are both extremely diverse and inclined to overlap and blur in ways which make a mockery of neat categorisation or reductive critical discussion. These sub-categories include feature films and television dramas; literary adaptations from contemporary novels or plays set in the past, and from older novels and plays with once-contemporary settings, including those that have accrued the status of 'classics'; productions based more or less loosely on 'real' historical figures or events, well-known or not; productions which claim authenticity to 'fact' or the source text and those which foreground imaginative licence; productions which reconstruct a distant past and those set within living memory. Nor do these subdivisions equate neatly with discrete *genres*: a whole range of recognised film genres and – more significantly – genre mixes may be found within each. Thus a costume film, literary adaptation or narrative derived from 'real' history may also be a melodrama, romance, comedy, satire, picaresque, fantasy, crime film, action adventure, political thriller, colonial epic, war film, horror or vampire film – or a mixture of more than one of these.

More than this, in the context of British cinema's subordination to Hollywood, the 'Britishness' or 'Englishness' of such films is never, nor has ever been, a straightforward matter. Historically and in the present, a contradictory situation has prevailed. The desire for cultural self-affirmation and the dream of a viable

British 'national' cinema ensure that the production and reproduction of British period films take place under the signs of national product differentiation, export-ability, and the projection of 'national' identity. Yet 'British' period film successes are repeatedly made by non-British personnel with non-British money, and meas-ured in terms of their reception and commercial performance abroad. Indeed, a case could be made that they have *characteristically* been products of international funding, migrancy or collaboration, in a lineage encompassing the Hungarian Alexander Korda's 1930s and 1940s productions at Denham; the European in-fluences at work at Gainsborough Studios in the 1940s (see Cook 1996: 80–115); the decades of BBC-TV costume dramas co-funded by US public-service television and re-broadcast transatlantically as *Masterpiece Theatre*; the 'English' literary adap-tations of the highly international self-styled 'wandering company' Merchant Ivory Productions; and the list of 1990s 'British' period film hits backed by Miramax and other US studios.

The points made above may seem obvious. My purpose in restating them here is to emphasise the field of 'British screen fictions set in the past' as a complex, hybrid and contradictory terrain, historically and in the present. It therefore de-mands a critical approach, or approaches, which acknowledge and engage with these complexities, hybridities and contradictions. In Britain since the late 1980s/early 1990s, however, academic discussion of recent cinematic representations of the past has been largely dominated by a debate which has tended to do the opposite: the debate around so-called 'heritage films' or 'heritage cinema'. In this debate, a perceived cycle of recent British (or 'British'?) films set in the past which critics attentive to differences of genre, theme and audience appeal might find disparate in many of the respects sketched above became the objects of a critical discourse which treated them as a unified entity – indeed, a genre – about which generalised claims could be made and to which a monolithic critique could be applied.

The idea, and critique, of heritage cinema first emerged in Britain in the late 1980s to early 1990s as a deferred response from the academic/intellectual left to certain British period films produced or released since the early 1980s – at the height of Thatcherite Conservatism – and argued to be ideologically complicit with it. The initial coinage and use of the term 'heritage film' – and contemporary synonyms for the same group of films, such as 'white-flannel films' – were openly pejorative and dismissive. 'Heritage films' were identified as a putative grouping in order that they might be collectively denounced, *a priori* of any more disinter-ested investigation, as 'all too familiar' (to borrow a phrase from Dyer and Vincendeau 1995); the 'far from imaginary work' of 'directors who know perhaps too well their audiences' expectations', in the words of one of their most hostile critics, Cairns Craig (1991: 10).

The academic most consistently cited in connection with the heritage-film debate is Andrew Higson, and the critique of heritage cinema with reference to the 1980s and 1990s is most fully developed in his work (primarily 1993 and 1996). However, the contours of heritage-film criticism cannot accurately be credited to a single author. Essentially similar arguments had already been presented in academic articles by Tana Wollen (1991) and Cairns Craig (1991); but the anti-heritage-film discourse emerged over a period of years from multiple origins – journalistic first, academic later. The critiques which preceded Higson's used terms other than 'heritage cinema' (Wollen, for instance, writes of 'nostalgic screen fictions', including *Brideshead Revisited* [Charles Sturridge, 1981] and *The Jewel in the Crown* [Christopher Morahan/Jim O'Brien, 1984] on British television), but all spoke with a strikingly similar voice. Heritage-film criticism, then, needs to be understood as a historically specific discourse, rooted in and responsive to particular cultural conditions and events. This is a crucial point I shall return to, for it is central to my argument in this chapter.

The films named as heritage films were typically set in an English, southern, middle- or upper-class past. They were usually period fictions rather than 'historical' films, and were frequently adapted from 'classic' literary sources, but typically ones which were popular and widely known. In terms of aesthetics, audience address and industrial status, heritage films were said to 'operate primarily as middle-class quality products', made and circulated with an 'emphasis on authorship, craft and artistic value' and typically 'valued for their cultural significance rather than their box-office takings' (Higson 1996: 232–3). The use of the term 'quality' here is negative. For heritage-film critics, the films were aesthetically conservative; uncinematic in that they favoured a static pictorialism rather than making the fullest use of the *moving* image; and their claims to 'quality' rested on a second-hand affiliation with 'high' literary and theatrical culture which flattered audiences while appealing to cultural snobberies. The films were identified with a particular aesthetic approach to the visualisation of the past: 'a museum look: apparently meticulous period accuracy, but clean, beautifully lit, and clearly on display' (Dyer and Vincendeau 1995). In relation both to this and to their literary sources, they were said to adopt a particular position in relation to the 'already canonic cultural properties adapted for the screen', summarised by Andrew Higson as a discourse of authenticity: 'the desire to establish the adaptation . . . as an authentic reproduction of the original' (Higson 1995: 26).

Early-1990s critics typically defined the field of heritage cinema as a distinct area of study by offering a *list* of disapproved 'heritage films'. This was usually followed by a shorter list of counter-example approved films, which were either 'set firmly in the present [in a] postimperialist and/or working-class Britain' (Higson 1993: 110) and perceived as realist, socially critical and/or politically engaged; or were held to engage more authentically or critically with 'historical reality', usually because they were set in a regional or working-class past. Thus the heritage film was defined negatively, and in binary terms.

The exact list of heritage films varied from critic to critic, but certain core films recurred consistently: *Chariots of Fire* (Hugh Hudson, 1981; original script by Colin Welland), *Another Country* (Marek Kanievska, 1984, adapted from Julian Mitchell's 1981 play), *A Passage to India* (David Lean, 1984, adapted from E. M. Forster's 1924 novel), and *Brideshead Revisited* director Charles Sturridge's *A Handful of Dust* (1988) and *Where Angels Fear to Tread* (1991), adapted from novels by Evelyn Waugh (1934) and Forster (1905) respectively. However, the core exemplars of heritage filmmaking were held to be the three adaptations from Forster's novels made by the producer-director team Ismail Merchant and James Ivory (Indian Muslim and Californian respectively), usually with their long-term screenwriting collaborator Ruth Prawer Jhabvala (of German and Polish Jewish parentage via Hendon, North London, and married to an Indian): *A Room with a View* (1985; novel 1908), *Maurice* (1987; novel published posthumously 1971)[1] and *Howards End* (1992; novel 1910).

The most-mentioned counter-example film set in the present was the multi-cultural hit comedy *My Beautiful Laundrette* (Stephen Frears, 1985). However, the period counter-examples cited were inconsistent to such an extent that some films – notably *Hope and Glory* (John Boorman, 1987), *Dance with a Stranger* (Mike Newell, 1985) and *Scandal* (Michael Caton-Jones, 1989) – have been declared heritage films by some critics and praised as non-heritage films by others.[2] This is perhaps the most obvious symptom of radical unclarity about what a heritage film is.

Notwithstanding their frequently international origins, heritage films were conceived as a 'genre' *centrally* engaged in the construction of *national* identity. The key charges directed against the films were as follows. First, they were said to project and promote a bourgeois or upper-class vision and version of 'the national past' which was organised around a narrow 'Englishness' rather than any notion of hybridity or regional diversity, and was both 'apparently more settled' and 'essentially pastoral' (Higson 1993: 110). Second, they were said to be 'fascinated by the private property, the culture and values of a particular class'[3] and this fascination was said to perform the ideological function of 'transform[ing] the heritage of the upper classes into the national heritage' (Higson 1993: 114). Third, as signalled by the reference to 'private property', the films were accused of reproducing only the seductive surface 'trappings' of the (bourgeois) past 'outside of a materialist historical context' (Higson 1993: 114). They were 'film as conspicuous consumption . . . [indulging] us in a perfection of style designed to deny everything beyond the self-contained world the characters inhabit' (Craig 1991: 10). The underpinning argument here, very clearly derived from mid-1980s critiques of the heritage industry (centrally, Patrick Wright 1985 and Robert Hewison 1987) was that, in rendering the past as 'an attractively packaged consumer item' (Hewison 1987: 144), the films promoted a false notion of historical reality.

As can be seen from the preceding quotations, the critique of heritage cinema depended on an insistent coupling – even conflation – of aesthetic and ideological claims. This coupling becomes explicit in the crowning charge directed at the films. The manner in which they visualise the past was said to '[invite] a nostalgic gaze that resists the ironies and social critiques so often suggested narratively' (Higson 1993: 109). In a later reformulation, it was suggested that the spectacular pleasures of the heritage film did not just produce a passive and uncritical viewing position but were intrin-sically ideological: 'one of the central pleasures of the heritage film' was stated to be 'the artful and spectacular projection of an elite, conservative vision of the national past' (Higson 1996: 233).

The construction of the idea of the 'heritage film' is interesting for its entangle-ment of political criticisms with a gut-level cultural–aesthetic aversion to the films on the part of many critics, which in turn has legitimised a wider cultural cringe around the films and, by implication, their audiences. Branded as middle-brow cultural products, heritage films have been disparagingly associated – rightly or wrongly – with middle-class, middlebrow, middle-aged and largely female audiences (see Monk 1999a). Precisely because of their 'quality', the hierarchies of film/critical culture have assigned them very low status as cinema. This gut distaste has lent an edge of hysteria and irrationality to some anti-heritage crit-icism. This can be seen in Craig's shuddering disgust at the films' excesses of bourgeois finery (1991: 10–11) – condemned by the literary scholar Alison Light as puritanical, killjoy and inaccurate (Light 1991: 63) – and in the *Sight and Sound* editorial accompanying Craig's article which, absurdly, accused the international Merchant–Ivory team of Anglocentric 'blind[ness] to the particularity of other cultures' (Dodd 1991: 3).

Equally, if we consider the films recurrently named as heritage films, it seems justifiable to conclude that the 'genre' has been defined by its consistent export – and especially North American – success with critics and (usually, 'discerning', niche) audiences as much as by any consistent ideological or aesthetic traits. The critical framing of heritage films as cultural *rather than* commercial products has always been questionable, and has been wholly invalidated by the wider commer-cialisation of British film culture since the 1990s, in which (US-backed) 'British' period hits from *Sense and Sensibility* (Ang Lee, USA/UK, 1996) to *Shakespeare in Love* (John Madden, USA, 1999) have played a central role. British period films of the past two decades which have not proved exportable – nor involved personnel associated with past successes – have tended not to be identified as heritage films or subjected to the attendant criticisms. Conversely, international success – typi-cally constructed as 'surprise' success, thus differentiating it from Hollywood big-marketing-spend successes, and accompanied by displays of national(ist) self-congratulation in the British media – has tended to trigger the application of the 'heritage' label in the face of clear aesthetic, thematic and ideological distinctions between films.

This can be illustrated amply with reference to the two 1980s films most frequently cited as central, undisputed examples of British heritage filmmaking, *Chariots of Fire* and *A Room with a View*. Both achieved high-profile critical acclaim and box-office success in the United States and multiple Academy Award victories. Both were therefore declared to belong to the same (heritage) genre. Yet the two films exhibit blatant differences of theme, readable ideological orientation or 'message', genre, audience appeal, and even aesthetics. *Chariots of Fire*, the film credited with kick-starting the 1980s British film 'renaissance' and 'grant[ing] British directors the confidence to confront English subjects' (Quart 1993: 26) was a boys'-own (and, in casting terms, virtually boys-only) fable which excavated Britain's 'forgotten' triumph in the 1924 Olympics with the primary effect of arousing indiscriminate national emotion in its international audience. By contrast, *A Room with a View* was a romance-cum-social comedy set among – and affectionately sending up – the Edwardian southern English middle classes. Unlike *Chariots of Fire*, its mix of romance, melodrama, visual pleasure and the encoded expression of sexuality marked it as a species of costume film, suggesting a particular appeal to female – and certainly 'non-masculine' – audiences (see Monk 1994 and 1995).

The commercialisation of British film culture since the mid-1990s, the increasing integration of British film production into the global entertainment industry, and related changes in British period films – calculated to realign perceptions of them and attract expanded and diversified audiences – have brought a curious reversal of critical attitudes to British period cinema. So too has the landslide election of Tony Blair's New Labour government in 1997 and the accordant shift in policies and ideologies surrounding cultural production and the projection of the nation. In 'New Britain', criticising commercial success has become bad form, and the dominant mood is one in which British film successes with period and contemporary settings alike are celebrated uncritically by almost everyone – regardless of whether or not critical scepticism or political criticism might, in fact, be richly deserved. Contrary to Cairns Craig's warning that 'it may be that the genre was viable only in the decade we have just left' (Craig 1991: 10), 'quality' period films exploiting British narratives, subjects and settings have continued to secure commercial and critical success in the global market, from *The Madness of King George* (Nicholas Hytner, 1995) to *Mrs Brown* (John Madden, UK/USA/Ireland, 1997), from *Sense and Sensibility* to *Shakespeare in Love* and the more innovative *Elizabeth* (Shekhar Kapur, 1998). In the age of vertically integrated multinational entertainment corporations, each of these 'British' successes has, of course been founded on US studio co-funding, big-distributor backing and/or international casting. But just as crucially, this continuing success has been achieved through conscious evolution rather than stasis. The subjects, favoured literary sources and even aesthetics and target markets – and marketing – of such films have shifted and diversified considerably since the 1980s in a self-conscious trend

I have termed 'post-heritage' cinema (Monk 1995). Indeed, 1980s Britain itself is now part of the 'past' available for cinematic plundering.

Amid these substantial changes, however, the term 'heritage film' continues to be applied and disseminated ever more widely. Heritage-film criticism has become as effective a commodity in the academy as heritage films have been in the cinema. One index of this academic institutionalisation is that the core claims of the early-1990s heritage debate are reproduced – in inevitably simplified form – in at least one introductory Film Studies textbook (Cooke in Nelmes [ed.] 1999: 368–9). Some of this expanded work has argued that at least some heritage films offer rather different pleasures, and are open to a wider range of valid readings, than those suggested by their detractors (Finch and Kwietniowski 1988; Dyer 1994; Monk 1994 and 1995). There have also been moves to reclaim the term heritage cinema for neutral rather than negative use and to reconceptualise it as a European rather than specific British phenomenon (Dyer 1995; Dyer and Vincendeau 1995), in both cases producing some clarification of definitional issues.

But, simultaneously, there has been a trend for recent discussions to claim an increasingly heterogeneous range of films as 'heritage films' while dodging awkward questions of definition – thereby extending the scholarly shelf-life of the term and ensuring a future for heritage-film criticism (and critics). Thus *Elizabeth* – a film whose style-consciousness, genre hybridity, appeals to multiple audiences and delight in historical anachronism epitomise all that has changed in British cinema since the 1980s – was welcomed in 2000 by an entire conference panel on the film as a sign of radical *changes in* the heritage film rather than the evolution of new forms of British period cinema.[4] Even the record-breakingly expensive, big-spectacle Hollywood blockbuster *Titanic* (James Cameron, USA, 1997) has been christened a 'heritage film'.[5] Those encountering such recent discussions might conclude that *all* recent period films – British and beyond – are 'heritage films'. Meanwhile Andrew Higson has sought to demonstrate (through a case study of Cecil Hepworth's 1923 filming of the popular Victorian novel *Comin' Through the Rye*) that the films have a historical lineage in British cinema which can be traced back to the 1910s (Higson 1995: 26–30). Though he stresses the historical specificity of *Comin' Through the Rye*'s particular strategies, a claim is clearly being staked that heritage films have a permanence within Britain's national film culture rather than being a historically distinct phenomenon.

The establishment of the idea of the heritage film as a key critical term, and its increasingly broad usage, give the impression that the heritage film is a clearly defined, agreed and workable category: that identifying a heritage film and establishing how it differs from 'non-heritage' films set in the past are relatively unproblematic matters. In this chapter I argue the contrary: that problems exist and persist around the definition of the heritage film and the methodology and claims of the heritage-film critique, despite its tendency to proceed as if they did not. These problems derive from the origins and nature of the heritage film as a critical construct, and have ramifications for its coherence and usefulness as a film category.

In particular, I will explore how the origins of the heritage-film idea and critique as a response to the specific cultural-political circumstances of the 1980s produce limitations. I will also suggest that the considerably changed industrial, cultural and political conditions within which all British films – not only period films – are produced and circulated since the mid-1990s raise new problems requiring new responses. In such a context, the insistence on interpreting an overly diverse range of period films under the heritage umbrella – or *exclusively* within a heritage framework – limits the debate and stymies new insights. Ultimately, I take the view that 'heritage cinema' is most usefully understood as a critical construct rather than as a description of any concrete film cycle or genre.

Problems of methodology and interpretation

Andrew Higson notes that heritage cinema 'seems to have become part of the common sense of film culture' (1996: 232). It has achieved this status, however, through empirical usage rather than rigorous theoretical definition. The heritage-film idea and the wider debate that emerged around it from the early 1990s were founded on three methodological problems. The first was the monolithic nature of the critique and its tendency to trample over significant differences between films at the textual level. This resulted in blanket claims being made about heritage films which are problematic enough when considered carefully in relation to the best-known 1980s heritage films (such as *Chariots of Fire* versus *A Room with a View*) and become still less credible with reference to today's liberally expanded heritage-film field.

Second, the derogatory coinage of the term 'heritage film', and the definition of the films in terms of ideological and aesthetic shortcomings, were symptomatic of the fact that heritage cinema was fundamentally defined from – and by – a top-down reading perspective which distanced itself from the films and their audiences. A related characteristic was that the heritage-film critique addressed a reader presumed to be already in agreement with it, and so constituted the reader as a member of a community of critics and intellectuals self-defined by their distaste for the films. This produced a lack of rigour in the debate, since preaching to the converted requires a less persuasive quality of evidence than convincing the unconvinced. Both problems undermine the credibility of treating heritage films as a genre, since it is a genre defined by those who define themselves by their distance from consumption or production of the films.

Third, and connected with this, the heritage-film critique depended on unspoken and unsubstantiated conjecture regarding the political-cultural orientation of the films' audiences and their reception of the films. Ironically, the critique has claimed to offer insights into 'how [the films'] representation [of the national past] works for contemporary spectators' (Higson 1993: 109); but in doing so it has relied centrally on textual evidence. One attempt to respond to this problem by '[taking] reception into account' can be found in Higson 1996 (242–4). But here, the media discourses cited as evidence are, again, produced from a top-down/ professional position, and it is neither a surprise, nor especially illuminating, that they reproduce and affirm the dominant discursive framing of the films already established by heritage-film critics. In short, the 'audience' posited in the heritage-film critique, like the spectator of early-1970s film theory, is nothing more than a product of the (supposed) textual operations of the heritage-film 'apparatus'. And through its undifferentiated and distanced conception of the films themselves, the heritage-film critique constructs this audience as an undifferentiated mass – and as 'other' than the heritage-film critic in their politics, tastes and responses to the films.

These are sufficiently obvious flaws that it is necessary to consider how heritage-film criticism was able to fall so easily into them. One answer of course concerns the practical and methodological difficulties involved in conducting research into, and interpreting data on, the responses of 'real' audiences. A second concerns the differences between the disciplinary histories and founding concerns of film studies and cultural studies, and the closer affinity of the heritage debate with the former (which has traditionally concerned itself with the workings of texts and left the study of 'real' audiences well alone) than the latter.

A third factor is that the burgeoning body of work produced on British cinema since the 1980s – of which the heritage-film discussion is part – has inherited from established British film-critical culture a notably binaristic and reductive evaluative framework. This framework has been in place since (at least) the emergence of the 'quality film' consensus among 1940s critics (see Ellis 1996). While the 'new' British cinema studies has devoted itself to reappraising British cinema and 'rediscovering' its forgotten or undervalued facets, the typical *modus operandi* has been to invert the established binary oppositions rather than breaking free of them. Thus where the 1940s critics insisted that 'quality', 'realism' and 'restraint' were the essential values of British cinema, recent work has rediscovered and celebrated British films, directors, cycles and genres seen to embody values of fantasy, surrealism, eroticism and/or excess. As Alan Lovell and, following him, David Sutton have pointed out, this new orthodoxy has the effect of reactively devaluing films and genres deemed to embody 'realism' or 'restraint' (Lovell 1997: 238–40). Meanwhile areas of British cinema displaying 'recalcitrance and awkwardness' in relation to this simplified model continue to be marginalised (Sutton 2000: 20–1). Thus the reactive binarisms of the heritage-film critique place it firmly within British cinema studies norms. The critical aversion to heritage films has often seemed to align itself with the backlash against middle-class 'quality' and 'restraint'. However, the contradictory discourse around the films – which carica-

Figure 12.1 National triumphalism and success through competition: members of the 1924 British Olympic team hold aloft the victorious Eric Liddell (Ian Charleson) in *Chariots of Fire* (1981) – one of the few 'heritage films' of the 1980s to articulate unambiguously an ideological ethos with clear Thatcherite affinities.
Source: British Cinema and Television Research Group archive, De Montfort University (TCF/Allied Stars/Enigma).

tures them for their supposed repression and sexlessness while condemning their seductive and ideologically pernicious spectacular excesses – suggests that their dismissal has as much to do with their troublesome resistance to such imposed binarisms.

A further trait of British film-critical culture noted by Lovell is the 'persistent linking of British film production with the question of national identity', a preoccupation he characterises as 'odd' (Lovell 1997: 241). The same can be observed of heritage-film criticism's over-privileging of 'the national', which colours virtually every claim made about the films' characteristics and effects – including, crucially, their pleasures – despite the films' hybrid creative origins and international address. Thus two of the central strategies of heritage films are named as 'the reproduction of literary texts, artefacts and landscapes *which already have a privileged status within the accepted definition of the national heritage*' and 'the reconstruction of a historical moment *which is assumed to be of national significance*' (Higson

Figure 12.2 The pleasures of female looking: teenage tourist Lucy Honeychurch (Helena
        Bonham Carter) borrows binoculars from the 'lady novelist' Miss Lavish (Judi
        Dench) during a sightseeing carriage ride in Italy in *A Room with a View* (1985).
        But the object of Lucy's gaze is the handsome driver kissing his 'sister', not
        the scenery.
Source: BFI Stills, Posters and Designs, courtesy of Merchant Ivory Productions.

1995: 27; my italics). As Lovell notes, 'that such a link exists is, at one level, a
truism', but he questions why writing on British cinema should so routinely '[take]
for granted both that the link exists and that it is a politically important one'
(Lovell 1997: 241). Attention to specific heritage films suggests that while some
(such as *Chariots of Fire*: see Quart 1993: 25–7) offer themselves plausibly for
interpretation in the light of specific 'official', 'national' (i.e. governmental) goals
and ideologies of the nation at the time of their release, others (such as *A Room with
a View*) do not. And, given the heritage films' address of an international audience,
it is not clear why they should function centrally as a vehicle for 'national' messages. This tension between the films' supposed national character and their international address may account for their contradictory construction by British critics
– who, while condemning the films for their conservative 'Englishness', nostalgically construct them as addressing 'the nation' as the cinema of the Second
World War did in 'our finest hour'.

Historicising the heritage-film idea

To contextualise the heritage-film debate, it is necessary to return to its origins, and to re-connect it with the specific historical, cultural and political climate out of which it evolved. In particular, it is necessary to recall the wider political and cultural battles in Britain since 1979, and the impact of these on the British film culture and criticism of the time. The critique of heritage films that emerged in the early 1990s was in no sense an immediate and spontaneous counter-response to the success of the films concerned. Some of the key films that would be denounced by anti-heritage-film critics – notably *Chariots of Fire* – predated the critique by half a decade or more. Others, notably *A Room with a View*, were received warmly by critics of most political/aesthetic persuasions on their release – including a positive review from the Communist Party newspaper the *Morning Star* (Dignam 1986: 2) – yet became widely excoriated by the early 1990s.[6] Clearly this reversal of reception requires an explanation for which it is necessary to look beyond the films themselves.

The term 'heritage cinema' was originally coined by Charles Barr with reference not to 1980s films but to certain patriotic British films of the 1940s which had drawn upon aspects of the 'national heritage', from *This England* (David MacDonald, 1941) to *Henry V* (Laurence Olivier, 1945) to *A Canterbury Tale* (Michael Powell and Emeric Pressburger, 1944). An important point is that the films identified by Barr were not invariably set in past historical periods; nor, even though some of the films he named were officially-sponsored propaganda – which the 1980s and 1990s heritage films were not – was he concerned to denounce them (Barr 1984: 12). Anti-heritage-film criticism began to emerge journalistically in 1987–8, doubtless in reaction against the media saturation surrounding *A Room with a View*. It was initially confined to publications addressing serious cinephiles such as the *Monthly Film Bulletin* (see, for example, Forbes 1987), cultural and intellectual elites, and/ or the left (particularly the *New Statesman* and the late London listings magazine *City Limits*). Equally, though, some of the first objections to the films emerged from publications associated with the Conservative right, notably the *Spectator* (Ackroyd 1986; Mantel 1987), and from writers aligned with an aristocratic perspective (Hollinghurst 1987; Christiansen 1988). In short, anti-heritage-film criticism was from the outset an elite rather than popular phenomenon, but not an exclusively left-wing one.

It is clear from its timing and content that the emergent critique was heavily inspired by recent and much-publicised books and articles criticising the cultural policy of the Thatcher government (or rather, its repudiation of any such thing) and, specifically, the National Heritage Acts of 1980 and 1983. The Acts set in statute Thatcherism's wider official national promotion of a heritage industry defined by the preservation of the landscapes and private-built properties of the past by means of their commodification and commercial exploitation. (For the main critical writings on this, see Wright 1985 and Hewison 1987. For criticisms of the 'heritage-baiting' position, see Samuel 1994: 259–73.) For Wright and his contemporaries, a national heritage was constructed by installing and maintaining a particular dominant conception of the national past. The activities of the conservation lobby were the central tool of this hegemonic process. Their activities were said to identify with the private property of the upper classes as in the public interest, and thus to secure public acceptance of the values and interests of the propertied classes as national values and the national interest (see Higson 1995: 42). Hewison echoed the same concerns, but also linked the promotion of heritage with the withdrawal of public funding from artistic or cultural activity which sought to engage with or comment on the present.

Despite its explicit focus on the activities of the conservation lobby – and on official support for these at the level of national policy – this critique was applied to 'heritage films' with virtually no translation. This appropriation of an off-the-peg critique already widely circulated and discussed in the 'quality' media explains the heritage-film critique's lack of rigour, since it presumed a reader who was already broadly acquainted with anti-heritage-industry arguments and predisposed to agree with them. However, this strategy neglected to consider differences between the display of the built or landscaped environment for public consumption and the operations of films, in which the 'heritage' *mise-en-scène* is only one element and potential site of pleasure among many, including the pleasures of narrative, character, performance, humour, sexuality, and so on. The undifferentiated equation of the films with the state-promoted heritage industry may also explain the heritage-film critique's odd insistence on portraying 1980s British cinema – hardly the dominant mass medium of the time – as an Althusserian ideological state apparatus 'by which the dominant representations of the past are reproduced and secured' by means of presentation to 'the public gaze' (Higson 1995: 42).

What is perhaps less well remembered today is the extent to which the vicious polarisation and combativeness of 1980s British politics infected the fields of cultural debate and production. By the end of the 1980s, the Thatcher government's friends in the media had emphatically defined both the British political landscape and the field of British cultural production – and hence film – in highly polarised and combative terms. 'The chattering classes' (the middle-class liberal intelligentsia) in general – and public figures in the cultural sphere (such as the novelists Salman Rushdie and Margaret Drabble) who voiced disquiet about government policies – were subjected to co-ordinated attack from the New Right press, as in this sneering example from the Rupert Murdoch-owned *Sunday Times*:

> Many of the leading luminaries of the country's intellectual and cultural establishment can barely contain themselves to words that are printable when it comes to Mrs Thatcher . . . These are the voices of the dispossessed – an

elite brought up to believe it would inherit the earth which has in reality
ended up out in the cold . . . What a shock to discover that in Mrs Thatcher's
Britain hardly anyone in a position of power takes much notice of them.

(Editorial, *Sunday Times*, 24 January 1988)

The aim seemed to be to demoralise and silence anti-Tory opinion among those
sections of the population equipped to articulate it most lucidly. The critic Graham
Fuller noted at around the same time that a 'climate of censorship . . . has been
stifling the basic democratic of thought and information throughout Mrs Thatcher's
current term' (Fuller 1988: 66).

In January 1988, British films became an explicit target of the New Right. The
binaristic simplifications of the heritage-film critique begin to make more sense
if understood as a defensive response to the terms of debate activated by the right
at that moment. Under the headline 'Through a lens darkly', the *Sunday Times*
devoted an entire broadsheet page plus overmatter to an incoherent attack by the
right-wing Oxford historian Norman Stone on six recent low-budget independent
British films. The films attacked by Stone varied greatly in style, audience appeal
and box-office success. They ranged from the crude Comic Strip farce *Eat the Rich*
(Peter Richardson, 1987); via *My Beautiful Laundrette* and its sequel *Sammy and
Rosie Get Laid* (Stephen Frears, 1987); to Derek Jarman's desolate avant-garde
response to current social and political oppressions, *The Last of England* (1987).
What they shared, though, was a firm location in a contemporary, culturally and
sexually diverse and socially divided Britain far away from the corridors of power,
the wealth of the City or the complacent prosperity of the shires. All six were
condemned by Stone as 'worthless and insulting' and 'riddled with left-wing bias':

> They are all very depressing, and are no doubt meant to be. The rain pours
> down; skinheads beat people up; there are race riots; there are drug fixes in
> squalid corners; there is much explicit sex, a surprising amount of it homo-
> sexual and sadistic; greed and violence abound; there is much grim concrete
> and much footage of 'urban decay'; on and off there are voice-overs by Mrs
> Thatcher, Hitler, etc. . . . The done thing is to run down Mrs Thatcher, to
> assume that capitalism is parasitism, that the established order of this country
> is imperialist, racist, profiteering.

(Stone 1988)

The films' crime, then, was to offer representations of contemporary Britain (or,
in Stone's terms, 'sick scenes from English life') which chose to focus on 'the
minority of the British people [who] live in conditions of some wretchedness
[rather than celebrating] a Government which has done so much for individual
liberty socially and economically' (editorial in support of Stone, *Daily Telegraph*,
28 January 1988).

As Fuller noted, Stone's attack 'reeked of provocation' (Fuller 1988: 63). More-over, the prominence it was given by the *Sunday Times* – and the extensive space subsequently devoted by the paper to the inevitable acrimony it generated (from Jarman and *Laundrette/Rosie*'s screenwriter Hanif Kureishi among others) – amply support suspicions that it had been strategically commissioned, and that its true target was somewhat larger than a group of low-budget films. Surprisingly, the films shortly to be vilified as heritage films featured little in Stone's article. In his penultimate paragraph, he briefly praised three recent 'very good films of a tradi-tional kind' which 'show what can be done' (Stone 1988). They were *Hope and Glory*, *A Passage to India* and *A Room with a View*. Those whom Stone had attacked, however, were not slow to link his favoured films with the political agenda his article sought to advance on behalf of the Conservative government.

It can be seen from the Stone episode that the reductive terms of debate which I have complained impoverish critical analysis of heritage films – and the wider terrain of British cinema over the past two decades – were initiated in the 1980s by the New Right, only to be reactively replicated by anti-Thatcherite critics and filmmakers. In comparing heritage films adversely with British films 'set firmly in the present . . . in an unstable and socially divided postimperialist and/or working-class Britain' (Higson 1993: 111), their academic critics were merely reversing the binary oppositions proposed by Stone. In such a climate, the heritage-film critique's dubious leaps of logic – '*by* turning their backs on the industrialised, chaotic present [the films] nostalgically construct an imperialist and upper-class Britain' (Higson 1993: 110; my italics) – and its tacit conflation of all films with contemporary settings, a working-class focus and anti-Conservative politics were unlikely to come under critical scrutiny from within.

These binaristic, conflationary tendencies generated a particularly simplistic politics of representation which is central to the logic of heritage-film criticism despite its nominally more sophisticated concern with iconography and represen-tation. In a climate in which it was necessary to defend films set in the present and featuring working-class protagonists, it became a corollary that all films set in the past and which focused on the comfortable bourgeoisie or upper classes must be politically conservative or 'bad'. In this context, heritage films were declared politically objectionable as much *because* they showed the 'middle and upper classes at home and abroad before they were drowned by the flood of the First World War and the end of Empire' (Craig 1991: 10) as because of *how* they showed them.

Again, this position needs to be understood in relation to the wider British film culture. Historically, British cinema has exhibited a huge middle-class bias – in personnel as much as representation. Consequently, British films and film move-ments seeking to represent the working class have often been valorised reactively in terms of a naïve politics of representation which conflates the act of *showing* the working class with presumed expression of a working-class perspective or a specifically 'working-class' (left-wing) political position. This simplification has become ingrained in British film culture through the interventions of filmmakers themselves as well as critics (see the stated objectives of the Documentary Movement in the 1930s or Free Cinema in the 1950s) and persist today: see much of the review coverage of the recent working-class hits *The Full Monty* (Peter Cattaneo, 1997) and *Billy Elliot* (Stephen Daldry, 2000). This is despite the fact that most British film representations of the working class were, and are, produced by a middle-class elite – and so, whatever their intentions, are clearly not products of working-class self-representation or self-determination – and that neither their political perspective nor their ideological workings can simply be read off from their subject-matter.

My claims may seem strange given that heritage-film criticism appears to place a central importance on aesthetics and representational strategies. However, the critique's interest in these matters is almost entirely displaced into a generalised critique of the heritage aesthetic and heritage iconography, which are then given explanatory primacy in interpretation of the films. By contrast, matters such as patterns of sympathy or identification with (or against) characters; the films' operations within the conventions of popular cinema or industry-recognised genres; or iconography which supports themes and meanings excluded by the 'heritage' discursive framework are ignored. Or rather, they are judged irrelevant, since they belong to the sphere of meanings that the viewer's conservative, consumerist 'nostalgic gaze' – supposedly fascinated by 'country houses . . . crystal decanters . . . all those objects' (Craig 1991: 10–12) rather than human bodies, behaviour or desires – is alleged to override. One example of such 'excluded' areas of meaning is the consistent emphasis throughout *A Room with a View* on the pleasures of female looking – at men, other women, and the burgeoning attraction between them. Such voyeurism is endemic among the film's characters, from the teenage protagonist Lucy (Helena Bonham Carter) to the 'lady novelist' Miss Lavish (Judi Dench) and Lucy's spinster chaperone Charlotte Bartlett (Maggie Smith), and is central to the development of its narrative and themes. Another example is the knowing use of phallic iconography and *double entendres* in *Maurice* to melodramatise gay male desire, which was illegal and therefore literally 'unspeakable' by more overt means in the Edwardian period in which the film is set.[7]

Genre, interpretation and power

In the changed British political and cultural conditions of the early 2000s, somewhat different concerns have supplanted 1980s worries about dominance by a conservative 'heritage culture'. Despite this, heritage-film criticism continues to treat the heritage industry as providing the most valid interpretative framework for studying the films, consigning other approaches to, or perspectives on, the films – such as those I have sketched briefly above – to marginal status (see Higson

1996: 241–4). Such alternative readings, however, begin to seem less marginal if we consider the nature of genres and how they are formed – and the formation of the heritage 'genre' in particular by uneven discursive power relations.

Given the historically specific origins of the heritage-film idea and its resultant points of weakness, a central question is whether heritage films can be said to constitute a valid and coherent genre – and how far this 'genre' has any usefulness outside the circumstances in which it was first defined. Andrew Higson has argued that it is feasible to treat heritage films as a genre or sub-genre (in his view, 'of the historical romance or costume drama' [Higson 1995: 27]), albeit one that 'we should not try to regulate . . . too closely or too loosely' (Higson 1996: 235).

There are, of course, differing theoretical approaches to the definition and analysis of genres. However, a key problem regarding the heritage film is that its attributed 'genre' characteristics are centrally organised around its *ideological* character, and around its supposed *raison d'être* as the projection of dominant 'national' values and a specific version of the 'national' past which serves a bourgeois, southern-English hegemony. It seems questionable whether a genre (or sub-genre) can be defined pre-eminently by such ideological and national functions, since such matters are highly dependent on the interpretative judgement of the viewer; certainly, such a genre will be a particularly unstable and contested proposition. Moreover, as illustrated by my earlier *Chariots of Fire* versus *Room with a View* example, many heritage films exhibit highly diverse 'genre' characteristics in other respects. And it is not clear how an ideologically defined category can be a sub-genre of other distinct period genres or genre mixes, such as the costume film, which are defined in non-ideological terms. If heritage films do share common ideological and 'national' traits, it seems more useful to conceive of these 'heritage' characteristics as pan-generic, potentially present across a range of period genres. An important possibility this raises is that 'heritage' ideologies – and ideological functions – are not specific to films set in the past.

A recent article by Mark Jancovich offers a perspective on how genres are produced which helps to pinpoint why the heritage film is unsatisfactory as a 'genre' category. As Jancovich notes: '[The] technique of classification does not simply identify some pre-existing essence. Instead, *it produces what it purports to identify.*' Thus 'genre definitions are produced more by the ways in which films are understood by those who produce, mediate and consume them, than they are by the internal properties of the films themselves' (Jancovich 2001: 33; my italics). Such a model obscures one problem, however:

> [It presupposes] the existence of a collective consensus – about the definition of particular genres within any given period. *But such a consensus may not have actually existed.* We need, therefore, to study . . . how definitions of genre . . . operate within the intense struggles between different taste formations.
>
> (Jancovich 2001: 33–4; my italics)

This emphasis on genre definition as a site of intense contestation is particularly salient to the formation of the heritage 'genre'. In Jancovich's terms, the heritage film is a genre defined exclusively by those who professionally mediate films, not by those who produce or consume them. Additionally, the specific critical and political anxieties that have constituted the heritage 'genre' seem particularly detached from an industry or audience/fan perspective. Yet, despite this, the critique of heritage films has most often proceeded as if the films, their ideological workings and the pleasures they offer to audiences are all adequately knowable from the hostile critic's viewpoint.

There have been attempts to demonstrate that the heritage film has some kind of industrial/institutional substance (Higson 1996: 234). However, it is clear that the industry *position* on the films will differ radically from the critical position. Indeed, in recent years the film industry has been intensively engaged in a – largely successful – attempt to reverse discursive power relations in the heritage-film debate. The marketing, promotion and indeed textual strategies of recent British period films – discernible even in the relatively conservative *Howards End* or *Sense and Sensibility* and more emphatically in *Elizabeth* or *The Wings of the Dove* (Iain Softley, UK/USA, 1998) – have worked hard, and with considerable strategic sophistication, to project the films as 'not heritage films' (see also Sargeant 2000: 306–7). Their efforts have persuaded much critical and academic opinion as well as audiences.

Whether or not *The Wings of the Dove* (a radical adaptation of Henry James's novel) or *Elizabeth* are labelled heritage films, their strategic aesthetic self-differentiation from 1980s heritage (which include their surface nods towards contemporaneity and democratisation) – which a cynic might see as little more than a Blairite image makeover – have been widely accepted as a 'progressive' transformation in ideological substance. *The Wings of the Dove* is acceptable to a certain liberal/left British critical taste formation not because of a discernible political stance but because of its liberties with the book, which permit a dark and decadent visual splendour,[8] the depiction of Kate Croy's father (Michael Gambon) as a derelict opium addict, and a sexual coupling between Kate (Helena Bonham Carter) and her impoverished lover Merton Densher (Linus Roache) in a London Underground lift. Similarly, *Elizabeth*'s deliberate inauthenticities of fact and location, and its portrayal of the Virgin Queen as a construct, are celebrated, amid widespread analytical uninterest in the ways in which the film's preoccupation with English sovereignty may speak to populist conservative anti-Europeanism and post-devolution English angst.

Conclusion

At the same time, however, the successful dissemination of the dominant critical discourse around heritage films ensures its (re)production and acceptance (at least in universities), even as shifting industry strategies render its relationship to current British period films increasingly incoherent. Meanwhile the preoccupation with the national/ideological which continues to shape academic and critical discourse around the films leaves audience and fan perspectives on both 'old' and 'new' (or post-) heritage films almost wholly unvoiced. The effect is to invalidate what would surely be a useful and relevant focus on how the films might work as popular cinema, within genres in which the period setting provides an opportunity for specific pleasures which are not *all* reducible to ideology.

But, from the perspective of the present, the overarching difficulty is that the critique of heritage films thus produced can be seen to have been historically specific to the context of its time, the tail-end of the Thatcher era. The ideological purposes required of or fulfilled by a genre or individual films, and the 'national' vision they work on behalf of, will change in different cultural-political or national contexts and across time. The drift from the early-1990s conceptualisation of heritage cinema – defined by a very specific political orientation and ideological function – to the loss of this specificity in much recent work both responds and testifies to this difficulty. Yet these specific ideological claims were so central to the original conceptualisation of the heritage film that much of its coherence as a category is lost if they are simply abandoned.

In this respect, the attempt to endow the heritage film with a pre-history in the early decades of British cinema has itself been ahistorical. It also shows a strange amnesia about the heritage film's more recent prehistory, in the living memories of its audiences, particularly since the 1960s – a topic which surely merits investigation, and which I intend to follow up elsewhere.[9] To give one example, heritage-film criticism has yet to explain why Merchant Ivory's English literary adaptations since the mid-1980s are objectionable when their American literary adaptations of the late 1970s and early 1980s, *The Europeans* (1979) and *The Bostonians* (1984) – enjoyed by the same (if smaller) audiences in the same cinemas – were not. Reviewers' responses to these films on their release – and to contemporaneous British period films such as *The French Lieutenant's Woman* (Karel Reisz, 1981) which are today barely mentioned due to their non-conformity with the heritage debate – make fascinating reading today.

At the start of the twenty-first century, under Britain's first Labour government since the 1970s, the term heritage film is still being widely applied to recent British period films. However, the heritage film was originally conceived in terms of its performance of hegemonic functions on behalf of the Thatcherite Conservative government – no longer in power – and the heritage industry, which, while still vulnerable to the old criticisms, has reconfigured itself in significant ways over the past decade. It seems logical to conclude either that the heritage film was a genre – or critical construct – historically specific to the Thatcher era, or that the ideological character of heritage films since the mid-1990s will have mutated in response to changed current conditions. Either way, the ideological critiques of heritage films produced in the early 1990s will no longer apply to current British period films. A polite conclusion would be either that the heritage film has lost its ideological substance (which would explain the increasingly liberal use of the term in recent work) or that the heritage-film critique has lost its currency.

More importantly, different films and film cycles have today taken on ideological functions on behalf of the entrepreneurial, 'cool', 'New British' identity promoted by the New Labour government. Meanwhile Moya Luckett's analysis of the workings of national identity in post-1997 British cinema is suggestive regarding the recent migration of 'heritage' functions into a very different body of films. Luckett identifies a new 'alternative heritage' British canon, constituted from a mixture of retrospective rediscoveries – *The Long Good Friday* (John Mackenzie, 1979), *Get Carter* (Mike Hodges, 1971) and *Quadrophenia* (Franc Roddam, 1979) – and image-conscious pretenders such as *Lock, Stock and Two Smoking Barrels* (Guy Ritchie, 1998). This new canon is masculine, populist and closely affiliated to youth-orientated style culture; it thus addresses a very different audience from the 'older', female-dominated middle-class faction associated with the traditional heritage film. For Luckett, these films '[express] the energy, style and sexuality of British culture' (Luckett 2000: 88). However, the appropriation of the 1970s films – and *Lock, Stock*'s *faux* East End gangland – are also indisputably nostalgic in ways that can be read as profoundly reactionary (see Monk 1999b: 172–5). A point not made by Luckett is that many of these films appeal to (or have been appropriated in ways that legitimise) a reactive 'Englishness' which is politically conservative and expressly white.

And, as I have myself discussed elsewhere, highly ideological projections of the nation can be found in a wider range of recent British films set in the present (Monk 2000). Some, such as *The Full Monty*, project upbeat, pro-enterprise messages – disavowing that poverty is a *social* problem – despite their nominal affinity with the working-class social-realist milieu generally favoured by anti-heritage critics. Others, such as *Notting Hill* (Roger Michell, USA/UK, 1999) and *Bridget Jones's Diary* (Sharon Maguire, US/UK, 2001) project a vision of the nation so uniformly young, white, wealthy, narcissistic and implicitly conservative, within a *mise-en-scène* cleansed of the urban poor, the homeless and ethnic minorities, that by contrast the 1980s heritage film looks like a paragon of socially inclusive, low-budget liberal filmmaking. Significantly, in its obligatory rural interlude, *Bridget Jones's Diary* embraces the heritage aesthetic, and the well-heeled country house and National Trust village iconography, with a shamelessness unseen in any period heritage film, and entirely without the heritage films' social critique or sense of irony. In such circumstances, the routinisation of the heritage-film idea seems a dangerous diversion from more urgently needed new critical responses and debates.

Notes

1 Jhabvala did not adapt *Maurice*, but did have advisory input into the script (by Ivory and Kit Hesketh-Harvey) (Emmet Long 1992: 147–50).
2 All three films are approvingly contrasted with the 'bourgeois' heritage film by Higson (1996: 235–6). However, Wollen differs on *Hope and Glory* (1987: 179). More recently, Marcia Landy has named *Dance with a Stranger* and *Scandal* as heritage films (Landy 2001: 10). Her second judgement seems peculiar given *Scandal*'s subject-matter and overtly anti-Tory orientation (see also Sargeant, Chapter 13).
3 The heritage-film critique typically conflates the bourgeoisie and aristocracy into a single class rather than making analytical distinctions between them.
4 The third Popular European Cinema conference, 'PEC 3: The Spectacular', University of Warwick, UK, March 2000. Pamela Church Gibson (2000) also discusses *Elizabeth* and *The Wings of the Dove* in terms of 'changes' in the heritage film, although in more recent work she refers instead to its demise (*Journal of Popular British Cinema*, 5, forthcoming 2002).
5 Discussion at the *Titanic* Conference, University of Southampton, UK, July 2000.
6 For analysis of the British print media reception of *A Room with a View*, see Monk 1994: 40–9.
7 For fuller discussion of these aspects of *A Room with a View* and *Maurice*, see Monk 1994, especially 16–24, 26–8 and 34–7. For a summary, see Monk 1995.
8 The film's flourishes of costume and decor are legitimised by its updating of James's narrative from 1902 to 1910 (see Church Gibson 2000: 120).
9 See C. Monk 'Heritage film audiences', doctoral thesis, Middlesex University, forthcoming.

Bibliography

Anon. (1988) 'From argument to abuse' [editorial], *Sunday Times*, 24 January 1988: B2.
Anon. (1988) 'A dismal chorus' [editorial], *Daily Telegraph*, 28 January 1988: 12.
Ackroyd, P. (1986) 'Pictures from Italy' [review of *A Room with a View*], *Spectator*, 19 April 1986: 38.
Ashby, J. and Higson, A. (eds) (2000) *British Cinema, Past and Present*, London: Routledge.
Barr, C. (1984): 'Introduction: amnesia and schizophrenia' in C. Barr (ed.) *All Our Yesterdays: 90 Years of British Cinema*, London: BFI: 1–30.
Christiansen, R. (1988) 'Biting the dust', *Harpers and Queen*, June 1988: 119–21.
Church Gibson, P. (2000) 'Fewer weddings and more funerals: changes in the heritage film' in Murphy (ed.) (2000): 115–24.
Cook, P. (1996) *Fashioning the Nation: Costume and Identity in British Cinema*, London: BFI.
Cooke, L. (1999) 'British cinema' in J. Nelmes (ed.) *Introduction to Film Studies*, second edition, London: Routledge: 347–80.
Craig, C. (1991) 'Rooms without a View', *Sight and Sound*, June 1991: 10–13.
Dignam, V. (1986) 'The English abroad' [review of *A Room with a View*], *Morning Star*, 11 April 1986: 2.
Dodd, P. (1991) [editorial] 'An English inheritance', *Sight and Sound*, June 1991: 3.
Dyer, R. (1994) 'Feeling English', *Sight and Sound*, March 1994: 16–19.

—— (1995) 'Heritage cinema in Europe' in G. Vincendeau (ed.) *Encyclopedia of European Cinema*, New York: Facts on File Inc. in association with London: Cassell/BFI: 204–5.

Dyer, R. and Vincendeau, G. (1995) [leaflet] 'European "Heritage" Film Workshop Conference', Coventry: University of Warwick, June 1995.

Ellis, J. (1996) 'The quality film adventure: British critics and the cinema, 1942–1948' in Higson (ed.): 66–93.

Emmet Long, R. (1992) *The Films of Merchant Ivory*, London: Viking.

Finch, M. and Kwietniowski, R. (1988) 'Melodrama and *Maurice*: homo is where the het is', *Screen*, 29, 3: 72–80.

Forbes, J. (1987) '——' [review of *Maurice*], *Monthly Film Bulletin*, November 1987: 338–9.

Friedman, L. (ed.) (1993) *British Cinema and Thatcherism: Fires Were Started*, London: University College London Press.

Fuller, G. (1988) 'Battle for Britain', *Film Comment*, July/August 1988: 62–8.

Hewison, R. (1987) *The Heritage Industry: Britain in a Climate of Decline*, London: Methuen.

Higson, A. (1993) 'Re-presenting the national past: nostalgia and pastiche in the heritage film' in Friedman (ed.): 109–29.

—— (1995) *Waving the Flag: Constructing a National Cinema in Britain*, Oxford: Oxford University Press.

—— (1996) 'The heritage film and British cinema' in Higson (ed.): 232–48.

—— (ed.) (1996) *Dissolving Views: Key Writings on British Cinema*, London: Cassell.

Hollinghurst, A. (1987) 'Suppressive nostalgia', *Times Literary Supplement*, 6–12 November 1987: 1225.

Jancovich, M. (2001) 'Genre and the audience: genre classifications and cultural distinctions in the mediation of *The Silence of the Lambs*' in M. Stokes and R. Maltby (eds) *Hollywood Spectatorship: Changing Perceptions of Cinema Audiences*, London: BFI: 33–45.

Landy, M. (2001) 'Introduction' in M. Landy (ed.) *The Historical Film: History and Memory in Media*, Piscataway, NJ: Rutgers University Press.

Light, A. (1991) 'Englishness' [letter], *Sight and Sound*, July 1991: 63.

Lovell, A. (1997) 'The British cinema: the known cinema?' in R. Murphy (ed.) *The British Cinema Book*, London: BFI: 235–43.

Luckett, M. (2000) 'Image and nation in 1990s British cinema' in Murphy (ed.) (2000): 88–99.

Mantel, H. (1987) 'Tasteful repro' [review of *Maurice*], *Spectator*, 21 November 1987: 87–8.

Monk, C. (1994) 'Sex, politics and the past: Merchant Ivory, the heritage film, and its critics in 1980s and 1990s Britain', unpublished MA dissertation, London: British Film Institute/Birkbeck College, University of London.

—— (1995) 'Sexuality and the heritage', *Sight and Sound*, October 1995: 32–4. Reprinted in G. Vincendeau (ed.) (2001) *Film/Literature/Heritage: A Sight and Sound Reader*, London: BFI.

—— (1999a) 'Heritage films and the British cinema audience in the 1990s', *Journal of Popular British Cinema*, 2: 22–38.

—— (1999b) 'From underworld to underclass: crime and British cinema in the 1990s' in S. Chibnall and R. Murphy (eds) *British Crime Cinema*, London: Routledge: 172–88.

—— (2000) 'Underbelly UK: the 1990s underclass film, masculinity, and the ideologies of "new" Britain' in Ashby and Higson (eds): 274–87.

Murphy, R. (ed.) (2000) *British Cinema of the 90s*, London: BFI.

Quart, L. (1993) 'The religion of the market: Thatcherite politics and the British film of the 1980s', in Friedman (ed.): 15–34.

Samuel, R. (1994) *Theatres of Memory*, London: Verso.

Sargeant, A. (2000) 'Making and selling heritage culture: style and authenticity in historical fictions on film and television', in Ashby and Higson (eds): 301–15.

Stone, N. (1988) 'Through a lens darkly', *Sunday Times* 10 January 1988: C1–C2.

Sutton, D. (2000) *A Chorus of Raspberries: British Film Comedy 1929–1939*, Exeter: University of Exeter Press.

Wollen, T. (1991) 'Over our shoulders: nostalgic screen fictions for the 1980s' in J. Corner and S. Harvey (eds) *Enterprise and Heritage: Crosscurrents of National Culture*, London: Routledge: 178–93.

Wright, P. (1985) *On Living in an Old Country*, London: Verso.

13 The content and the form

Invoking 'pastness' in three recent retro films

Amy Sargeant

Past absolute

In the early 1990s, the Conservative government intervened in the teaching of history in British schools by recommending that the syllabus be confined to events more than thirty years distant.[1] At first glance, especially to those of us brought up in the liberal belief that one reason for studying the past was to draw lessons for the present, the proposed limit seemed arbitrary. One could not help but suspect that the gap (of clear blue water or whatever) was a specious attempt to place the past at a 'safe' distance and render it less open to contention than it might otherwise be. From one perspective, this intervention could be seen as a reaction against the idea of contemporary history *per se*. However, the thirty-year limit also happened to match the juncture after which the cabinet papers of British governments are released into the public domain. This coincidence is suggestive as to which matters and 'certainties' were thought worthy of study by the government of the time, what was judged to constitute a primary source, what sorts of documents were deemed valid and which protagonists were acknowledged as important. Meanwhile, some British cabinet ministers have written diaries intending them for publication, and other politicians (notably the Labour veteran Tony Benn) have kept audio diaries over many years as a pre-emptive alternative to a more official record.

Concurrently and subsequently, there have been calls for a return to a Sellar and Yeatman version of history, foregrounding a correct chronology of events and regional and national rulers – prompted in part by a series of surveys revealing ignorance of such matters among British schoolchildren.[2] This last demand seems finally to have been answered by Simon Schama's television series *A History of Britain* (BBC-TV, 2000), its accompanying website and various associated publications. Although history was here somewhat differently conceived from Schama's earlier *Landscape and Memory* (BBC-TV, 1995), both series share with much popular treatment of historical subject-matter a strong sense of narrative structure and capacity. Indeed, if we regard history as the narration of the past and not simply as a repository of available source material – as Roland Barthes, Umberto Eco and especially Hayden White have demonstrated – then films and television should be considered as media which produce history rather than just record or represent it, and which deploy their various means to particular purposes. Hayden White observes that the effect of the emplotment (the chosen mode or system of meaning production) may be regarded as an explanation – as opposed to a 'scientific' account – of the events of which it speaks:

> In its origins, historical discourse differentiates itself from literary discourse by virtue of its subject matter ('real' rather than 'imaginary' events) rather than its form. But form here is ambiguous, for it refers not only to the manifest appearance of historical discourses (their appearance as stories) but also to the systems of meaning production (the modes of emplotment) that historiography shared with literature and myth. This affiliation . . . should provide no reason for embarrassment, however, because the systems of meaning production shared by all three are distillates of the historical experience of a people, a group, a culture . . . In the historical narrative, experience distilled into fiction as typifications are subjected to the test of their capacity to endow 'real' events with meaning.
>
> (White 1987: 44–5)

Thus history is not something absolutely contained in the past, entire unto itself, but is made, tested and remade in the present.

The representation of events more than thirty years past in contemporary film and television in many respects differs little in form and content from the treatment of more immediate matters in drama documentary and docu-drama. The latter are thought of as potentially more dangerous, perhaps, and to have a greater burden of responsibility, because they often touch people who are living who may take offence or take legal or more direct action where necessary. The likelihood of this depends, it seems to me, on how deeply and closely one feels one's own past at a personal level, or the remoter past of a group with which one identifies, and the ends to which one is prepared to resort to right social and political wrongs.

There are also, perhaps, more people likely to consider themselves qualified to pronounce upon events which happened relatively recently. Such commentators on film and television representations of the recent past have been as wont to dwell upon inaccuracies in superficial details as have supposedly expert criticisms of period reconstruction. Certainly some objected to the bio-pic of the late cellist Jacqueline du Pré and her sister, *Hilary and Jackie* (Anand Tucker, 1998) – including, prominently, du Pré's husband Daniel Barenboim – even though the film showed distinct 'Hilary' and 'Jackie' takes on a single story. But all histories, as Karl Popper noted, by definition present particular stories as more plausible or authoritative than their alternatives, and good historians should seek to have their expectations refuted (Popper 1960: 88, 98). And all narratives (as Hayden White asserted) are fundamentally sustained by morality (White 1987: 23).

Controversy reigns over the instability and hybridity of these forms in film and over filmmakers' handling of their supposed material. Michael Winterbottom's film *Welcome to Sarajevo* (1997) used a combination of staged material, 'faked' and actual footage in its reconstruction of television journalist Michael Nicholson's own account of the war in former Yugoslavia. Writer Peter Flannery's *Shoot the Revolution* (directed by Jane Howell, BBC-TV, 1990), which consciously referred to the official authorisation of a particular history and the place of alternative tales, comprised material collected by Flannery in Romania in the preceding year. Sometimes conflicting accounts of the overthrow of President Ceausescu (in which television itself was a vital participant) are staged as monologues direct to camera, alongside stock footage and dramatic reconstructions and speculations. The execution of the former head of state and his consort, as the culmination of this history, is displaced to hearsay, in favour of showing a single, typical death of the child of two peasant farmers.

Then again, there are other media which take a similar degree of licence. Craig Raine's epic poem *History: The Home Movie* carries the usual qualification: 'All the characters . . . are fictitious and any resemblance to actual persons, living or dead, is purely coincidental'. But this work, spanning a century and a continent, is populated by characters whose names are familiar (Lenin, Edward VII and Edward VIII, Eliot and Yeats) and events which are corroborated elsewhere (the execution of Meyerhold, Bergen–Belsen, the Blitz) alongside a more personal family record of births, marriages and deaths. Jonathan Coe's novel *The Rotters' Club* sets a story of 1970s adolescence against a first-hand history of Bilbo Baggins posters, the Grunwick strike, the death of Blair Peach, the Rock Against Racism initiative, the Birmingham pub bombing and John Stonehouse ('They did things properly back then') and a secondhand history of Danish Jewry (Coe 2001: 177).

Ken Loach's Spanish Civil War film *Land and Freedom* (1995, UK/Spain/ Germany) opens in the present with the death of the protagonist David Carne (Ian Hart), and his granddaughter Kim (Suzanne Maddock) sorting through a box of memorabilia: a handful of stony earth wrapped in a red kerchief; a black-and white-photograph of a woman; photos of David with the militia; newspaper cuttings; leaflets; letters; poems. Loach announces the film as 'A Story from the Spanish Revolution' rather than from a civil war, and briefly outlines the circumstances in February and July 1936 which led the elected Spanish government's supporters 'to fight for their democratic rights'. The film repeatedly cuts to Kim sifting through this material, as if the story is disclosed progressively through these documents. Conversely, the film's historical narrative makes sense of the objects already seen. Documents are not merely to be taken at face value: Dave reports the arrival of false propaganda from Franco, intended to demoralise his opposition, and the *Daily Worker* headline 'Spanish Trotskyites plot with France' conveys the approved

Stalinist position which Dave himself comes to distrust. The personal account counters the published record. At the end, the funeral of David's Spanish Militia comrade Blanca (Rosana Pastor) is paired with David's funeral in Liverpool, where Kim throws the earth onto the coffin and reads from William Morris.

A private rite of passage often coincides in a historical narrative with a shared social and national crisis, as occurs also in such 'Home Front' films as *Hope and Glory* (John Boorman, 1987) and *The Land Girls* (David Leland, 1998). *Another Time, Another Place* (Michael Radford, 1983) refers by its title to the foreignness of the past to the present as 'another country'. But it also suggests the longing of its protagonist Janie (Phyllis Logan), caught in a remote Scottish crofting community enlivened only by the presence of Italian prisoners-of-war, for 'other times . . . and other places' – and what might have been for its characters if they had indeed met in 'another time, another place'. Meanwhile, the 'purer' genres of television arts features and current-affairs broadcasting frequently use dramatic reconstruction alongside their display of visual evidence. Here, again, Schama's series provides some notable examples: archaeological remains; stylised, silhouetted enactments of hand-to-hand battle; allegorical figures (the white peacock); inky signatures (the characteristically embellished mark of Elizabeth I); Schama himself delivering his authoritative commentary.

In *The Clothing of Clio*, Stephen Bann discusses the exhibition of history in written accounts, paintings, museum installations and film. Following Barthes, he notes that all these forms narrate a past and present, a notion of what constitutes history, in their selection and ordering of events and privileging of protagonists. Bann observes that history films, like many films of contemporary life, strive to achieve an effect of reality in their scripting and *mise-en-scène* (Bann 1984: 166). More significantly, they strive for correspondence with some known referent and for coherence between the various means employed. Elsewhere (and similarly a comparison may be drawn with literary and cinematic practice), Bann draws a hierarchical distinction between different genres of historical depiction:

> ['Historical genre'] was a term invented and popularised in order to cope with an irrepressible intrusion into the traditional hierarchy of pictorial genres . . . a hybrid between 'history painting' in the grand Post Renaissance style and the inferior practice of 'genre' [painting] . . . [The] concept denotes the response of academic painting to the contagious influence of multiple historical narratives, which themselves became strengthened and authenticated by the proliferation of well-researched images of the remote past . . . Historical genre [made] authentic detail both the sign and proof of a correspondence to the historical real. Whether seen on the walls of the Salon, or glimpsed between the pages of a book, the historical image claimed unprecedented access to the plenitude of the past event, 'as it really happened'.
>
> (Bann 2000: 1)

In the remainder of this chapter I intend to explore a number of British films in the light of these twists and turns in recent thinking about history and its representation. Some of these films negotiate the distinction between the public and private realm in the past; some may lay claim to being historical by dint of their procedures or a moral which one may choose to draw. All are concerned with events, more or less real or imaginary, set in the past of living memory. All employ a variety of visual, aural and structural means to create a correspondence with the past and a relation between past and present.

Past perfect

Michael Caton-Jones's *Scandal* (1989) is ostensibly concerned with the Profumo case of 1963. The British War Minister John Profumo was discovered to have had a transient affair with Christine Keeler, a part-time prostitute and friend to society osteopath and procuror Stephen Ward ('Just a jumped-up little pimp from Torquay', says a Detective Chief Inspector in the film) who was responsible for introducing her also to Eugene Ivanov, a Soviet naval attaché. The episode led to Profumo's resignation and seriously damaged the Conservative government of the time. Amidst numerous instances and rumours of extra-marital affairs in the Conservative British cabinet of the late 1980s – which simultaneously publicly advocated a 'return to family values' – the film had immediate contemporary resonance on its release, even in the absence of an equivalent threat to national security. Few of the 1980s cabinet ministers concerned matched Profumo's contrition (Campbell 1987: 272–5).

The credit sequence of the film consists of a series of monochrome newsreel images, blue-tinted, dissolving into the first colour frame of the film proper. We see Harold Macmillan on the steps at Downing Street, a scene from the Highland Games, the comedian Ken Dodd, a cookery demonstration and a child bundled into a woollen bobble-hat and anorak looking querulously into the camera. The announcement of Harold Macmillan's third term as Prime Minister occurs during the course of the film, and a comedian repeats his slogan, 'You've never had it so good', at a rally of the faithful attended by Ward and Keeler. Newsreel and newspaper images of astronauts, Fidel Castro, John F. Kennedy, Martin Luther King and The Beatles are interspersed with 'fabricated' documents (Ian McKellen as John Profumo, 'the rising star of the Conservative Party', making a television appearance; Joanne Whalley-Kilmer as Christine Keeler and John Hurt as Stephen Ward appearing under banner headlines on the *Daily Express*, *Daily Sketch* and London *Evening Standard*, alongside Prince Philip).

The poster for *Scandal* replicated Lewis Morley's 1963 nude photographic portrait of Keeler, sitting astride an Arne Jacobsen chair. There are references in the script to *Animal, Vegetable or Mineral?* (a contemporary radio quiz show) and to D. H. Lawrence's *Lady Chatterley's Lover* (publicly banned in Britain until 1960)

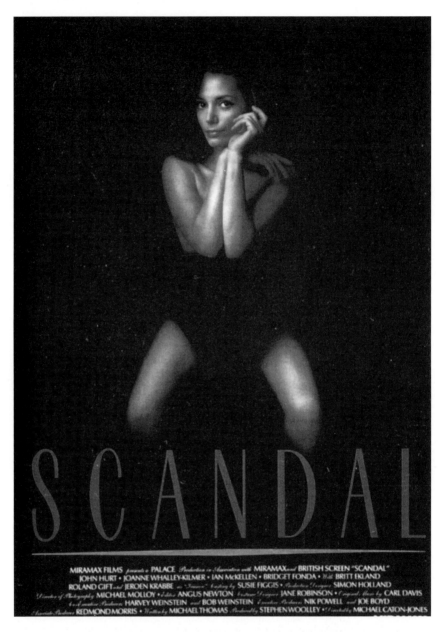

Figure 13.1 Joanne Whalley-Kilmer poses as call-girl Christine Keeler on the poster for *Scandal* (1989) in a reconstruction of Lewis Morley's iconic 1960s portrait of the latter.

Source: The Ronald Grant Archive (Palace Pictures).

in addition to excerpts from the transcript of Mandy Rice-Davies's performance in court (of Lord Astor's denial of impropriety, she famously remarked 'Well, he would, wouldn't he?') and of Profumo's speech in the House of Commons, recorded in *Hansard* (Parliamentary Debates 1962–3: 809–10). Harewood House in Yorkshire appears as Cliveden. The soundtrack underpins both the location in time and space and the action: Peter Sellers and Sophia Loren singing *Goodness Gracious Me* in *The Millionairess* (Anthony Asquith, 1960); ska for sequences in Westbourne Grove, west London, renowned, like nearby Notting Hill, for its association with Britain's Caribbean community; The Beatles (*Please Please Me*); Sinatra's *Witchcraft* (1957) for the credit sequence; and The Shadows's 1960 *Apache* as brunette Christine (all in black) and blonde Mandy (all in white) harness themselves into basques and suspenders and apply lipstick and eye-liner for a night on the town.

As is customary, the film closes with written captions bringing the viewer up to date with the story thus far: Stephen Ward has died unmourned; Profumo has devoted his life to charity work and has been duly rewarded with a CBE. In 1988, the proceeds from Christine's memoirs (a source credited at the end) have long since disappeared and she lives alone in London, while Mandy has established herself as something of a nightclub celebrity in Florida. In the meantime, Keeler has renewed allegations that she was no more than the scapegoat in a much larger conspiracy to protect the powerful and influential. 'It may be false, it may be true but nothing has been proved', sings 1960s icon Dusty Springfield with 1980s icons the Pet Shop Boys as the end credits roll. But, thematically, the true moral of the story has been confided already by Eugene Ivanov to Stephen and by Stephen to Christine. One resorts to metaphor, the other to an anecdotal parable from his own past, to account for his preferring to 'get to himself' before he is got at: 'Because I was the nearest they picked on me . . . "Someone had to have a thrashing, Ward – it just happened to be you."'

Past pluperfect

Scandal begins with a pre-credits mock footage sequence of Keeler being mobbed and jostled by reporters on the steps of the Old Bailey, repeated towards the end of the film. Even without any *a priori* knowledge of the Profumo case, one may infer that the story is likely to end badly for her. Otherwise, the film's narrative is arranged in a straightforward chronological manner with date codes judiciously introduced to indicate time ellipsis between significant episodes. Any relevance of the Profumo scandal to concerns of the late 1980s is never explicitly stated. By contrast, Todd Haynes's treatment of history in *Velvet Goldmine* (UK/USA, 1998) is a more ambitious project, cutting backwards and forwards from 1954 to 1974 and 1984, suggesting comparisons and indicating, at any rate, that events have causes in the past and ramifications for the future.

Superficially, *Velvet Goldmine* celebrates glam rock's androgyny and high camp and sets this against dowdiness and suppression endured in more ordinary lives in the 1980s. Of whatever order (simple, reflexive or interpretative), the bitter-sweet recollection of journalist/fan Arthur (Christian Bale) – whose retrospective investigation of the 1974 disappearance of his idol Brian Slade (Jonathan Rhys Meyers) shapes the narrative – sustains Fred Davis's diagnosis of nostalgia as a distinctive and particularly adolescent state of consciousness, even while it is a yet older Arthur who is viewing his own adolescence:

> During the developmental transition from adolescence to adulthood it is, on a mundane plane, anxieties, uncertainties and feelings of strangeness about the present and future that constitute the *figure* for youth while the *ground* is composed of familiar and likeable persons, places and identities from the past. 'Without really changing a thing' (and thus sparing one's being self-accusations of distortion or falsification) the nostalgic reaction inverts the perspective: the warmly textured past of memory that was merely a backdrop suddenly emerges as *figure* while the harshly etched silhouette of current concerns fades into *ground*.
>
> (Davis 1979: 58)

Certainly the film is trying to be more than a spectacular and aural evocation of the 1970s (however often the colour supplements in 1998 chose to invoke it as such) and nor do I find its disposition towards the past which it represents particularly ironic (however hackneyed the word has now become). But there is more than sleek Emma Peel leathers and clipped accents to distinguish *Velvet Goldmine* from *Austin Powers: International Man of Mystery* (Jay Roach, US, 1997), much as they employ similar means to achieve the effect of their respective originals. The latter presents us with the delights of Burt Bacharach and Nancy Sinatra; 'the electric psychedelic Pussycat Swingers' Club'; formation dance routines; crushed velvet, frilly cravats, Italian boots; a Union Jack-emblazoned E-type Jaguar; and a 1960s and 1990s model Michael York as spymaster Basil Exposition. As an ironic parody of Bond movies, *Austin Powers* seems entirely outwitted by the self-reflexivity of the 'real' Bond movie *The World is Not Enough* (Michael Apted, 1999). Sadly, I – like many commentators – think that *Goldmine* too fails to deliver on various counts. But I am interested to work out why this is the case, and am prepared to take its efforts seriously even while accepting its opening inflection of a routine disclaimer: 'Although what you are about to see is a work of fiction, it should nevertheless be played at maximum volume'. It may be that Haynes intends his message to be shouted from the rooftop on which Arthur and Curt eventually get together.

As a pop bio-pic, *Velvet Goldmine* might be compared with Iain Softley's specu-lative history of the fifth Beatle, *Backbeat* (1993), the 1970s 'Rutland Weekend

Figure 13.2 Glam as self-invention and the lost 1970s as mirage: fictitious glam-rock icon Brian Slade (Jonathan Rhys Meyers) flaunts his Maxwell Demon stage persona in *Velvet Goldmine* (1998) before staging his own disappearance.
Source: The Ronald Grant Archive (Zenith/Killer Films).

Television' mockumentary *The Rutles* (BBC-TV), Julian Temple's 1979 Sex Pistols feature *The Great Rock 'n' Roll Swindle*, and Nick Broomfield's 1998 documentary *Kurt and Courtney*. Temple's feature-length documentary on the Pistols, *The Filth and The Fury* (2000), was a more regular composite of home movies, contemporary interviews and news reports. *Velvet Goldmine* advisedly gives its leading protagonists the names of fictitious characters: Brian Slade is here a surrogate for David Bowie, and his Maxwell Demon incarnation an allusion to Bowie's adoption and shedding of his Ziggy Stardust persona. In 2000, BBC-TV offered the audience the choice of the real thing by scheduling Alan Yentob's 1975 *Omnibus* documentary *Cracked Actor: David Bowie* opposite the Channel Four screening of *Goldmine*. But just as Alex Cox armed himself against potential criticism by claiming that *Sid and Nancy* (1986) was a love story rather than a history of The Sex Pistols, glam star Brian and his US counterpart Curt Wild (Ewan McGregor) are modelled by Haynes – and commodified by Jerry Divine (Eddie Izzard) – after Barbie and Ken, employing dolls and miniatures in a similar style to Haynes's *Superstar: The Karen Carpenter Story* (US, 1987). *Velvet Goldmine* is for Mandy (Toni Colette), Brian's wife, a riches-to-rags story, and for journalist Arthur a story of compromised adolescent desire and hopes disappointed. Izzard plays Bijou Records boss Divine as the wicked uncle and eponymous goldminer; Shannon (Emily Woof), Brian's devoted personal assistant, is transformed from country mouse in tweed to sequinned glamour-puss – and finds her prince. *Goldmine* endorses the popular myth that drugs, sex, expensive cars and outlandish behaviour are part and parcel of a rock 'n' roll career.

It seems worth considering the means employed by *Goldmine* alongside retrospective exhibitions and features which have taken the style of a decade and the notion of a *Zeitgeist* as their subject. I am especially interested here in the manner in which particular visual and aural materials are understood necessarily to correspond, cohere and be recognised as compatible by dint of their historic coincidence. The *Rock Style* show at the Barbican Arts Centre in London (2000), exhibited alongside *The Wilde Years* (but only cursorily drawing a comparison), brought together costumes (as worn or donated by the stars), advertising material, record sleeves and the music itself; sometimes it indicated quotation from within the style from one performer or from one generation to another. Alexander McQueen's 1990s coat for Bowie, for example, cut from a scorch-marked, faded and bayoneted Union Jack, referred both to Spice Girl Geri Halliwell's micro-dress (worn at the Brit Awards in 1996 and auctioned by Sotheby's in 1998) and the brash appropriations of the flag in the 1960s and 1970s. Ted Polhemus's archaeological and anthropological survey *Street Style*, curated for London's Victoria and Albert Museum in 1994, astutely mapped currents and crosscurrents between the catwalk and the sidewalk and across different concurrent tribal and eclectic styles in dress and music. Sometimes the political content of a choice of identification was manifest, sometimes it appeared more aesthetically or socially motivated. 1970s style (as *Velvet Goldmine* too observes) was eclectic in its borrowings from Regency and Edwardian dandyism, from 1940s angularity and from exotic, ethnic imports (Steele 1997: 280). The accompanying *Street Style* publication was not merely an inventory but a catalogue matching image to appropriate co-ordinated soundtrack, recommending films for further viewing and support groups for devotees.

BBC-TV's wearisome archive-based series *I Love the Seventies* (2000) and *I Love the Eighties* (2001) included reminiscences and commentary, music, dance, fashion, films, television, household objects and toys, but said noticeably little of Grunwick, Blair Peach and John Stonehouse. In October 1997, the UK edition of *Elle* magazine advised its readers to 'shrug on your shoulder pads, slick on your fuchsia gloss and slip into your stilettos – the '80s are back' (page 36). In November 1996, British *Vogue* announced: 'Home Girl: Seventies sitcom style – bobble hats, Tom Baker scarves and chunky jumpers – is back for winter' (page 135). In 2001, the poster advertisement for Sky Digital's 1980s pop nostalgia series (showing British pop performers Toyah, Limahl, Adam Ant and Steve Strange) invited us to consider trends in hairstyling.

In their linear ordering, these television series are akin to annals. They 'do not conclude, but simply terminate' (White 1987: 8 and 17); in their very self-

quality bestowed by the heavens and invested in a magical talisman exchanged between the favoured few, 'singled out for a great gift' (here represented as queerness): in the film, Oscar Wilde's pin is acquired by Jack Fairy (alternatively Guardian and Avenging Angel), from whom it passes to Brian to Curt and thence to Arthur. Precisely what use Arthur makes of it is open to conjecture. Whether Wilde would approve of his successors one can but surmise. Oscar, Jack, Brian and Curt all worked to manufacture and sustain a public image of themselves and were promoted accordingly but whereas Wilde (the non-fictitious character) answered for his personal and political convictions, Brian escapes from notoriety into an alias and sells out to President Reynolds ('he's doing great work') while Curt reconciles himself to ignominy and defeat. The comparison is never fully justified nor explored – merely, like much else in the film, gesturally invoked.

Past imperfect

The Cement Garden (Andrew Birkin, UK/Germany/France, 1992), adapted from Ian McEwan's 1978 novel, is indeterminate in its location in both time and space. Like *Velvet Goldmine* it mixes period references but to very different effect. Here, a sense of a generalised pastness is invoked rather than of any one single particular past or disparate pasts. Whereas *Goldmine* may strive to invoke a moment in time, *Cement Garden* conveys a profound effect of a place in a Never Land and of time suspended. 'Everything seems still and fixed', says Julie (McEwan 1997: 134) – the older daughter of the family, and one half of the brother–sister relationship at the core of the source novel and the film. Both films are nostalgic, but the sites and states of longing of the narrative's protagonists are differently expressed.

The Cement Garden's soundtrack is remarkably uncluttered and consists mostly of speech. The cast speaks with a variety of accents, even among the family who are the narrative's hermetic focus. The father (Hanns Zischler) is dubbed, the mother (Sinead Cusack) is Irish, Charlotte Gainsbourg (daughter of Jane Birkin and Serge Gainsbourg, playing Julie, is locatable nowhere in particular. Appropriately enough, the reading of Commander Hunt's adventures in space by Julie's unhappy adolescent brother (and eventual lover) Jack (Andrew Robertson) is voiced over in American. Julie's boyfriend (Jochen Horst) – from Jack's perspective, the intruder into the family whose presence hovers as a constant threat that its secrets will be unmasked – has a German accent. Occasionally the void is interrupted by the weather report and identifiable tracks leaking from a classic Roberts portable radio.

The desaturated colour of the exterior shots, bleached by the long, hot summer and matching the tone of the grey, austere flat-fronted house in its nondescript surroundings, contrasts with the depth of colour and the personal clutter of the interior. With its simple Crittall windows, the house resembles a child's drawing, it looks, says McEwan, like 'the face of someone trying to remember' (McEwan

1997: 23). Plaster flying ducks, commonplace framed prints and patterned wall-papers are mixed with the deep mauve of the hallway. On one side of the parents' bed is a light which could have been bought from any number of high-street shops at any time between 1972 and 1992; on the other is an Art Deco-style lamp. In the living room there is a hardy-perennial paper and bamboo lampshade sold by the first-ever Habitat shop in the Fulham Road in the 1960s as an exclusive de-signer item, since retailed *en masse* and now ubiquitous. Products seem peculiarly carefully displaced or not placed. The school uniforms are worn unadorned by Nike, Reebok, Gola, Adidas or any other recognisable brand of trainer.

We could, perhaps, read this accumulation of superficially contradictory mater-ial simply as the expression of homeliness. As Mark Stephenson, designer of the family drama series *In a Land of Plenty* (BBC-TV, 2001), and Michael Riley, one of its producers, have commented, much was made of the crew's own memories in the course of filming this forty-year saga: 'We don't want to chime with the times too obviously. A lot of television drama is over-designed with period biscuit tins everywhere and streets full of vintage motors' (Garratt 2001: 48). For many of us, the familiar stuff of nostalgia is indeed a conglomerate of new, borrowed and inherited, there by choice and there by neglect or accident, and there by reasons other than cosmetic. But the style of *The Cement Garden*, highly co-ordinated across its various aspects, appears to serve a larger symbolic purpose (Zander 1993: 41). This family is nuclear: as Jack says, 'there are no aunts or uncles, nothing like that'. After both parents die in quick succession, Julie and Jack take on their parenting role as protectors of this nuclearity.

Some reviews of the film at the time of its release discussed its fidelity to Ian McEwan's source novella, while also commenting upon its transposition in time (Beard 1993: 41). Some noted that Bernd Lepel's 'quirky production and costume design, part fifties, part nineties', was not 'wholly grounded in a "British look"' (Elley 1993: 61). However, the original is hardly marked by its specificity, apart from a couple of references to costuming: 'In the evenings [Julie] often stayed at home to wash her hair and iron the pleats in her navy-blue school skirt. She was one of a handful of daring girls at school who wore starched white petticoats beneath their skirts to fill them out and make them swirl when they turned on their heel. She wore stockings and black knickers, strictly forbidden' (McEwan 1997: 20). Lepel matches McEwan's low, red car for Derek, the boyfriend, and selects a vulgarly over-sized watch to characterise him as a bit flash. Jack's and Julie's younger sister Sue (Alice Coulthard) is enthralled, but Jack is resentful and unimpressed by Derek's presumptuous efforts to ingratiate himself.

It seems to me to be useful to refer the film to others which have used children as a means of commenting upon social structures, conventions and sanctions, such as *Lord of the Flies* (Peter Brook, 1963), *Our Mother's House* (Jack Clayton, 1967) and Birkin's own television study, *J. M. Barrie and The Lost Boys* (directed by Rodney Bennett, BBC-TV, 1978). These are concerned with children performing as adults and replicating behaviours and exploring desires and fears through games. In *The Cement Garden*, Jack and Julie have played at doctors and nurses with the younger Sue, and play at mummies and daddies once their parents have gone. Tom (Ned Birkin), the youngest child, and his friend William (Gareth Brown) in turn subsequently dress up to play at being Jack and Julie. Sometimes Tom wants to dress as a girl, and Julie reprehends Jack for thinking ill of it. But the spaces too are emblematic: Jack's isolated iron bedstead in the 'dark sanctuary' of his den, from which he is cast away into the distant cosmos or escapes into orgasmic oblivion; the cot to which Tom habitually returns when he wants to be babied; the school gates; the cement-filled tomb in the cellar where Jack buries his mother after her death. Alongside these are a number of rituals and rites of passage performed in the family: Mum's birthday; the arrival of the boyfriend; the initiation of Jack into the game shared by Julie, Sue and Tom.

Rather than reading the children's reaction to their mother's death as callous (Street 1997: 110) it seems clear to me that this nuclear family opts for self-preservation. The burial of Mum in cement is equated with Dad's burial in sand shown in flashback (as flickering home-movie) as part of an idealised past of holidays on the beach and the flying of red kites. Dad is 'tucked up' in the ambulance blanket as if for sleep (McEwan 1997: 9). The self-conscious flashback scenes, not in the novella, are peculiarly evocative (Turim 1989: 2). In his 1821 essay 'Why distant objects please', William Hazlitt remarked that he could:

> never see a child's kite in the air, but it seems to pull at my heart . . . [It is to me a] 'thing of life'. I feel the twinge at my elbow, the flutter and palpitation, with which I used to let go the string of my own, as it rose in the air and towered among the clouds. My little cargo of hopes and fears ascended with it; and as it made a part of my own consciousness then, it does so still, and appears 'like some gay creature of the element', my playmate when life was young, and twin-born with my earliest recollections.
>
> (Hazlitt 1970: 152)

The pistachio green of the older Julie's bikini prompts Jack's memory of a perhaps more innocent childhood. As Julie recollects, her sexual intimacy with Jack – on which the boyfriend eventually intrudes – has gone on for ages and ages. This is at once an exceptional, highly personal – indeed, incestuous – past and one which is shared by anyone who has experienced adolescent and prepubescent anxieties in a family with siblings. Alliances in the family (Dad, Mum, Julie, Jack, Sue, and not forgetting Tom) are formed and re-configured after the parents' deaths. 'What are you all laughing about?' says Tom on first seeing Mum's body, the last one to know what has happened. Jack begrudges Mum's having confided in Julie and not 'you lot' ('She's been dying for months', she says) and is fascinated and intimidated by Julie's worldliness, her secrets and her sexual difference, emasculated by the sight of her crotch as she performs handstands at Mum's party. Sue and Julie giggle together over the increasing smelliness of their spotty adolescent brother, but Jack becomes a participant in their game, rather than an outside observer, when he wears the ribbon; he is again excluded from Julie's confidence when the ribbon is cut. The family reunites in another shared subterfuge when the boyfriend threatens to uncover their secret. The film seems, simultaneously, out of time and archetypically for all time, in a state of perennial return. Its visual referents, it seems to me, far from disorientating the spectator, lead one to this more abstract conclusion.

In his study of Roland Barthes's conception of the 'reality effect' in the depiction of history in a range of media, Stephen Bann has suggested that:

> In the case of visual representations, the 'effect' is also in a sense one of redundancy: it is precisely the authentic detail which appears *almost* gratuitous – which passes *almost* unnoticed – that will confirm and enhance the historical realism of the image. But since there is no precise equivalent in visual representation for the binding coherence of narrative, the danger is that such authentic details will be *completely* gratuitous – that will make their impression brutally and disrupt the historical milieu . . . We require the persistence of the effect or at least its non-contradiction; and that implies the persistence of a discourse in which such an effect can echo and reverberate.
>
> (Bann 1984: 57–8)

It is this persistence for which most television and film representations of history and the historical have generically striven, have drawn material from declared sources, conventionally delivered in particular composite forms and have bolstered by subsequent associated publications, exhibitions and so forth across a variety of media. *Scandal* corresponds closely to this tightly co-ordinated model, and the proximity in time of its content or the contentiousness of its conclusions in no way disqualifies it from being discussed as valid history. *Velvet Goldmine*'s putative narratives, it seems to me, are undermined rather than served by the hybridity of its stylistic references and, in spite of its gestural invocations of a larger historical scenario, it is unclear to what sort of history it aspires. *The Cement Garden*'s details, taken individually, are *almost* gratuitous but cohere alongside the narrative to convey a sense of a generalised pastness beyond any particular moment in time.

Notes

1 See Jenkins and Brickley (1991), declaring history to be 'the most overtly "political" of the subjects on the National Curriculum list', and Richard Aldrich's response (1991a). The Conservative cabinet minister Kenneth Clarke, after deciding on the thirty-year

moratorium, later announced that for the purposes of the National Curriculum history ends a mere twenty years from the present. As Aldrich queried: 'Why, for example, in the unit on "Life in Britain since 1930" are references made to unemployment limited to the 1930s and not to later periods? Why does the study of "Britain in the Twentieth Century" stop at 1969 while studies of Europe, particularly Eastern Europe and Russia, of Black Africa and China reach well into the 1980s?' (Aldrich 1991b: 24). Aldrich notes ambivalence on the part of the then Prime Minister Margaret Thatcher herself on this issue, and differences of opinion expressed in the 1980s by Conservative cabinet ministers Keith Joseph and Kenneth Baker as well as Clarke.

2 See, for instance, the most recent of such surveys, commissioned by educational publishers Osprey, 'Children who think Hitler was British' (reported by Lightfoot 2001). Sellar and Yeatman (1930), 'A memorable History of England, comprising all the parts you can remember, including 103 Good Things, 5 Bad Things and 2 Genuine Dates', is, of course, the best-known British spoof of school history style, delivery and misrecorded howlers.

Bibliography

Aldrich, R. (1991a) 'Always historicise?', *Teaching History*, October 1991: 8–12.

—— (1991b) (ed.) *History in the National Curriculum*, London: Kogan Page.

Bann, S. (1984) *The Clothing of Clio*, Cambridge: Cambridge University Press.

—— (2000) Introduction to Delaroche special issue, *Word and Image*, January–March 2000.

Beard, S. (1993) '*The Cement Garden*', *Empire*, November 1993: 41.

Campbell, B. (1987) *The Iron Ladies*, London: Virago.

Coe, J. (2001) *The Rotters' Club*, London: Viking.

Davis, F. (1979) *Yearning for Yesterday: A Sociology of Nostalgia*, New York: Free Press.

Elley, D. (1993) 'The Cement Garden' [review], *Variety*, 8 March 1993: 61–2.

Frith, S. (1983) *Sound Effects: Youth, Leisure, and the Politics of Rock*, London: Constable.

Garratt, P. (2001) 'Within these walls', *BBC Homes and Antiques*, February 2001: 46–9.

Hazlitt, W. (1970) 'Why distant objects please' [1821], in Ronald Blythe (ed.) *Selected Writings*, Harmondsworth: Penguin.

Hobbs, C. (1999) interviewed in Peter Ettedgui (ed.) *Production Design and Art Direction*, Crans-près-Céligny: Roto Vision.

House of Commons (1963) *Parliamentary Debates* 674, 22 March 1963.

Jenkins, K. and Brickley, P. (1991) 'Always historicise: unintended opportunities in National Curriculum history', *Teaching History*, January 1991: 8–14.

Lightfoot, L. (2001) 'Children who think Hitler was British', *Daily Telegraph*, 18 January 2001.

McEwan, I. (1997) *The Cement Garden* [1978], London: Vintage.

Morley, P. (1981) 'Glam: the very dream of smartness' in Tony Stewart (ed.) *Cool Cats: Twenty-Five Years of Rock 'n' Roll Style*, London: Eel Pie Publishing.

Polhemus, T. (1994) *Street Style*, London: Thames and Hudson.

Popper, K. (1960) *The Poverty of Historicism*, London: Routledge and Kegan Paul.

Romney, J. (1995) 'Access all areas: the real space of rock documentary' in J. Romney and A. Wootton (eds) *Celluloid Jukebox*, London: BFI.

Sellar, W. C. and Yeatman, R. J. (1930) *1066 And All That*, London: Methuen.

Steele, V. (1997) 'Anti-fashion: the 1970s', *Fashion Theory*, September 1997.

Street, S. (1997) *British National Cinema*, London: Routledge.

Turim, M. (1989) *Flashbacks in Film*, London: Routledge.

White, H. (1987) *The Content of the Form: Narrative Discourse and Historical Representation*, Baltimore, MD: Johns Hopkins University Press.

Zander, H. (1993) '*Der Zementgarten*', *Film Echo/Film Woche* 31, 6, August 1993: 41.

14 Taking liberties with the monarch

The royal bio-pic in the 1990s

Kara McKechnie

The relationship between film and history is less cozily opposed than it used to be. It was a relatively straightforward matter some years ago for historians to criticize the misrepresentation of dramatized versions of the past . . . Allowances had to be made for the screen, which of course was much more the creature of historical pressures in the present than academic history was – a delusion still to be found in some corners of the academy. Commerce had to have its due: the stars were there for the box office and so were the plots. The costume department, though, should try to get things right.

(Barta 1998: x)

In her 1994 book on the British costume film, Sue Harper demonstrates the difficulties posed by attempting a precise definition of the genre of films with historical content. Very generally, one can distinguish between the history film, which, although not a blueprint for historical accuracy, is concerned with actual historical figures, and the costume film, which is set in a recognisable historical period, but with fictional characters. Within the history film category there is a small but distinctive number of films about monarchs. Although these films are often associated with the 1930s, for example, *The Private Life of Henry VIII* (Alexander Korda, 1933), *Victoria the Great* (Herbert Wilcox, 1937), *Sixty Glorious Years* (Wilcox, 1938), *Tudor Rose* (Robert Stevenson, 1936) and *Fire over England* (William K. Howard, 1937), the tradition of the monarchy film has undergone periodic revival and endures to the present day.

In the most recent films, the concern with 'getting things right' seems to be more important than ever. The precision with which period images are reconstructed in contemporary history films has even led to the question of whether the preference for a more visually based – and therefore widely distributed and immediately accessible[1] – history over 'traditional' ways of conveying historical knowledge can contribute towards a nation's sense of identity. As Moya Luckett, writing about *Elizabeth* (Shekhar Kapur, 1998), one of the most successful of the recent royal bio-pics, argues:

> *Elizabeth* . . . narrates a new history, one that reinforces the power of images over archival knowledge, and thereby legitimises a similar strategy for more contemporary narratives. The film might be seen in the context of Tony Blair's attempts to update the monarchy by demonstrating how the image of a monarch might produce national renown, even in the face of very real domestic problems and their potential threat to nationhood. *Elizabeth* suggests, then, how a reconceived history – both as a discipline and as a specific narrative – might have practical efficacy in pre-millennial Britain. If 'authentic images' replace contested facticity, then the nation might find its identity again.
>
> (Luckett 2000: 91)

The discussion on the role of 'historical truth' within history films, the 'accuracy debate',[2] has been featuring in film magazines and journals ever since the genre came into existence. While there is consensus among filmmakers on the necessity and marketability of visual period accuracy, the role of the 'historical truth' within the film's narrative and its parameters has always met with a more ambivalent response from critics and audiences. Whatever the current fashion in monarchy films, the expectation is always that it will represent history 'as it really happened', but the key to convincing audiences that historical truth is being represented appears to lie in the film's ability to reproduce accurately the look of the period.

One is constantly reminded by academics that criticising a monarchy film for historical inaccuracy is inappropriate. A multitude of arguments lead on from this: there can only ever be versions of history; the narrative has needs that hardly ever conform to historical developments; a history film tells us more about the time in which it was made than about the time in which it is set. History films made during the Second World War are an obvious example of this: films like *Henry V* (Laurence Olivier, 1945) and *Fire Over England* clearly stress similarities between their period and the time of war for purposes of propaganda and the restoring of public morale. There is widespread agreement about the necessity to take history on screen with a pinch of salt on the basis of the above commonplace arguments. This agreement is, however, nearly always theoretical. Not only do academics not practise what they preach in analysing films, but viewers will frequently give as a reason for their liking or disliking of a text its success in 'getting things right'. If a film does not conform to the particular viewer's concept of 'what really happened' or 'what it looks like in pictures', the film will be seen as a disappointment.

Intriguingly, Alan Bennett, author of *The Madness of King George* (Nicholas Hytner, 1995), expresses criticism of the approach to history in *Elizabeth*: 'I hated [it], I'm afraid', because none of it 'happened like that at all' (Bennett in Wu 2000: 89–90). This shows that one cannot put the reaction described above down to audience naïveté. The expectations are formed through highly subjective personal experience and selective recollection of previously acquired knowledge. If one remembers from history lessons that Henry VIII had six wives, one will be more gratified by a film about his private life than by one that foregrounds the social and economic determinants of the reformation. The first internationally successful British monarchy film, *The Private Life of Henry VIII*, drew on this potential of selective knowledge, satisfying expectations by presenting the well known and familiar.

For the non-professional historian, knowledge – particularly in the case of monarchs – is generally based on school textbooks, previous media texts and the viewing of famous period portraits. Audiences will only accept Henry VIII as 'authentic' if he looks as he does on the 1536–7 portrait by Holbein the Younger. Makers of recent successful films with historical content recognise that the conscious evocation of period through production design is essential to the suspension of a spectator's disbelief.[3] This obligatory accuracy of appearance can provide the necessary level of authenticity, so that greater narrative freedom can be taken. The disadvantage is that the appearance of the *mise-en-scène* with its convincing period settings is often discarded as unworthy of critical attention, as having a merely decorative function. A history film with emphasis on the visual is often automatically categorised as a 'heritage film', suggesting an unhealthy and conservative concern with nostalgia.[4] Visually displayed history and the very fact that films are set in the past result in accusations of apolitical superficiality and aloofness from relevant contemporary issues.

It is these contemporary issues, of course, which have provided the impetus for the recent revival of the monarchy film. The problems of the Crown in the 1990s were both personal and political: a royal family beset with scandal – as in *The Madness of King George* and *Mrs Brown* (John Madden, USA/UK/Ireland, 1997) – and an unstable constitutional position created by the demands of devolution (as in *Elizabeth*).

Two statements are invariably made by critics of the history film, and they seem to contradict each other. First, there is the charge that the films are irrelevant to the present and merely 'dress up' a past and shape it into convenient tableaux that usually exclude the lower social classes. Second, there is a consensus that sees history films as highly valuable historical documents about the period in which they were made.[5] How can the history film be both relevant and irrelevant to the present at the same time? Cairns Craig makes the first point in his critique of heritage films:

> The audience is invited to understand the plot of the films as though we are contemporary with the characters, while at the same time indulging our pleasure in a world which is visually compelling precisely because of its pastness. If these were films whose content was as much of today as yesterday, their translation into our own time would challenge us with the modernity of the

issues raised. But they never do: instead we are placed back in a world whose evasions and silences are accepted as natural.

(Craig 1991: 12)

This criticism addresses itself mainly to heritage films such as *A Room with a View* (James Ivory, 1985) and *Howards End* (James Ivory, 1992), where the past that is displayed is not the kind of past which critics like Craig wish to see. He argues for the depiction of a past that displays inequalities and questions the validity of ideologies, according to the problems of the present. The films are not seen to promote or generate change. Mere depiction of a distant past is seen as unnecessary historical ballast and as perpetuating a conservative hegemony. Hence they are both irrelevant and dangerous.

This criticism may undervalue the ability of audiences to make their own meanings and bring their own critical approaches to the text. Historical occurrences on screen invite audiences to detect parallels with the present; sometimes these parallels heavily influence the way a film is produced. *Tudor Rose*, for example, underlines the need for self-sacrifice in times of crisis, as well as providing a romantic plot that satisfies escapist urges. Seeing history repeating itself and discovering the existence of similarities between past and present may therefore provide the viewer with a sense of reassurance and placate the urge for change. The production of history films in times of crisis and uncertainty has the potential to put present problems in perspective and the resulting 'appeasement' can play into the hands of the ruling regime.

Equally, parallels with the present in the history film may have the opposite effect and intensify feelings of dissatisfaction with present conditions in the audience, because the lessons of history are seen not to have been learned. Modern monarchy films seem to be steering the audience's opinion less tightly than was the case in the 1930s. The loosening of censorship and the government no longer using film as a medium for propaganda contribute to this opening up of interpretative possibilities.

Looking at the historical development of the monarchy films, we see how the filmic depiction of the monarch always depended on the contemporary situation. When the privations of the Depression created an audience demand for comic relief, the outrageousness and unrestrained behaviour of the King in *The Private Life of Henry VIII* satisfied the demand, exploiting prurient interest in the King's relationships and foregrounding their sensationalist aspects.

When the public lacked confidence in the stability of the monarchy, as was the case at the time of the 1938 Abdication Crisis, films like *Victoria the Great* and *Sixty Glorious Years* provided reassurance. By contrast, when stability prevailed, after the coronation of Elizabeth II, weak and ridiculous monarchs could be shown on screen without danger, as in *Beau Brummell* (Curtis Bernhard, 1954). In times of relative stability, the monarchy film seems to lose its significance as a way of articulating issues and reassuring anxieties, and it is therefore worth noting that there were far fewer monarchy films in the decade after *Beau Brummell*. When they returned in the 1960s, films like *Becket* (Peter Glenville, 1964) and *A Man for All Seasons* (Fred Zinnemann, 1966) positioned the ruler as antagonist and, in keeping with the mood of the times, emphasised principled resistance to authority. When the rise of feminism and female self-assertion demanded representation on screen, films like *Anne of the Thousand Days* (Charles Jarrott, 1969) and *Mary Queen of Scots* (Jarrott, 1972) adapted the monarchy film to this need.

During the 1980s the taste for historical subjects was principally satisfied by the kind of literary adaptations which provoked the heritage label, but, after a hiatus of nearly twenty years, monarchy films came back in the mid-1990s, evidently responding to a need arising from the public mood of the time. Just as *Victoria the Great* was influenced by the real royal drama that unfolded during its production, both *The Madness of King George* and *Mrs Brown* responded to the crisis in the monarchy that dominated the media in the 1990s. At this time, the monarchy was rapidly losing its function as a role model: fairytale marriages ended, dated rituals were questioned and public reluctance to provide for the extravagance of a dysfunctional and distant family unit grew. The significance of the monarchy as a symbol of a unified nation had waned and had been substantially replaced by a kind of royal soap opera. The public's increasing appetite for gossip and insight into the royal family's private life seemed to revive the genre of royal bio-pics. Together with the constant of the American market's fascination with all films British and historical,[6] this meant a favourable climate for success.

With varying degrees of obviousness, the three films discussed here index the real royal crisis unfolding in the House of Windsor through historical parallels. As the odd one out, *Elizabeth* (Shekhar Kapur, 1998) does not point out these parallels as clearly as the other two films. The reception of *Mrs Brown* and, to a certain extent, the production of *Elizabeth*, were influenced by the prevailing atmosphere after the Princess of Wales's death in August 1997. As Cate Blanchett, the Australian actress cast as Elizabeth, commented:

> It was incredible to begin filming two days after her death. The first line of the shoot was 'The Queen is dead. Long live the Queen!' And it was just very odd, very odd.
>
> (quoted in de Lisle 1998: 2)

Feelings of voyeuristic guilt and questions about the royal right to happiness were the dominant issues of the day. The three films mirror this public awareness of the discrepancy between private and public, while showing different approaches towards visual and 'factual' authenticity. *The Madness of King George* is a screen adaptation of Alan Bennett's stage play (Royal National Theatre, 1991). Bennett, originally a historian, and the film's director Nicholas Hytner, a regular collaborator, show awareness of the delicate balance between historical fact and the needs of the genre of history film. *Mrs Brown* is a film based on historical fact that makes use of the sketchiness of a particular episode. Screenwriter Jeremy Brock wants to tell a story that is based on particular, unconfirmed choices in the framework of a broadly 'true' story. The public versus the private, in a narrative that cleverly juxtaposes speculation with documented fact, is displayed with the utmost attention given to visual period reproduction. *Elizabeth* is a radical departure from the conventions of the history film, visually invoking the period in detail, but not giving the same importance to telling the story in a way that conforms to the current state of historical knowledge. Instead, the narrative's needs are given prime importance, and with this priority in mind, it is advantageous for the film's purposes that certain biographical questions are ultimately unanswerable. What was the nature of the relationship between the Queen and the Earl of Leicester? Was the Queen really a virgin? In the film, these questions are fitted with an imaginative answer, which factual documentation is unable to confirm.

Without wishing to generalise, it is worth noting that the trend during the four-year period in which all three films were made – 1994–8 – seems to move against rigid inclusion of archival facts and towards more importance being given to 'getting things right'. The re-creation of visually accurate historical spectacle is now easier to achieve than in previous decades. The development of this trend for spectacle is in tune with the needs of a culture with a preference for the image over the written word and seems appropriate for audiences with a decreasing attention span.

The three films have in common that they are based on 'real' historical narratives and have at their centre monarchs in crisis, especially in relation to the discrepancy between their public and private personae. They can be regarded as case studies for the state of visual and historical display in which we are able to observe current tendencies in the representation of history. Just as King George III and Queen Victoria are closer relations to one another than to Elizabeth I (both Hanoverians: George III was Victoria's grandfather), so *The Madness of King George* and *Mrs Brown* have much in common with one another stylistically, while *Elizabeth* marks a significant departure.

Mad king?

> George the First was always reckoned
> Vile, but viler George the Second
> And what mortal ever heard
> Any good of George the Third?
> When from earth the fourth descended
> God be praised, the Georges ended.
> Walter Savage Landor

Unlike Victoria and Elizabeth I, George III is not a monarch who has been accorded much respect in British cinema. So tarnished has been his reputation that Curtis Bernhard's highly unflattering depiction of his mental illness in *Beau Brummell* was thought suitable for screening to the young Elizabeth II as the Royal Film Premiere of 1954. As the mad monarch, Robert Morley plays on the farcical elements of lunacy, eyes rolling, attacking the wimpish Prince of Wales (Peter Ustinov) and behaving in a way that makes the Regency the lesser of two evils. In spite of the eagerness with which her Hanoverian ancestors are shown as incompetent rulers, the young Queen was said to have been amused.[7] This demonstrates the liberties that can be taken in times of stability.

Alan Bennett's portrayal of George III in *The Madness of King George* shows a similar lack of respect and unconcern with keeping up appearances, but offers more sympathy for the King's condition. Based on Bennett's stage play *The Madness of George III*,[8] the film shows an awareness of the thin line between historical fact and the needs of the genre and the medium, the latter grudgingly given preference when the need arises.

Nigel Hawthorne as the King in Bennett's version of royal madness shows the depths and desperation of his illness. His portrayal exposes the absurdity and sometimes farcically comic side to his suffering, reflecting Bennett's psychologically enlightened approach and his detailed knowledge of the state of academic research on George III. The very probable hypothesis that the King suffered from the hereditary disease porphyria (Bennett 1995a: xix) makes the issue of madness more complex and turns the King into a victim, who suffers as much from his doctors' incompetence as he does from a disturbed mind.[9] In contrast with *Beau Brummell*, the audience's sympathy is firmly with the King.

Bennett used a very wide range of sources in the writing of *The Madness of George III*. Bennett had probably never felt the clash of his two professions – historian and playwright – so acutely. The more detailed knowledge he acquired, the more responsible he felt for the accurate presentation of these findings. Bennett the historian aimed for greatest possible authenticity, often adapting or directly using contemporary sources, such as letters by one of the King's equerries, Greville, or contemporary accounts of the speech of mad people (Bennett 1995b: xviii). Bennett the author and theatre practitioner found it problematic to satisfy the narrative needs of drama which demand coherence rather than authenticity and have little tolerance for the twists and turns of 'real' history. Bennett had to telescope developments, exaggerate characters to make them types, and to convey the necessary historical information without characters saying 'what they know in their bones' (Bennett 1995b: xiii). His troubled attitude towards the obligations of artistic freedom is not only due to his being a historian; he also explains it with his insecurities as a writer, which undermine his concept of the kind of playwright he would like to be:

I find I write naturalistically, while wanting to be much more impressionistic . . . I long to be more abstract, to play on an empty stage, and not to be trammelled by naturalistic considerations. But it's seldom I can break away from it.

(Bennett in Wu 2000: 86)

Two important factors had to be considered for the adaptation from stage to screen. First, Bennett and director Nicholas Hytner believed there were two ways of producing the text; one seemed to be more suitable for the stage, the other more appropriate for the screen:

With *George III*, it immediately became apparent that you could either do everything, and make it the biggest pile of scenery ever seen on the London stage, or do nothing – so we did nothing. [The film version] was everything. Yes. Because that's what films are.

(Hytner in Wu 2000: 101)

Secondly, and soberingly, the expectations of American audiences influenced the adaptation from stage to screen. Joseph O'Mealy describes the changes that took place in order to 'crack' the market overseas (O'Mealy 1998). Box-office figures and award nominations[10] suggest that Bennett's and Hytner's approach maximised the film's appeal in the USA. Just as viewers of historical films have a concept of what is 'authentic', very generally speaking, the American audiences seem to have a definite concept of what for them constitutes Britishness. In this niche of the market, 'royalty' and 'history' must be included – and the concept will not sell without lavish period display.

In its stage version, Bennett's play relied on a minimal set and strongly emphasised the psychological drama inherent in the King's fall from monarch to patient. The conscious decision in the film to prominently include historical settings and landscapes for a more naturalistic reading of the text led to charges of dumbing down from O'Mealy and other critics. The at times condescending tone of their comments highlights the resistance to engaging critically with history on screen, which for many critics equates to a 'worthless' cinema of heritage. In the case of *The Madness of King George*, there has been little acknowledgement by critics of the film's complexities of coding, for instance the visually expanded parallels with and references to *King Lear*. The film gains from its period setting a complex dramaturgy of colour and a more poignant sense of political crisis:

I never felt that I managed to get the sense of political crisis in the stage as sharply as we got it on film. But that's because we had to do the House of Commons in a very impressionistic way with just a couple of spotlights, or whatever, whereas on film you did actually see the whole house.

(Bennett in Wu 2000: 83)

Throughout the film, the progress of the King's illness is expressed through changes in colour and lighting. The film's opening revels in royal red and navy blue; but as his mental instability escalates, the light becomes bright and disturbing. This development culminates in the King's rise at the first light of dawn, escaping and running across a heath with his servants struggling to keep up with him. He is wearing a long white night-dress and incessantly talking, culminating in a confused prayer. Parallels with the mad Lear on the heath are obvious. Once the King has descended into the depths of madness, with bleak, wintery shots in blue and grey, the camera and lens almost *become* his eyes, and we see the world with his failing sight and blurred mental vision. As sanity gradually returns, the colours become soothing, lighter and warmer. The turning point is a reading of Act IV, Scene 6 of *King Lear*, with the King as Lear and Thurlow as Cordelia. Mad Lear has been captured, put into fresh clothes and is just awaking from deep sleep, all traces of madness gone, to see once again his banished daughter Cordelia. Accordingly, here we see a mild-mannered monarch directing the reading, who no longer soils his clothes, scratches at his sores, or hurls abuse while he is escaping from those trying to restrain him.

Bennett is thankful that the reading of Lear is documented to have taken place, as it has such dramaturgical value for his work, but admits he would have never included it otherwise:

> The Lear scene I wouldn't have been able to invent. I'm quite timid, imaginatively speaking; the fact that Willis did actually read *King Lear* with George III, is actually a fact. If he'd read *Twelfth Night* or something like that, I wouldn't have had the wit to change it to *King Lear*, so I'm glad he got it right.
>
> (Bennett in Wu 2000: 88)

Just as the King and his doctor kindly 'got it right' to provide a subtext to George III's crisis, the film gets it right in its display of period imagery. Although it does not refer to particular portraits, as *Elizabeth* does, the landscape shots and their relation to human beings often seem inspired by paintings. The enclosed idyll hardly ever shows solitary landscapes, but a 'controlled' environment, populated by peasants and animals, which provides a perfect backdrop for the interests of the King – or 'Farmer George' as he was affectionately known (see also Bermingham 1986: 40–1). The looks and costumes of some of the characters in the court scenes seem slightly exaggerated, invoking contemporary satirical works by artists such as William Hogarth and Charles Williams.

Overall, *The Madness of King George* constitutes a highly complex text, which manages to make statements about period imagery, behaviour as performance and the function of royalty, with definite links to the Windsors of the 1990s. The film's generic indeterminacy derives from the aim to satisfy diverse target groups and potential critics, and, not least, includes elements of a heritage film, a study of mental illness and a family melodrama.

Monarch of the glen?

Like her grandfather George III, Queen Victoria seems to be fashioned for the screen according to the need of the age. This becomes evident when comparing Herbert Wilcox's two films about Victoria produced in the 1930s, *Victoria the Great* and its successor *Sixty Glorious Years*, with 1997's *Mrs Brown*. All three films thematise the tension between the private and the public lives of the monarch. The older films construct the Queen for propaganda purposes as wedded not only to Albert, but also to her duty as the figurehead of Empire. The newer version deconstructs her propaganda image by showing her shrinking from this duty and exploring a post-marital friendship.

Victoria the Great balances the virtual canonisation of the Queen on the centenary of her accession against Victoria as the model of a devoted wife and mother. Wilcox was influenced during the planning stages of the film by the upheaval of the Abdication Crisis of 1936 (Harper 1994: 53). The sixty-four years of Victoria's reign are presented in the film in terms of a celebration of the monarchy's lasting endurance – a necessary measure so soon after the Crisis if the public's confidence in their rulers was to be restored (Harper 1994: 183). Given that Edward VIII was perceived as having given up his throne for love, both *Victoria the Great* and *Sixty Glorious Years* carry reassuring messages concerning the stability of the family as well as the monarchy, foregrounding the successful combination of royal duty and a happy married life. As propaganda films, both strongly promote social stability, imperial glory and patriarchal rules, and can also be seen as satisfying the audience's escapist yearnings for a glorified past in a period of high unemployment and political uncertainty. Their visual reliance on tableaux give the two films a static pace, making them more like animated picture books.

If the link that made Wilcox's Victoria films relevant to their contemporary audience was the Abdication Crisis, it was the death of Princess Diana in August 1997 that enhanced *Mrs Brown*'s impact, even though this connection could be made only after the film's release around the time of the Princess of Wales's funeral. *Mrs Brown* was released first in the USA (18 July 1997), then in the UK (5 September 1997). American reviewers, in particular, compared Queen Victoria's dilemmas to those of Princess Diana:

> The inescapable image is of Diana striding into the new century with a coltish grace that left the Royal family rooted in the past. She showed Britain the same spirit that John Brown sought to instil in Victoria. This graceful, witty movie now assumes an awful sadness.

(Ellis 1998)

The outpouring of public grief and guilt after Diana's death made audiences sympathetic to the theme of *Mrs Brown* – a monarch's pursuit of personal freedom and happiness. In this new context, the relationship between the Queen (Judi Dench) and her favourite servant, John Brown (Billy Connolly), the subject of so much disapproval by surrounding officials and family members, unwittingly invoked similar tensions within the royal family of the 1990s.

The Brown-affair was a destabilising factor for the royal family. After Queen Victoria's reclusive and intense period of mourning in the early 1860s, following the death of Albert, she refused to undertake any public duties for several more years and built a close relationship with her 'Highland Servant' John Brown. Their apparent closeness and his growing privileges and responsibilities led to rumours of a secret marriage, satirisation in *Punch* and the nickname 'Mrs Brown'.[11] The Queen's absence from public life provoked calls to dissolve the monarchy, and her unwillingness to put duty before a personal relationship was perceived as disloyalty to her people as well as her family, as expressed in a riddle circulated in the film: 'Why is the Queen penny-wise and pound-foolish? Because she looks after the Browns and lets the sovereigns take care of themselves' (Brock 1997: 34).

Although the consequences of the monarch's absence are not ignored in the film, its unfavourable portrayal of the upper and political classes ensures that the audience is conspiratorially enlisted on the side of the relationship between Queen and commoner. One 'Society Lady' is described in the script as 'thick as shit' (Brock 1997: 35), and the Prime Minister, Benjamin Disraeli (Antony Sher), is portrayed as endlessly duplicitous. There is a very poignant contrast between the refined southern English courtiers and the ruddy Scotsman, who 'speaks as he finds' (Brock 1997: 13) and seems to be the embodiment of 'the honest man, tho' e'er sae poor, [who is] King o' Men, for a' that' (Burns 1993: 489).

For much of the film, audience sympathy is denied to the 'other camps': Parliament, the press, the Queen's family – notably the Prince of Wales, who resents being reprimanded by Brown on behalf of his mother – and the senior servants, who resent Brown's privileged position. The film alternates scenes of the deepening friendship with scenes of parliamentary debate, showing how the clashes between pro- and anti-royalist parliamentarians increase the pressure on the Queen and Brown's relationship. *Mrs Brown* lacks the sense of martyrdom of films like *Tudor Rose* or *Anne of the Thousand Days* (Charles Jarrott, 1969), but it still dramatises the impact of politics on private happiness. Gradually, in what seems to be a distant reminder of the monarchy film's traditional theme of self-sacrifice, support for the Queen's behaviour is withdrawn, and the two protagonists' less appealing personal qualities are displayed: the Queen's self-centred stubbornness and Brown's alcohol-fuelled paranoia. The simple, mythologised image of *Victoria the Great* is replaced by a more complex representation which includes psychological insights and the element of scandal.

Mrs Brown's director John Madden and scriptwriter Jeremy Brock approach their historical material with more ease than Alan Bennett in *The Madness of King George*, drawing upon sources such as the Queen's letters and historical biographies. They are happy, in the absence of exhaustive historical data,[12] to suggest a conspiracy to conceal the truth. This is in keeping with the postmodern treatment of history: subjectivity and selectivity, 'facts' subordinated to the needs of the narrative, and an underlying mood of paranoia and conspiracy theories. Although the visual approach of the film is not overtly postmodern, the way its love story is foregrounded over the 'demands' of history and biography takes advantage of gaps in historical recording. *Mrs Brown* does not take its historical responsibility lightly; but rather than merely reproducing, it interprets.

However, the story of the Queen and her ghillie is not a well-known one, and the audience will therefore not detect what is fact and what is fiction. The relative obscurity of the plot can be explained with reference to the obscurity of the facts: the existence of Brown's diary, used as a narrative device in the film, is not historically confirmed. It is easy for Brock and Madden to justify the sparsity of information about the affair through the disappearance of the diary, plotted by Brown's enemies, Ponsonby and Jenner (Brock 1997: 78). Their suppression of Brown's account of the story therefore stands for a suppression of history itself.

Mrs Brown has greater stylistic coherence than *The Madness of King George*. It also has clearer stylistic heritage credentials: *Mrs Brown*'s pace, its camerawork and especially its visual style make it as much a continuation of the likes of *Howard's End* as it is of the royal bio-pic. Visually, the film evokes connections with several contemporary paintings, notably those of Sir Edwin Landseer. *Queen Victoria at Osborne House* (1865–7) shows the Queen, clad in mourning black, on horseback, reading a letter, her black horse held by Brown. *Mrs Brown* was partly shot on location in the grounds of Osborne House on the Isle of Wight; and the film's Queen and Brown look very similar to their depictions in the painting both in dress and in pose, the only difference being the colour of the Queen's horse. Furthermore, in a central scene of the film, the Queen takes her letters from Prince Albert to read on horseback, with Osborne House in the background of the shot (Brock 1997: 19). The film's theme of the beleaguered ruler and its use of lavish landscape shots recall two of the Victorian age's most popular paintings: Landseer's *The Monarch of the Glen* (1851) and *The Stag at Bay* (1846). The former majestically depicts a stag proudly overseeing his 'kingdom'; the latter is a painting of a stag hunted down by hounds and nearing the end of his life in freedom. The pictures function as a powerful metaphor, given the film's emphasis on the sharp contrast between the freedom the Queen enjoys in the company of Brown, riding in the Scottish Highlands, and the oppression public life holds for her.[13]

As with many recent period films, many audiences and critics have perceived *Mrs Brown* as a nostalgic and escapist film that is little more than pleasant on the eye. Part pragmatic, part playful, *Mrs Brown* represents a middle way between the historically careful but at times timid approach of *The Madness of King George* and the flamboyance with which history is treated in *Elizabeth*.

Virgin queen?

Queen Elizabeth's appearances as a protagonist of films invariably have a significant connection with the state of the nation at particular historical moments. Flora Robson in *Fire over England* shows an ageing Queen, who is aware of her decline, but still protects the unified nation effectively against foreign intrusion. Shekhar Kapur's film *Elizabeth* is a story 'of a journey from innocence to loss of innocence' (Kapur in de Lisle 1998: 1) and, in focusing on the monarch's unification of Scotland and England, perhaps encourages viewers to reflect upon its current reversal through devolution (Luckett 2000: 91).

Fire over England is in essence a propaganda film, its dialogue heavy with historical information. It takes the task of visual period reproduction seriously, but from the perspective of today, its stylistic clashes give the film a somewhat parodic, clichéd, doublet-and-hose image. As the film has the Spanish Armada at its centre, the focus is on the ageing Virgin Queen. By contrast, *Elizabeth*'s time-frame spans the period from the reign of Mary Tudor (1553–8), persecutor of Protestants, to the beginnings of the Virgin Queen cult. The film's visuality is firmly based on the construction of the Virgin Queen image and corresponding period portraits.

Elizabeth is very significant for the genre of the monarchy film. Some of its critics categorise it as a heritage film, albeit a groundbreaking one: 'the juxtaposition of different generic elements and the creation of new possibilities for heritage were taken still further in *Elizabeth*' (Church Gibson 2000: 122). It is believed here, however, that *Elizabeth* does not constitute a variation on 'typical' heritage-film style, but a departure from it. The film shows a preoccupation with the reconstruction of period imagery, but fails to conform to any of the heritage film's other – admittedly loosely established – conventions.[14] Like *Mrs Brown* but unlike the majority of heritage films, *Elizabeth* is not a literary adaptation and, although it revels in the composition of compelling images, it is not idyllically picturesque and does not create a calm-flowing stylistic unity to maximise appreciation of its imagery. Its visual concept is based on 'violent juxtapositions' between 'beauty and violence' (Hirst 1998: 9) and the resulting stylistic clashes reflect the tension and conflict that characterise the film's events. *Elizabeth*'s camerawork and narrative follow the conventions of the political thriller: angled, rapidly changing shots and perspectives, and many parallel plotlines, with constant reference to the political and social consequences of royal actions. In the very first scene, for instance, Protestants are shown being tortured under the Catholic 'Bloody Mary's' instructions. Shot from above, a woman's head is shaved so brutally that it bleeds, anticipating the Queen's transformation at the end of the film in shot style and content.

Of the films discussed here, *Elizabeth* takes the most extreme approach to period display. As in *The Madness of King George* and *Mrs Brown*, locations are transformed into period settings reminiscent of paintings. The look of costumes and make-up in the other two films is very much based on contemporary portraiture, but *Elizabeth* takes this one step further. Not only are famous portraits of Queen Elizabeth meticulously re-created, but two of those portraits are used to frame the narrative: the Coronation portrait (1559, in the National Gallery, London) and the Ditchley portrait by Marcus Gheeraerts (1592, in the National Portrait Gallery, London). The film explains the visual and behavioural changes in the monarch in the period between the two portraits: Elizabeth's transformation from young, exuberant monarch, into Virgin Queen. Moya Luckett argues that through the clever use of shots which resemble these and other surviving portraits, the film reassures viewers by foregrounding visual 'authenticity' even though in many respects it shows 'scant respect for actuality' (Luckett 2000: 90).

The portraits have the right kind of popular appeal and familiarity, but their authenticity does not necessarily reflect the 'real' appearance of Queen Elizabeth. Elizabethan iconography was not in the first instance concerned with the reproduction of a naturalistic image of the Queen, but must be understood as part of an 'alliance of art and power' (Strong 1995: 5). The portraits sanctioned by the Queen and her parliament were the Elizabethan equivalent of 1990s 'spin'. The portraits' original rhetorical function is preserved in Kapur's use of them to 'sell' his story to the audience. In addition to the two 'framing' portraits, there is a free adaptation of a third picture: the Rainbow portrait (attributed to Marcus Gheeraerts, *c.*1600). In this portrait the Queen's cloak is adorned with eyes and ears, representing those of her servants, seeing and hearing everything of possible interest or vital importance on behalf of their mistress: 'Many things she sees and hears through them, but the Judgement and Election are her own' (Davies in Strong 1995: 14).

In the film, this cloak is reproduced as fabric draped around the Queen's bed. It is brought to our attention in a love scene between Elizabeth and Leicester: reversing its original meaning, it does not represent the monarch's omnipresent eye, but is a metaphor for constant observation and scrutiny of the Queen by enemies, allies and cinema audiences alike. This is underlined by the see-through quality of the fabric. An image adapted from contemporary portraiture therefore gains a meaning convenient to the concept of the film. The imagery is used to emphasise the political power of the Queen's advisors rather than of the monarch. The reconstruction of the Ditchley portrait at the end of the film reasserts her political authority and firmly establishes the invention of the Virgin Queen as a deliberate, carefully staged campaign.

But before constructing his image of the Virgin Queen, Kapur paradoxically undermines the myth that Elizabeth was sexually inactive. In the final sequences of the film, we see Elizabeth transform herself, by shaving her head (an action closely associated with the taking of religious orders) and applying white make-up (a symbol of purity and virginity), into England's chaste bride. 'I have become a

Figure 14.1 The Ditchley portrait of Elizabeth I (Marcus Gheeraerts, 1592): one of several
contemporary portraits which serve as important visual references for the film
Elizabeth (1998).

Source: Courtesy of the National Portrait Gallery.

Figure 14.2 From carefree, spirited – and sexually active – young monarch to Virgin
          Queen: Cate Blanchett as *Elizabeth* (1998).
Source: BFI Stills, Posters and Designs (Polygram/Channel Four Films/Working Title)

virgin', she declares, emphasising the constructed nature of her new identity.[15] In
the Ditchley portrait, the Queen is seen to be standing on a map of England. In its
filmic adaptation, she is almost identical to the portrait in dress and make-up,
framed by curtains in royal red, standing in front of the royal coat of arms. Strangely,
it does not carry Queen Elizabeth's motto *Semper Eadem*, but one that begins with
Video ('I see'), which ties in with the established theme of the all-seeing eye. The
Queen's statement to Lord Burghley – 'Observe, my Lord, I am married to England' – shows that the makers of *Elizabeth* have decided on a definite line of narrative, whereas there is historical speculation over, and no ultimate proof for, the
reason for the Queen's reluctance to marry. From the beginning, this moment of
transformation was going to be the final climactic image of the film: 'the moment
at which Elizabeth became historical' (Hirst 1998: 7).

Although they interpret differently, Elizabethan iconography and the film *Elizabeth* share similarities of approach: they do not necessarily show what was, but show images constructed as appropriate vehicles for the allegorical meanings they wish to present. Neither of them has any ultimate historical reliability. The narrative liberties afforded by apparent visual authenticity offended people who believe that 'what really happened' should be displayed on screen. Kapur, his ambition directed towards making a film 'raw with emotion' (Hirst 1998: 10), was more interested in relating to the audience's perennial interest in the hidden private lives of monarchs and the way this links with royal propaganda:

> Whether she [Elizabeth] was or wasn't a virgin I think is unimportant. I was interested in the idea that people made such a big thing of it. It must have gone beyond a physical fact. She made a declaration of virginity as a political statement. So then you ask, what was behind that? . . . History has not proved she was not a virgin . . . I had to make a choice: whether I wanted the details of history or the emotions and essence of history to prevail.
>
> (Kapur in de Lisle 1998: 1)

The audacity with which Kapur and his collaborator Michael Hirst ask the 'what if?' question is admirable, but clashes with audience perceptions surrounding the presentation of history on screen. *Elizabeth* is based in places on historically confirmed facts, while taking the liberty to depart from them whenever the need arises: 'It is a film, not a documentary' (Hirst 1998: 7). For this approach, the choice of Shekhar Kapur was decisive, as he brought with him no preconceptions about Elizabeth I and lacked any protective feelings towards the image of the Virgin Queen. Kapur and Hirst are, however, playfully rather than painfully aware of having to fulfil visual expectations. They thus embrace the heritage principle of authentic pictorial detail, while rejecting or subverting other heritage conventions in order to gain freedom for *Elizabeth*'s narrative inventions.

Conclusion

In conclusion, these three films do not differ in the historical weight they carry. In terms of both artistic ambition and their use of historical documents and period works of art, the films aim high: they want visual authenticity, and to invoke the values of historical artworks, as well as psychological depth, political conspiracy and family melodrama. *The Madness of King George* exploits an ancient myth: the fall of a powerful ruler. That this myth is acted out in surroundings accurate to the 1780s period does not affect its impact. What does, however, is Bennett's aim to please everybody, thereby depriving the film of a strong single focus and watering down both its psychological and its historical value. *Mrs Brown* has a stronger focus on its aim to emphasise love in a cold climate, cleverly echoing similar events in the contemporary monarchy. It manages to leave its central question – was there an intimate relationship? – open, just as the final proof is lacking in historical documents.

Where John Madden leaves questions open, Shekhar Kapur's film is highly opinionated, even though the decisions made are not always sustainable historically. *Elizabeth* is concerned with finding its own path through a vast area of speculation and embraces the postmodern approach to history more forcefully than the other two films discussed. Its makers stress the need to be selective in order to meet the demands of drama, and do not apologise for inaccuracies, but exploit the source material for the benefit of entertainment.

Although ironically intended, the following statement communicates how the makers of recent British historical films do not want to be reduced to simple reporters of a historical occurrence:

> I would like this film to be a masterpiece, if it can be arranged.
>
> (Bennett 1995b: xvii)

Notes

1 My use of the term 'accessible' here refers to the immediacy with which historical contexts are available when presented in a filmic context. But of course their accessibility can be deceptive: settings in historical films are often closely based on period imagery that is itself not a straightforward representation and requires decoding: see this chapter's section on *Elizabeth*.

2 This debate was initiated by the release of *The Private Life of Henry VIII* in 1933 and was largely conducted by newspapers (mainly the *Daily Mail* and the *Daily Herald*) and 'lowbrow' film journals such as *Film Weekly* and *Picturegoer*. For a comprehensive account see Harper 1994: 56 onwards.

3 See, for example, Ridley Scott's comments on the importance of detailed visual period reconstruction in the documentary *The Making of Gladiator* (transmitted on ITV, 4 May 2000).

4 For summaries of the British debate on heritage film, see Hill 1999: 73–98, and Claire Monk's chapter in this volume (Chapter 12).

5 'Movies, especially popular ones, comprise a record of the aspirations, obsessions, and frustrations of those who spend time and money making or viewing them' (Andrew 2000: 179).

6 Like numerous British period film successes before them, *The Madness of King George* and *Mrs Brown* opened in the United States before they opened in Britain. This, together with the change made to *King George*'s title for the benefit of US audiences (see note 8), indicate the profitable appreciation of British period films in the US.

7 At the royal screening, Stewart Granger recalls Prince Philip asking him whether he thought the film was appropriate for Her Majesty, to which he replied 'If you could manage to distract her attention when Robert Morley appears, it might be better, Sir.' On the way out, Prince Philip remarked to Granger that the mad scene with George III has been Her Majesty's 'favourite scene' (Granger 1981: 312).

8 The alteration of the title from *The Madness of George III* to *The Madness of King George* was a marketing decision. There were concerns that, had 'George III' remained in the title, US viewers would have come out of the film wishing they had seen the first two in the series as well (Bennett 1995a: xiii–xiv).

9 For a more detailed account on the royal madness, see my chapter 'Mrs Brown's mourning and Mr King's madness' in D. Cartmell, I. Q. Hunter and I. Whelehan (eds) (2001) *Retrovisions – Reinventing the Past*, London: Pluto Press.

10 For example: Academy Award Nominations 1995: Best Actor: Nigel Hawthorne; Best Supporting Actress: Helen Mirren; Best Writing, Screenplay based on material from another medium: Alan Bennett; Best Art Direction – Set Decoration: Ken Adam and Carolyn Scott (won).

11 A satirical Court Circular published in *Punch* is mentioned in the film: 'On Tuesday, Mr John Brown enjoyed a display of sheep-dipping by local farmers' (Brock 1997: 41–2).

12 There is no evidence to support the thesis of an intimate relationship between Queen Victoria and John Brown, so any decision on whether or not to display such a relationship would be based on speculation. Elizabeth Longford states that 'Queen Victoria, naïve and obstinate as ever, kept providing fresh evidence of her infatuation', but argues: 'That the Queen was neither John Brown's mistress nor his morganatic wife should be clear from a study of her character' (Longford 1964: 330).

13 I am grateful to Steve Chibnall for pointing out the significance of these paintings.

14 For an extended discussion of the instability of the heritage film as a category, see Claire Monk's chapter in this volume (Chapter 12).

15 One critic argued: 'Perhaps it's a sign that the transformation has not been entirely successful that your sympathies are focused more on the decline in her sense of a decent hairstyle, than on the consumption of her spirit by experience and cunning' (Gilbey 98).

Bibliography

Andrew, D. (2000) 'Film and history' in J. Hill and P. Church Gibson (eds) *Oxford Guide to Film Studies*, Oxford: Oxford University Press.

Barta, T. (ed.) (1998) *Screening the Past: Film and the Representation of History*, London: Praeger.

Bennett, A. (1995a) *The Madness of George III*, London: Faber and Faber.

—— (1995b) *The Madness of King George*, London: Faber and Faber.

Bermingham, A. (1986) *Landscape and Ideology*, Berkeley, CA: University of California Press.

Brock, J. (1997) *Mrs Brown* [screenplay], London: Methuen.

Burns, R. (1993) *Poems, Songs and Ballads*, London: Chancellor Press.

Church Gibson, P. (2000) 'Fewer weddings and more funerals: changes in the heritage film' in R. Murphy (ed.) *British Cinema of the 90s*, London: BFI: 115–24.

Coward, R. (1998) 'Birthday Soup', *The Guardian*, 14 November 1998.

Craig, C. (1991) 'Rooms without a view', *Sight and Sound*, June 1991: 10–13.

Ellis, J. (1997) '*Mrs Brown*' [review], Nebadoon, http://ellis.nebadoon.com/docs/joined_reviewfiles/MRS_BROWN.html [10 April 2000].

Gilbey, R. (1998) 'The tale of a royal hair-raiser', *The Independent*, 1 October 1998.

Granger, S. (1981) *Sparks Fly Upward*, London: Granada.

Harper, S. (1994) *Picturing the Past: The Rise and Fall of the British Costume Film*, London: BFI.

Hill, J. (1999) *British Cinema in the 1980s*, Oxford: Oxford University Press.

Hirst, M. (1998) *The Script of Elizabeth*, London: Macmillan.

de Lisle, R. (1998) 'Shekhar Kapur – the original Elizabethan' [interview], *Independent on Sunday*, 27 September 1998.

Longford, E. (1964) *Victoria R. I.*, London: Weidenfeld and Nicholson.

Luckett, M. (2000) 'Image and nation in 1990s British cinema' in R. Murphy (ed.), *British Cinema in the 90s*, London: BFI.

O'Mealy, J. (1998) 'Royal family values: the Americanisation of Alan Bennett's *The Madness of George III*', *Film and Literature Quarterly*, 5: 90–6.

Strong, R. (1995) *The Tudor and Stuart Monarchy*, Woodbridge: Boydell Press.

Wu, D. (2000) *Making Plays*, London: Macmillan.

Selective filmography

Compiled by Darren Kerr, Claire Monk and Amy Sargeant

This filmography lists all British and Irish films and television programmes and series mentioned within the text which are either set in the past (in the case of fiction films and television dramas/drama serials) or which deal – in some sense or another – with 'historical' subjects. Films and television programmes/films/series are listed if they are British or Irish and fall into the following categories:

1   Fiction films and television dramas, one-off films or drama serials which were set in the past at the time when they were made, including those belonging to recognised period or historical film or television genres (historical, costume, heritage or retro films, television historical or costume dramas/serials, etc.).
2   Factual film documentaries or television programmes/series on historical subjects.
3   Films or television programmes/series recording or exploring contemporary events from a historical perspective.

Films set in recent or temporally non-specific pasts are included (e.g. *The Cement Garden*). Also included is the documentary *A Queen Is Crowned*, which constructs the 1953 coronation of Elizabeth II as a contemporary historical (and historic) event, while locating it with reference to earlier English history.

In cases where the 'Britishness', 'Irishness' or 'historical' status of a given film or television programme/series is ambiguous or contentious, our principle has been to include the film or programme/series concerned. Primarily, the filmography lists films and television productions which are British or Irish in production origin and/or funding. However, productions made and/or funded by non-British/non-Irish companies, or with substantial input from non-British/non-Irish personnel, are included if they are 'British' or 'Irish' in their subject-matter, source narratives, events depicted and/or settings. For example, the many 'British' colonial adventures or 'Irish' (melo)dramas produced by Hollywood studios and directed by US directors are included, as is Orson Welles's *Chimes at Midnight*, a Shakespearean film featuring British actors but made as a Swiss/Spanish co-production, and Kenneth Branagh's US-funded but partly British-cast *Love's Labour's Lost*, even though Branagh transposes Shakespeare's narrative to 1930s America. Baz Lurhmann's *William Shakespeare's 'Romeo + Juliet'* is, however, not included, since it is set in the present-day USA. We have also excluded a small number of productions which are British-funded but non-British in every other significant respect (production personnel, subject and setting).

Films and television productions cited in the text but not listed here (i.e. those which are non-British and non-Irish, and/or which are set in the present and/or deal with non-historical subjects) can be located via the index.

• Entries are listed alphabetically by title.
• Film titles are indicated in capitals (*ACES HIGH*).
• Titles of television programmes or series, or feature-length television dramas/films, are indicated in upper and lower case (*Brideshead Revisited*).

Data for each entry is presented in the following order:

UK title; year (usually the date of the first public screening); production company/ies; registered country/ies of origin; director (D); producer (P); scriptwriter(s) (S) and literary source, if any; leading cast (C); a brief description, indicating genre, subject and period setting.

Where any details are omitted, this is because they have proved unavailable.

The following abbreviations are also used:

BBC   British Broadcasting Corporation
BFI   British Film Institute
ITV   Independent Television network, UK
LWT   London Weekend Television
MGM   Metro-Goldwyn-Mayer
PoW   Prisoner of war
RTE   Radio-Television Eireann (Ireland)
TV   Programme/film/series produced for television and never screened in cinemas
UA   United Artists
UK   United Kingdom
USA   United States of America
UTV   Ulster Television (Northern Ireland)
WW1   First World War (1914–18)
WW2   Second World War (1939–45)

The information in this filmography has been compiled from a variety of sources. These include: the British Film Institute's SIFT database, *Monthly Film Bulletin* (to 1991) and *Sight and Sound* (from 1991); Denis Gifford's *British Film Catalogue 1895–1985*, Rachael Low's *History of the British Film* seven volumes (1948–85), London: Allen & Unwin, spanning 1896–1939; and the Internet Movie Database (www.imbd.co.uk).

ACES HIGH (1976)
EMI/Fisz. UK/France. D: Jack Gold.
P: S. Benjamin Fisz/Jacques Roitfeld. S: Howard Barker, from R. C. Sherriff's stage play *Journey's End*. C: Malcolm McDowell, Christopher Plummer, Simon Ward, Peter Firth, John Gielgud, Trevor Howard.
WW1 drama: British airforce.

THE ADVENTURES OF DICK TURPIN, THE KING OF HIGHWAYMEN (1912)
UK. C: Percy Moran, Ernest Trimmingham. No further details.

ALFRED THE GREAT (1969)
MGM. UK. D: Clive Donner
P: Bernard Smith. S: Ken Taylor, James R. Webb. C: David Hemmings, Michael York, Prunella Ransome, Colin Blakely, Julian Glover.
Historical monarchy drama aimed at youth market: in AD 871, Alfred supersedes his weak older brother as king.

ANGELS AND INSECTS (1995)
Playhouse International/Samuel Goldwyn Co. UK/USA. D: Philip Haas.
P: Joyce Herlihy, Belinda Haas. S: Belinda Haas, from A. S. Byatt's novella *Morpho Eugenia*.
C: Mark Rylance, Kristin Scott Thomas, Patsy Kensit, Douglas Henshall, Jeremy Kemp.
Victorian drama about social class, entomology, Darwinism and incest.

ANNE OF THE THOUSAND DAYS (1969)
Universal. UK. D: Charles Jarrott.
P: Hal B. Wallis. S: John Hale, Bridget Boland, from Maxwell Anderson's stage play.
C: Richard Burton, Genevieve Bujold, John Colicos, Irene Papas, Anthony Quayle.
Historical drama; Henry VIII's marriage to Anne Boleyn.

ANOTHER COUNTRY (1984)
Goldcrest. UK. D: Marek Kanievska.
P: Alan Marshall. S: Julian Mitchell, from his stage play. C: Rupert Everett, Colin Firth, Michael Jenn, Robert Addie.
1930s drama: the public-school memories of a homosexual defector from Britain to the Soviet Union (based on the spy Guy Burgess).

ANOTHER TIME, ANOTHER PLACE (1983)
Channel Four Films/Scottish Arts Council. D: Michael Radford.
P: Simon Perry. S: Jessie Kesson, Radford. C: Phyllis Logan, Giovanni Mauriello, Denise Coffey, Tom Watson, Gian Luca Favilla, Claudio Rosini.
Romantic WW2 drama: Italian PoWs in rural Scotland.

AS YOU LIKE IT (1992)
Sands Films. UK. D: Christine Edzard.
P: Richard Goodwin. S: Uncredited, from William Shakespeare's stage play. C: Andrew Tiernan, Emma Croft, Don Henderson, Celia Bannerman, Griff Rhys Jones.
Shakespearean romantic comedy.

BACKBEAT (1993)
Film Four/Polygram. UK/Germany. D: Iain Softley.
P: Stephen Woolley, Finola Dwyer. S: Softley, Michael Thomas. C: Stephen Dorff, Ian Hart, Sheryl Lee, Gary Bakewell.
1960s pop bio-pic of Stuart Sutcliffe, fifth member of The Beatles.

THE BANDIT OF ZHOBE (1959)
Columbia. UK. D/S: John Gilling.
P: Irving Allen. C: Victor Mature, Anne Aubrey, Anthony Newley, Norman Wooland.
Colonial action-adventure: 19th-century India under British rule.

BATTLE OF BRITAIN (1969)
UA/Spitfire. UK. D: Guy Hamilton.
P: Harry Saltzman, S. Benjamin Fisz. S: James Kennaway, Wilfrid Greatorex. C: Laurence Olivier, Robert Shaw, Michael Caine, Christopher Plummer, Kenneth More, Susannah York.
WW2 drama: the air attacks on Britain of summer 1940.

THE BATTLE OF JUTLAND (1921)
British Instructional Films. UK. P: H. Bruce Woolfe.
WW1 battle reconstruction: the May 1916 naval battle.

THE BATTLE OF THE SOMME (1916)
British Topical Committee for War Films/War Office. UK. P: William F. Jury.
WW1: official briefing film for instruction of troops.

THE BATTLES OF THE CORONEL AND FALKLAND ISLANDS (1927)
British Instructional Films. UK. P: H. Bruce Woolfe.
Battle reconstructions.

BEAU BRUMMELL (1954)
MGM. UK/USA. D: Curtis Bernhard.
P: Sam Zimbalist. S: Karl Tunberg, from Clyde Fitch's stage play. C: Stewart Granger, Elizabeth Taylor, Peter Ustinov, Robert Morley.
Regency historical romance about the famous dandy.

BECKET (1964)
Paramount. UK. D: Peter Glenville.
P: Hal B. Wallis. S: Edward Anhalt, from Jean Anouilh's stage play. C: Richard Burton, Peter O'Toole, John Gielgud, Donald Wolfit.
Epic historical drama about Henry VI's archbishop Thomas à Becket.

THE BEGGAR'S OPERA (1953)
Imperadio. UK. D: Peter Brook.
P: Herbert Wilcox, Laurence Olivier. S: Dennis Cannan, Christopher Fry, from John Gay's opera. C: Laurence Olivier, Stanley Holloway, Dorothy Tutin, Daphne Anderson, Mary Clare.
Drama based on Gay's 1726 low opera: a highwayman imprisoned in London's Newgate jail writes an opera based on his exploits.

BILLY ELLIOT (2000)
Working Title/BBC Films/Arts Council of England/Tiger Aspect. UK. D: Stephen Daldry.
P: Greg Brenman, Jon Finn. S: Lee Hall. C: Jamie Bell, Gary Lewis, Julie Walters, Jamie Draven.
Working-class/male ballet drama set in County Durham, north-east England, during the 1982 miners' strike.

Blackadder (TV) (1983)
BBC-TV. UK. D: Mandie Fletcher, Martin Shardlow.
P: John Lloyd. S: Rowan Atkinson, Richard Curtis. C: Atkinson, Brian Blessed, Peter Cook, Robert East.
Historical spoof comedy.

Blackadder II (TV) (1986)
BBC-TV. UK. D: Mandie Fletcher.
P: John Lloyd. S: Richard Curtis, Ben Elton. C: Rowan Atkinson, Tim McInnerny, Tony Robinson, Miranda Richardson.
Historical spoof comedy: the Elizabethan court.

Blackadder the Third (TV) (1987)
BBC-TV. UK. D: Mandie Fletcher.
P: John Lloyd. S: Richard Curtis, Ben Elton. C: Rowan Atkinson, Tony Robinson, Hugh Laurie, Helen Atkinson-Wood.
Historical spoof comedy.

Blackadder Goes Forth (TV) (1989)
BBC-TV. UK. D: Richard Boden.
P: John Lloyd. S: Richard Curtis, Ben Elton. C: Rowan Atkinson, Tony Robinson, Stephen Fry, Hugh Laurie.
Historical spoof comedy: WW1.

BLEAK HOUSE (1920)
Ideal. UK. D: Maurice Elvey.
S: William J. Elliot, from Charles Dickens's novel. C: Constance Collier, Berta Gellardi, E. Vivian Reynolds, Norman Page.
Victorian satire on inheritance and the legal profession.

BONNIE PRINCE CHARLIE (1923)
Gaumont-British Screencraft. UK. D: C. C. Calvert.
S: Alice Ramsay. C: Adeline Haydn Coffin, Gladys Cooper, Lewis Gilbert, A. B. Imeson.
Historical drama about Charles Edward Stuart, Scottish leader of the 1745–6 Jacobite uprising.

THE BOY FRIEND (1971)
MGM/Russfix. UK. D/P: Ken Russell.
S: Russell, from Sandy Wilson's stage musical. C: Twiggy, Christopher Gable, Max Adrian, Tommy Tune, Barbara Windsor.
1920s backstage musical drama.

Brideshead Revisited (TV) (1981)
Granada TV. UK. D: Michael Lindsay-Hogg, Charles Sturridge.
P: Derek Granger. S: John Mortimer, from Evelyn Waugh's novel. C: Anthony Andrews, Jeremy Irons, Diana Quick, Laurence Olivier, Claire Bloom.
13-part serial: upper-class family drama set between WW1 and WW2.

THE BRIGAND OF KANDAHAR (1965)
Hammer. UK. D/S: John Gilling
P: Anthony Nelson Keys. C: Oliver Reed, Ronald Lewis, Duncan Lamont, Yvonne Romain.
Colonial action-adventure: 19th-century India under British rule.

CAPTAIN BOYCOTT (1946)
Individual Pictures. UK. D: Frank Launder.

P: Sidney Gilliatt, Launder. S: Wolfgang Wilhelm, Launder, Paul Vincent Carroll, Patrick Campbell, from Philip Rooney's novel. C: Stewart Granger, Kathleen Ryan, Alistair Sim, Robert Donat, Cecil Parker.
1880s Irish historical drama: impoverished Irish farmers rebel against English landowners.

CARAVAGGIO (1986)
BFI. UK. D/S: Derek Jarman.
P: Sarah Radclyffe. C: Nigel Terry, Sean Bean, Dexter Fletcher, Tilda Swinton, Nigel Davenport.
Speculative bio-pic of the homosexual Italian painter (1571–1610).

THE CARD (1952)
British Film Makers/Rank. UK. D: Ronald Neame.
P: John Bryan. S: Eric Ambler, from Arnold Bennett's novel. C: Alec Guinness, Petula Clark, Glynis Johns, Valerie Hobson.
Edwardian comedy-drama set in the Staffordshire Potteries.

CARRINGTON (1995)
UK. D/W: Christopher Hampton.
C: Emma Thompson, Jonathan Pryce, Jeremy Northam, Samuel West.
Bloomsbury Set bio-pic: love affairs of artist Dora Carrington and her agonised relationship with gay biographer Lytton Strachey in 1920s England.

CARRY ON CLEO (1964)
Anglo Amalgamated. UK. D: Gerald Thomas.
P: Peter Rogers. S: Talbot Rothwell. C: Sidney James, Kenneth Williams, Kenneth Connor, Amanda Barrie.
Historical comedy spoof of Roman film epics, especially *Cleopatra* (1963).

CARRY ON COLUMBUS (1992)
Comedy House/Island World Pictures/Peter Rogers Productions. UK. D: Gerald Thomas.
P: John Goldstone. S: Dave Freeman. C: Jim Dale, Bernard Cribbins, Peter Richardson, Maureen Lipman.
Historical comedy: the 15th-century Italian explorer's 1492 discovery of the (supposed) New World.

CARRY ON COWBOY (1965)
Anglo Amalgamated. UK. D: Gerald Thomas.
P: Peter Rogers. S: Talbot Rothwell. C: Sidney James, Jim Dale, Charles Hawtrey, Joan Sims.
Comedy: spoof Western.

CARRY ON DICK (1974)
Rank. UK. D: Gerald Thomas.
P: Peter Rogers. S: Talbot Rothwell. C: Sidney James, Kenneth Williams, Barbara Windsor, Hattie Jacques.
Historical comedy: the 18th-century English highwayman Dick Turpin.

CARRY ON DON'T LOSE YOUR HEAD (1966)
See *DON'T LOSE YOUR HEAD* (1966)

CARRY ON ENGLAND (1976)
Rank. UK. D: Gerald Thomas.
P: Peter Rogers. S: David Pursall, Jack Seddon. C: Kenneth Connor, Windsor Davies, Patrick Mower, Judy Geeson.
Comedy: the Home Front during WW2.

CARRY ON FOLLOW THAT CAMEL (1966)
See *FOLLOW THAT CAMEL* (1966)

CARRY ON HENRY (1971)
Rank. UK. D: Gerald Thomas.
P: Peter Rogers. S: Talbot Rothwell. C: Sidney James, Kenneth Williams, Charles Hawtrey, Joan Sims.
Historical comedy: spoof of recent historical films and TV dramas about Henry VIII.

CARRY ON JACK (1963)
Anglo Amalgamated. UK. D: Gerald Thomas.
P: Peter Rogers. S: Talbot Rothwell. C: Bernard Cribbins, Juliet Mills, Charles Hawtrey, Kenneth Williams.
Seafaring comedy: spoof of C. S. Forester's Hornblower adventure novels set during the Napoleonic Wars.

CARRY ON SCREAMING (1966)
Anglo Amalgamated. UK. D: Gerald Thomas.
P: Peter Rogers. S: Talbot Rothwell. C: Harry H. Corbett, Kenneth Williams, Fenella Fielding, Joan Sims.
Comedy: spoof of Hammer horror films.

CARRY ON UP THE JUNGLE (1970)
Rank. UK. D: Gerald Thomas.
P: Peter Rogers. S: Talbot Rothwell. C: Frankie Howard, Sidney James, Charles Hawtrey, Joan Sims.
Jungle adventure comedy.

CARRY ON UP THE KHYBER (1968)
Rank. UK. D: Gerald Thomas.
P: Peter Rogers. S: Talbot Rothwell. C: Sidney James, Kenneth Williams, Charles Hawtrey, Roy Castle.
Comedy: spoof of British Empire adventure literature and films, especially Kipling.

THE CEMENT GARDEN (1992)
Constantin Film/Torii Productions/Sylvia Montalti/Laurentic. UK/Germany/France. D: Andrew Birkin.
P: Bee Gilbert, Ene Vanaveski. S: Birkin, from Ian McEwan's novel. C: Andrew Robertson, Charlotte Gainsbourg, Alice Coulthard, Ned Birkin, Sinead Cusack, Hanns Zischler.
Family/sibling incest drama set in an indefinite recent past: the teenage son and daughter of dead parents take on parental roles to preserve the family.

THE CHARGE OF THE LIGHT BRIGADE (1968)
UA/Woodfall. UK. D: Tony Richardson.

P: Neil Hartley. S: Charles Wood. C: Trevor Howard, John Gielgud, David Hemmings, Vanessa Redgrave, Harry Andrews.
Revisionist military drama: the Crimean War, 1854.

CHARIOTS OF FIRE (1981)
Allied Stars/Enigma. UK. D: Hugh Hudson.
P: David Puttnam. S: Colin Welland. C: Ben Cross, Ian Charleson, Ian Holm, Cheryl Campbell, Alice Krige.
Biographical sporting drama: personal struggles of British athletes Harold Abrahams and Eric Liddell leading to national triumph at the 1924 Olympics.

CHIMES AT MIDNIGHT (1965)
Internacional Films Espanola/Alpine. Spain/Switzerland. D: Orson Welles.
P: Alessandro Tasca. S: Orson Welles, from William Shakespeare's history plays. C: Orson Welles, John Gielgud, Margaret Rutherford, Jeanne Moreau.
Shakepearean drama telescoping characters and events from several plays.

THE COLDITZ STORY (1954)
British Lion. UK. D: Guy Hamilton.
P: Ivan Foxwell. S: Hamilton, Ivan Foxwell, from Pat Reid's book. C: John Mills, Eric Portman, Christopher Rhodes, Lionel Jeffries, Bryan Forbes.
WW2 PoW drama.

Colour Blind (TV) (1998)
Festival Film and Television for Carlton. UK. D: Alan Grint.
P: Ray Marshall. S: Gordon Hann, from Catherine Cookson's novel. C: Niamh Cusack, Tony Armatrading, Joe Caffrey, Elspeth Charlton.
Inter-racial romance set between WW1 and WW2.

COMIN' THROUGH THE RYE (1923)
Hepworth Picture Plays. UK. D/P: Cecil M. Hepworth.
S: Blanche McIntosh, from Helen Mathers's novel. C: Alma Taylor, Shayle Garner, Eileen Dennes, Ralph Forbes, Francis Lister.
Romantic drama set in Victorian England.

COMRADESHIP (1919)
Stoll. UK. D: Maurice Elvey.
S: Jeffrey Bernerd, Louis N. Parker. C: Lily Elsie, Gerald Ames, Guy Newall, Peggy Carlisle.
WW1 drama.

THE CRUEL SEA (1953)
Ealing. UK. D: Charles Frend.
P: Leslie Norman. S: Eric Ambler, from Nicholas Monsarrat's novel. C: Jack Hawkins, Donald Sinden, Stanley Baker, John Stratton, Virginia McKenna.
WW2 naval drama.

Culloden (TV) (1965)
BBC-TV. UK. D/P: Peter Watkins.

S: John Prebble, Watkins.
Docu-drama reconstructing the 1746 Battle of Culloden, the final engagement of the Scottish Jacobite uprising.

THE DAM BUSTERS (1954)

Associated British Picture Corporation. UK. D: Michael Anderson.
P: Robert Clark. S: R. C. Sherriff, from books by Guy Gibson and Paul Brickhill.
C: Michael Redgrave, Richard Todd, Basil Sydney, Derek Farr, Patrick Barr.
WW2 drama: 1946 destruction of the Rühr dam by British bouncing bombs.

DANCE WITH A STRANGER (1985)

Goldcrest/NFFC/First Picture Co. UK. D: Mike Newell.
P: Roger Randall-Cutler. S: Shelagh Delaney. C: Miranda Richardson, Rupert Everett, Ian Holm, Matthew Carroll.
Biographical drama: the life and *crime passionel* of Ruth Ellis, last woman to be hanged in Britain.

DAWN (1928)

British and Dominions Film Corporation. UK. D/P: Herbert Wilcox.
S: Wilcox, Robert Cullen, from Reginald Berkeley's stage play. C: Sybil Thorndyke, Marie Ault, Mary Brough, Haddon Mason.
WW1 drama: the activities of Nurse Edith Cavell, Brussels 1914.

THE DEMI-PARADISE (1943)

Two Cities Films. UK. D: Anthony Asquith.
P/S: Anatole de Grunwald. C: Laurence Olivier, Penelope Dudley Ward, Marjorie Fielding, Margaret Rutherford, Leslie Henson.
Satirical comedy: A Russian inventor observes 1939 Britain.

THE DEVILS (1971)

Warner/Russo. UK. D: Ken Russell.
P: Robert H. Solo, Russell. S: Russell, from John Whiting's play and Aldous Huxley's book. C: Vanessa Redgrave, Oliver Reed, Dudley Sutton, Max Adrian, Gemma Jones.
Historical drama: sexual hysteria among nuns, religious persecution and torture in 17th-century Loudun, France.

DON'T LOSE YOUR HEAD (1966)

Rank. UK. D: Gerald Thomas.
P: Peter Rogers. S: Talbot Rothwell. C: Sidney James, Kenneth Williams, Jim Dale, Charles Hawtrey.
Historical comedy: *Carry On* spoof of French Revolution historical films, especially *The Scarlet Pimpernel*.

THE DRUM (1938)

London Films. UK. D: Zoltan Korda.
P: Alexander Korda. S: Lajos Biró, Arthur Wimperis, Patrick Kirwan, Hugh Gray, from A. E. W. Mason's novel. C: Sabu, Roger Livesey, Raymond Massey, Valerie Hobson, Desmond Tester.
Colonial adventure set during British rule in India.

DUNKIRK (1958)
Ealing. UK. D: Leslie Norman.
P: Michael Balcon. S: W. P. Lipscomb, David Divine. C: John Mills, Bernard Lee, Richard Attenborough, Robert Urquhart.
WW2 drama: evacuation of the British Expeditionary Force from Dunkirk, 1940.

EDWARD II (1991)
Working Title/BBC/British Screen. UK. D: Derek Jarman.
P: Steve Clark-Hall, Anthony Root. S: Jarman, from Christopher Marlowe's stage play.
C: Steven Waddington, Andrew Tiernan, Tilda Swinton, Nigel Terry.
Queer historical drama: the 12th-century British monarch falls foul of political plotting prompted by his gay relationship with commoner Piers Gaveston.

1871 (1990)
Film Four International. UK. D: Ken McMullen.
P: Stewart Richards. S: Terry James, James Leahy, McMullen. C: Jack Klaff, John Lynch, Roshan Seth, Ana Padrão, Ian McNiece.
Avant-garde historical drama: the establishment of the 1871 Paris Commune after the Franco–Prussian War.

ELIZABETH (1998)
Channel Four Films/Polygram/Working Title. UK. D: Shekhar Kapur.
P: Tim Bevan, Eric Fellner, Alison Owen. S: Michael Hirst. C: Cate Blanchett, Joseph Fiennes, Geoffrey Rush, Christopher Eccleston.
Historical/political thriller: the metamorphosis of Elizabeth I from princess to 'Virgin Queen'; 16th century.

ELIZABETH IS QUEEN (1953)
Associated British Pathé. UK. D: Uncredited.
P: Howard Thomas. S: John Pudney. Narrated by Leo Genn.
Documentary: the coronation of Elizabeth II, 1953.

The Far Pavilions (TV) (1984)
Acorn/ITV. UK. D: Peter Duffell.
P: Geoffrey Reeve. S: Julian Bond, from M. M. Kaye's novel. C: Ben Cross, Amy Irving, Omar Sharif, Rossano Brazzi, Benedict Taylor.
Drama serial: India under British colonial rule, late 19th century.

THE FILTH AND THE FURY (2000)
Film Four/The Sex Pistols. UK/USA. D: Julien Temple.
P: Anita Camarata, Amanda Temple. With Paul Cook, Steve Jones, Glen Matlock, John Lydon, Sid Vicious.
Feature-length punk rock documentary: the Sex Pistols's story.

FIRE OVER ENGLAND (1937)
London Films/Pendennis. UK. D: William K. Howard.
P: Erich Pommer. S: Clemence Dane, Sergei Nolbandov, from A. E. W. Mason's novel.
C: Flora Robson, Laurence Olivier, Lesley Banks, Vivien Leigh, Raymond Massey.
Historical drama: Elizabeth I and her navy defeat the Spanish Armada (1588).

THE FLAG LIEUTENANT (1926)
Astra–National. UK. D: Maurice Elvey.
S: P. L. Mannock. C: Henry Edwards, Fred Raynham, Fewlass Llewellyn, Lionel D'Aragon, Lilian Oldland.
Period naval drama.

FLAMES OF PASSION (1922)
Graham–Wilcox Productions. UK. D: Graham Cutts.
P: Herbert Wilcox. S: Wilcox, M. V. Wilcox. C: Mae Marsh, Herbert Langley, Allan Ainsworth, Eva Moore, C. Aubrey Smith.
Period costume melodrama.

FOLLOW THAT CAMEL (1966)
Rank. UK. D: Gerald Thomas.
P: Peter Rogers. S: Talbot Rothwell. C: Phil Silvers, Jim Dale, Peter Butterworth, Charles Hawtrey.
Historical comedy: *Carry On* spoof of French Foreign Legion films, especially *Beau Geste*.

FOOLS OF FORTUNE (1990)
Film Four/PolyGram/Working Title. UK. D: Pat O'Connor.
P: Tim Bevan, Sarah Radclyffe. C: Iain Glen, Julie Christie, Mary Elizabeth Mastrantonio, Michael Kitchen.
Family chronicle set against a backdrop of 1920s Anglo-Irish conflict.

FOR QUEEN AND COUNTRY (1988)
Zenith/Working Title. UK/USA. D: Martin Stellman.
P: Tim Bevan. S: Stellman, Trix Worrell. C: Denzel Washington, Dorian Healy, Amanda Redman, Sean Chapman.
Political drama; a black British paratrooper returns from the 1982 Falklands/Malvinas War to south London and threatened repatriation to the Caribbean.

THE FOUR FEATHERS (1939)
London Films. UK. D: Zoltan Korda.
P: Alexander Korda, Irving Asher. S: R. C. Sherriff, Lajos Biró, Arthur Wimperis. C: John Clements, Ralph Richardson, C. Aubrey Smith, June Duprez, Allan Jeayes.
British colonial adventure set in 1890s Sudan.

FRANTZ FANON: BLACK SKIN, WHITE MASK (1996)
Normal Film/BBC/Arts Council of England/L'Institut National de l'Audiovisuel. UK/France. D: Isaac Julien.
P: Mark Nash. S: Julien, Nash. C: Colin Salmon.
Documentary blending archive footage, dramatisation, commentary and interviews: the work and ideas of the Martinique-born psychiatrist and pioneer theorist of colonialism (1925–61).

THE FRENCH LIEUTENANT'S WOMAN (1981)
UA/Juniper. UK. D: Karel Reisz.
P: Leon Clore. S: Harold Pinter, from John Fowles's novel. C: Jeremy Irons, Meryl Streep, David Warner, Leo McKern, Patience Carver.

Romantic drama about Victorian sexual/social attitudes set in 19th-century Lyme Regis, Dorset.

A FUNNY THING HAPPENED ON THE WAY TO THE FORUM (1966)
UA/Quadrangle. UK. D: Richard Lester.
P: Melvin Frank. S: Frank, Michael Pertwee, from Burt Shevelove, Larry Gelbart and Stephen Sondheim's stage musical. C: Zero Mostel, Phil Silvers, Michael Crawford, Michael Hordern.
Farce set in Ancient Rome.

GANDHI (1982)
Goldcrest/Indo-British/International Film Investors/National Film Development Corporation of India. UK. D: Richard Attenborough.
P: Attenborough, Rani Dube. S: John Briley. C: Ben Kingsley, Rohini Hattangadi, Roshan Seth, Candice Bergen, Edward Fox.
Bio-pic: the life of the Indian lawyer, Indian independence activist and statesman Mahatma Gandhi from 1914 to his assassination in 1948.

THE GO-BETWEEN (1970)
EMI/World Film Services. UK. D: Joseph Losey.
P: John Heyman, Norman Priggin. S: Harold Pinter, from L. P. Hartley's novel. C: Alan Bates, Julie Christie, Dominic Guard, Michael Redgrave, Michael Gough.
Edwardian drama: the cross-class affair of a wealthy young woman and a local farmer conducted via a child messenger.

GREAT EXPECTATIONS (1946)
Cineguild. UK. D: David Lean.
P: Anthony Havelock-Allan, Ronald Neame. S: Neame, Lean, Havelock-Allan, Kay Walsh, Cecil McGivern, from Charles Dickens's novel. C: John Mills, Bernard Miles, Finlay Currie, Martita Hunt, Valerie Hobson.
Victorian drama: a young boy's encounter with an escaped convict brings strange consequences.

Great Expectations (TV) (1999)
BBC-TV. UK. D: Julien Jarrold.
P: David Snodin. S: Tony Marchant, from Charles Dickens's novel. C: Ioan Gruffudd, Charlotte Rampling, Bernard Hill, Justine Waddell.
Victorian drama.

THE GREAT ROCK 'N' ROLL SWINDLE (1979)
Kendon Films/Matrixbest. UK. D/S: Julien Temple.
P: Don Boyd, Jeremy Thomas. C: Malcolm McLaren, Sid Vicious, Johnny Rotten, Steve Jones, Paul Cook.
Eclectic punk rock feature: the Sex Pistols's story (1976–9) told as English profane comedy, mixing documentary footage, fictional sequences, set pieces and animation.

GUNGA DIN (1939)
RKO. USA. D/P: George Stevens.
S: Joel Sayre, Fred Guiol, Ben Hecht, Charles MacArthur. C: Cary Grant, Victor McLaglen, Douglas Fairbanks Jr, Sam Jaffe.
Colonial action/adventure/comedy: India, the North-West Frontier, 19th-century.

HAMLET (1997)
Castle Rock. USA. D: Kenneth Branagh.
P: David Barron. S: Branagh, from William Shakespeare's stage play. C: Branagh, Julie Christie, Derek Jacobi, Kate Winslet.
Shakespearean tragic drama updated to 19th-century Denmark.

A HANDFUL OF DUST (1988)
LWT/Stagescreen. UK. D: Charles Sturridge.
P: Derek Granger. S: Tim Sullivan, Granger, from Evelyn Waugh's novel. C: James Wilby, Kristin Scott Thomas, Rupert Graves, Judi Dench, Anjelica Huston, Alec Guinness.
Tragic drama: 1930s upper-class adultery, betrayal and decline.

HEAT AND DUST (1982)
Merchant Ivory Productions. UK. D: James Ivory.
P: Ismail Merchant. S: Ruth Prawer Jhabwala, from Jhabwala's novel. C: Julie Christie, Greta Scacchi, Shashi Kapoor, Christopher Cazenove, Jennifer Kendal.
Drama alternating between colonial India in the 1920s and independent India in the present.

HENRY V (1945)
Two Cities Films. UK. D/P: Laurence Olivier.
S: Olivier, Arthur Dent from William Shakespeare's stage play. C: Olivier, Robert Newton, Leslie Banks, Renée Asherson, Esmond Knight.
Shakepearean historical/war drama.

HENRY V (1989)
Renaissance Films. UK. D: Kenneth Branagh.
P: Bruce Sharman. S: Branagh, from William Shakespeare's stage play. C: Branagh, Derek Jacobi, Brian Blessed, Ian Holm.
Shakepearean historical/war drama.

HIDEOUS KINKY (1999)
BBC Films/Film Consortium/Arts Council/Greenpoint/L Films/AMLF. UK/France. D: Gillies MacKinnon.
P: Ann Scott. S: Billy MacKinnon, from Esther Freud's novel. C: Kate Winslet, Saïd Taghmaoui, Bella Riza, Carrie Mullan.
Autobiographically inspired drama set on the early-1970s hippie trail in Morocco and Algeria.

HILARY AND JACKIE (1998)
Film Four/Intermedia Films/Oxford Film Company. UK. D: Anand Tucker.
P: Andy Paterson, Nicolas Kent. S: Frank Cottrell Boyce, from the book *A Genius in the Family* by Hilary and Piers du Pré. C: Emily Watson, Rachel Griffiths, James Frain, David Morrissey.
Bio-pic: the relationship between the cello prodigy Jacqueline du Pré and her sister Hilary, 1950s–1980s.

A History of Britain (TV) (2000)
BBC-TV/The History Channel. UK/USA.
Executive Producer: Martin Davidson. S and presenter: Simon Schama.
Eight-part factual history series.

THE HISTORY OF MR POLLY (1949)
Rank/Two Cities Films. UK. D: Anthony Pelissier.
P: John Mills. S: Pelissier, from H. G. Wells's novel. C: John Mills, Sally Ann Howes, Megs Jenkins, Finlay Currie, Betty Ann Davies.
Edwardian semi-comic drama about the metamorphosis of a draper's assistant.

HMS DEFIANT (1962)
Columbia/GW. UK. D: Lewis Gilbert.
P: John Brabourne. S: Nigel Kneale, Edmund H. North, from Frank Tilsley's novel *Mutiny*. C: Alec Guinness, Dirk Bogarde, Anthony Quayle, Tom Bell, Nigel Stock.
Naval drama: mutiny erupts on an 18th-century British ship.

HOPE AND GLORY (1987)
Goldcrest/Nelson. UK. D/P/S: John Boorman.
C: Sarah Miles, Susan Wooldridge, Ian Bannen, David Hayman, Derrick O'Connor.
WW2 Home Front drama: events in suburban London through the eyes of a young boy.

Hope in the Year Two (TV) (1994)
BBC-TV. UK. D: Bill Bryden. S: Trevor Griffith.
Historical drama: awaiting execution in 1794 on Robespierre's orders, Georges Danton looks back on the events of the French Revolution.

HOWARDS END (1992)
Channel Four Films. UK. D: James Ivory.
P: Ismail Merchant. S: Ruth Prawer Jhabvala, from E. M. Forster's novel. C: Emma Thompson, Anthony Hopkins, Helena Bonham Carter, Vanessa Redgrave, Samuel West, James Wilby.
Drama of two families with contrasting values set in Edwardian London and south-east England.

HUNGRY HILL (1947)
Two Cities Films. UK. D: Brian Desmond Hurst.
P: William Sistrom. S: Daphne du Maurier, Terence Young, Francis Crowdy, from du Maurier's novel. C: Margaret Lockwood, Dennis Price, Michael Denison, F. J. McCormick, Dermot Walsh.
Costume melodrama: an Irish family feud over three generations.

In a Land of Plenty (TV) (2001)
BBC-TV. UK. D: Hettie MacDonald, David Moore.
P: John Chapman, Claire Hirsch, Michael Riley. S: Neil Biswas, Kevin Hood, from Tim Pears's novel. C: Robert Pugh, Helen McCrory, Shaun Dingwall, Lorraine Ashbourne.
Family saga: the fortunes of a northern English industrial family from 1950s to the present.

IN THE NAME OF THE FATHER (1993)
Universal/Hell's Kitchen. Ireland/UK/USA. D/P: Jim Sheridan.
S: Terry George, Sheridan, from Gerry Conlon's autobiography *Proved Innocent*. C: Daniel Day-Lewis, Pete Postlethwaite, Emma Thompson, John Lynch, Corin Redgrave.
Bio-pic of Gerry Conlon: one of the 'Guildford Four' wrongly convicted for the 1974 IRA bombing of a pub in Guildford, England.

The Irish RM (TV) (1983–5)
Channel Four TV/RTE/Rediffusion/UTV. UK/Ireland. D: Roy Ward Baker, Robert Chetwyn and others.
P: Barry Blackmore, Adrian Hughes, James Mitchell. C: Peter Bowles, Bryan Murray, Doran Godwin, Lise Ann McLaughlin, Sarah Badel.
Period comedy-drama series: an English major becomes a Resident Magistrate in Ireland.

The Jewel in the Crown (TV) (1984)
Granada TV. UK. D: Christopher Morahan, Jim O'Brien.
S: Ken Taylor, from Paul Scott's *Raj Quartet* novels. C: Tim Piggott-Smith, Peggy Ashcroft, Geraldine James, Susan Wooldridge, Art Malik, Charles Dance.
Fourteen-part colonial drama serial: the British in India, pre-independence 20th century.

J. M. Barrie and the Lost Boys (TV) (1978)
BBC-TV. UK. D: Rodney Bennett.
P: Louis Marks. S: Andrew Birkin. C: Ian Holm, Maureen O'Brien, Ann Bell, Tim Piggott-Smith, Anna Cropper.
Biographically based single drama set in the 1900s: the Scottish writer (creator of Peter Pan) and his obsessive friendship with the five sons of Arthur and Sylvia Llewellyn-Davies.

JOURNEY'S END (1930)
Gainsborough/Welsh–Pearson/Tiffany–Stahl. USA/UK. D: James Whale.
P: George Pearson. S: Joseph Moncure March, Gareth Gundrey, from R. C. Sherriff's stage play. C: Colin Clive, Ian MacLaren, David Manners, Billy Bevan, Anthony Bushell.
WW1 drama set in the French trenches, 1917.

KHARTOUM (1966)
UA. UK. D: Basil Dearden.
P: Julian Blaustein. S: Robert Ardrey. C: Charlton Heston, Laurence Olivier, Ralph Richardson, Richard Johnson.
Colonial action adventure/bio-pic: the last years of General Gordon, 1880s Sudan.

Kim (TV) (1984)
London Film Productions. UK. D: John Howard Davies.
P: Peter Manley, Jean Walter. S: James Braboza from Rudyard Kipling's novel. C: Ravi Sheth, Peter O'Toole, Bryan Brown, John Rhys-Davies.
Colonial action adventure: a British military orphan in India.

KIND HEARTS AND CORONETS (1949)
Ealing. UK. D: Robert Hamer.
P: Michael Relph. S: Hamer, John Dighton, from Roy Horniman's novel *Noblesse Oblige*. C: Dennis Price, Alec Guinness (x 8), Valerie Hobson, Joan Greenwood.
Black comedy: class, inheritance and murder in Edwardian England.

KING AND COUNTRY (1964)
BHE. UK. D: Joseph Losey.
P: Norman Priggen, Losey. S: Evan Jones, from John Wilson's stage play *Hamp*. C: Dirk Bogarde, Tom Courtenay, Leo McKern, Barry Foster.
WW1 court-martial drama.

KIPPS (1921)
Stoll. UK. D: Harold M. Shaw.
S: Frank Miller, from H. G. Wells's novel. C: George K. Arthur, Edna Flugrath, Christine Rayner, Teddy Arundell, Norman Thorpe.
Edwardian period comedy about an upwardly mobile draper's assistant.

KIPPS (1941)
Twentieth Century–Fox. UK. D: Carol Reed.
P: Edward Black. S: Sidney Gilliat, from H. G. Wells's novel. C: Michael Redgrave, Phyllis Calvert, Diana Wynyard, Arthur Riscoe, Max Adrian.
Edwardian period comedy about an upwardly mobile draper's assistant.

Kurt and Courtney (1998)
Strength Ltd for BBC-TV. UK. D/P: Nick Broomfield.
Documentary: the director tracks down US rock performer turned actress Courtney Love after the overdose of her husband, Nirvana vocalist Kurt Cobain.

LADY JANE (1986)
Paramount. UK/USA. D: Trevor Nunn.
P: Peter Snell. S: David Edgar, Chris Bryant. C: Helena Bonham Carter, Cary Elwes, John Wood, Michael Hordern, Jill Bennett, Jane Lapotaire.
Historical drama/romance: the story of Lady Jane Grey, Queen of England for nine days after Edward VI's death in 1553.

LAND AND FREEDOM (1995)
Parallax Pictures/Messidor Films/Road Movies Dritte. UK/Spain/Germany. D: Ken Loach.
P: Rebecca O'Brien. S: Jim Allen. C: Ian Hart, Rosana Pastor, Icíar Bollaín, Tom Gilroy.
Historical drama: the fight of the anti-Franco International Brigade in the Spanish Civil War (1936–9), particularly its British volunteers.

THE LAND GIRLS (1998)
InterMedia. UK. D: David Leland.
P: Simon Relph. S: Leland, Keith Dewhurst, from Angela Huth's novel. C: Catherine McCormack, Rachel Weisz, Anna Friel, Steven Macintosh.
WW2 Home Front drama: lives and loves of three land girls (agricultural workers).

Landscape and Memory (TV) (1995)
BBC-TV. UK. D: Various. S: Simon Schama.
Five-part factual series illustrating the relationship between culture and the natural environment.

LAWRENCE OF ARABIA (1962)
Horizon. UK. D: David Lean.
P: Sam Spiegel. S: Robert Bolt, from T. E. Lawrence's memoirs. C: Peter O'Toole, Omar Sharif, Jack Hawkins, Donald Wolfit, Anthony Quayle, Alec Guinness, Anthony Quinn.
Epic bio-pic of the desert adventurer T. E. Lawrence, who helped to lead the Arab revolt against the Turks in the Middle East during WW1.

THE LIFE STORY OF LLOYD GEORGE (1918)
UK. D: Maurice Elvey.
S: Sydney Low. C: Douglas Munro, Norman Page, Alma Reville, Ernest Thesiger.
Bio-pic: achievements to date of the Liberal statesman David Lloyd George, Chancellor of the Exchequer (1908–16) and Prime Minister (1916–22).

THE LION IN WINTER (1968)
Avco Embassy/Haworth. UK. D: Anthony Harvey.
P: Martin Poll. S: James Goldman, from his play. C: Katherine Hepburn, Peter O'Toole, Jane Merrow, John Castle, Anthony Hopkins.
Historical drama: domestic rows between Henry II and Eleanor of Aquitaine over the royal succession in 1183.

LIVES OF A BENGAL LANCER (1934)
Paramount. USA. D: Henry Hathaway.
P: Louis D. Lighton. S: Waldemar Young, John F. Balderston, Achmed Abdullah, Grover Jones, William Slavens McNut, from Francis Yeats-Brown's book. C: Gary Cooper, Franchot Tone, Richard Cromwell, Sir Guy Standing, C. Aubrey Smith.
British-in-India colonial adventure.

THE LONG DUEL (1967)
Rank. UK. D/P: Ken Annakin.
S: Ernest Borneman, Peter Yeldham, Geoffrey Olme, from Ranveer Singh's story. C: Trevor Howard, Yul Brynner, Harry Andrews, Charlotte Rampling.
Colonial action adventure: the North-West Frontier, India, 1920s.

LOOKING FOR LANGSTON (1988)
Sankofa/BFI/Channel Four TV. UK. D/P/S: Isaac Julien.
C: Ben Ellison, Matthew Baidoo, John Wilson, Akim Magaji.
Poetic visual fantasy about the lives of black gay men during the Harlem Renaissance, 1920s New York, centred around the poet Langston Hughes.

LOVE'S LABOUR'S LOST (1999)
Shakespeare Film Company/Intermedia/Pathé. UK/France/USA. D: Kenneth Branagh.
P: David Barron, Branagh. S: Branagh, from William Shakespeare's stage play. C: Branagh, Allesandro Nivola, Adrian Lester, Alicia Silverstone, Natascha McElhone.
Shakespearean romantic comedy reworked as a 1930s Hollywood musical.

THE MADNESS OF KING GEORGE (1995)
Samuel Goldwyn Co./Channel Four Films/Close Call Films. UK. D: Nicholas Hytner.
P: Stephen Evans, David Parfitt. S: Alan Bennett, from his play. C: Nigel Hawthorne, Helen Mirren, Ian Holm, Rupert Graves, Amanda Donohoe, Rupert Everett.
Monarchy drama: the temporary insanity of George III from 1788, and resultant political machinations around him.

MADONNA OF THE SEVEN MOONS (1944)
Gainsborough. UK. D: Arthur Crabtree.
P: R. J. Minney. S: Roland Pertwee, Brock Williams, from Margery Lawrence's novel.
C: Phyllis Calvert, Stewart Granger, Patricia Roc, Peter Glenville, John Stuart.
Escapist romantic fantasy: a wife and mother leads a double life as a sensual gypsy.

THE MAGIC BOX (1951)
Festival Films/British Lion. D: John Boulting.
P: Ronald Neame. S: Eric Ambler, from Ray Allister's biography. C: Robert Donat, Margaret Johnson, Maria Schell, John Howard Davies, Renée Asherson, Richard Attenborough.
Episodic bio-pic of British cinema pioneer William Friese-Green.

A MAN FOR ALL SEASONS (1966)
Columbia/Highland. UK. D/P: Fred Zinnemann.
S: Robert Bolt, from his stage play. C: Paul Scofield, Wendy Hiller, Susannah York, Robert Shaw, Orson Welles.
Historical drama: Sir Thomas More opposes Henry VIII's divorce, leading to More's execution.

THE MAN IN GREY (1943)
Gainsborough. UK. D: Leslie Arliss.
P: Edward Black. S: Margaret Kennedy, Arliss, Doreen Montgomery, from Lady Eleanor Smith's novel. C: James Mason, Margaret Lockwood, Phyllis Calvert, Stewart Granger.
Regency costume melodrama.

MANSFIELD PARK (1999)
Miramax HAL/BBC Films. USA/UK. D: Patricia Rozema.
P: Sarah Curtis. S: Rozema, from Jane Austen's novel, letters and journals. C: Frances O'Connor, Jonny Lee Miller, Embeth Davidtz, Alessandro Nivola, Harold Pinter, Lindsay Duncan.
Early-19th-century social/romantic drama: the eldest daughter of an impoverished father reaches adulthood in the household of her wealthier uncle and aunt.

MARY, QUEEN OF SCOTS (1971)
Universal. UK. D: Charles Jarrott.
P: Hal B. Wallis. S: John Hale. C: Vanessa Redgrave, Glenda Jackson, Patrick McGoohan, Timothy Dalton.
Tudor historical drama: Mary Stuart's opposition to Elizabeth I, leading to imprisonment (1567) and execution (1587).

MAURICE (1987)
Merchant Ivory Productions. UK. D: James Ivory.
P: Ismail Merchant. S: Kit Hesketh-Harvey, James Ivory, from E. M. Forster's novel. C: James Wilby, Hugh Grant, Rupert Graves, Billie Whitelaw, Judy Parfitt, Simon Callow.
Social melodrama/romance: the personal struggles and eventual fulfilment of a young gay man in Edwardian England.

MICHAEL COLLINS (1996)
Geffen/Stephen Woolley. USA. D: Neil Jordan.
P: Stephen Woolley. S: Neil Jordan. C: Liam Neeson, Julia Roberts, Alan Rickman, Aidan Quinn, Stephen Rea.
Irish historical/political drama: bio-pic of the IRA's director of intelligence in the 1920s Anglo-Irish War and head of the Irish Free State.

The Monocled Mutineer (TV) (1987)
BBC-TV. UK. D: Jim O'Brien.
P: Richard Broke. S: Alan Bleasdale. C: Paul McGann, Cherie Lunghi, Penelope Wilton, Timothy West.
Political WW1 drama about resistance among ordinary soldiers.

MONS (1926)
British Instructional Films. UK. D: Walter Summers.
P: H. Bruce Woolfe.
WW1 battle reconstruction.

MORNING DEPARTURE (1950)
Rank/Jay Lewis. UK. D: Roy Baker.
P: Leslie Parkyn. S: William Fairchild, from Kenneth Woolard's stage play. C: John Mills, Richard Attenborough, Nigel Patrick, Lana Morris, Peter Hammond.
WW2 naval tragedy: a crippled submarine is hit by a mine.

MRS BROWN (1997)
BBC Scotland/Ecosse Films. UK/USA/Ireland. D: John Madden.
P: Sarah Curtis. S: Jeremy Brock. C: Judi Dench, Billy Connolly, Geoffrey Palmer, Anthony Sher.
Monarchy drama: Queen Victoria's withdrawal from public life and close friendship with her Scottish ghillie John Brown after Prince Albert's death in 1861.

MUTINY ON THE BOUNTY (1935)
MGM. USA. D: Frank Lloyd.
P: Irving Thalberg, Albert Lewin. S: Talbot Jennings, Jules Furthman, Carey Wilson, from the first two books of the Charles Nordoff and James Norman Hall trilogy. C: Charles Laughton, Clark Gable, Franchot Tone, Movita, Dudley Digges.
18th-century British naval adventure.

MUTINY ON THE BOUNTY (1962)
MGM/Arcola. USA. D: Lewis Milestone.
P: Aaron Rosenberg. S: Charles Lederer. C: Trevor Howard, Marlon Brando, Richard Harris, Hugh Griffith, Tarita.
18th-century naval adventure remake.

MY LEFT FOOT (1989)
Granada/Ferndale Films. UK. D: Jim Sheridan.
P: Noel Pearson. S: Shane Connaughton, Sheridan, from Christy Brown's autobiography. C: Daniel Day-Lewis, Ray MacAnally, Brenda Fricker, Ruth McCabe, Fiona Shaw.
Bio-pic of the Irish writer/artist Christy Brown, born with cerebral palsy, Dublin 1930s–1950s.

The Naked Civil Servant (1975)
Thames TV. UK. D: Jack Gold.
P: Barry Hanson. S: Philip Mackie, from Quentin Crisp's autobiography. C: John Hurt.
One-off biographical drama: the persecution and bravura of the gay, defiantly camp civil servant – and later writer – Quentin Crisp, mid-20th century onwards.

NELL GWYNNE (1926)
British National Films/WM Productions. UK. D/P: Herbert Wilcox.
S: Wilcox, from Marjorie Bowens's novel. C: Dorothy Gish, Randall Ayrton, Juliet Compton, Sydney Fairbrother.
Monarchy drama/romance: Charles II and his actress mistress (1650–87).

NELSON: THE STORY OF ENGLAND'S IMMORTAL NAVAL HERO (1919)
Apex/Master International Exclusive. UK. D: Maurice Elvey.
P: Low Warren. S: Eliot Stannard, from Robert Southey's book. C: Donald Calthrop, Malvina Longfellow, Ivy Close, Ernest Thesiger.
Bio-pic of the British admiral (1758–1805) renowned for his victories during the early years of the Napoleonic Wars.

The 1940s House (TV) (2001)
Channel Four TV. UK. D/P: Simon Shaw.
Five-part 'reality TV' historical simulation series: a British family volunteer to experience domestic life during WW2.

The 1900 House (TV (1999)
Wall to Wall for Channel Four TV. UK.
Nine-part 'reality TV' historical simulation series: a British family volunteer to live as if in 1900.

NORTHWEST FRONTIER (1959)
Rank. UK. D: J. Lee Thompson.
P: Marcel Hellman. S: Robin Estridge. C: Kenneth More, Lauren Bacall, Herbert Lom, Ursula Jean, Wilfrid Hyde White.
Colonial action adventure: India, 1905.

OH! WHAT A LOVELY WAR (1969)
Paramount/Accord. UK. D: Richard Attenborough.
P: Brian Duffy, Richard Attenborough. S: Len Deighton, from Joan Littlewood and Charles Chilton's musical play. C: Ralph Richardson, Meriel Forbes, John Gielgud, Kenneth More, John Mills.
WW1 musical satire.

OLIVER! (1968)
Warwick/Romulus. UK. D: Carol Reed.
P: John Woolf. S: Vernon Harris, from Lionel Bart's stage musical of Charles Dickens's novel. C: Ron Moody, Oliver Reed, Mark Lester, Shani Wallis, Jack Wild, Harry Secombe.
Musical: adventures of a Victorian foundling drawn into London's criminal underworld.

OLIVER TWIST (1948)
Cineguild. UK. D: David Lean.
P: Ronald Neame. S: Lean, Stanley Haynes, from Charles Dickens's novel. C: Alec Guinness, Robert Newton, John Howard Davies, Francis L. Sullivan, Kay Walsh.
Drama: adventures of a Victorian foundling drawn into London's criminal underworld.

ORLANDO (1992)
Adventure Pictures/Lenfilm/Rio/Mikado/Sigma. UK/Russia/France/Italy/Netherlands.
D: Sally Potter.
P: Christopher Sheppard. S: Potter, from Virginia Woolf's novel. C: Tilda Swinton, John
Wood, Lothaire Bluteau, Charlotte Valandrey, Quentin Crisp.
Modernist costume drama spanning five centuries to the present: a melancholy young
male Elizabethan aristocrat travels through time and changes gender.

A PASSAGE TO INDIA (1984)
Thorn–EMI/Columbia/HBO. UK. D: David Lean.
P: John Brabourne, Richard Goodwin. S: Lean, from E. M. Forster's novel. C: Judy
Davis, Victor Bannerjee, Peggy Ashcroft, Alec Guinness, James Fox.
British Raj drama: India, 1920s.

THE PICKWICK PAPERS (1952)
Renown/George Minter. UK. D: Noel Langley.
P: Bob NcNaught. S: Langley, from Charles Dickens's novel. C: James Hayter, James
Donald, Donald Wolfit, Hermione Baddeley, Hermione Gingold.
Episodic Victorian comedy.

THE PLOUGHMAN'S LUNCH (1983)
Goldcrest/Greenpoint/AC & D. UK. D: Richard Eyre.
P: Simon Relph, Ann Scott. S: Ian McEwan. C: Jonathan Pryce, Tim Curry, Rosemary
Harris, Frank Finlay, Charlie Dore.
Media drama: an ambitious BBC journalist is commissioned to write a book on the 1956
Suez crisis during the 1982 Falklands War.

PRICK UP YOUR EARS (1987)
Zenith/Civilhand. UK. D: Stephen Frears.
P: Andrew Brown. S: Alan Bennett. C: Gary Oldman, Alfred Molina, Vanessa Redgrave,
Wallace Shawn.
Bio-pic: the life and death of gay playwright Joe Orton and his less-successful partner
Kenneth Halliwell in late 1950s/1960s London.

Pride and Prejudice (TV) (1995)
BBC-TV. UK. D: Simon Langton.
P: Sue Birtwhistle. S: Andrew Davies, from Jane Austen's novel. C: Colin Firth, Jennifer
Ehle, Susannah Harker, David Bamber, Crispin Bonham Carter.
Social comedy/romantic costume drama: early 19th-century England.

THE PRIVATE LIFE OF HENRY VIII (1933)
London Films. UK. D: Alexander Korda.
P: Korda, Ludovico Toeplitz. S: Arthur Wimperis, Lajos Biró. C: Charles Laughton,
Robert Donat, Binnie Barnes, Elsa Lanchester, Merle Oberon, Wendy Barrie.
Historical drama: Henry VIII's various marriages, affairs and divorces.

QUADROPHENIA (1979)
The Who Films/Polytel. UK. D: Franc Roddam.

P: Roy Baird, Bill Curbishley. S: Dave Humphries, Martin Stellman, Roddam. C: Phil Daniels, Lesley Ash, Philip Davis, Marc Wingett, Toyah Wilcox, Sting.
Retro youth drama: mods and rockers do battle in 1964 Brighton.

A QUEEN IS CROWNED (1953)
Rank. UK. D/P: Castleton Knight. Narrated by Laurence Olivier.
Feature-length documentary: the coronation of Elizabeth II.

THE QUIET MAN (1952)
Republic/Argosy. USA. D: John Ford.
P: Ford, Merian C. Cooper. S: Frank Nugent, from a story by Maurice Walsh. C: John Wayne, Maureen O'Hara, Barry Fitzgerald, Victor McLaglan, Ward Bond.
Irish comic drama.

REACH FOR THE SKY (1956)
Rank/Pinnacle. UK. D· Lewis Gilbert.
P: Daniel M. Angel. S: Gilbert, from Paul Brickhill's biography of Douglas Bader. C: Kenneth More, Muriel Pavlow, Lyndon Brook, Lee Patterson, Alexander Knox.
Bio-pic of paraplegic WW2 airforce hero Douglas Bader.

REGENERATION (1997)
Rafford Films/Norstar Entertainment/BBC Films. UK/Canada. D: Gillies MacKinnon.
P: Allan Scott, Peter Simpson. S: Scott from Pat Barker's novel. C: Jonathan Pryce, James Wilby, Jonny Lee Miller, Stuart Bunce, David Hayman, Dougray Scott.
WW1 drama: the incarceration of officers, war poets and anti-war critics Siegfried Sassoon and Wilfred Owen, Edinburgh 1917.

A Respectable Trade (TV) (1998)
BBC-TV/Irish Screen. UK. D: Suri Krishnamma.
P: Ruth Baumgarten. S: Philippa Gregory, from her novel. C: Warren Clarke, Anna Massey, Emma Fielding, Ariyon Bakare.
Historical drama: an 18th-century British slave-trading family and their slaves.

RESURRECTED (1989)
St Pancras Films. UK. D: Paul Greengrass.
P: Adrian Hughes, Tara Prem. S: Martin Allen. C: David Thewlis, Rudi Davies, Lorraine Ashbourne, Tom Bell, John Bowe.
Military drama: an amnesiac soldier who went missing during the 1982 Falklands War and was presumed dead resurfaces – and meets with abuse and victimisation from the British army.

REVEILLE (1924)
Gaumont/Welsh-Pearson. UK. D/P/S: George Pearson.
C: Betty Balfour, Stuart Rome, Ralph Forbes, Sydney Fairbrother.
WW1 drama.

RHODES OF AFRICA (1936)
Gaumont. UK. D: Berthold Viertel.

P: Geoffrey Barkas. S: Michael Barringer, Leslie Arliss, Miles Malleson, from Sarah Millin's book. C: Walter Huston, Oscar Homolka, Basil Sydney, Peggy Ashcroft, Frank Cellier. Historical bio-pic of the British-born South African statesman Cecil Rhodes (1853–1902).

RICHARD III (1955)
London Films. UK. D/P: Laurence Olivier.
S: Olivier, Alan Dent, from William Shakespeare's stage play. C: Olivier, Claire Bloom, Ralph Richardson, Cedric Hardwicke, Stanley Baker.
Shakespearean historical tragedy.

RICHARD III (1995)
British Screen/Bayly Paré. UK. D: Richard Loncraine.
P: Lisa Katselas Paré, Stephen Bayly. S: Ian McKellen, Loncraine, from Richard Eyre's adaptation of William Shakespeare's stage play. C: McKellen, Annette Bening, Kristin Scott Thomas, John Wood, Nigel Hawthorne.
Shakespearean historical tragedy, relocated to 1930s Britain and rendered as a political thriller.

A ROOM WITH A VIEW (1985)
Merchant Ivory Productions/Goldcrest. UK. D: James Ivory.
P: Ismail Merchant. S: Ruth Prawer Jhabvala, from E. M. Forster's novel. C: Maggie Smith, Denholm Elliot, Helena Bonham Carter, Judi Dench, Julian Sands, Daniel Day-Lewis, Simon Callow, Rupert Graves.
Edwardian social comedy/romantic drama: the English middle classes in Italy and at home.

RYAN'S DAUGHTER (1970)
MGM/Faraway. UK. D: David Lean.
P: Anthony Havelock-Allan. S: Robert Bolt. C: Sarah Miles, Robert Mitchum, Christopher Jones, Trevor Howard, John Mills.
Irish melodrama/romance: 1916 rural Ireland under British rule.

THE SAILOR'S RETURN (1978)
Euston Films. UK. D: Jack Gold.
P: Otto Plaschkes. S: James Saunders, from David Garnett's novel. C: Tom Bell, Shope Shodeinde, Mick Ford, Paola Dionisotti, George Costigan.
Inter-racial tragic romance set in mid-19th-century rural Dorset.

SANDERS OF THE RIVER (1935)
London Films. UK. D: Zoltan Korda.
P: Alexander Korda. S: Lajos Biró, Jeffrey Dell, Arthur Wimperis, from Edgar Wallace's stories. C: Leslie Banks, Paul Robeson, Nina Mae McKinney, Robert Cochran.
African colonial adventure.

SCANDAL (1989)
Palace Pictures/British Screen. UK. D: Michael Caton-Jones.
P: Stephen Woolley. S: Michael Thomas. C: John Hurt, Joanne Whalley-Kilmer, Bridget Fonda, Ian McKellen.
Political drama: the early-1960s scandal surrounding British Conservative war minister John Profumo's affair with showgirl Christine Keeler.

THE SCARLET PIMPERNEL (1934)
London Films. UK. D/P: Alexander Korda.
S: Robert E. Sherwood, Sam Berman, Arthur Wimperis, Lajos Biró, from Baroness Orczy's novel. C: Leslie Howard, Merle Oberon, Raymond Massey, Nigel Bruce, Bramwell Fletcher. Swashbuckling 18th-century adventure: in the early days of the French Revolution, an English dandy rescues aristocrats from the guillotine.

SCOTT OF THE ANTARCTIC (1948)
Ealing. UK. D: Charles Frend.
P: Sidney Cole. S: Ivor Montagu, Walter Meade, Mary Hayley Bell. C: John Mills, James Robertson Justice, Derek Bond, Harold Warrender, Reginald Beckwith.
Heroic historical adventure/tragedy: Captain Scott's ill-fated 1912 expedition to the South Pole.

SCROOGE (1970)
Cinema Center/Waterbury. UK. D: Ronald Neame.
P: Richard H. Solo. S, music and lyrics: Leslie Bricusse, from Charles Dickens's *A Christmas Carol*. C: Alec Guinness, Albert Finney, Michael Medwin, Edith Evans, Kenneth More.
Musical version of Dickens's tale of the reformed miser.

SENSE AND SENSIBILITY (1996)
Columbia/Mirage Entertainments. USA/UK. D: Ang Lee.
P: Lindsay Doran. S: Emma Thompson, from Jane Austen's novel. C: Emma Thompson, Kate Winslet, Greg Wise, Hugh Grant, Alan Rickman.
Social/romantic costume drama: late 18th-century England.

SHAKE HANDS WITH THE DEVIL (1959)
UA/Troy/Pennebaker. Ireland. D/P: Michael Anderson.
S: Ivan Goff, Ben Roberts, from Rearden Connor's novel. C: James Cagney, Glynis Johns, Don Murray, Dana Winter, Michael Redgrave.
IRA melodrama: the 1921 Irish rebellion.

SHAKESPEARE IN LOVE (1999)
Miramax/Universal. USA. D: John Madden.
P: David Parfitt, Donna Gigliotti, Harvey Weinstein, Edward Zwick, Marc Norman. S: Marc Norman, Tom Stoppard. C: Joseph Fiennes, Gwyneth Paltrow, Judi Dench, Ben Affleck, Geoffrey Rush.
Romantic bio-pic: the Elizabethan playwright William Shakespeare.

Shoot the Revolution (TV) (1990)
BBC-TV. UK. D: Jane Howell.
P: George Faber. S: Peter Flannery.
Documentary/drama mix: the collapse of Communism in Romania and the overthrow of the dictator Ceausescu, 1989.

SID AND NANCY (1986)
Zenith/Initial. UK. D: Alex Cox.
P: Eric Fellner. S: Cox, Abbe Wool. C: Gary Oldman, Chloë Webb, David Hayman, Debbie Bishop.

1970s punk bio-pic: the love, heroin abuse and death of Sex Pistols bassist Sid Vicious and his US girlfriend Nancy Spungen.

633 SQUADRON (1964)
UA/Mirisch. UK. D: Walter E. Grauman.
P: Cecil F. Ford. S: James Clavell, Howard Koch, from Frederick E. Smith's novel. C: Cliff Robertson, George Chakiris, Maria Perschy, Harry Andrews.
WW2 airforce drama: Mosquito jets try to destroy a munitions factory in Norway, 1944.

SIXTY GLORIOUS YEARS (1938)
Imperator. UK. D/P: Herbert Wilcox.
S: Robert Vansittart, Miles Malleson, Charles de Grandcourt. C: Anna Neagle, Anton Walbrook, C. Aubrey Smith, Walter Rilla.
Episodic historical drama and sequel to *Victoria the Great*: further scenes from the life of Queen Victoria.

SOME MOTHER'S SON (1996)
Castle Rock/Hell's Kitchen. Ireland/USA. D: Terry George.
P: Jim Sheridan/Arthur Lappin/Edwin Burke. S: George, Sheridan. C: Helen Mirren, Aidan Gillen, David O'Hara, John Lynch, Fionnula Flanagan.
Northern Ireland prison drama: the 'dirty protests' and hunger strikes in H-block at Long Kesh prison, 1981.

Staying On (TV) (1979)
ITV. UK. D: Silvio Narizzano.
P: Irene Shubik. S: Paul Scott, from his novel. C: Trevor Howard, Celia Johnson, Saeed Jaffrey, Pearl Padamsee.
Post-colonial drama: the fortunes of an English couple who stayed on in India following Independence in 1947.

Surviving the Iron Age (2001)
BBC-TV. UK. P: Peter Firstbrook.
'Reality TV' historical simulation series: volunteers experience reconstructed Iron Age life.

TELL ENGLAND (1931)
British Instructional Films. UK. D: Anthony Asquith, Gerald Barkas.
P: H. Bruce Woolf. S: Asquith, from Ernest Raymond's novel. C: Carl Harbord, Fay Compton, Tony Bruce, Gerald Rawlinson, Wally Patch.
WW1 drama: British schoolfriends join up, fight and are mostly killed in the Allies' 1915 invasion of Gallipoli.

A TERRIBLE BEAUTY (1960)
UA/Raymond Stross. UK/USA/Ireland. D: Tay Garnett.
P: Raymond Stross. S: Robert Wright Campbell, from Arthur Roth's novel. C: Robert Mitchum, Anne Heywood, Dan O'Herlihy, Cyril Cusack, Richard Harris.
IRA melodrama set at outbreak of WW2.

TERRITORIES (1984)
Sankofa/BFI/Channel Four TV. D/P/S: Isaac Julien.
Radical documentary: the Notting Hill Carnival as an expression of diaspora culture; finding
a language to tell black British histories.

TESS (1979)
Renn–Burrill. France/UK. D: Roman Polanski.
P: Claude Berri. S: Polanski, Gerard Brach, John Brownjohn, from Thomas Hardy's novel.
C: Nastassja Kinski, Leigh Lawson, Peter Firth, John Collin.
Tragic rural drama set in 19th-century Wessex. A peasant girl tries to prove her noble
ancestry.

THAT HAMILTON WOMAN (1941)
Alexander Korda Films. USA. D/P: Alexander Korda.
S: Walter Reisch, R. C. Sherriff. C: Vivien Leigh, Laurence Olivier, Gladys Cooper, Alan
Mowbray, Sarah Allgood.
Bio-pic: Admiral Lord Nelson's affair with Lady Emma Hamilton.

THIS ENGLAND (1941)
British National Pictures. UK. D: David MacDonald.
P: John Corfield. S: Emlyn Williams, A. R. Rawlinson, Bridget Boland. C: John Clements,
Emlyn Williams, Constance Cummings, Morland Graham, Roland Culver.
Episodic drama: conflict between landowner and labourer through five periods of English
history.

THIS HAPPY BREED (1944)
Two Cities Films/Cineguild. UK. D: David Lean.
P: Noel Coward, Anthony Havelock-Allan. S: Ronald Neame, Lean, Havelock-Allan, from
Coward's stage play. C: Robert Newton, Celia Johnson, John Mills, Kay Walsh.
Family drama: lower-middle-class life between WW1 and WW2, suburban south
London.

THE TICHBORNE CLAIMANT (1998)
Bigger Picture Company/Swiftcall International Telephone Co. UK. D: David Yates.
P: Tom McCabe. S: Joe Fisher. C: Robert Pugh, John Kani, Stephen Fry, Robert Hardy,
John Gielgud.
Inheritance drama set in the 1870s: a black family servant searches for a missing heir, but
brings back an imposter.

TOM JONES (1963)
Woodfall. UK. D/P: Tony Richardson.
S: John Osborne, from Henry Fielding's novel. C: Albert Finney, Susannah York, Hugh
Griffith, Edith Evans, Joan Greenwood.
Picaresque drama: the adventures of a foundling in 18th-century England.

THE TRENCH (1999)
Blue PM/Skyline Films/Galatée Films/Arts Council. UK/France. D/S: William Boyd.
P: Steve Clark-Hall. C: Paul Nicholls, Daniel Craig, Julian Rhind-Tutt, Danny Dyer.
WW1 drama.

TUDOR ROSE (1936)
Gainsborough. UK. D: Robert Stevenson.
S: Stevenson, Miles Malleson. C: Cedric Hardwicke, Nova Pilbeam, John Mills, Felix Aylmer, Leslie Perrins.
Historical drama: the brief life and nine-day reign in 1553 of Lady Jane Grey.

Tumbledown (TV) (1988)
BBC-TV. UK. D: Richard Eyre.
P: Richard Broke. S: Charles Wood. C: Colin Firth, Paul Rhys, David Calder, Barbara Leigh-Hunt.
1982 Falklands War drama.

Vanity Fair (TV) (1998)
BBC-TV/Arts and Entertainment Network. UK. D: Marc Munden.
P: Gillian MacNeill. S: Andrew Davies, from William Makepeace Thackeray's 1847–8 novel. C: Natasha Little, Nathaniel Parker, Frances Gray, Philip Glenister.
Picaresque drama set in the early 19th century: the fortunes of two friends of contrasting backgrounds, Becky Sharpe and Amelia Sedley.

VELVET GOLDMINE (1998)
Channel Four Films/Miramax. UK/USA. D/S: Todd Haynes.
P: Christine Vachon. C: Jonathan Rhys Meyers, Ewan McGregor, Christian Bale, Toni Collette, Eddie Izzard.
Queer 1970s glam rock drama.

VICTORIA THE GREAT (1937)
British Lion/Imperator. UK. D/P: Herbert Wilcox.
S: Miles Malleson, Charles de Grandcourt, from Laurence Houseman's play *Victoria Regina*. C: Anna Neagle, Anton Walbrook, H. B. Warner, Walter Rilla, Mary Morris.
Episodic historical drama: scenes from the life of Queen Victoria.

WAR REQUIEM (1988)
Anglo International/BBC. UK. D/S: Derek Jarman.
P: Don Boyd. C: Nathaniel Parker, Tilda Swinton, Laurence Olivier, Patricia Hayes.
Non-narrative film mourning WW1, merging Benjamin Britten's choral *War Requiem* with Wilfred Owen's war poems.

WELCOME TO SARAJEVO (1997)
Channel Four Films/Miramax/Dragon Pictures. UK/USA. D: Michael Winterbottom.
P: Graham Broadbent, Damian Jones. S: Frank Cottrell Boyce, from Michael Nicholson's book *Natasha's Story*. C: Stephen Dillane, Woody Harrelson, Marisa Tomei, Emira Nusevic, Kerry Fox.
War drama: a British TV journalist reporting on the war in Bosnia-Herzegovina, 1992, adopts a local child assumed to be an orphan.

WHERE ANGELS FEAR TO TREAD (1991)
Stagescreen. UK. D: Charles Sturridge.
P: Derek Granger, Jeffrey Taylor. S: Tim Sullivan, Granger, Sturridge, from E. M. Forster's novel. C: Helena Bonham Carter, Judy Davis, Rupert Graves, Giovanni Guidelli, Helen Mirren, Barbara Jefford.

Tragi-comic Edwardian drama: an English widow marries a younger Italian. After she dies in childbirth, her disapproving in-laws travel to Italy intending to snatch the baby.

WHO NEEDS A HEART? (1991)
Black Audio Film Collective/Channel Four TV/ZDF. UK. D/S: John Akomfrah.
P: Lina Gopaul.
Documentary: investigation of the 1960s life and times of British Black Power leader Michael X.

THE WICKED LADY (1945)
Gainsborough. UK. D: Leslie Arliss.
P: R. J. Minney. S: Arliss, Aimée Stuart, Gordon Glennon, from Magdalen King-Hall's novel. C: Margaret Lockwood, James Mason, Patricia Roc, Griffith Jones.
17th-century costume adventure/drama. A bored wife turns highwaywoman.

THE WICKED LADY (1983)
Cannon. USA. D: Michael Winner.
P: Menahem Golan, Yoram Globus. S: Leslie Arliss, Winner, from Magdalen King-Hall's novel. C: Faye Dunaway, Alan Bates, John Gielgud, Denholm Elliott, Prunella Scales.
17th-century costume adventure/drama remake.

THE WINGS OF THE DOVE (1998)
Miramax/Renaissance Dove. USA/UK. D: Iain Softley.
P: David Parfitt, Stephen Evans. S: Hossein Amini, from Henry James's novel. C: Helena Bonham Carter, Linus Roache, Alison Elliott, Alex Jennings, Charlotte Rampling.
Noir costume drama: desire, friendship, scheming and betrayal updated to 1910s London and Venice.

WOMEN IN LOVE (1969)
UA/Brandywine. UK. D: Ken Russell.
P: Larry Kramer. S: Kramer, from D. H. Lawrence's novel. C: Glenda Jackson, Jennie Linden, Alan Bates, Oliver Reed.
Relationship drama: two sisters in a 1920s Midlands colliery town grapple with sex and love.

YOUNG LOCHINVAR (1923)
Stoll. UK. D: Will P. Kellino.
S: Alicia Ramsay, from Walter Scott's ballad. C: Gladys Jennings, Owen Nares, Dick Webb, Cecil Morton York.
Scottish highland period drama.

THE YOUNG MR PITT (1942)
Twentieth Century Productions. UK. D: Carol Reed.
P: Edward Black. S: Sidney Gilliat. C: Robert Donat, Geoffrey Atkins, Jean Cadell, Robert Morley, Phyllis Calvert, Raymond Lovell.
Period bio-pic of the 18th-century politician.

YOUNG SOUL REBELS (1991)
BFI/Film Four. UK/France/Spain/Germany. D: Isaac Julien.

P: Nadine Marsh-Edwards. S: Paul Hallam, Julien, Derek Saldaan McClintock. C: Valentine Nonyela, Mo Sesay, Dorian Healy, Frances Barber, Sophie Okonedo.
Multicultural urban youth-culture drama: the black soul scene in 1977 punk-era London.

YPRES (1925)
British Instructional Films. UK. D: Walter Summers. P: H. Bruce Woolf.
WW1 drama.

ZARAK (1956)
Columbia/Warwick. UK. D: Terence Young.
P: Phil C. Samuel. S: Richard Maibaum. C: Victor Mature, Michael Wilding, Anita Ekberg, Finlay Currie, Bernard Miles.
British colonial adventure: India, the North-West Frontier.

ZINA (1985)
Looseyard Productions. UK. D: Ken McMullen.
S: Terry James, McMullen. C: Domiziana Giordano, Ian McKellen, Philip Madoc, Paul Geoffrey, Maureen O'Brien.
Biopic/drama: the traumas of 20th-century history distilled through the psychic disturbances of Trotsky's daughter, Zina, under analysis with Sigmund Freud in 1930s Berlin.

ZULU (1964)
Paramount/Diamond. UK. D: Cy Endfield.
P: Stanley Baker, Endfield. S: John Prebble, Endfield. C: Stanley Baker, Jack Hawkins, Ulla Jacobsson, Michael Caine, James Booth, Nigel Green.
Zulu War action drama: the 1879 Battle of Rorke's Drift, southern Africa.

ZULU DAWN (1979)
Samarkand/Zulu Dawn NV. USA/Netherlands. D: Douglas Hickox.
P: Barry Saint Clair. S: Cy Endfield, Anthony Storey. C: Burt Lancaster, Denholm Elliott, Peter O'Toole, John Mills, Simon Ward.
Zulu War action prequel: 1878, the massacre of British troops at Isandlwhana, southern Africa.

Index